MW01485867

ManageFirst®
Human Resources
Management and Supervision
Competency Guide

Upper Saddle River, New Jersey 07458

Disclaimer

Table of Contents

A Message from the National Restaurant Association

Founded in 1919, the National Restaurant Association is the leading business association for the restaurant industry. Together with the National Restaurant Association Educational Foundation (NRAEF) and National Restaurant Association Solutions (NRA Solutions) our goal is to lead America's restaurant industry into a new era of prosperity, prominence, and participation, enhancing the quality of life for all we serve.

As one of the nation's largest private-sector employers, the restaurant, hospitality and foodservice industry is the cornerstone of the American economy, of career-and-employment opportunities, and of local communities. The overall impact of the restaurant industry is astounding. The restaurant industry is expected to add 1.8 million jobs over the next decade, with employment reaching 14.8 million by 2019. At the National Restaurant Association, we are focused on enhancing this position by providing the valuable tools and resources needed to educate our current and future professionals.

For more information on the National Restaurant Association, please visit our Web site at www.restaurant.org.

What is the ManageFirst Program™?

The ManageFirst Program is a management-training certificate program that exemplifies our commitment to developing materials by the industry, for the industry. The program's most powerful strength is that it is based on a set of competencies defined by the restaurant, foodservice, and hospitality industry as critical for success. For more information on the ManageFirst Program, visit www.managefirst.restaurant.org.

ManageFirst Program Components

The ManageFirst Program includes a set of Competency Guides, exams, Instructor Resources, certificates, a credential, and support activities and services. By participating in the program, you are demonstrating your commitment to becoming a highly qualified professional preparing either to begin or to advance your career in the restaurant, hospitality, and foodservice industry.

The Competency Guides cover the range of topics listed in the chart at right.

Competency Guide/Exam Topics

ManageFirst Core Credential Topics

Controlling Foodservice Costs

Hospitality and Restaurant Management

Human Resources Management and Supervision

ServSafe® Food Safety

ManageFirst Elective Topics

Customer Service

Food Production

Inventory and Purchasing

Managerial Accounting

Menu Marketing and Management

Nutrition

Restaurant Marketing

ServSafe Alcohol® Responsible Alcohol Service

Within the guides, you will find the essential content for the topic as defined by industry, as well as learning activities, assessments, case studies, suggested field projects, professional profiles, and testimonials. You can also find an answer sheet or an online exam voucher for a NRA Solutions exam written specifically for each topic. The exam can be administered either online or in a paper and pencil format (see inside front cover for a listing of ISBNs), and it will be proctored. Upon successfully passing the exam, you will be issued a customized certificate from NRA Solutions. The certificate is a lasting recognition of your accomplishment and a signal to the industry that you have mastered the competency covered within the particular topic.

To earn the ManageFirst Professional™ (MFP™) credential, you will be required to pass four core exams and one elective exam (to be chosen from the remaining program topics) and to document your work experience in the restaurant and foodservice industry. Earning the MFP credential is a significant accomplishment.

We applaud you as you either begin or advance your career in the restaurant, hospitality, and foodservice industry. Visit *www.managefirst.restaurant.org* to learn about additional career-building resources offered through the National Restaurant Association, including scholarships for college students enrolled in relevant industry programs.

ManageFirst Program Ordering Information

Review copies or support materials:
FACULTY FIELD SERVICES
Tel: 800.526.0485

Domestic orders and inquiries:
PEARSON CUSTOMER SERVICE
Tel: 800.922.0579
www.prenhall.com

International orders and inquiries:
U.S. EXPORT SALES OFFICE
Pearson Education International Customer Service Group
200 Old Tappan Road
Old Tappan, NJ 07675 USA
Tel: 201.767.5021
Fax: 201.767.5625

For corporate, government, and special sales (consultants, corporations, training centers, VARs, and corporate resellers) orders and inquiries:
PEARSON CORPORATE SALES
Tel: 317.428.3411
Fax: 317.428.3343
Email: managefirst@prenhall.com

For additional information regarding other Prentice Hall publications, instructor and student support materials, locating your sales representative, and much more, please visit *www.prenhall.com/managefirst.*

Acknowledgements

The National Restaurant Association Solutions is grateful for the significant contributions made to this competency guide by the following individuals.

Frederic B. Mayo, MBA, PhD, CHE, CHT

In addition, we are pleased to thank our many other advisors, subject matter experts, reviewers, and contributors for their time, effort, and dedication to this program.

Teresa Marie Gargano Adamski	John Hart	James Perry
Ernest Boger	Thomas Kaltenecker	Patricia Plavcan
Robert Bosselman	Ray Kavanaugh	William N. Reynolds
Jerald Chesser	John Kidwell	Rosenthal Group
Cynthia Deale	Carol Kizer	Mokie Steiskal
Fred DeMicco	Holly Ruttan Maloney	Karl Titz
Johnathan Deustch	Cynthia Mayo	Terry Umbreit
John Drysdale	Patrick Moreo	David Wightman
Gene Fritz	Robert O'Halloran	Deanne Williams
John Gescheidle	Brian O'Malley	Mike Zema
Thomas Hamilton	Terrence Pappas	Renee Zonka

Features of the ManageFirst® Competency Guides

We have designed the ManageFirst competency guides to enhance your ability to learn and retain important information that is critical to this restaurant and foodservice industry function. Here are the key features you will find within this guide.

Beginning Each Guide

Tuning In to You

When you open a ManageFirst competency guide for the first time, you might ask yourself: Why do I need to know about this topic? Every topic covers key information you will need as you manage a restaurant or foodservice operation. Located in the front of each review guide, "Tuning In to You" is a brief synopsis of the reasons why the information contained in the guide is important to you. It contains real-life scenarios that you will face as a manager and how the concepts in the book will help you in your career.

Professional Profile

This is your opportunity to meet a professional who is currently working in the field associated with a competency guide's topic. This person's story will help you gain insight into the responsibilities related to his or her position, as well as the training and educational history linked to it. You will also see the daily and cumulative impact this position has on an operation, and receive advice from a person who has successfully met the challenges of being a manager.

Beginning Each Chapter

Inside This Chapter

Chapter content is organized under these major headings.

Learning Objectives

Learning objectives identify what you should be able to do after completing each chapter. These objectives are linked to the required tasks a manager must be able to perform in relation to the function discussed in the competency guide.

Test Your Knowledge

Each chapter begins with some True or False questions designed to test your prior knowledge of some of the concepts presented in the chapter. The answers to these questions, as well as the concepts behind them, can be found within the chapter—see the page reference after each question.

Key Terms

These terms are important for thorough understanding of the chapter's content. They are highlighted throughout the chapter, where they are explicitly defined or their meaning is made clear within the paragraphs in which they appear.

Throughout Each Chapter

Exhibits

Exhibits are placed throughout each chapter to visually reinforce the key concepts presented in the text. Types of exhibits include charts, tables, photographs, and illustrations.

Think About It...

These thought-provoking sidebars reveal supportive information about the section they appear beside.

Activities

Apply what you have learned throughout the chapter by completing the various activities in the text. The activities have been designed to give you additional practice and better understanding of the concepts addressed in the learning objectives. Types of activities include case studies, role-plays, and problem solving, among others.

Exhibit

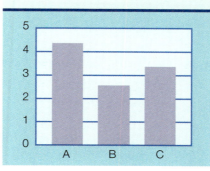

Exhibits are visuals that will help you learn about key concepts.

Think About It...

Consider these supplemental insights as you read through a chapter.

Activity

Activity

Types of activities you will complete include case studies, role-plays, and problem solving, among others.

At the End of Each Chapter

Review Your Learning

These multiple-choice or open- or close-ended questions or problems are designed to test your knowledge of the concepts presented in the chapter. These questions have been aligned with the objectives and should provide you with an opportunity to practice or apply the content that supports these objectives. If you have difficulty answering them, you should review the content further.

At the End of the Guide

Field Project

This real-world project gives you the valuable opportunity to apply many of the concepts you will learn in a competency guide. You will interact with industry practitioners, enhance your knowledge, and research, apply, analyze, evaluate, and report on your findings. It will provide you with an in-depth "reality check" of the policies and practices of this management function.

Tuning In to You

As your career grows and you become a manager, you will face many challenges and reap many rewards. Probably your most challenging and rewarding area as a manager will be dealing with the "people aspects" of your job. Understanding how to find and hire the right people and then develop, train, supervise, and motivate them will help you reach your full potential as a manager and turn your operation into the kind of place that attracts both customers and employees. In addition, learning about the laws that govern your workplace will help you protect the operation and yourself from legal disputes while ensuring that employees' and customers' rights are also protected. However, even if you are not yet a manager, understanding these management issues will help you become a better employee.

Working in the restaurant and foodservice industry can be very fulfilling. One of the best rewards in this industry is seeing the smiles on the faces of customers who are enjoying a good meal that is well served. You can enjoy the excitement of learning how to prepare a new dish, set up a new banquet, organize a special event, develop a new menu, or find a new pairing of a wine with an entrée. You also get the opportunity to work with and learn from a diverse range of people. This is a field where you will never learn all there is to know, which leaves plenty of room for your professional development and stimulation.

It is also exciting to be part of one of the largest industries in the United States—over $500 billion in sales in more than 925,000 locations. Given the size of the industry and its continuing growth pattern, there are plenty of jobs to explore and a range of career options in any size, structure, service level, or type of food operation. If you prefer fine dining, there are plenty of restaurants looking for talented employees. If you like chain establishments, they are growing so fast that they cannot find enough good staff members to fuel their growth. If you want to start your own restaurant, people are eating out with increasing frequency and are looking for good restaurants everywhere. Even if you cannot find your ideal job now, just wait: the industry is growing so fast, there will be new opportunities soon.

Professional Profile
Your opportunity to meet someone working in the field

Bob Luz

Executive Vice President, Human Resources & Training
Ninety Nine Restaurant & Pub
Woburn, MA

As the Executive Vice President, Human Resources & Training, for the Ninety Nine Restaurant & Pub, I live by its mission statement, "We treat people right." This means we treat everyone—employees, business partners and suppliers, guests, and the community—exactly the way we want to be treated. Our mission statement drives every business decision we make, and it's the reason why our company has the lowest turnover rate in the restaurant industry.

In the six years I've been with Ninety Nine Restaurant & Pub, a casual-dining restaurant company serving large portions of great food and drink, we have grown from forty-eight units with 2,500 employees to 107 units with 7,200 employees. During such a high growth phase, it would be expected for a company to have an increase in turnover. But just the opposite happened with us. Our turnover rate in the beginning of this phase was 58 percent—already lower than the industry standard of 125 percent—and it has dropped in each of the last six years. In 2004, our turnover rate was just 43 percent!

I think our success is based on the fact that our team does a lot of little things right. My contribution is to oversee the recruiting, selection, training and development, staffing, benefit programs, and legal proceedings for all employees. However, my greatest joy is seeing employees grow and develop their careers. Our industry allows people who want more than just a job to start as a dishwasher and become a kitchen manager, or to start out waiting on tables and then someday run a $3 million restaurant. Providing employees with the tools, paths, and opportunities to succeed is why I joined the Ninety Nine, and I know that this strategy works because of our results. Nineteen percent of our general managers, 71 percent of our kitchen managers, 38 percent of our assistant managers, and nine employees at director-level and above started in hourly positions. In fact, our president started as a bartender!

Our business results at the Ninety Nine have been the subject of numerous articles and industry awards, and I have received recognition for my work as well. In 2002, I was named the Steven Elmont HTM Alumnus of the Year by my alma mater, the University of Massachusetts. In 2005, I was awarded the Elliot Hospitality Motivator of the Year, a highly coveted HR award in the restaurant industry.

I think what has helped me to succeed is my love for helping people and the operations experience I gained early in my career. I started in the industry at age thirteen by working in a Jewish deli and in various foodservice establishments during high school, where I discovered that I had a passion for providing people with a great dining experience and realized that I wanted to incorporate this in some way in my professional career. When it came time for college, I chose the hospitality management program at the University of Massachusetts.

During college, I worked as a manager trainee at a Sheraton Hotel franchise. When I graduated in 1982, I accepted a position as a manager with the Rusty Scupper Restaurant Group. I wanted to gain experience as an industry manager, but my long-term goal was to move into HR, where I could use my experience to develop training programs that made sense.

Within two years of accepting the position, I became the general manager of a restaurant with an annual sales volume of $2.4 million. I positioned my restaurant as a training restaurant, which meant that the company would send new managers to my location to be trained by me. From here, the natural extension was for me to become involved in management recruiting.

By 1987, I was looking for a new challenge, so I accepted a position with an executive recruiting firm that specialized in hotel and restaurant personnel. I was successful there, but I missed the employee development aspects of my previous job. So in 1991, I became the vice president of human resources with the Back Bay Restaurant Group.

Then in 1993, a former client from my recruiting firm asked me to join his company, Applebee's Neighborhood Grill & Bar, which was a franchise of a new restaurant concept. I moved to Kansas and became the executive director of human resources, and in the next six years, the company grew from sixty-seven company-owned and two hundred franchised locations to 310 company-owned and 950 franchised locations. With this rapid growth, the nature of my work changed again, and instead of working in restaurants and listening to employees' needs, I was spending most of my time in the office. To get back to the work I loved, I took my current position with the Ninety Nine Restaurant & Pub.

What is my advice to anyone considering a career in human resources in the restaurant and foodservice industry? Love what you do, get a solid education, learn your business inside and out, and understand how your work affects others—this approach has served me well.

Building a Welcoming Work Environment and Encouraging Diversity

1

Inside This Chapter

- Overview of Human Resources from a Manager's Perspective
- Benefits of a Diverse Working Environment
- Avoiding Illegal Discrimination
- Prejudices, Stereotypes, Bias, and Cultural Tendencies
- How Prejudices and Stereotypes Affect the Work Environment
- Promoting Diversity

After completing this chapter, you should be able to:

- Define diversity as it relates to foodservice.
- Identify the benefits of a diverse workplace.
- List the ten categories of people protected from discrimination by federal equal employment opportunity (EEO) laws.
- Recognize federal laws that prohibit discrimination in the workplace.
- Differentiate between a cultural tendency and a stereotype.
- Identify how stereotypes and prejudices can affect a workplace.
- Recognize practices that promote diversity in the workplace.
- Describe ways to increase positive cross-cultural interaction and communication.

Test Your Knowledge

1 **True or False:** Equal employment opportunity laws protect everyone from every type of discrimination in the workplace. *(See p. 8.)*

2 **True or False:** Stereotypes and cultural tendencies are the same thing. *(See p. 10.)*

3 **True or False:** Promoting diversity among your employees can bring new customers to your restaurant or foodservice operation. *(See p. 6.)*

4 **True or False:** Holding people accountable for discriminatory behavior toward coworkers will create a hostile work environment. *(See pp. 16–17.)*

5 **True or False:** Discriminating among job applicants due to an applicant's certain characteristics is legal except when the discrimination is arbitrary. *(See p. 7.)*

Key Terms

Affirmative action programs

Applicants

Bias

Candidates

Cross-cultural interaction

Cultural tendencies

Discrimination

Diversity

Executive orders (EOs)

Hostile environment

Immutable characteristics

Prejudice

Protected categories

Protected classes

Protected groups

Stereotypes

Introduction

Working in the restaurant and foodservice industry gives you a chance to meet a wide variety of people as coworkers and as customers. It can be a very exciting place, in large part because it has always contained one of the most diverse workforces of any industry. Since most of us come from a limited ethnic, religious, and cultural background, the chance to work with and learn from a diverse group of people will broaden your horizon and expand your perspective. Working almost any job in a restaurant or foodservice operation that promotes and honors **diversity,** or the differences among people, will provide you with the opportunity to learn and grow as an individual and as a manager. In the restaurant industry, encouraging diversity means that you treat *all* people—employees, vendors, and guests—in a nondiscriminatory manner, without regard to race, color, national origin, or any other trait unrelated to that person's role at your establishment. (See *Exhibit 1a.*)

Think About It...

Restaurants employ more minority managers than any other industry.

Source: National Restaurant Association: Restaurant Industry 2005 Fact Sheet

Exhibit 1a

Bases of Possible Differences

Gender

Age

Group affiliation

Physical and learning abilities

Physical and mental disabilities

Nationality

Ethnic background

Skill level

Sexual orientation

Physical appearance

Economic level

Skin color

Political preferences

Career goals

Religion

Race

Diversity issues and anti-discrimination policies impact every aspect of human resources. As someone who is planning a career in the restaurant industry, you need to understand these various aspects of human resources from a manager's perspective.

Overview of Human Resources from a Manager's Perspective

Since the restaurant and hospitality industry is a people-oriented business, the most important assets are the employees—*not* the equipment and facilities that are considered to be assets on a balance sheet. Without caring employees who know how to do the work effectively and efficiently, no restaurant or foodservice operation could survive, much less grow and expand. Consequently, as a manager, you will spend more time on personnel issues than on any other area. Helping you realize the importance and principles behind the phases of finding, recruiting, screening, hiring, orienting, supervising, motivating, training, and developing employees is the purpose of this guide.

Recognizing that these challenges are part of a continuous cycle of personnel tasks will help you understand their importance and represents the first step in becoming a good manager. The employment cycle is a series of repeating activities that managers and human resources professionals perform to ensure their operations are fully staffed and their employees are productive. This cycle incorporates activities that happen before, during, and after a person works for a restaurant or foodservice operation. The graphic on the next page highlights each step of the employment cycle. As we progress through this text, this graphic will indicate where we are in the cycle.

- **Finding potential employees**—Before you can even persuade someone to apply for a job in your operation, you need to develop a system of disseminating information about the vacancy. Doing this work involves both identifying people and organizations that can help spread your message, and maintaining ongoing relationships with them.

- **Recruiting potential employees**—Once you have identified sources of potential employees, you can promote your operation's vacancies to attract interested job seekers.

- **Screening applicants**—After people apply for a job in your operation, you need to evaluate their skills and personality to see whether or not they are a good fit for the job and your operation.

You should develop and follow practices that help you identify the best **applicants,** the people who have applied for an open job, as well as ensure equal opportunity for all job **candidates,** the applicants who possess minimum job qualifications and are being considered for a job opening.

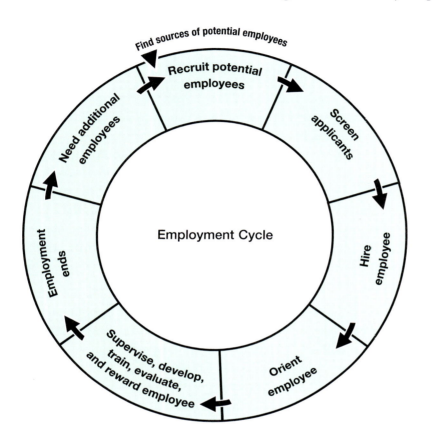

Find sources of potential employees

Recruit potential employees

Need additional employees

Screen applicants

Employment ends

Employment Cycle

Hire employee

Supervise, develop, train, evaluate, and reward employee

Orient employee

■ **Hiring employees**—Once you have selected a person to hire, you need to make a job offer that specifies the terms of employment. If your candidate accepts the position, there are many procedures that must be followed to make sure your new employee can legally work for you, and that he or she gets the wages and benefits you promised.

■ **Orienting employees**— New employees need a lot of information and help to learn their new jobs and become comfortable at work. An orientation program is a formal plan for welcoming new employees and getting them up to speed. In some operations, orientation programs include procedures for processing hiring-related documents, such as tax and benefit enrollment forms.

■ **Supervising employees**—Employee supervision is an ongoing activity to ensure that employees are productive, motivated, and supported in their work, so the operation runs smoothly and customers have the best possible experience.

■ **Training and developing employees**—Ongoing and as-needed training and employee development programs help employees remain productive and happy.

■ **Managing employee terminations**—When an employee permanently leaves your operation, you should conduct an exit interview to find out why the employee is leaving, even if the termination was not the employee's choice. Compiling and analyzing information from exit interviews will help you continuously improve your operation and reduce turnover.

Throughout this cycle, ongoing activities support the administration of benefits, policies, payroll, and other functions. In addition, a direct and often dramatic influence on most human resources-related activities are the various legislative, executive, regulatory, and judicial decisions concerning discrimination and fair employment practices. While laws and rules are incentives for avoiding illegal discrimination practices, the benefits of diversity are strong incentives in their own right.

Benefits of a Diverse Working Environment

Providing a welcoming environment for employees is a way to encourage each person to do his or her best. It is a commitment to your employees that you value the quality of their work, want their working situation to be hospitable, and recognize the benefits of diversity. This welcoming environment also should extend to guests and vendors.

Creating an environment in which all people are valued has many benefits beyond fulfilling legal obligations. Encouraging and honoring differences can mean a larger and higher-quality labor pool, a more enjoyable and productive environment, improved public relations, and ultimately, more customers. It is also the right thing to do in a cultural environment that increasingly recognizes the importance of protecting people from discriminatory treatment and honoring individual differences.

Creates a More Enjoyable and Productive Environment

A broad, diverse workforce means that employees with different backgrounds will look at the same situations and challenges from a variety of viewpoints. These diverse views can lead to a more productive work environment and better creative problem solving, an especially valuable commodity in the fast-paced environment of most restaurants.

Employees with different backgrounds can contribute their talents and be recognized for making a difference. In addition, all employees can learn from one another and appreciate the value of different ethnic, racial, and cultural backgrounds. Sometimes this learning translates to helping with the dietary requirements of some guests; sometimes it means recognizing different ways of celebrating religious beliefs; and sometimes it means just learning

Activity

Noticing Differences

Make a list of the differences among students and the types of diversity in your class. Consider differences that are not necessarily protected by federal law, such as hair color or what year of school you are in. Compare your list to other students' lists and see if you came up with similar items.

_____

_____

_____

_____

_____

_____

about the lives of coworkers, so that everyone enjoys and respects each other more fully. All of these benefits contribute to creating a positive workplace.

Attracts More Customers

Recruiting and hiring people from a range of areas, including the local community, will help ensure your staff mirrors the community. This practice often builds new business from customers who feel more comfortable patronizing establishments where the staff is drawn from their community, or who want to support diverse businesses.

Another benefit is the publicity about your operation. Word will get around quickly that you are an equal opportunity employer who hires from the community, and you will find people asking you for work.

Increases Labor Pool

When an operation encourages diversity and demonstrates that value by hiring a diverse staff, more people will likely seek employment in such a positive environment. When there are persons of many ethnic heritages working in and patronizing your operation, the person who comes from a relatively small minority will feel less unusual. Potential employees (and guests) will recognize diversity and will feel more comfortable about seeking employment in your operation. For all these reasons and other business benefits, promoting an environment in which diversity is encouraged and honored helps potential job seekers view your operation as a viable place of employment.

With a wider range of potential employees to consider, the labor pool increases, and the chances of finding good employees increase dramatically as well. Given the difficulty of finding qualified employees and the high rate of turnover in the industry, any program that improves the quality of the labor pool is worth pursuing.

Improves Legal Protection

Promoting diversity also helps you fulfill legal requirements and better positions you to defend against any claims of illegal discrimination. If you provide a welcoming environment and honor differences, then employees will be less likely to feel mistreated and file complaints. If you ever do find yourself with a complaint, your policies, processes, and actions will provide a strong defense.

To gain these benefits, you need to understand several aspects of diversity in the workplace. The first and most basic of these is complying with the laws and regulations that prohibit discrimination.

Avoiding Illegal Discrimination

Discrimination is the ability to notice differences, and it is very appropriate when deciding among competing options—whether they are menu items when you are dining, or job applicants when you are hiring employees for your operation. The act of drawing distinction is perfectly proper, legal, and appropriate. In fact, making good judgments based on distinctions is an essential part of managing all aspects of human resources. However, making a biased and prejudiced choice is not legal, nor is it good business practice. Making such an arbitrary distinction—without an objective and business-related reason, or according to a whim—is dangerous and could be unethical and illegal as well.

One reason to consider the issue of arbitrary distinctions derives from the range of laws that protect applicants and employees against various forms of discrimination. In essence, these laws stipulate that employers cannot recruit, screen, hire, train, promote, discipline, terminate, or take any other employment action affecting individuals on the basis of criteria protected against discrimination under applicable federal, state, or local law. In addition, employers cannot create or allow an environment that is hostile to people based on certain characteristics. (See *Exhibit 1b*.) A **hostile environment** is one in which someone is exposed to unwelcome, intimidating, offensive, or antagonistic behavior, that interferes with his or her ability to perform a job and is based on a protected characteristic.

Federal, state, and local laws and regulations protect people from discrimination based on protected characteristics and ensure they are given equal employment opportunities. While these EEO laws and rules can seem overwhelming or confusing, the best way to ensure that you comply with all of the laws that apply to your business is to treat everyone equally, without regard to traits that have nothing to do with an employee's work responsibilities.

Exhibit 1b

Federally Protected Characteristics

Race

Color

Religion

Sex

National origin

Age (40 or older)

Disability

Military service

Pregnancy

Citizenship

Federal Equal Opportunity Employment Laws

The U.S. Equal Employment Opportunity Commission (EEOC) and other federal agencies enforce federal laws prohibiting discrimination on the basis of race, color, religion, sex, national origin, age (forty or older), disability, pregnancy, citizenship, and military service. These areas are known as federally **protected categories.** Individuals who share one of these characteristics, such as women or minorities, are called federally **protected classes** or **groups,** even though the protection is extended to all people. For example, discriminating against a white male because of his color or gender is just as illegal as discriminating against a member of a protected group based on color or gender.

The federal legislation that established a framework for practices prohibiting employment discrimination includes the following:

- **The Equal Pay Act of 1963** prohibits paying different wages to men and women on the basis of gender, if they are doing the same jobs in the same establishment.

- **The Age Discrimination in Employment Act of 1967 (ADEA)** prohibits employment discrimination on the basis of age for persons forty years or older.

- **Title I of the Americans with Disability Act of 1990 (ADA)** protects qualified individuals with a disability from discrimination with regard to any term, condition, or privilege of employment.

- **Title VII of the Civil Rights Act of 1964, as amended,** outlaws employment discrimination on the basis of race, color, religion, sex, and national origin. This act, as amended, also provides extensive remedies for such discrimination, which includes sexual harassment.

- **The Pregnancy Discrimination Act** is an amendment to Title VII stating that employment discrimination based on pregnancy, childbirth, or related medical conditions is prohibited as a form of sex discrimination.

- **The Immigration Reform and Control Act (IRCA)** outlaws discrimination based on national origin or citizenship and requires companies to verify citizenship for all employees.

- **The Uniformed Services Employment and Reemployment Rights Act (USERRA)** prohibits discrimination against people who serve or have served in the Armed Forces Reserve, National Guard, or other uniformed services, and protects their right to return to their civilian jobs after being away for military service or training.

These laws, along with others that affect daily operations, are covered in more detail in Chapter 12.

Think About It...

"If we cannot end now our differences, at least we can help make the world safe for diversity."

—John F. Kennedy

Rules Affecting Businesses That Contract with the Federal Government

Some operations also may be governed by additional EEO rules that further protect individual characteristics. These operations include:

- Businesses that contract with the federal government

- Businesses that provide services or supplies as a subcontractor to a business that contracts with the government

- Organizations that accept federal grants or funds, such as schools and hospitals

For example, foodservice operations that supply federal government facilities such as airports, and restaurants that operate within these facilities, may be required to follow additional rules.

The rules are specified in federal statutes and by executive orders that apply to certain businesses, generally based on the dollar amount of the business's government contract, or grants or funds received from the government. **Executive orders (EOs)** are proclamations issued by the President of the United States, with implementing regulations issued by federal agencies such as the U.S. Department of Labor. Executive orders and federal statutes often require **affirmative action programs** that actively take positive steps to eliminate existing, remedy past, and prevent future discrimination. For example:

- Executive Order 11246 requires affirmative action for minorities and women.

- Section 503 of the Federal Rehabilitation Act of 1973 mandates affirmative action for individuals with disabilities.

- The Vietnam Era Veterans' Readjustment Assistance Act of 1974 imposes affirmative action for veterans of the Vietnam era and certain disabled veterans.

While these additional federal rules apply to only some restaurants and foodservice operations, all businesses must follow any additional state and local EEO laws for their area.

State and Local Equal Employment Opportunity Laws

Most state and some local EEO laws also prohibit discrimination in the workplace, and these laws are often broader and more extensive than federal law. For example, some state and local laws prohibit workplace discrimination based on sexual preference, marital status, parental status, and appearance. In addition, these laws, while

Exhibit 1c

As a manager, you should nurture an environment that reinforces positive behavior and encourages diversity.

providing remedies similar to federal law, often provide penalties beyond what may exist under federal law and offer different administrative procedures in settling or resolving claims.

In a sense, equal opportunity laws define the floor of unacceptable discriminatory behavior in employment practices. As a manager, however, you want to promote positive behaviors and nurture an environment that recognizes differences and treats everyone well at all times. (See *Exhibit 1c*.)

To effectively and courageously promote diversity and manage diversity issues, you need to be able to distinguish between cultural tendencies that should be respected and factors that lead to arbitrary discrimination.

Prejudices, Stereotypes, Bias, and Cultural Tendencies

Since the field of hospitality employs many diverse groups, it can be easy to get caught in an atmosphere in which differences are stereotyped and prejudice is rampant. **Stereotypes** are generalizations that individuals make about particular groups which assume that all members of that group are the same. Stereotypes are often hard to change since they are usually not based on actual experience, and once embedded, take a lot of contrary experience to alter. For example, people who think that a certain group of people are always late, stupid, or not trustworthy are caught in stereotypes. In fact, all of these people are hurt by stereotyping—those who are inappropriately labeled by stereotypes, and those who think stereotypes are true. If you believe in stereotypes, these beliefs will cheat you out of genuine relationships with people and will cloud your personal and business judgment in untold ways.

Stereotypes produce **prejudice** or **bias**—a general attitude toward a person, group, or organization on the basis of judgments unrelated to abilities. Some of us are brought up in an environment in which we learn to like certain people and groups, and dislike others. Sometimes the prejudice comes from our own experience, and sometimes from the lessons taught by family members and other adult role models.

On the other hand, many groups of people do have common beliefs, such as religion, or share common ways of acting. These groups have **cultural tendencies** to do some things based on their beliefs and their habits. In contrast, stereotypes do not distinguish between what a group of people may tend to do or believe and what an individual does or believes.

Activity

Learning About Stereotypes

Consider the following statements and how you might complete them. Write your thoughts and feelings (on a separate piece of paper if needed), and then discuss them with your class. Are any of the statements stereotypes? Are any of them cultural tendencies?

1. Doctors are _____

2. Baptists are _____

3. Muslims are _____

4. African-Americans are _____

5. Plumbers are _____

6. Secretaries are _____

7. Computer professionals are _____

8. Short-order cooks are _____

9. New Englanders are _____

10. Texans are _____

Since there are many different groups of people employed in restaurants and foodservice operations, you want to set a climate in which you honor cultural tendencies and break down stereotypes. Building a team that works well together means helping everyone understand and value the strengths that individuals bring to work and exposing prejudice and stereotypes as the problems that they are. If you fail to do this, there will be many negative and, often, illegal consequences.

How Prejudice and Stereotypes Affect the Work Environment

In the restaurant and foodservice environment, prejudice and stereotyping have no place, but unfortunately, they are as alive and well here as they are in the broader society. People who do not want to work with a person from another culture, race, religious group, or specific gender are caught in habits and beliefs that run counter to honoring diversity and often are contrary to law. This is something that you, as a manager, cannot tolerate. You need to expose prejudice and bias whenever they occur and set the expectation that they will not be tolerated in your workplace.

To allow harassment means that employees will learn it is acceptable to treat each other as less than equals and colleagues; it also opens the door for the development of a culture of distrust and frustration—the opposite of what you want in your operation. If employees do not feel trusted or welcome, they will not work hard, their productivity will fall, and their willingness to help each other will diminish dramatically. The lower the morale, the higher the chances for conflict and turnover. The resulting malaise will mean a poorly

Think About It...

In what ways have you seen or heard people being mocked or teased because of their differences? How did that make you feel? What are some things you can do to change these situations?

functioning operation in which food will not be prepared well or on time, and customers will be unhappy. (See *Exhibit 1d.*)

Since discriminatory treatment in many cases is illegal, allowing it to happen in your operation opens you to the possibility of a complaint, investigation, or possible lawsuit. Current case law recognizes the importance of an environment free from harassment, in which an employee feels comfortable to do his or her job without being mocked, criticized, or mistreated on the basis of his or her differences from other employees. As a child, you may have observed the shorter, taller, or fatter child, or the one from a different area of town, or the one from a different religion being picked on because he or she was different. It was not good then, and it is not something to tolerate now in your workplace.

Promoting Diversity

Building a work environment in which people are honored for their contributions makes a real difference in an operation. It is important for employees to know that they are not being judged by immutable characteristics—those such as race and sex that cannot be changed, or their membership in some group, or their similarity to you as the manager or even the majority of your employees. To promote this culture of mutual respect and realize the benefits of diversity, you need to help break down the stereotypes that people hold and manage activities that impact diversity. These activities include actively recruiting for members of minority groups, increasing cross-cultural communication among employees, educating employees about diversity and discrimination, setting and communicating expectations for positive (or at least neutral) behavior, and holding employees and the organization accountable to these expectations.

Recruiting for Diversity

Recruiting members of minority groups is an active process that demonstrates your commitment to honor differences and encourage diversity while still trying to find the best qualified person regardless of race, color, national origin, or other differences. Your goal in recruiting should be to employ a diverse workforce, regardless of the diversity of the local community and your customer base. Sometimes accomplishing this takes a very active recruiting effort. For more information on recruiting practices, see Chapter 3.

Exhibit 1d

Prejudice versus Diversity

Effects of Prejudice	Effects of Diversity
Limits the labor pool	Increases the labor pool
Increases turnover; lowers morale	Promotes the operation as a viable employer
Stifles new ideas, talents, and perspectives	Encourages new ideas, talents, and perspectives
Increases conflict and misunderstanding	Encourages appreciation of other cultures
Decreases productivity	Creates a positive work environment
Decreases profitability	Builds business with new customers
Decreases customer service	Creates an environment where a diverse group of customers is comfortable
Increases likelihood of discrimination claims and litigation	Fulfills regulatory guidelines

Increasing Cross-Cultural Interaction and Communication

Encouraging **cross-cultural interaction,** or meaningful communication among employees from diverse cultures and backgrounds, helps break down stereotypes and prejudices and improves the workplace environment.

There are many ways to develop cross-cultural interaction. One way is to establish policies and procedures that clearly promote these goals. These policies and procedures should be based on a mission statement that integrates diversity into the operation's mission. From this foundation, other policies and procedures may be defined to encourage diversity and discourage prejudice and harassment.

Policies and procedures that recognize diverse backgrounds in a positive manner and do not tolerate harassment make it clear that all employees are valued and treated equally. Aggressive recruiting practices that seek out people of both genders from various cultural backgrounds, religions, physical conditions, races, colors, and national origins also convey the message that these differences are valued.

However, merely assembling a diverse staff is not enough on its own to foster positive cross-cultural interaction. As an individual manager, you can do many things to help employees of all cultures feel comfortable in your operation. One of the most important is modeling the behavior you expect from employees. If you participate in teasing, joke telling, or other behaviors that show you tolerate or even encourage stereotyping and discrimination, you will be sending the message that these behaviors are acceptable. In contrast, demonstrating how to encourage and honor diversity goes a long way toward establishing a hospitable and welcoming environment for all employees.

In addition to offering positive role models, holding diversity training sessions for people helps them overcome their fears and unfamiliarity of other cultures, especially if the training is a reward or enrichment rather than a punishment for violating diversity policies. In some operations, the manager conducts ongoing diversity training by learning then sharing facts about the customs, languages, and habits of different employees' cultures. (See *Exhibit 1e.*) By doing this, you can demonstrate that differences are fun to learn about and not something to be hidden, feared, or ashamed of. Each time you lead a diversity training session, you can contribute to making the work environment positive and welcoming.

Other activities that help increase positive cross-cultural interaction involve improving communication among various groups of people. The presence of many languages, primarily in the kitchen, can be an enriching environment that enables everyone to learn other languages. Learning at least a few key words of the languages spoken by employees in your operation can help these employees feel welcome and more comfortable. Using posters and charts with the languages spoken by your staff also improves communication, and offering training in relevant languages ensures that important knowledge and skills are learned. These multilingual materials also show the value of diversity in your operation.

Since language competency may vary among your employees, providing educational opportunities for those who want to learn English and improve their reading and writing skills can affect how well your employees interact as a group. However, sometimes employees are embarrassed to admit they have literacy problems. In these cases, try to arrange for classes or tutors to work with employees in private locations or at such times when other employees are engaged in other tasks.

Increasing cross-cultural interaction is an important part of reaping the benefits of diversity for your operation. This interaction is key to breaking down stereotypes and encouraging diverse groups of people to work as a team. To reap the full benefits of diversity, however, you need to promote it even more.

Exhibit 1e

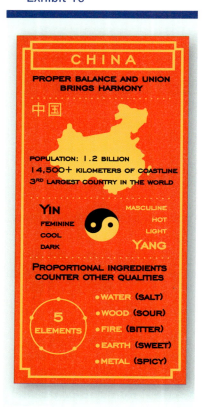

Cross-cultural education enhances awareness and understanding.

Activity

Sharing Cultures

Make a short list of facts about your own culture and share them with the class. If you do not identify with a particular ethnic group or culture, remember that even people from majority groups come from cultures.

_____

_____

_____

_____

Think About It...

Regular and periodic training programs work better than just annual splashes of diversity or anti-harassment training.

Educating Employees and Setting Expectations

Given the fast pace of restaurants and foodservice operations and the range of experience and educational levels among employees, reminding them to honor differences can be a constant struggle. Regrettably, kitchens and dining rooms are sometimes places where people are teased or mocked because of their race, religion, gender, sexual orientation, disabling condition, age, or other traits. Sometimes that behavior builds a team culture of "us versus them," but unfortunately, the cost of this type of team building is detrimental to employees, and the behavior is sometimes illegal.

Part of promoting diversity is educating employees about the value of tolerance and teamwork and the inappropriateness of hostility and harassment on any basis. Employees must be educated about which behaviors are acceptable in the workplace and which are not. As a manager, you must set the expectation that harassment, hostility, prejudicial treatment, and stereotyping have no place in your operation.

As part of this effort, most organizations post their policies about harassment, honoring differences, and recruiting. In addition, the EEOC requires companies to post a notice about laws prohibiting discrimination. Some organizations also hold periodic meetings or training events about diversity and promoting tolerance. Common topics for these events include avoiding and managing sexual harassment and racial stereotyping. In your establishment, you will know what needs to be done, given the different backgrounds of employees and the culture of your operation.

Regardless of your company's approach, communicating a consistent message of tolerance and expectations is important. As a manager, you should provide continuing education about the value of diversity and encourage tolerance in every way that you can. One way to show that you are serious about this is to make honoring diversity a criterion on the employee performance evaluation form.

Once employees understand the benefits of diversity, your company's policies on discrimination and harassment, and the behavior expected of them, you will need to hold them accountable for any hostile or unacceptable behavior. In fact, the law requires this.

Addressing Issues and Holding People Accountable

Beyond communicating policies, you must take steps to stop, prevent, and address any issues of discrimination or hostility that arise and hold people accountable for their actions. Prompt attention to the issues and holding people accountable for their actions are critical to promoting diversity and protecting the operation from liability.

As a manager, you need to be diligent about ensuring your operation welcomes all people equally. You should actively look for signs of discriminatory behavior or elements of a hostile environment, such as inappropriate joking, teasing, comments, or name-calling or improper cartoons, posters, or notes posted in common places. (See *Exhibit 1f*.) Stop discriminatory behavior as soon as you see it—do not wait until someone complains. Also, encourage your employees to come to you with their concerns. Reinforce that there will never be retaliation against them for coming forward with a concern.

If you see or hear about discriminatory behavior, address the issue promptly. Consistently follow your operation's guidelines and policies for investigating and managing these issues in a fair and reasonable manner. When warranted, hold employees accountable for their behavior. A consistent record of addressing these issues shows that you really do mean what you say and that you want the work environment to be tolerant.

Sometimes, intervening can put you in the middle of a conflict. In these cases, it is helpful to focus on the issue and not on the personalities of the people involved. Remember your long-range goals, and focus on correcting and reshaping employees' behavior. Also keep in mind that some people mean well but may not understand how their behavior discourages a welcoming environment. Others may know better but have not learned what is and is not tolerated in your workplace. As previously mentioned, continuing education and communication help to reduce the possibility of these situations occurring.

Exhibit 1f

Improper cartoons should not be posted in common work areas.

Whenever you intervene to correct a behavior, your actions can have a tremendous impact on the entire workforce. Other employees soon will learn that you are serious about antidiscrimination policies and a welcoming environment, and they will act accordingly. Hopefully, establishing the right tone will eliminate the need for intervention, but this may be necessary to create the welcoming and hospitable environment that you want.

Activity

Dealing with Intolerance

Assume you are a supervisor in a multiunit restaurant operation. Sabrina, a new employee, complains to you that a coworker has been mocking her since he saw her praying while on her break several days ago. How will you handle her complaint?

_____

_____

_____

Summary

The restaurant and foodservice industry contains one of the most diverse workforces. In this industry, encouraging diversity means you treat *all* people—employees, vendors, and guests—in a nondiscriminatory manner; that is, without regard to race, color, national origin, and any other trait not related to that person's role at your establishment. Diversity issues and antidiscrimination policies impact every aspect of human resources, from finding and recruiting potential employees to managing employee terminations.

Creating an environment in which all people are valued has many benefits. Encouraging and honoring differences can mean a larger and better quality labor pool, a more enjoyable and productive environment, improved public relations, and most important, more customers. Promoting diversity also helps you fulfill regulatory guidelines and better positions you to defend against any claims of illegal discrimination.

Discrimination is appropriate when deciding among competing options, but making arbitrary distinctions could be unethical and illegal. Employers cannot base employment actions on characteristics protected under applicable federal, state, or local laws against discrimination. In addition, employers cannot create or allow an environment that is hostile to people based on these characteristics.

Federal law prohibits workplace discrimination based on race, color, religion, sex, national origin, age (forty or older), pregnancy, citizenship, disability, and military service. In addition, organizations that contract with the federal government, provide services or supplies as a subcontractor to a business that contracts with the government, or accept federal grants or funds may be governed by additional equal employment opportunity rules.

To promote and manage diversity, you need to be able to distinguish among stereotypes and prejudice, which should be discouraged, and cultural tendencies, which should be respected. Stereotypes are generalizations that individuals make about particular groups and the assumptions that all members of that group are the same. Stereotypes produce prejudice or bias, a general attitude toward a person, group, or organization on the basis of stereotypes unrelated to abilities. In contrast, many groups of people have cultural tendencies, or common beliefs and ways of acting. The main difference between stereotypes and cultural tendencies is that stereotypes do not distinguish between what a group of people may tend to do or believe, and what an individual actually does or believes.

Since discriminatory treatment often is illegal, allowing it to happen in your operation exposes you to the possibility of a complaint, investigation, or possible lawsuit. In addition, when discrimination and harassment are allowed, a culture of distrust and frustration is likely to develop. Employee productivity will fall, and their willingness to help each other will diminish dramatically. Morale will drop, and conflict and turnover will increase. Ultimately, these conditions will result in a poorly functioning operation.

To promote a culture of mutual respect, you need to help break down the stereotypes that people hold and manage activities that impact diversity. These activities include actively recruiting for members of minority groups, increasing cross-cultural communication among employees, educating employees about diversity and discrimination, setting and communicating expectations for positive (or at least neutral) behavior, and holding employees and the organization accountable to these expectations.

Review Your Learning

1 List the ten categories of people protected from discrimination by federal equal employment opportunity (EEO) laws.

_____

_____

_____

_____

_____

_____

_____

_____

_____

_____

2 List four ways that stereotypes and prejudice can affect a workplace.

_____

_____

_____

_____

3 List four benefits of diversity.

_____

_____

_____

_____

4 List three ways to increase positive cross-cultural interaction and communication.

_____

_____

_____

5 Which of these laws prohibits discrimination against five of the federally protected categories?

A. Title VII of the Civil Rights Act

B. Vietnam Era Veterans' Readjustment Assistance Act

C. Rehabilitation Act

D. Equal Pay Act

6 Which of these statements best describes how diversity relates to foodservice?

A. Diversity means ignoring the presence of stereotypes or discriminatory beliefs even when they result in higher turnover, reduced profits, and discrimination claims.

B. Diversity means asking employees to ignore their own and their coworkers' cultural customs at work to ensure that everyone acts as part of a team.

C. Diversity means preventing harassment and being responsible for ensuring a safe environment free from crime and other illegal behavior.

D. Diversity means recognizing and respecting the differences among people and treating employees, vendors, and guests in a nondiscriminatory way.

7 Which of these practices are critical for promoting diversity in the workplace?

A. Recruiting for diversity and promoting people based on their protected characteristics

B. Addressing diversity issues and holding people accountable

C. Acting as a role model for both positive and negative behavior

D. Increasing cross-cultural interaction and keeping records of this interaction

Notes

Defining Job Descriptions

2

Inside This Chapter

- What Is a Job Description?
- Related Documents and Terminology
- Function of Job Descriptions
- Analyzing a Job
- Developing Job Descriptions
- Distinguishing between Exempt and Nonexempt Positions
- Maintaining Job Descriptions

After completing this chapter, you should be able to:

- Define job description.
- Identify the functions of a job description.
- Identify the minimum information needed for a good job description.
- Explain how the Americans with Disabilities Act (ADA) affects the information in a job description.
- Recognize the differences between exempt and nonexempt positions.
- Recognize the importance of periodically reviewing job descriptions.

Test Your Knowledge

1. **True or False:** The job description is a form developed for human resources professionals. *(See p. 23.)*

2. **True or False:** Job specifications and job descriptions are the same thing. *(See p. 24.)*

3. **True or False:** Job descriptions can support many functions in an operation. *(See pp. 25–27.)*

4. **True or False:** A job description should include the actual responsibilities of a job. *(See pp. 23, 29.)*

5. **True or False:** An exempt job is not eligible for overtime pay. *(See p. 35.)*

Key Terms

Back of the house (BOH)

Bona fide occupational
    qualifications (BFOQ)

Class

Competencies

Essential functions

Exempt

Front of the house (FOH)

Grade

Hourly

Job analysis

Job description

Job specifications

Nonexempt

Performance standards

Reasonable accommodation

Salaried

Scope of a job

Undue hardship

Introduction

Job descriptions have often been one of the lowest priority items for managers of restaurant and foodservice operations. These documents take a lot of time to prepare, are often ignored in the reality of daily operations, and sometimes seem designed for other audiences rather than the people doing the work. However, well-written job descriptions provide employees with a clear sense of the scope of their work. In addition, one document provides everyone—managers, employees, human resources professionals—with information that explains what a person needs to do and to whom a person reports. Because of this, good job descriptions can be the foundation of many functions in both large and small operations.

Applications of the Job Description in the Employment Cycle

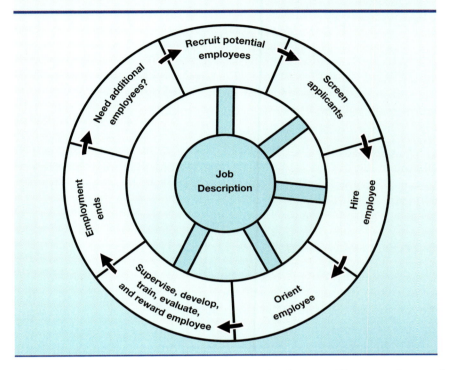

Job Description

Recruit potential employees

Screen applicants

Hire employee

Orient employee

Supervise, develop, train, evaluate, and reward employee

Employment ends

Need additional employees?

What Is a Job Description?

A job description is a document that defines the work involved in a particular assignment or position. A job description includes the position title and the responsibilities or duties of a position. The responsibilities include both essential and nonessential functions performed by the person holding that position. As depicted in *Exhibit 2a,* the job description is a helpful tool for human resources and management in recruiting and maintaining employees.

Many job descriptions also include educational and legal requirements for holding the position, such as a diploma or sanitation certificate, and organizational information, such as to whom the position reports. Other organizational information commonly included is the class or salary grade of the position.

Because a job description identifies the scope of a job, it helps set employees' expectations. Job descriptions also define the boundaries between positions so there is no confusion about who is responsible for doing what.

How Much Can You Remember?

See how much you can remember about a foodservice job you held. What were your day-to-day duties? What special responsibilities did you have? On a separate piece of paper, write a brief summary of the job. You may find you did a lot more on the job than you thought you did.

Related Documents and Terminology

To have a clearer understanding of what a job description is and what it is not, it helps to be familiar with related documents and terminology.

Job Descriptions and Job Specifications

Some job descriptions include job specifications—the qualifications a person should have to do the job. These qualifications may specify the education or experience required, as well as the mental, emotional, and physical skills necessary to do the job. Attitudes, especially for positions in the dining room, or front of the house (FOH), may be specified as well. (The kitchen and other areas where customers do not go are known as the back of the house [BOH].) Job specifications can be included in a job description or can appear in a separate document.

Job Descriptions and Performance Standards

The duties that make up a job description are also used in performance standards. Typically, job descriptions identify the duties that comprise a job, while performance standards identify *how well* and possibly *how often* or *how quickly* a duty must be completed. *Exhibit 2b* lists a few examples of different duties written as job descriptions and as performance standards. Performance standards are usually not part of a job description, although some operations may include them.

Exhibit 2b

Duties as Job Descriptions and Performance Standards

Duty as a job description	Duty as a performance standard
Greet drive-through customers.	Greet drive-through customers using the standard greeting within fifteen seconds of their arrival at the drive-through board.
Clean and stock the restrooms.	Clean and stock the restrooms once per shift so that toilet paper and soap dispensers are full; empty any full waste receptacles; and clean the vanities, mirrors, commodes, and floors according to house standards.
Prepare the station for work.	Set up a cutting board, sanitation solution, appropriate equipment, and ingredients according to standards and within fifteen minutes of starting the shift.
Stock a side stand in the dining room.	Check the contents of the side stand, replace all equipment up to par level, and ensure that all equipment is clean and ready to use.

Function of Job Descriptions

There is a wide range of reasons for clear and thorough job descriptions. Job descriptions provide employees with a clear definition of what their position entails. Additionally, job descriptions provide a critical foundation for many other functions in an operation, from recruiting to termination, as well as salary administration, safety, union relations, and legal issues.

Recruiting and Screening

Job descriptions are useful for recruiting and screening possible new employees because of their clarity and comprehensiveness. The educational background and work history expectations that are often included in job descriptions provide information that can be used to advertise the position and help candidates self-screen. In screening activities, the job description provides a foundation for evaluating job applicants and developing legally defensible interview questions and screening practices.

Hiring and Orientation

In hiring and orienting new employees, the job description helps clarify for the new hire what the job entails and provides direction for both the hiring and orientation programs. This direction is also extended to training and employee development programs.

Employee Development and Training

When evaluating employee performance as part of a training or employee development program, managers often go back to the job description, not only to see how an individual's performance compares to work expectations, but also to consider areas that need more training. In addition, having clear job descriptions makes it easier to identify how to develop or groom employees for other positions.

Performance Programs and Evaluations

A job description plays an integral role in performance programs because it provides basic information and regular expectations for that position. This information can provide useful benchmarks for evaluations, but a better use is to build on that information and create a performance program for each employee. This includes establishing goals for the employee based on the job description duties, extending those goals where appropriate, or focusing on areas where the employee is not performing so well.

Exhibit 2c

Job descriptions provide a foundation for performance programs and a starting point during performance evaluations.

A job description used during performance evaluations provides a starting point for a conversation about the work performed during the evaluation period. (See *Exhibit 2c*.) However, the performance evaluation usually covers more topics than just the job description, such as teamwork with colleagues and adherence to and support for the policies of the operation.

Salary Administration

Job descriptions, along with job specifications, can provide the basis for structuring compensation or salary ranges for positions. The descriptions provide a starting point for pooling jobs into grades and classes. **Grades** are categories of jobs that fit into a defined salary range. **Classes** are clusters of jobs that have common information bases or skill areas. For example, all culinary positions would be in a culinary class. (See *Exhibit 2d*.) In some operations, the terms *class* and *grade* are used interchangeably. For related information, see the section *Distinguishing between Exempt and Nonexempt Positions* on pp. 34–35.

Exhibit 2d

Example of Classes and Grades

	Classes		
Grades	**Culinary**	**Dining Room Staff**	**Administration**
Executive	Executive chef	Dining room manager	Director, human resources
Managerial	Sous chef	Captain	Human resources manager
Specialist	Baker	Sommelier or wine steward	Human resources specialist
Senior	Senior line cook	Senior waitstaff	Senior personnel administrator
Mid-level	Line cook	Waitstaff	Personnel administrator
Entry level	Prep cook/dishwasher	Busser	Personnel assistant

Job descriptions and job specifications make it easier to compare positions both within an operation and outside an operation. For example, the title "dining room manager" can encompass vastly different responsibilities depending on the operation. Job comparisons are done primarily by large organizations that use compensation specialists to set up or study job classifications and grades. However, even small operations can use job descriptions informally to help determine if the salaries they offer are competitive.

Exhibit 2e

Job descriptions can define responsibilities for safety and security.

Safety and Security

Job descriptions can formally define responsibilities for ensuring safety and security and preventing injuries. For example, a cook position might include duties for ensuring food safety, such as "Handle, prepare, and store food following HACCP guidelines." A manager position might include duties for ensuring security while closing a restaurant, such as ensuring that the facility is locked and the alarm is set. (See *Exhibit 2e*.)

Union Relations

Job descriptions are often the subject of intense scrutiny when misunderstandings occur between a union employee and his or her supervisors, or when there are union grievances. In addition, job descriptions clarify the **scope of a job**—the range of responsibilities a person is expected to undertake—which is sometimes a factor during contract negotiations.

Legal Proceedings

Ultimately, job descriptions are consulted in any kind of lawsuit, administrative hearing (for discrimination claims), or other legal proceedings. The better these documents are written, the more protection an operation has against claims.

Analyzing a Job

Developing a job description can be challenging because the document serves so many functions. Before you can begin to write a good job description, you need to have a clear picture of all aspects of the position. This is where a job analysis comes in. Typically conducted by supervisors, human resources professionals, or the persons doing the job, a **job analysis** identifies the following information (see *Exhibit 2f*):

Exhibit 2f

Employees may be involved in the job analysis.

- Detailed breakdown of the duties involved in a position

- Skills, knowledge, attitudes, and experience a person should bring to the position

- Environmental conditions of the job

Once the duties are identified, you can organize them into statements that accurately summarize the responsibilities of the position. However, not all of the information identified in a job analysis may be used in the job description.

Developing Job Descriptions

From the job analysis, you can develop a job description. A well-written job description includes not only the minimum information needed to understand the job, but also presents the information in a carefully worded way. First, the job description should be free of discriminatory language. Second, the job description—especially the responsibilities—needs to strike a balance between being too specific and not specific enough. The description should be specific enough to give people a good idea of what the job entails and to support the various functions in an operation. However, the job description should not include so much detail that it defines the job in rigid or narrow terms. A narrow job description can be hard to maintain, become quickly outdated, and discourage teamwork.

Components of a Good Job Description

A good job description is comprised of the following minimum components. Each is identified by a numbered red box on the sample job descriptions in *Exhibits 2g* and *2h* on pp. 31–32.

O*NET, a consortium sponsored by the U.S. Department of Labor, Employment and Training Administration (ETA), publishes a Web site that provides occupational information geared toward schools, employers, students, and job seekers. The O*NET Web site *(online.onetcenter.org)* provides lists of tasks, job titles, knowledge, skills, and abilities needed for various jobs, which can be used as the basis for job descriptions or résumés.

1 **Job identification information**—Includes the job title and other identifying information used by the operation, such as the job grade or class.

2 **Position supervisor**—Indicates to whom the position reports. (The supervisor is expressed as another title, not as an actual person's name.) Sometimes information about other work relationships is included, such as other positions the position works closely with. For example, a cook may be supervised by the executive chef but may work very closely with other cooks, the dishwasher, butcher, dining room staff, and sous chef. This particular type of information might be included when teamwork is one of the key values of the operation.

3 **Job summary**—A short paragraph that explains the core duties of the position. It provides an overall view of what the job entails and is often used in advertisements for job openings. These summaries can vary in style from organization to organization and can provide a lot of information or very little.

4 **Responsibilities**—The duties or major responsibilities of the job that describe what a person in this position does. Duties often start with "action verbs" that identify something visible or demonstrable—for example, "cook," "serve," or "prepare." Duties for positions that have the same title can vary greatly from operation to operation. In some cases, the duties include references to safety and sanitation policies, company procedures, and teamwork goals because these policies and procedures are so important. Such references can have the added benefit of helping to protect an operation in case of legal problems related to safety, liability, or discrimination.

5 **Job specifications**—Typically used by larger operations, the job specification indicates the background, education, or skills a person should bring to the job or the mental, emotional, or physical skills associated with the position. Sometimes, job specifications are expressed as **competencies,** the general capabilities needed to perform a duty.

Some organizations also include the following information in a job description:

6 **Job setting information**—Includes a physical description of the primary locations of the job, such as the kitchen or dining room. Sometimes this information includes descriptions about the work setting, such as a hot and noisy kitchen or a dimly lit dining room.

7 **Publication information**—Identifies who wrote the description or who is responsible for its content, and the date it was approved or published. This information helps to identify how recently a job description was reviewed.

Information to Leave Out

The value of a job description lies in its clarity—how well it defines a job for the person doing the job and the supervisor of that job. This clarity depends on the information included in the description and the information left out. Too much information can make the job description cumbersome and difficult to maintain, which reduces the chances of it being kept up to date.

However, there is other information that is just as important for employees to understand, but which is not normally found in the job description. This information includes the various operational policies and procedures on such topics as promptness, illness, food sanitation, uniform and dress code, cleanliness, cordiality, and theft. These policies are often addressed in employee handbooks and policy statements, or they may be addressed in a multitude of other documents, including operation standards, performance standards, various checklists, and training documents. Some of these documents are explained in more detail in later chapters.

Since most of these policies and procedures apply to many or all employees, putting them in every job description would be redundant, even though they are important and often part of employee evaluations. Safety and sanitation responsibilities, for example, should be included because they are critical responsibilities. In a job description, this information is often covered by tasks that reference general policies or other documents. A few examples of these types of references might be:

■ "Follows all policies and procedures as stated in the Employee Handbook."

■ "Cleans and sanitizes work areas following company sanitation practices."

Exhibit 2g

Sample Job Description 1

Position Title: **Expeditor** ─── 1

Reports to: Restaurant manager ─── 2 **Works closely with:** Cooks, sous chef, waitstaff

Position Summary ─── 3

The expeditor functions as the communication link among the various food production areas in the kitchen, and ensures the coordination and smooth flow of quality products as they are produced and assembled, so that servers may deliver meal orders to dining room patrons in a timely manner.

Duties and Competencies ─── 4

1 Sets up the food production line by checking the worktable, counter, broil station, fry station, and line freezer to ensure they are properly stacked prior to the mean production period. *Competencies: Resources* ─── 5

2 Checks all assembly stations for presence of appropriate small equipment, assembler materials, and stock levels. *Competencies: Resources*

3 Monitors all food production areas for safety and sanitation practices and procedures. Checks walk-in refrigerators and dry-storage area for cleanliness and orderliness, and provides direction/takes action as necessary. *Competencies: Resources, Information, Systems*

4 Sets up production cycles, ensures proper inventory levels are available, and calls to replenish items as necessary. *Competencies: Resources, Interpersonal*

5 Reads order tickets as they arrive, calls out orders to line stations in order of sequence (appetizer, salad, entrée item, etc.). Tracks cooking time on all orders, checks finished product for proper degree of doneness and appearance, and passes on items and order tickets to cook assemblers. *Competencies: Interpersonal, Information, Systems*

6 Controls flow of work, determines when to call out orders to production personnel, and gives tickets to assemblers based on volume and individual employee capacity to handle production. *Competencies: Interpersonal, Information, Systems*

7 Checks assemblers' work for quality and presentation. *Competencies: Resources, Interpersonal*

8 Periodically monitors production to see which individuals need assistance, checks food and material supplies, takes action as necessary. *Competencies: Resources, Information*

9 Communicates clearly and efficiently to food production personnel, receives information and feedback from them on their needs, and takes action based on observation and information received. *Competencies: Resources, Interpersonal, Systems, Information*

10 Cleans and sanitizes work stations on an ongoing basis during meal preparation periods and at the end of the meal period. Monitors work of kitchen staff in the completion of their close-down duties and responsibilities. *Competencies: Resources, Interpersonal, Systems*

Prerequisites ─── 5

High school diploma desired, some college beneficial. Must be able to communicate clearly and effectively and understand the primary languages used in the work area.

Experience: Previous experience in food production essential, dining room service experience beneficial, as are demonstrated organizational and management skills.

Physical: Requires bending, climbing, and reaching for periods of up to four hours at one time; ability to move expeditiously around the kitchen and storage areas; and carrying items up to twenty-five pounds on a regular and routine basis. Must possess visual acuity and communication ability.

Exhibit 2h

Sample Job Description 2

Position Title: Waitstaff

1

Job Title:	Waiter/Waitress
Location:	Dining room — **6**
Reports to:	Dining room manager — **2**
Level/Grade:	C3

Type of position:
- ☒ Full-time
- ☐ Part-time
- ☐ Contractor
- ☐ Intern

Hours: _40–50/week_

- ☐ Exempt
- ☒ Nonexempt

General Description — **3**

Welcomes customers, takes food and beverage orders, and serves orders. Presents professional and friendly image to customers at all times. Maintains side stands and prepares tables for service. Communicates and works effectively with other waitstaff and kitchen staff.

Duties — **4**

- Learns and explains menu items
- Welcomes customers in a hospitable manner
- Provides information about beverages and food items promptly and positively
- Records orders
- Checks customers' identification to make sure they can legally consume alcohol
- Serves tables promptly and professionally
- Maintains high service standards of the restaurant
- Sets up side stands

5

- Collects and polishes flatware and glassware for tables
- Sets all tables with linens, plates, glasses, flatware, and accessories according to dining room standards
- Prepares tables for service at the beginning of each shift
- Maintains personal hygiene
- Works effectively with other waitstaff and kitchen staff
- Uses professional practices in all situations
- Performs other tasks as assigned

Work Experience Requirements

- Two years of waiting on tables in à la carte settings or two years of banquet/catering waiting experience
- Experience with customer service
- Knowledge of dining room procedures and practices

7

Education Requirements

- High school diploma
- Over twenty-one years old
- College education a plus

Reviewed by

[signature] Date: Aug 23

Human Resources Manager

Approved by

[signature] Date: 08-23-08

Executive Chef, Director of Food and Beverages, General Manager

Avoiding Discrimination in Job Descriptions

Writing a job description takes care and sensitivity since you need to avoid defining a job in a discriminatory way. One challenge is to write job descriptions in a way that helps you comply with the Americans with Disabilities Act (ADA). To do this, focus on the results or outcomes of a duty, identify the essential functions of the position, and describe them in clear and neutral language. **Essential functions** are the key duties that an individual must be able to perform in order to do the work. For example, the job description for a sauté cook might include these essential functions:

- Identifies and prepares selected cuts of meat, poultry, shellfish, fish, or vegetables for sautéing

- Prepares items for sautéing

- Sautés and prepares appropriate sauces

- Plates sautéed items with appropriate garnishes

- Maintains a well-organized and sanitary workstation

Exhibit 2i

Employers may need to accommodate some employees.

Honoring the spirit and intent of the ADA legislation means that managers may be asked to clarify what is involved in specific duties and whether there are alternate ways to accomplish them. These alternate ways are known as **reasonable accommodation,** which is defined by the Equal Employment Opportunity Commission as "a change in the job application process, a change in the way a job is performed in the work environment, or a change to other parts of the job (like employer-sponsored training, benefits, or social events) that enables a person with a disability to have equal employment opportunities." (See *Exhibit 2i.*)

However, an employer does not need to accommodate a person if doing so would cause an **undue hardship,** which is defined as an action that is excessively costly, extensive, or substantial in relation to an employer's size and financial resources, or that would fundamentally alter the nature or operation of the business. Providing reasonable accommodation is discussed in more detail in Chapter 5.

The clearer the job description, the easier it will be to address questions of accommodation and to distinguish among those parts of the job where accommodation is not possible. For example, if a person has an allergic reaction to meat or the inability to hold a knife and use it, then that person cannot be a butcher even if he or she applies, since there is no way to accommodate for that allergy and the lack of that motor skill. However, a busser in an institutional foodservice setting may not be able to carry heavy trays, but can make more trips or be provided with a cart to use in clearing tables. (For more information on the Americans with Disabilities Act, see Chapter 11.)

Finally, when including job specifications for a job, make sure they identify only the **bona fide occupational qualifications (BFOQ)** for the job—the realistic range of skills or credentials needed to perform the essential functions of the job. For example, you cannot specify gender as a job specification unless it is necessary for performing the functions of the job, such as specifying a female for the position of women's restroom attendant. A good job description provides information about the tasks in such a way that the physical and intellectual requirements are honest and accurate.

Activity

Writing a Job Description

You are a manager who needs to develop job descriptions for your employees. As a class, conduct a job analysis by interviewing one student about his or her current job. Afterward, write your own job description for this position on a separate piece of paper. Be prepared to share your job description with the class.

Distinguishing between Exempt and Nonexempt Positions

In developing a job description, you may need to distinguish between exempt employees and nonexempt employees. These categories are defined by the Fair Labor Standards Act (FLSA), which provides different rules for paying employees based on the duties of their jobs and other factors. For positions that are covered under this law, it

Think About It...

According to the U.S. Department of Labor, Bureau of Labor Statistics, restaurant foodservice managers held about 386,000 jobs in 2002. Most of these positions were salaried, and almost three-fourths of these salaried jobs were in full-service restaurants or limited-service eating establishments, such as quick-service restaurants and cafeterias. Conversely, about one-third of the 346,000 foodservice manager jobs were self-employed positions in independent restaurants or other small foodservice establishments.

specifies a minimum wage and when overtime pay is required. Positions that are **exempt**—not covered under this law—are not legally entitled to overtime pay or the minimum wage established by the FLSA. Exempt positions are also known as **salaried** positions because their compensation is based on a set salary rather than an hourly wage. Conversely, positions that are covered by the FLSA are known as **nonexempt** or **hourly** positions.

Exempt employees are normally managerial employees with the authority to discipline, evaluate, and terminate others under the policies of the operation, and they carry responsibility for planning and management. They exercise independent judgment and often have significant discretional decision-making authority. However, there are nonmanagerial employees who are also exempt. In general, exempt employees should not spend more than 50 percent of their time performing the same work as hourly employees, though this is not the only test for exempt status. Federal and state rules can be complex on this issue, it is always advisable to seek advice from your human resources official or legal counsel about determining status.

On the other hand, nonexempt employees can be paid overtime since they are regular employees doing the bulk of the work in an operation. Normally, they operate within clear boundaries and do not have broad authority. Assistant managers, however, have a certain amount of decision-making authority, yet they are normally considered nonexempt. From an employee's point of view, being nonexempt means that you can be paid overtime at state and federal rates (e.g., time-and-a-half for normal days and double-time for holidays). Depending on their hours, nonexempt employees can make significantly more money than exempt employees. *Exhibit 2j* on the next page lists some of the qualifications that constitute exempt and nonexempt positions. Cooks, dishwashers, wait staff, bussers, janitors, catering staff, catering sales persons, clerical staff, receptionists, and hostesses are typically nonexempt employees. Dining room managers, executive chefs, banquet chefs, pastry chefs, and general managers are typically exempt.

Maintaining Job Descriptions

Often, reviewing a job description can be an eye-opening experience both for an employee and a supervisor, especially if they have been working together successfully for some time and have not bothered to refer to the document. This phenomenon occurs because the responsibilities and other information for a position can change over time.

Exhibit 2j

Exempt versus Nonexempt Positions

Traits	Exempt Positions	Nonexempt Positions
Typical jobs	Managers and specialists	Staff members and assistant supervisors
Pay structure	Salaried—not eligible for overtime pay	Hourly—eligible for overtime pay at state and federal rates
Duties	Can spend as much as 20 percent of the day performing the tasks of a nonexempt (hourly) employee	May perform some management duties
Range of responsibility	Can hire, discipline, evaluate, and terminate other employees according to company policy	Hiring, disciplining, evaluating, and terminating other employees is generally not part of their responsibilities
Planning roles	Are responsible for planning and management	Not generally responsible for planning and management
Use of judgment	Use discretion and judgment as a routine part of their jobs	Not expected to use a lot of discretion and judgment in their jobs

Some of the reasons job descriptions may change include:

- Responsibilities or reporting structures may change as an operation grows or changes.

- Responsibilities may change as an employee's abilities grow or change (assuming the employee keeps the same position and title).

- Job specifications and responsibilities may change to accommodate new regulations.

- New equipment may affect responsibilities or job specifications.

- New menu items or modes of operation may affect responsibilities or job specifications.

- New union contracts may change responsibilities or job specifications.

Periodically reviewing job descriptions and updating them as needed is a good practice. Typically, job descriptions are reviewed at least once a year when they are used as part of the annual evaluation of employees. Most human resources policies call for supervisors to review the job description at that time and make suggestions for amendments or changes.

Summary

Job descriptions are documents that define the work involved in a particular assignment or position. Job descriptions are primarily intended as a tool to help an employee understand his or her job. However, they also support recruiting, screening, hiring, orienting, development, training, performance programs and evaluations, salary administration, safety, union relations, and legal support.

A good job description starts with a thorough job analysis. A well-written job description includes at least the following information: (1) job identification information, which may include whether a position is exempt or nonexempt; (2) position supervisor information; (3) job summary; (4) responsibilities; and (5) job specifications. Some job descriptions also include job setting and publication information. The responsibilities should be written as duties and may include performance standards, although most operations do not do this.

A good job description avoids discriminatory language. Doing this involves writing the description honestly with a focus on the duties and bona fide occupational qualifications and using neutral language. To ensure job descriptions stay relevant, they should be reviewed periodically and updated as needed.

Review Your Learning

1 Which statement best describes a job description?

A. Document used by auditors to determine payroll tax exemptions

B. Series of documents that define what a person is supposed to do on the job

C. Document that defines the work involved in a particular assignment or position

D. Document that defines the work a person is supposed to do in an evaluation period

2 Circle the letter next to each type of information that should be included in a good job description.

A. Position supervisor

B. Salary or wage

C. Name of operation owner or president

D. Job creation date

E. Job identification information

F. Uniform requirements

G. Responsibilities

H. Smoking and break policies

I. Job summary

J. Job specifications

K. Career path information

L. Benefit information

3 It is important to periodically review job descriptions because the

A. employee can outgrow the position over time.

B. position's salary and benefits can change.

C. person doing the job or the supervisor can change.

D. responsibilities and other information can change.

4 Circle the letter next to each function that a job description can support.

A. Public relations and operation marketing

B. Legal proceedings

C. Employee development and training

D. Paid and unpaid leaves of absence

E. Safety and security

F. Performance programs and evaluations

G. Menu planning

H. Benefit administration

I. Hiring and orientation

J. Shift management

K. Union relations

L. Operational goal setting

M. Customer service

N. Salary administration

5 What is the best way to avoid using discriminatory language in a job description?

A. Include a disclaimer on the job description stating that the operation is an equal opportunity employer.

B. Write the duties in the briefest way possible and summarize the job using clear and neutral language.

C. Write in a clear and neutral way and focus on identifying how well the duties should be performed.

D. Write in a clear and neutral way and focus on the essential functions and bona fide occupational qualifications.

6 Which statement best describes an exempt position?

A. Salaried position with the authority to discipline, evaluate, and terminate others

B. Hourly position requiring specialized skills

C. Any position with the authority to discipline, evaluate, and terminate others

D. Position that is eligible for overtime pay

Finding and Recruiting New Employees

After completing this chapter, you should be able to:

- Identify information that can be used to forecast staffing needs.
- Identify common sources of potential employees in the restaurant and foodservice industry.
- Communicate a job opening to internal and external audiences.
- Describe methods for maintaining relationships with sources of potential employees.
- Avoid using discriminatory language in advertisements for job openings.
- Describe how to track and analyze the results of recruiting.

Test Your Knowledge

1 **True or False:** The goal of building connections with local schools, technical training organizations, and colleges is to have a chance to guest lecture. *(See pp. 53–54.)*

2 **True or False:** Internal recruiting means hiring employees already on staff. *(See pp. 45–47.)*

3 **True or False:** If you do a good job at forecasting staffing needs, you can predict when to recruit, hire, and train employees, so they can be productive when you need them. *(See p. 42.)*

4 **True or False:** In a job advertisement, identifying a job as "ideal for students" is discriminatory. *(See p. 60.)*

5 **True or False:** Networking is the least productive method of recruiting. *(See p. 49.)*

Key Terms

Blind ads	Intranet	Promoting from within
Cost-benefit relationship	Job postings	Recruiting
Employee referral programs	Longevity	Return on investment (ROI)
External sources	Networking	Screening
Forecast	New hires	Sources
Internal sources	Open house	
	Perquisites (perks)	

Introduction

Locating potential employees is a constant process in an industry with a very high average turnover of employees. Part-time employees are often short-time workers—either they move on, find a different job, or become full-time employees—and full-time employees move often for better salaries and working conditions. As a result, managers and human resources professionals are always looking for applicants for various jobs.

Finding new employees for any organization involves a variety of tasks. Two of the most important are recruiting and screening. Recruiting is a series of activities designed to bring the largest number of *qualified* persons to apply for a job at your organization. However, an ongoing prerequisite to recruiting is finding appropriate sources of potential new employees and building and maintaining relationships with these sources. After recruiting comes screening, the process of reviewing the skills, experience, attitudes, and backgrounds of people who have applied to work at your restaurant or foodservice operation.

Sometimes, recruiting and screening work against each other. If you are expected to recruit, you may use every activity and skill you know to find prospective new employees and encourage them to apply. Talking to the widest range of individuals, soliciting in the broadest pool of organizations, and disseminating information about vacancies as widely as possible may yield a high quantity of possible employees. However, without care, recruiters can encourage applications from many people who will not match the needs of the organization. This situation makes screening more difficult and time-consuming because every application needs to be processed. In this way, screening and recruiting activities can work at cross-purposes, something that can be avoided if you follow good recruiting practices.

In small restaurant or foodservice operations, recruiting and screening are often accomplished by the same person—the general manager, the dining room manager, or the chef. In large organizations, human resources management staff complete many of these tasks, especially the initial screening. Regardless of the operation, everyone is usually involved to some degree in recruiting new employees.

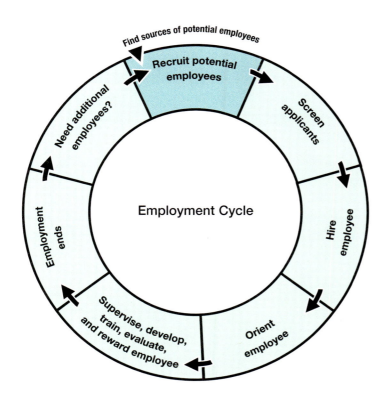

The Recruiting Process

Good recruiting is not just a matter of creating a few signs and advertisements and hoping for the best. It takes careful planning, analysis, and implementation, as well as an honest approach to presenting information about the restaurant or foodservice operation and its vacancies. Ideally, the recruiting process works so that an operation finds well-qualified employees and these employees find an operation where they will be happy, productive, and successful.

The tasks of organizing the recruiting process cover many areas, from considering what is needed in new employees to deciding how, when, and where to present that information in a format that encourages good applicants. These tasks include:

■ Deciding what vacancies exist in the organization, ideally based on the staffing levels planned for the year or anticipated for the future

■ Establishing what skills and backgrounds are needed in the new employees

■ Clarifying what the organization can offer to prospective employees

■ Identifying sources of potential employees

■ Communicating the vacancies in the most productive way to build a talent pool of qualified people

Throughout the entire cycle—and between cycles—you also need to build and maintain ongoing relationships with the sources of potential employees. This activity lays a critical foundation for some of the best recruiting methods.

While communicating or advertising the vacancies is perhaps the most visible part of the recruiting process, it actually starts when you identify the need for one or more additional employees. Ideally, you will know ahead of time when to hire people so you can train them and get them up to speed as you need them. The art and science of this timing is based on good forecasting.

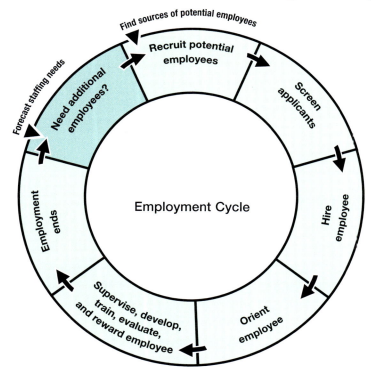

Forecasting Staffing Needs

The timing of recruiting efforts can have a huge impact on an operation's ability to hire and train new employees to be ready for work at the right time. Managers or human resources professionals normally analyze the past staffing needs of their business and other information to **forecast,** or predict based on this analysis, when they will need to hire additional employees.

From this analysis, they can develop and implement a recruiting plan to provide for those needs.

Analyzing staffing needs often involves examining a variety of information about your operation, similar operations, and the labor market in your area. As a manager, you should consider the following information to forecast your staffing needs:

■ **Last year's sales and staffing pattern**—Determine how much business the operation did and the number of staff that were used. Comparing the number of staff, the cost of the staff, the amount of overtime, and the shortages helps provide a picture of how many staff will be needed in the future and suggests the need for **new hires**—people newly employed by an operation.

■ **History of turnover in your establishment**—Determine how often positions need to be filled and at what times of year. This information helps organize the seasonality of recruiting and suggests when to start adding new employees so you can train them before experienced employees leave.

Exhibit 3a

Local outdoor festivals can affect staffing needs.

■ **Current and seasonal staffing schedules**—Identify the periods of peak demand and low demand for staff. In some locations, the difference in staff needs varies dramatically from one season to another. For example, your establishment's involvement in outdoor festivals or community celebrations may cause a peak in demand. (See *Exhibit 3a*.) This information is critical to helping managers know whether to hire seasonal staff members, part-time employees, or permanent full-time staff. Examining new assumptions about how the business may increase (or decrease) also provides information about when to hire additional staff to accommodate expected growth.

■ **Staffing patterns, guidelines, and formulas for similar establishments**—See what staff other operations have hired and need to operate successfully. Because labor costs are a significant aspect of any operation, ensuring that you have the right number of people—without having too many people—and the right balance of skills can make a real difference in your bottom line. Therefore, you may want to compare your staffing patterns with those of other operations and use industry guidelines and formulas for forecasting staffing needs. To find this information, use resources such as the National Restaurant Association or state and local restaurant associations. Also, try networking with other local foodservice professionals to learn how they handle their staffing needs.

■ **Local labor market realities**—Recognize what sets of skills you can find locally and who is competing for new employees. Knowing this information may dramatically change the ways in which you recruit for new employees.

Once you have forecasted your staffing needs and identified when you need to begin hiring and training new employees, you can develop a recruiting plan. Part of this plan includes determining the skills and abilities you want in the people you would like to hire and the advantages and compensation your operation can offer in exchange.

Determining the Skills You Need and What You Can Offer

Whenever you prepare to recruit new employees, you must have a clear picture of the skills, knowledge, and abilities you want in the people you are recruiting. Having written job descriptions will put you well ahead of the game. If you do not have job descriptions already available, you will need to analyze each job, determine the duties or responsibilities involved, and develop a clear picture of each position you want to fill.

You also need to have a clear picture of what your operation can offer prospective employees so you can market the job as effectively as possible. This picture should extend beyond wages and benefits. For example, what kind of environment does your operation have? Can you offer training and opportunities for advancement? How flexible are your work schedules? When assessing what you can offer prospective employees, it is important to be honest. If you sell a position based on false or misleading information, your new employee will not stay very long, and you will have wasted time and money in recruiting, hiring, orienting, and training that employee.

Identifying Sources of Potential Employees

Once you have identified the skills and abilities you want in prospective employees and what your operation can offer them, you are ready to start thinking about promoting the job openings. Promoting a job opening involves marketing your recruiting message to appropriate sources of potential employees. As a manager of a restaurant or foodservice operation, you have a wide variety of **sources**—places, organizations, and individuals—you can draw on to find new employees. The sources and methods you use for recruiting should vary based on the position or positions you are trying to fill. For example, if you are hiring people to clean a quick-service operation, you might post signs at the restaurant, ask employees to refer friends and family, collect applications on a continuing basis, and place a few advertisements in local papers. If you are looking for cooks to work in a white-tablecloth restaurant, you might develop good contacts and communicate with local high schools or colleges that have programs in the culinary arts. Finding managers and chefs can be even more complex, since the candidates need to bring a broader collection of knowledge, skills, and experience to their work. In such a case, you might look within the operation for candidates you can promote or use various sources outside the operation.

These examples suggest two main categories of sources: internal sources and external sources. **Internal sources** of potential employees come from within your operation, such as existing employees you promote or people referred by employees. **External sources** of potential employees come from outside your operation, such as people referred by employment agencies or recruited through advertising, open houses, and networking activities.

Recruiting from Internal Sources

Internal sources of potential employees include people referred by employees and the employees themselves. A big advantage of recruiting from internal sources is that job applicants are more familiar with your operation than most of those recruited through external sources.

Restaurant and foodservice operations typically use a combination of methods for internal recruiting. Some operations have a policy of informing current employees of any vacancies before searching outside the operation. This way, current employees may apply for the job or refer their family or friends before the general public can apply. Many operations also have **employee referral programs,** where they provide a bonus or reward for employees who refer candidates. Sometimes the bonus is paid when the individual is hired; sometimes it is paid after the new employee makes it through a trial employment period. Employee referral programs such as these provide employees with an added incentive to find good, new employees. Typically these programs are very cost-effective methods of recruiting.

People tend to recommend others like themselves, which may discourage diversity if your staff is not already diverse. Therefore, internal recruiting as the only recruiting method may limit employment opportunities at your operation to certain groups of people. Such practices may be interpreted as discriminatory and can result in claims of discrimination. However, if you let your staff

Exhibit 3b

Place job postings in a common area where employees are likely to see them.

know that you are looking to increase diversity, chances are they can help in this effort.

Regardless of an operation's formal policies and programs, the most common way to let current employees know about job openings is through regular employee communication methods, such as crew meetings, company newsletters, and postings. Notices about jobs, or **job postings,** often are placed on a bulletin board located in the staff lounge, changing area, or other areas frequented by employees. (See *Exhibit 3b.*) When an operation has a private Web site, or an internal computer network called an **intranet,** job information is commonly posted there. In some cases, an operation may include notices of vacancies or reminders of the employee referral program in paycheck envelopes.

Employee Referrals

The value of employee referrals is that current employees already know the operation's working conditions and have a sense of how the prospective employee will fit within the culture. Even new hires can provide this benefit. Employees also serve as filters or prescreeners, since they are not likely to suggest people they do not want to work with or who they do not think will fit into the operation. In fact, new employees recruited through this method usually have the highest **longevity,** or length of stay.

An important factor in the success of internal recruiting is to create and maintain the kind of relationship with your employees that encourages them to help with recruiting. If your employees like working in your operation, they are far more likely to want friends and family members to work there as well.

Also, use every opportunity to remind employees of your employee referral program—including any incentives—or the need for new employees. Be sure to announce new employees who were recruited through referrals and publicly and privately thank the employee who made the recommendation.

Promoting from Within

When you promote current employees into open positions, you save time and costs compared to hiring people who are new to your operation. This practice, called **promoting from within,** offers many benefits to both employers and employees. Promoting from within rewards employees for good performance, motivates others to improve their performance, and encourages all employees to consider long-term opportunities at your operation. Of course, promoting from within still creates another vacancy, but that vacancy usually is a less specialized position that can be filled more easily with an external hire. However, if internal recruiting is not handled carefully and fairly, employees who applied for a job and did not get it may be resentful.

Potential problems can occur if you advertise internally for a position and then do not seriously consider the internal applicants—for example, if you are looking to hire a dining room manager and several servers apply, but you do not even interview them. If this happens, they will feel disregarded and suspicious of any further internal promotions. To avoid this, some organizations have a policy of interviewing all internal applicants for an internally advertised vacancy. If you do not provide these interviews or some feedback, or if you advertise after you already decided who to promote, applicants will get discouraged and not apply again, even if they are talented persons you hope to promote in the future. Other employees also may lose faith in the system of internal recruiting and may stop applying or encouraging people outside the operation to apply.

Recruiting from External Sources

There are a variety of external sources where you can find new employees. Sometimes the strategies for recruitment differ, but there are common sources to which managers can go when recruiting all employees.

External Sources of Potential Employees

The range and number of sources from which to potentially recruit prospective employees depends in large part on the location of your operation. In rural and suburban areas, for example, the local chamber of commerce can be a good place to network and build relationships, while access to other organizations might be limited. Conversely, in large urban areas, professional and other organizations would probably provide better opportunities than the local chamber of commerce. *Exhibit 3c* on the next page lists common external sources of potential employees.

In any location, recruiting needs to be targeted to find the best applicants possible, regardless of race, gender, national origin, age, religion, or other nonessential traits. To ensure your operation gives everyone a fair chance at employment, you may want to target external sources that encourage a diverse labor pool. For example, in addition to advertising in the local newspaper, you might advertise in a local foreign language newspaper or through a social service organization that works with disabled people to help them find employment opportunities.

Exhibit 3c

Common External Sources of Potential Employees

- Culinary schools
- Other schools, especially those with culinary programs:
  - High schools
  - Colleges and universities
  - Vocational and technical training centers
  - Proprietary schools
- Student organizations
- Federal, state, and local government agencies and programs, such as:
  - Employment agencies and programs
  - Work-release and other programs for persons in jail, on parole, or on probation
  - Departments of labor
  - Social service departments
- Business organizations
- State and local chambers of commerce
- Community organizations and clubs, such as:
  - Youth groups
  - Career and vocational centers
  - Women's centers
  - Men's centers
  - Senior citizen centers
  - Student organizations
- Private employment agencies
- Temporary employment agencies
- Welcome organizations
- Former employees
- Past applicants
- Health clubs, YMCAs, YWCAs, and exercise facilities

- Local sports teams
- Not-for-profit social service organizations, such as:
  - Literacy-related organizations
  - Job placement centers in human service organizations
  - Employment programs for disabled or emotionally challenged individuals
- Churches, synagogues, mosques, and other religious institutions
- Local hospitality-oriented professional organizations, such as:
  - Local chapters of the National Restaurant Association
  - Local hospitality and lodging associations
  - Les Amis du Vin
  - Les Dames d'Escoffier
  - Local chapters of the American Culinary Federation
  - The Federation of Dining Room Professionals
  - La Chaîne des Rôtisseurs
- Unions
- Competitors, other foodservice operations, and other businesses
- Internet-based job databases and services, including:
  - Company Web sites
  - Professional or business organization Web sites
  - Privately owned Web sites such as Monster.com and CareerBuilder.com
- Suppliers and salespeople

External Recruiting Methods

The methods for recruiting from external sources are nearly as varied as the sources themselves. These include networking with various sources, sponsoring various programs, marketing to organizations, advertising in various ways, recruiting from competitors, participating in job or career fairs, holding open houses, and giving tours.

Networking with Various Sources

Historically, one of most powerful ways to find new employees for all positions is **networking.** (See *Exhibit 3d.*) This is the practice of building and maintaining ongoing communication with individuals who you can help and who can help you. Good networking produces referrals and word-of-mouth advertising. The keys to successful networking include making contacts with people in the industry and nurturing the professional relationships you form with those people. Regular communication is important for maintaining these relationships. Communication may be by phone, email, letters, fax, or through meetings. Once you have built a successful network, you can use it to communicate job openings at your operation.

Exhibit 3d

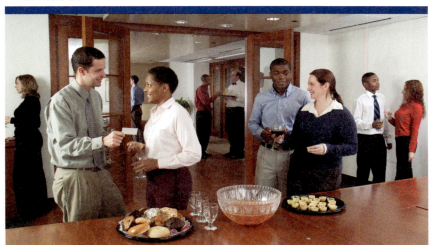

Networking is one of the best ways to recruit people from outside your operation.

Sponsoring School, Community, and Professional Programs

Sponsoring or participating in various school and organizational programs and activities builds your network and provides opportunities for advertising vacancies. An added bonus is the good publicity and public relations these opportunities provide. Programs and events vary widely depending on the type of organization you are working with. For example, you might sponsor a meeting for a professional or community organization. For a school, you might participate in an internship program or sponsor a joint school-industry program.

Marketing to Professional and Community Organizations

Ongoing, general marketing to professional and community organizations increases name recognition of your operation both as a place to visit and a place to work. With all possible sources of referrals, your chance of maintaining interest in your operation increases when you regularly communicate with them. To this end, some organizations have established electronic newsletters or their own email lists targeted for guests. Others send information through their local business organization or chamber of commerce or distribute a hard-copy newsletter.

Advertising Through Traditional Media

When you think of advertisements you have seen for job openings, you probably remember ads from traditional media, such as radio, television, newspapers, magazines, and other publications. Of these, advertisements in local newspapers and other publications are commonly used by the restaurant and foodservice industry. These ads are a common source of hourly employees, and sometimes they are effective in recruiting salaried employees as well.

While local newspapers and other publications can reach a large number of people, the success of your advertising depends in part on how well the publication audience matches the type of people you are trying to recruit. For example, some operations find that regular advertisements in high school and college newspapers are the most effective way to recruit entry-level employees, especially when the schools have culinary, foodservice, or hospitality programs.

Radio and television can also help with recruiting. Like newspapers, these media can reach broad audiences, and the success of the advertising depends in part on how well the audience matches the people you are trying to reach. However, radio and television are more expensive than print advertising.

One disadvantage of print and broadcast advertisements can be the cost, which is very high in urban areas. Another is the possibility of attracting negative attention for a restaurant in need of new employees. To avoid creating this perception, some operations run **blind ads,** which omit the company name and other identifying information. Often a post office box or publication reply number is given for the company address. This fear of appearing unsuccessful is sometimes overblown. If you are hiring for expansion, the advertisement may in fact promote a positive perception of your operation. Seasonal growth advertisements are often expected and have little or no negative impact on public perception, and they may be excellent sources of high school and college student applicants.

Other disadvantages of advertisements include the challenge of getting all the information into a short printed or oral advertisement and the task of making sure the ad is printed or read accurately. Depending on the publication in which the ad runs, another disadvantage can be the limited area it covers.

Exhibit 3e

"Help wanted" signs are one method of advertising.

Advertising Through Other Media

Signs and postings in and around your operation, postings on public bulletin boards, and postings on Web sites offer other ways to advertise job openings. These methods have the advantage of being easy to implement and relatively inexpensive compared to advertising through traditional media. However, they take more work on the part of applicants to find the advertisements and postings.

Posting help wanted signs and other advertising in and around your operation may not be appropriate for all types of operations, but it does disseminate information to the people who visit your establishment and have some sense of what you do. Signs in the window or notices on a marquee also encourage people who live nearby or who visit your area to apply. (See *Exhibit 3e.*) If your operation has a large turnover of hourly positions with low skill levels, this form of recruiting may be very successful at providing a continuous flow of potential new employees. Furthermore, if a guest or walk-in applicant asks for an application, you have the chance to meet the applicant, form an initial impression, and perhaps even screen or interview the applicant on the spot.

A similar way to advertise is posting advertisements on public bulletin boards, such as those found in stores, coffee shops, copy shops, diners, and laundry facilities. Community bulletin boards, boards in local chamber of commerce offices, and outside post offices can also be ways to post advertisements for free.

Finally, today's technology offers other options for posting job notices and advertisements. If your company has a public Web site, chances are you can post job openings there. In addition, employment Web sites sponsored by various organizations offer a variety of recruiting services. Many professional, business, and community organizations provide Web sites in which their members or the communities they serve can post job openings or résumés. In addition, college placement offices, chambers of commerce, and town governments often will allow you to post job notices on their Web sites. For a fee, other Web sites that specialize in connecting employers and job seekers are available, such as Monster.com or CareerBuilder.com. Sites like these often provide sophisticated tools for recruiting and job hunting, such as résumé searches and networking features.

Actively Recruiting Competitors' Employees

Sometimes, you can find prospective employees who may not even be looking for a job. When you visit other operations, and even businesses that are not in the hospitality industry, look for people who demonstrate the skills and abilities you want in prospective employees. For example, you might find an efficient server who has great customer service skills at a competitor's operation. Or you might find a bagger at a grocery store or a person in the childcare facility where you take your child who has the spirit and intelligence you are looking for in your entry-level help. When you find people like this, approach them in a discreet way and ask if they might be interested in interviewing for a position in your operation. Leave your business card or contact information and ask them to contact you.

Participating in Career Development Events

Career development events, such as job fairs, provide an easy way to meet many prospective employees in a short time period. At a job fair you typically set up a booth or table and job seekers stop by to learn about your employment opportunities. Events like this enable you to screen applicants when they submit their applications.

Sometimes these events are organized and coordinated by colleges to serve their students or a regional area, and sometimes they are arranged by organizations, such as chambers of commerce, departments of labor, and other agencies. Participating with a table or booth and appropriate display materials both demonstrates your ongoing commitment to hire local people and builds a following among the people who will refer potential employees to you. Networking with other people hosting booths can also help you learn what is happening in the local labor market, what new developments may affect your operation, and what strategies have helped others recruit new employees.

Holding Open Houses and Giving Tours

Holding open houses and giving tours can showcase your operation as a good place to work and to patronize. (See *Exhibit 3f.*) An **open house** is a designated time for people to visit your operation. Normally, you provide food, drinks, and tours for the people who visit your facility. The event allows visitors an opportunity to meet you and the staff, have a tour, see the menu, taste your food, admire the atmosphere and location, and mix with others who come to the open house. You can hold an open house for any reason, but operations often do this to exhibit recent changes in equipment, furnishings, or menu items. Special souvenirs are often presented to visitors as well.

Exhibit 3f

Hosting an open house is one way to showcase your operation as a good place to work and patronize.

Think About It...

The U.S. Chamber of Commerce indicates that, according to the Bureau of Labor Statistics, U.S. employment will increase by approximately 15 percent from 2002 to 2012, while the labor force will grow by only 12 percent.

These events build good public relations, often lead to temporary increases in business, and cement the relationship with people or organizations that visited your business. During these events, distributing materials that explain what it is like to work in your organization can help convert these general goodwill-building events to recruiting events.

To successfully use many of the external recruiting methods just discussed, you first must build and maintain relationships with external sources. The most productive external sources include schools, government agencies, and professional and community organizations.

Building and Maintaining Relationships with External Sources

One of the most effective ways to find potential new employees through external sources is to build and maintain good relationships with a number of key people in your local area. These people can be members of various organizations, faculty or administrators at local schools, administrators of government agencies, or informal community leaders. The more people that you know and feel confident calling about job openings, the more likely you are to find prospective employees who fit your needs and work well in your operation.

As a manager, you should build relationships with a variety of these people or organizations so you can draw from different populations of potential employees. Having a wide base like this can also provide an added bonus: whenever you are active in the community, you are promoting your operation not only as a good place to work, but also as a good place to visit.

Relationships with Schools

The most productive external sources of potential employees are schools, technical training organizations, and colleges; their students often study fields related to your operation, such as business, culinary arts, or hospitality.

Therefore, these sources can provide:

1 Prepared groups of part-time or even full-time employees

2 Sources of employees for limited periods through co-ops or internships

3 Full-time employees when the students graduate

The normal mechanisms for building relationships with individuals in these organizations include networking with key people, hosting open houses, sponsoring events and programs, participating in job fairs, and coordinating or participating in joint activities.

Networking with the people who can recommend job placements or who can provide information to students about good places to work requires continuous contact and communication. As a restaurant manager, you have many ways to develop this contact. For example, periodically meeting with faculty and staff, sending newsletters or other regular communications, and working with these people on common projects can be excellent uses of your time.

The best way to network with these key people and to publicize your operation as a good place to work is by becoming involved. Most schools, training organizations, and colleges are always looking for support for their activities, whether through scholarships, suppliers, money, prizes for student competitions, resources for student clubs, or funds for lectures and demonstrations. Being part of the group that sponsors some of these activities will bring you into closer contact with key people in these institutions and give you an opportunity to get to know them better. Working with them on these events also will build connections beyond just writing a check.

Similarly, coordinating joint events between your operation and your local educational institution can also win you many friends. (See *Exhibit 3g.*) Hosting a culinary competition, a recipe contest, or a local American Culinary Federation (ACF) meeting with the local school or college increases your visibility, enhances your reputation, and builds your brand recognition, all of which will lead to increased applications when you have vacancies.

Other ways to build relationships with educational sources include teaching a class, being a guest speaker, and serving on an advisory committee.

Exhibit 3g

Hosting a culinary competition sponsored by a local college can build relationships.

Relationships with Government Agencies

Many local, regional, state, and federal government programs hire and train employees for the local workforce. These job training and retraining programs, welfare-to-work programs, and local job referral networks are places to learn about and support, since they may provide a steady stream of well-trained employees for some positions at your operation.

To work with these agencies, learn about the requirements for participating in the programs by talking with local officials and getting on the distribution list for agency or program newsletters. Visiting their offices is also a good way to learn what guidelines they use in recommending people to businesses, especially restaurant and foodservice operations. Finally, regularly communicate your business needs to these agencies so they can refer appropriate candidates.

Relationships with Organizations

There are many other organizations to consider when building a collection of external referral sources. Sometimes, excellent sources can include community, business, and professional organizations; religious institutions; and social service agencies that are looking to find employment for members or people in their program. In each of these situations, building personal relationships with key people and providing regular communication, such as email or newsletters, are effective strategies.

Creating relationships with a variety of professional and community organizations also provides a chance to develop them as sources of referrals for potential new employees. Building these relationships usually involves attending meetings, participating in committees, and getting involved in the work of those organizations. The advantage can be professional development for you as a manager, as well as developing your reputation in the community. This strategy can yield referrals since many job seekers want to work for good bosses in organizations where they are treated with respect.

Getting involved in an organization means you participate in and support the organization in various ways. One creative way is to offer your facility as a meeting space, especially if you have a private dining room. (See *Exhibit 3h*.) You might also offer reduced-cost dinners for local charities to raise funds. While these activities can promote your operation by encouraging people to visit, they also trigger thoughts among the attendees of working there or of suggesting names of possible applicants. Another way to be involved is to host an open house or give tours, especially if these activities help support the mission of the organization.

Exhibit 3h

Becoming involved in organizations can build your network and referral sources.

To support an organization less directly, but still have an impact, advertise your operation in the organization's newsletter and regularly attend meetings. If the organization provides time for announcements at meetings, take this opportunity to publicize events or news related to your operation, announce job openings, and ask for referrals.

Activity

Developing a Recruiting Plan

You are the manager of a full-service restaurant that operates year-round with a fairly steady business. Holidays are peak times, but summer is the busiest because the restaurant is located near a park. In the summer, you open the deck, which has a wonderful view of the lake and draws a lot of adults as well as families, whose children are attracted to the play section you added. In the late summer evenings, the place is busy with a singles crowd and married couples.

One of your responsibilities is developing and implementing a recruiting plan. You have analyzed staffing, turnover, and sales data. Based on this information, you have forecasted your staffing needs for the next year. Your business typically increases during the summer months, and you use seasonal help to handle the increase. It takes about a month to get new hires trained and up to speed for most of the positions. To get your new employees trained for the busy season, you need to hire them during May and early June. By September, the seasonal employees leave. Attrition continues at a slow pace throughout the fall. Unless you hire a few more people in the fall, you will be short on help in November, when the busy holiday season begins.

You need to hire for the following positions in the next year:

May	July	August	November
■ Eight full-time, seasonal servers	■ One full-time server	■ Three part-time servers	■ Two part-time servers
■ Three part-time, seasonal bussers	■ One full-time dishwasher	■ Two part-time bussers	■ One part-time busser
■ One full-time dishwasher		■ One full-time cook	■ One part-time bartender
■ Two full-time cooks		■ One part-time bartender	
■ Two part-time bartenders			
■ One part-time assistant manager			

Based on these needs, write a plan for recruiting to fill these positions on a budget of $2,000. Assume your restaurant is located in or near your current residence. Include the *actual* sources and methods you would use to recruit for each period and when you would conduct each recruiting activity. That is, identify specific recruiting methods that will work where you are living, and find out the actual costs of newspaper ads, open houses, membership in the chamber of commerce, etc. For example, if you live in Harpers Ferry, West Virginia, you might place a classified advertisement in the weekly *Spirit of Jefferson Farmer's Advocate* newspaper for the first two weeks of April at a cost of $18.00.

Use the table on the next page as a template for your plan or create your own format on a separate piece of paper. Be prepared to explain in class why you chose the methods you did.

Plan for Ongoing Recruiting (for all recruits)	
Recruiting Methods and Timing	Cost

For May Recruits	
Recruiting Methods and Timing	Cost

For July Recruits	
Recruiting Methods and Timing	Cost

For August Recruits	
Recruiting Methods and Timing	Cost

For November Recruits	
Recruiting Methods and Timing	Cost
Total Cost	$

Communicating a Job Opening

When you are ready to let people know about a job opening, you need to communicate this information in an effective way. You also need to make sure that the way you communicate the opening complies with equal employment opportunity regulations.

A job opening can be communicated orally or in writing. In any case, you need to gear your message toward your audience and include enough information to attract applicants while helping people decide if the job sounds right for them.

Elements of a Job Posting or Advertisement

A good job posting or advertisement entices people who are a good match for the position to apply for it. For each advertisement or job posting, you should include certain information. The exact information you include and the depth of this information may vary based on whether the notice or advertisement is intended for internal or external sources and how much space or time you have.

Job or Position Title

The job or position title can provide a succinct way to describe the position when it is a common one, such as line cook, dishwasher, or server. In other cases, this information is important for internal recruiting because the title will have more meaning to current employees than external applicants. When including the job title, be sure to use gender-neutral language whenever possible.

Desired Qualifications or Skills

Including the qualifications and skills needed for the position is important because it helps potential employees self-screen for the position. As with the job or position title (and job description), you must be careful of the language you use to describe the qualifications and skills. In small ads, this information can be very simple.

Company Name

The company name is most important when advertising to external sources. Including your logo, when possible, continues the general promotion of your operation. However, as mentioned previously, some companies run blind ads when advertising externally. These ads omit the company name and identifying information and provide only a post-office box number or reply number at the newspaper to ensure privacy.

Benefits

If your company provides benefits, such as health insurance, including this information in the job posting or advertisement can encourage more applications. In addition, if you have the space, include information about any incidental benefits, called **perquisites** (or **perks** for short), such as formal training, flexible scheduling, and opportunities for advancement.

Work Location

Include the location where the person will be working in all notices and ads. This information is especially important when there are multiple units in your company. For internal postings, you can include the department, region, or other location information as appropriate.

Ways to Respond

This information instructs potential applicants on how to apply for the job. For example, should the job seeker apply in person or send in a résumé or application? If you want people to apply in person, include the time and date to apply, what information to bring, and the street address of your operation. If you want people to apply in other ways, tell them what information to send and where; include the email address, the Web site address, mailing address, or fax number you want them to use.

While asking people to apply in person is a legitimate way to screen people (especially for front-of-the-house positions), you cannot use this practice to avoid hiring or considering anyone based on race, color, age, disability, national origin, gender, religion, or any traits that have nothing to do with bona fide occupational qualifications (BFOQ) for the job. Employers who screen in this manner are discriminating illegally. If you do this, you will create resentment in the people you send away, and you will expose your operation to potential discrimination claims and bad publicity.

Equal Employment Opportunity (EEO) Statement

A statement in your advertisement or posting that identifies your operation as an equal opportunity employer will encourage a diverse range of applicants. This statement is not limited to a standard "EEO Employer" tag line. If you have the time or space, include a more descriptive statement, such as "Maynard's Chop House encourages all applicants for this position without regard to race, religion, sex, national origin, age, sexual orientation, disability, or other traits." If your operation's vision or mission statement illustrates a commitment to diversity, you might include one of these instead.

Be aware, however, that merely including an EEO statement in your advertisement does not make your operation an equal employment opportunity employer. You still must treat all applicants and employees fairly.

Avoiding Discriminatory Language

The information in job postings and advertisements needs to be written in a manner that not only provides clear information about the job, but avoids discriminatory language as well. The Equal Employment Opportunity Commission (EEOC) and other government agencies enforce laws that ensure everyone, regardless of race, age, gender, religion, national origin, color, or ability/disability, gets a fair chance at any job opening. This means you should not write the notice or advertisement in any way that eliminates or discourages certain groups of people from applying.

Following are guidelines for avoiding discriminatory language in job postings and advertisements:

- **Avoid gender-specific titles and other language.** Instead, use gender-neutral language or gender-inclusive language. For example, for a position that involves waiting on tables, use "server," both "waiter" and "waitress," or "waitstaff" instead of just "waiter" or just "waitress."

- **Avoid references to groups of people that imply age, race, color, religion, gender, national origin, physical traits, disabilities, sexual orientation, or other traits that do not relate to BFOQ or essential functions.** For example, instead of advertising a position that is good for "homemakers," "retirees," or "students," advertise the hours or seasonality of the job.

- **Focus on the actual skills, knowledge, and abilities needed on the job.** For example, instead of advertising a position as a "man's job," state the actual requirement, such as "must be able to lift fifty pounds."

As in job descriptions, describing the duties a person might have to do on the job—so long as they are actually true—provides honest information and fair warning to each applicant and encourages the broadest range of qualified applicants. Including this information also helps protect you and your operation from possible claims of discrimination.

Activity

Identifying and Eliminating Discriminatory Language

Review these advertisements for discriminatory language. If the advertisement does not contain discriminatory language, write "OK" next to the ad. If it contains discriminatory language, rewrite the portion that contains discriminatory language.

ORPHA*S   NOW HIRING

WAITSTAFF, BUSBOYS, DISHWASHERS FULL- AND PART-TIME. FLEXIBLE HOURS; FUN, BUSY ATMOSPHERE; UNIFORMS PROVIDED. EXPERIENCE HELPFUL BUT NOT REQUIRED. APPLY IN PERSON OR CALL LEE (555) 555-1234. 1237 EAST WASHINGTON STREET.

WANTED!

SUNDAY BRUNCH Buffet Attendants

Monitor, replenish, and clean buffet and drink stations. Must work holidays. Perfect for non-Christians.

Apply in person, Mondays 1:00 p.m.–4:00 p.m. Stockton's Family Restaurant, 8900 Luther Dr.

Part-time counter and **drive-thru** help needed for lunch or dinner hours at two Springfield locations. Some weekends. Good customer service skills, clear speaking voice, and **attention to detail** desired. Restaurant experience not necessary. Complete an application at either **Sandwich Sally's** location: 7801 N. Jackson St. or 890 Central St, Springfield. For more information, visit our Web site: **www.sandwichsallys.com.**

CINQVE TERRE

The Primo Italian Restaurant in the Heart of Downtown

Now hiring a Maitre d' and Line Cooks. Experience required. Italian heritage a plus. Competitive pay and good benefits. Fax or mail résumé by 6/1 to Mr. Broccolo, 150 N. Minton Ave, Seattle, WA 98110. Fax: (555) 555-7890.

Reflecting the Character of Your Operation

When preparing printed information for external recruiting, such as advertisements or signs, you need to match the tone and style of this information to the tone and style of your organization. Although this task may seem unnecessary, you need to provide a clear image of your operation to prospective applicants so they can make an intelligent decision about applying for the vacancies advertised. In addition, you never want to miss an opportunity to communicate the image of your operation. Typically, a consistent image involves using the logo, ink color, paper, and fonts that people associate with your operation, but it may include providing the mission statement or vision of the organization as well.

Activity

Communicating a Job Opening

You are a manager for Fred's Food Firm, an innovative restaurant popular with business people during the day, families during the early dinner hour, and young singles and couples later in the evening. Your restaurant has a private room that is often booked for parties and business functions. You need to hire an additional server who can work flexible hours in both the dining room and the private room.

On a separate sheet of paper, write how you would communicate an opening for this job through the following methods:

1 Internal job posting on a bulletin board—no space limit

2 Job notice for the placement office of a local culinary school—no space limit

3 Classified advertisement for the local newspaper—fifty-word limit

4 Job posting for a store bulletin board—unspecified physical space (but you need to compete with other postings for space and attention)

5 Oral announcement for a meeting of a local, general business organization—one minute or less (around 150–175 words)

As you write these notes, consider how much physical space or announcement time you have for each notice, how many words you can fit in the space or time, the minimum information you need to include to get good responses, and the people you are likely to reach using each of these methods. Also consider how to communicate the character and culture of your operation and how to encourage the best number and quality of responses.

Evaluating Recruiting Methods

Considering the work involved in finding prospective employees and the importance of this work, it is not surprising that most operations assess the effectiveness of their recruiting activities. A good evaluation identifies which recruiting activities are most useful for which vacancies. For example, in quick-service restaurants, signs on doors and tabletops may encourage the right applicants for counter and kitchen help. In a more formal, fine-dining establishment, networking may produce the best candidates for kitchen employees, and internal recruiting might produce the best pool for table service staff. The method and depth of assessment often varies from location to location and from one type of establishment to another.

In small restaurants, managers often informally reflect on whether certain activities have produced the right kinds of applicants. Typically, these managers are quite aware of the recruiting methods that are most effective for particular positions. This assessment may be based on intuition and some anecdotal evidence, but it is still used to decide what kinds of efforts to support or expand and what efforts to drop.

Large organizations normally evaluate their recruiting activities in a more thorough manner. Like typical **return on investment (ROI)** calculations, which measure the profits of a program or event against the costs of implementing it, the work involves determining the cost-benefit relationships of various activities. A **cost-benefit relationship** is a comparison of the total direct and indirect recruiting costs against the number (and sometimes quality) of applicants produced. Of course, other considerations belong in the final analysis, including the loss of productivity during a vacancy, the extra cost for other employees to cover shifts, the longevity of various employees relative to the way they were recruited, and their learning curve in becoming productive.

It takes significant work to collect these actual expenses and overhead costs—tasks more easily completed when the financial data is easily accessible or there are dedicated staff members to conduct the analysis. However, weighing the full costs of a recruiting activity against the number and quality of applicants it produced enables an operation to improve its recruiting efforts.

Summary

Recruiting is an ongoing activity that encompasses many tasks. These include deciding what vacancies exist in the organization, establishing the skills and backgrounds needed in new employees, clarifying what your operation can offer to prospective employees, identifying sources of potential employees, and communicating the vacancies in the most productive way to build a talent pool of qualified people. You also need to build and maintain ongoing relationships with the sources of potential employees.

To identify when to increase recruiting efforts, you can forecast your staffing needs. Forecasting involves examining a variety of information about your operation, similar operations, and the labor market in your area. Once you have determined when to increase recruiting and for which jobs, you can identify the skills, knowledge, and abilities you want in potential employees and what your operation can offer in return.

Promoting a job opening involves marketing your recruiting message to appropriate sources of potential employees. These sources may be internal or external to your operation.

For internal recruiting, operations typically use a combination of recruiting methods, including job postings and regular employee communications. Employee referral programs often provide an incentive to current employees to refer friends and family to apply for new positions. The practice of promoting from within encourages employees to apply for other jobs within the operation.

For external recruiting, the range and number of sources depend in large part on the location of your operation. To successfully use many of the external recruiting methods, you first must build and maintain relationships with the external sources. The most productive external sources include schools, government agencies, and professional and community organizations.

In any type of recruiting effort, be sure to communicate the information in an effective way that complies with equal employment opportunity regulations. Avoid gender-specific titles and other discriminatory language, and avoid references to specific groups of people. Focus on the actual skills, knowledge, abilities, and responsibilities needed for the job. Include a diversity statement to encourage everyone who is interested in the job to apply.

To identify how successful a recruiting strategy is and whether the recruiting efforts need to be adjusted, analyze and evaluate the recruiting methods. This analysis should consider the costs of recruiting versus the benefits or results of the recruiting.

Review Your Learning

1 Which is *not* a common source of potential employees in the foodservice industry?

   A. Government agencies and programs

   B. Schools, colleges, and technical training organizations

   C. Community and professional organizations

   D. Human resources and benefit consulting firms

2 Which can be used to build and maintain relationships with sources of potential employees?

   A. Forecasting

   B. Networking

   C. Screening

   D. Web surfing

3 How should you evaluate a recruiting method?

   A. Compare the recruiting costs against the number and quality of applicants produced.

   B. Compare the recruiting costs against the number of people hired and trained.

   C. Compare the recruiting costs against the recruiting costs of similar operations.

   D. Use industry-accepted standards to analyze media costs and application processing costs.

4 Which is considered discriminatory language in a job advertisement?

   A. Good schedule for retirees

   B. Bilingual/Spanish language a plus

   C. Must have good work ethic

   D. Perfect job for energetic person

5 Which is *not* considered when forecasting staffing needs?

   A. Past sales and staffing patterns

   B. Turnover history

   C. Current and seasonal staffing schedules

   D. Competitors' average check per table

Notes

Screening Potential Employees

Inside This Chapter

- The Screening Process
- Screening Tools and Techniques
- Avoiding Illegal Discrimination in Screening
- Managing and Evaluating the Initial Application Documents
- Conducting Screening Interviews
- Testing Work Skills and Using Personality Tests
- Planning for Job Interviews
- Conducting Job Interviews
- Conducting Reference Checks

After completing this chapter, you should be able to:

- Describe the steps in the screening process.
- Recognize standard tools and techniques to screen job applicants.
- Identify examples of discriminatory language and practices related to screening.
- Describe typical methods for testing work skills and assessing personality traits.
- Recognize different types of interviews and when to use them.
- Develop a list of interview questions to use when screening an applicant.
- Describe common methods for checking references.

Test Your Knowledge

1 **True or False:** The goal of screening applicants is to find the best person for the job in your restaurant or foodservice operation. *(See p. 72.)*

2 **True or False:** Employees screen themselves just by applying for or accepting a job. *(See p. 68.)*

3 **True or False:** Legal issues make it impossible to hire the best person for a job opening. *(See p. 72.)*

4 **True or False:** It should not take more than one interview to screen an applicant for a job in a restaurant or foodservice operation. *(See p. 74.)*

5 **True or False:** One way to make sure applicants are treated fairly is to require all applicants to complete an application form. *(See p. 73.)*

Key Terms

Group interview

Interview schedule

Job interview

Preinterview

Realistic job preview

Screening

Screening interview

Sous chef

Successive interviewing

Introduction

Have you ever applied for a job and then been called for an interview? When you applied for that job and talked with your potential employer, you did your best to make a good impression and convince the interviewer that you were the right person for the job. Meanwhile, your interviewer was evaluating you and your skills—screening you— to determine whether you were a good fit for the job. Every day, this scenario is repeated many times in restaurant and foodservice operations all over the country. As someone starting a new career, you will have an advantage over others if you understand how operations screen job applicants to find people they want to hire.

As your career grows and you become a manager in an industry with significant turnover rates, one of your routine responsibilities will be to screen people who apply for jobs at your operation. Hiring the right people will make a dramatic difference in the success of your business. Sloppy screening can mean that inappropriate persons are hired, which may entail extra time and effort in orientation and training, as well as potentially difficult terminations. Careful screening can help you avoid this long and costly process.

In addition, if you do a good job in screening and hiring employees, you can reduce turnover and its negative impact on profits, employee morale, and customer service. You also help protect your business in the event it must defend itself against a discrimination or wrongful termination lawsuit. Finally, hiring the right people is the starting point for making your operation the place where both customers and employees want to be.

The Screening Process

Once you have collected applications through the recruiting process, the next step is screening the people who applied for your job openings. Screening must be done carefully to ensure a process free from discriminatory practices, to defend the operation from potential lawsuits, and to ensure that the best applicants are considered for the job opening. The screening process is complex because it involves federal and state (and sometimes local) regulations and builds on the recruiting activities of multiple people. Compared to recruiting, screening is a more focused process that includes the following activities:

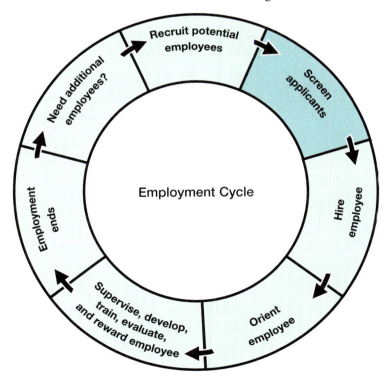

- Reviewing documents, such as the application form, cover letter, résumé, or other materials

- Conducting preliminary interviews, called screening interviews, by telephone or in person

- Assessing skills, experience, and personalities through testing or other simulations

- Interviewing to determine knowledge, skills, abilities, and appropriateness for the job opening

- Investigating backgrounds and fitness through reference checks, background checks, and other means

At any stage in this process, an operation may determine that an individual is not suited for the job opening. However, to protect

From 2001 to 2002, the number of applications for hourly positions increased by 40 percent for table-service restaurants and by one-third for quick-service operators, according to the National Restaurant Association's *Restaurant Industry Workforce Study*.

both the individual and the operation, all of this work needs to happen in a manner that is hospitable and welcoming, careful and comprehensive, and fair and equitable.

In large operations, human resources professionals conduct several activities in the screening process, although a manager and possibly other employees may be involved in some of the interviewing. In small companies, the general manager accomplishes all the screening activities or delegates these activities to the supervisor of the area that has the job opening. In any case, everyone involved in screening needs to know the various steps in the process and the legal regulations that affect screening.

Screening Tools and Techniques

Screening involves a range of tools and techniques. These include, but are not limited to, the following:

- **Initial application form**—Form used by businesses to collect all appropriate and legally allowable information in a standard format so every individual who applies is treated equally (See *Exhibit 4a.*)

- **Cover letter and résumé**—Letter from prospective applicants indicating their interest in the position and their list of work experience and education

- **Proof of eligibility to work**—Required part of the hiring process, typically not required in the screening process but sometimes included as part of the application form

- **Screening interview**—Discussion intended to determine whether an individual meets basic requirements before the business invests more time and resources in evaluating him or her for a job opening

- **Testing**—Personality, ability, aptitude, or skill tests to determine an individual's suitability for a position (more often used by large operations)

- **Work assessments or simulations**—Shadowing or completion of actual tasks under real-life or simulated conditions to evaluate the skills of an individual

- **Job interview**—Interview with the potential supervisor and/or other employees—sometimes conducted in a one-on-one discussion or sometimes in a group—intended to gather additional information about an individual and to give the individual a realistic idea of what the job entails

Exhibit 4a

Every individual who applies for a job should complete an application form.

- **Reference and background checks**—Investigation of an individual's previous employment and other information, including credit history and possible criminal records

- **Medical tests and records**—Information from physicians (including drug tests) that indicates the health and physical abilities of the individual as they relate to the job

Although operations may not all use the same tools and techniques or use them in the same order, these techniques are important. Even small restaurant and foodservice operations use them in some way. For example, the initial application and screening interview often happen at the same time when an individual applies for an entry-level job opening and the manager is available to meet him or her. Combining these techniques can be an efficient way to cover a lot of information quickly and determine whether the person is worth pursuing through the next steps of the screening process.

Other aspects of the screening process may happen in different sequences, depending on the operation's practices, the urgency of the situation, and the type of position being filled. In the case of managerial candidates, they sometimes participate in screening interviews, testing procedures or simulations, and a job interview before the reference and background checks are completed. Reference checks generally are done last because of the need for confidentiality and secrecy during the screening and hiring processes. In other cases, hourly employees may be interviewed first, and then references are checked and other final checks are conducted during the hiring process. In situations in which there is some urgency to hire a person, the operation may make a job offer contingent on the results of reference checks or other factors while moving ahead with the process. If the references are not satisfactory, the job offer may be withdrawn.

Background checks and other investigations, such as medical and drug tests, cost money and are time-consuming. When these methods are used, they are often done after an operation has decided to hire a candidate—just before a job offer, after the job offer but before the new hire starts, or just after the new hire starts the job. If these checks provide information that contradicts information supplied by the candidate or new hire, the operation has grounds to withdraw the offer or terminate the new hire, assuming it has appropriate policies for handling such situations.

Avoiding Illegal Discrimination in Screening

The goal of any screening process is to find the best-qualified person—regardless of age, race, color, religion, gender, national origin, or other traits—and to give every person a fair chance to be considered for a vacancy. To do this, you will be making judgments about people and you should do so carefully to find the right employees for your restaurant or foodservice operation. However, your judgments should not be arbitrary. You cannot use discriminatory practices that adversely affect any of the protected classes of people or that deny *any* individual an equal and fair chance for consideration. Throughout the screening and hiring processes, be extremely careful to ensure all individuals have a fair chance and that you are complying with the applicable laws.

When you conduct interviews, administer tests, and evaluate individuals, you need to comply with federal, state, and local regulations for screening and hiring practices. The best way to do this is to make sure your screening techniques focus on the essential skills of the job and the person's ability to perform them. To ensure this focus, have a clear and comprehensive knowledge of the job description and the Bona Fide Occupational Qualifications (BFOQ). Understand the actual skills of the job that are connected to the job description and the realistic range of skills that are needed to perform the job.

In honoring the spirit and the specifics of legislation that apply to screening, you need to be careful of what you say, how you say it, and when you say it. This means watching your personal judgments, being open to alternative ways that a person may have acquired the skills and experience to do the job, being open to alternative ways that a person may be able to perform the essential functions, and helping the rest of your colleagues refrain from inappropriate personal judgments of possible new employees. These principles apply throughout the screening process which begins when you receive the initial application documents.

Managing and Evaluating the Initial Application Documents

When an individual first applies for a job at your restaurant or foodservice operation, he or she may complete an application form or submit a résumé and cover letter. (See *Exhibit 4b.*) Reviewing the form or cover letter and résumé is the first step in the screening process.

There are many reasons to review these initial documents:

- To become familiar with the person's work history, background, and skill level to determine whether he or she may be able to master the tasks required to do a good job
- To identify what extra experience or information the individual can bring to enrich your restaurant or foodservice operation
- To ascertain the individual's reading and writing skills—even if these skills are not required for the job—to determine whether special job training or literacy education might be needed once the person is hired

Using a Standard Application Form

Providing a standard application form and requiring all individuals interested in the job to complete it ensures that you obtain equivalent types of information from each and every person. This equal treatment protects you and your restaurant or foodservice operation from potential criticism or even claims or lawsuits for discriminatory screening practices.

Exhibit 4b

Sample Hourly Employee Application

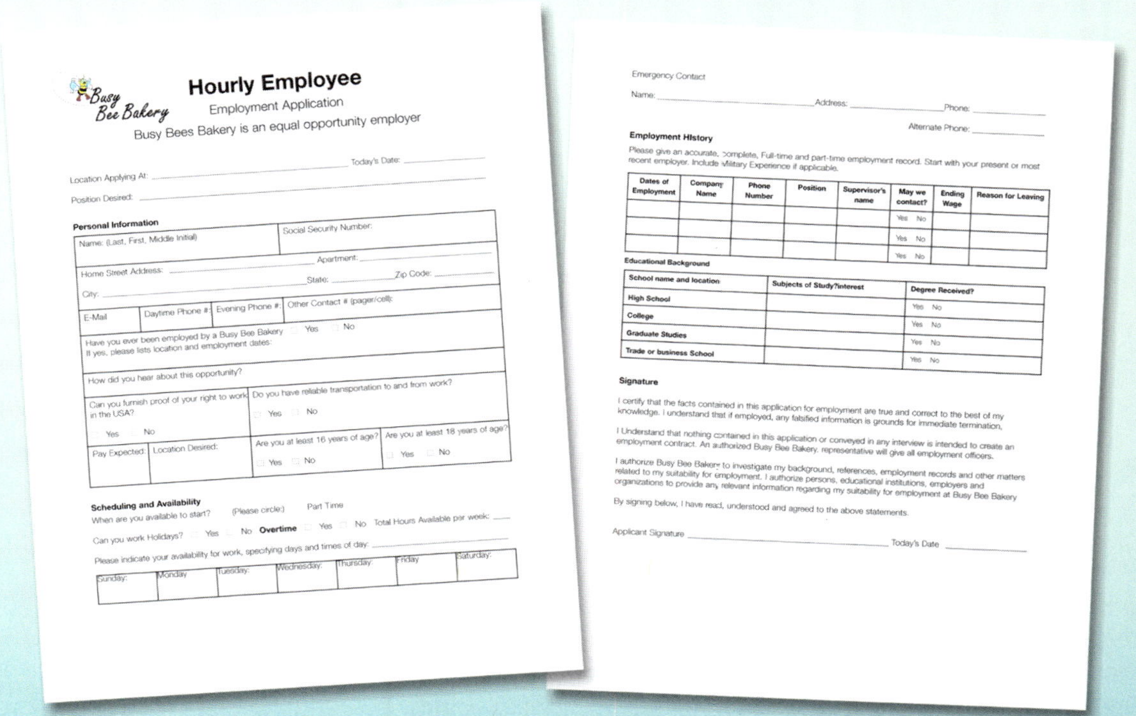

Busy Bee Bakery

Hourly Employee
Employment Application
Busy Bees Bakery is an equal opportunity employer

Location Applying At: ____ Today's Date: ____
Position Desired: ____

Personal Information

Name: (Last, First, Middle Initial)			Social Security Number:
Home Street Address: ____ Apartment: ____ City: ____ State: ____ Zip Code: ____			
E-Mail	Daytime Phone #:	Evening Phone #:	Other Contact # (pager/cell):
Have you ever been employed by a Busy Bee Bakery ☐ Yes ☐ No If yes, please lists location and employment dates:			
How did you hear about this opportunity?			
Can you furnish proof of your right to work in the USA? ☐ Yes ☐ No		Do you have reliable transportation to and from work? ☐ Yes ☐ No	
Pay Expected:	Location Desired:	Are you at least 16 years of age? ☐ Yes ☐ No	Are you at least 18 years of age? ☐ Yes ☐ No

Scheduling and Availability
When are you available to start? (Please circle:) Part Time ☐ Yes ☐ No Total Hours Available per week: ____
Can you work Holidays? ☐ Yes ☐ No **Overtime**
Please indicate your availability for work, specifying days and times of day: ____

Sunday:	Monday	Tuesday:	Wednesday:	Thursday:	Friday	Saturday:

Emergency Contact
Name: ____ Address: ____ Phone: ____
Alternate Phone: ____

Employment History
Please give an accurate, complete, Full-time and part-time employment record. Start with your present or most recent employer. Include Military Experience if applicable.

Dates of Employment	Company Name	Phone Number	Position	Supervisor's name	May we contact?	Ending Wage	Reason for Leaving
					Yes No		
					Yes No		
					Yes No		

Educational Background

School name and location	Subjects of Study?interest	Degree Received?
High School		Yes No
College		Yes No
Graduate Studies		Yes No
Trade or business School		Yes No

Signature

I certify that the facts contained in this application for employment are true and correct to the best of my knowledge. I understand that if employed, any falsified information is grounds for immediate termination.

I Understand that nothing contained in this application or conveyed in any interview is intended to create an employment contract. An authorized Busy Bee Bakery, representative will give all employment officers.

I authorize Busy Bee Bakery to investigate my background, references, employment records and other matters related to my suitability for employment. I authorize persons, educational institutions, employers and organizations to provide any relevant information regarding my suitability for employment at Busy Bee Bakery

By signing below, I have read, understood and agreed to the above statements.

Applicant Signature ____ Today's Date ____

To use an application form this way, even individuals who submit résumés should complete the form and then attach their résumés to it. In some managerial and other screening situations, this form is completed at the end of the process and not at the beginning.

Most application forms include important statements or notices that individuals must sign to help protect your operation from potential legal claims. One statement explains that providing false information is grounds for dismissal. Another obtains the person's permission to check references and other background information.

Keeping Applications on File

Using a standard application form also enables you to keep the application on file for future vacancies, which increases the return on your recruiting investment. A pool of job applications always represents a possible new hire. Because of this possibility, you should avoid writing on the application form. Writing on the application may limit a person's chances for a fair review in a different hiring situation. For example, suppose a person applies for a kitchen position and is not qualified, but might be a good candidate for a front-of-the-house position. Notes written on the application about why the person is not qualified for the kitchen position may make it harder for that person to get a fair chance to be considered for the front-of-the-house position.

Exhibit 4c

Most organizations conduct screening interviews via the telephone.

Conducting Screening Interviews

As part of the screening process, businesses often conduct a variety of interviews, including a screening interview and a job interview. Sometimes these interviews are combined due to the lack of time or staff or the level of the position. Most often, these interviews are separate meetings conducted at different points during the screening process. Most organizations conduct screening interviews via the telephone. (See *Exhibit 4c.*)

Screening interviews are conducted early in the screening process. The main purpose of a screening interview is to determine whether the person meets basic requirements and warrants further screening. It is also used to gather information about the person applying for a position, to make him or her feel welcome and comfortable, and to build some interest in the restaurant or foodservice operation. In large operations, human resources professionals often conduct screening interviews. In operations that do not have a human resources department, the manager typically conducts these interviews. Screening interviews are sometimes called preinterviews because they precede the job interview. This type of interview also sets the tone for future testing, interviews, and the hiring process.

Complying with Regulations during Screening

When you conduct a screening interview, regulations require you to conduct the interview and your subsequent evaluation in an effective and fair manner. To do this, you must understand the questions that you can and cannot ask potential new employees. You must also compare results across the various interviews.

Topics for Interview Questions

Asking the right kinds of questions requires a clear and comprehensive knowledge of the job description. It also requires focusing on the BFOQ and using language that pertains specifically to the job. Asking questions about a candidate's past behaviors as they relate to the job is one way to do this. Focusing on the skills, knowledge, and abilities required for the job helps ensure you evaluate people based on their qualifications instead of making arbitrary judgments.

When asking questions in an interview, you cannot ask questions about certain areas of information. However, questions relating directly to the job can be asked. *Exhibit 4d* on the next page shows the areas of inquiry you need to avoid and provides examples of acceptable topics.

In addition, there are other topics that you may want to avoid, such as personal finances, transportation (unless relevant to an essential job function), political memberships, child-care arrangements, and union membership. While it is legal to ask about some of these topics, bringing them up can leave your operation vulnerable to charges of discrimination because such discussions can give the impression that these areas are factors in your hiring decision.

You do have the right to ask about a person's ability to perform the job, such as the required job hours and expectations for coming to work on time and in all kinds of weather. Therefore, instead of asking about transportation or child care, you can ask, "Is there anything I should know about your ability to be here on time and work for the full shift during all times of the year and in all types of weather?" In short, you can ask questions that relate directly to the *skills, knowledge, abilities,* and *requirements* of the job for which the person is applying.

Exhibit 4d

Topics for Interview Questions

Forbidden Topics	Acceptable Topics
Birthplace or birthplace of parents	Current place of residence and length of stay in that location is acceptable.
Age	If the person is hired, you must ask the new employee to provide proof of eligibility to work, which will provide the person's age.
National origin or ancestry	Languages spoken and extent of skills are permissible, especially if they relate to the languages in the kitchen or dining room or among the restaurant's customers.
Religion or religious beliefs	You cannot bring up this topic, but you can respond if the applicant mentions this area.
Gender	You cannot bring up this topic unless gender is a BFOQ, which is typically not the case in restaurant or foodservice operations.
Marital status	None—this topic is not relevant to hiring.
Parental status, sexual orientation	These topics are not relevant to hiring and should be avoided. After explaining the hours and other functions expected to perform the job, you may ask, however, if the applicant can fulfill the job obligations.
Disability or disabling conditions	If there are any disabling conditions that a person has that would make it difficult or impossible to perform the work involved, you may ask what accommodations may be made in order for the applicant to perform the essential job functions.
Criminal record	If relevant to the job functions, you may ask about the number and kinds of convictions, when they occurred, and whether the applicant has completed any required sentencing obligations. You may not ask about arrests or criminal charges if a criminal conviction did not (or has not) occurred.
Height, weight, or other physical characteristics unless they are BFOQ	You can ask this information if it is directly relevant to the job; for example, you can ask whether a person can reach the top shelf in the cooler or carry heavy pots, if these skills are essential to doing the job.

Testing Work Skills and Using Personality Tests

Businesses often use different types of tests or assessments to find out how suited an applicant may be for a job. More often used by large operations, these instruments can assess an individual's personality, ability, aptitude, or skills. Testing may be done before or after a job interview.

To be fair to each individual and comply with regulations, operations that use tests need to follow these guidelines:

- Give every applicant—or every applicant in a certain category, such as all managerial positions—the same test.

- Use a test that is culturally neutral, so the testing process does not adversely affect any of the protected classes of people.

- Each inquiry must be about a BFOQ—related to the specific duties or necessary skills to perform the job.

- Administer the test in a fair and consistent manner.

- Evaluate the test results against clear criteria.

Beyond pen-and-pencil personality or interest tests, operations more often use real assessment vehicles to determine an individual's skills and aptitude. Actual work assessments that measure the individual's real skills range from simple keyboard tests (for clerical and administrative staff), to machine operation, table setting, and food preparation tests. Sometimes these tests involve real machines, dining room tables, and food. Other times, they are organized as simulations.

While real testing situations provide a more thorough and lifelike assessment, simulations can be done at any time and do not require an empty dining room or a kitchen that is not in production. When these tests are administered by a person who will be making or influencing the hiring decisions, there is often a period of discussion after the test in which individuals are asked what they did, why they did it, how they think they did, and what they would have done differently. Usually, you can learn as much from the discussion after the testing process as you can from observing and analyzing the results of the actual test.

Planning for Job Interviews

To make an interview successful, you need to plan for it. The clearer you are about what you want to learn during the interview, the more successful you will be. When planning, consider the space you will use when interviewing people, the time you want to allot for the interview, what you will say at the beginning of the interview, what notes you will take, and what interview format you want to use and why.

To protect yourself from using questions that open you to possible liability and to make sure you get all the information you want, develop and use a standard list of questions. This list is often called an **interview schedule.** A sample is shown in *Exhibit 4e*. Use the same interview schedule for every candidate you interview for the same position. Use one for each interview.

Without an interview schedule, you might not gather the information to make sure an individual is the right person for the job. Developing your own list can be a useful way to ensure that you obtain the information you want and need.

Exhibit 4e

Interview Schedule for Professional Candidates

SUSHI IZAGAYA
425 West 52ⁿᵈ Street
New York 10019

INTERVIEW SCHEDULE

BACKGROUND INFORMATION

- Tell me about your current job. What do you do? How do you like working there?
- What do you do best in that work environment?
- Tell me about yourself.
- Is there anything that will make it difficult for you to get to work on time? Is there anything that would prevent you from working shifts that may change from week to week?

JOB INTEREST AND EXPERIENCE

- What appeals to you about this job? Why are you interested in it?
- Why are you thinking about leaving your current job?
- What do you know about this company? What do you like about this company?
- What are the skills or strengths you can bring to our company?
- How would you do ? (? is relevant to the skills of the job for which the candidate is being considered)
- What are the most important qualities that you look for in a supervisor?
- Tell me about a decision-making or problem-solving situation you were in at work, how you handled it, and what you learned from it.

SELF-PERCEPTION

- How would your current team members or colleagues describe you as a coworker?
- What does your current supervisor think are your greatest strengths at work? What areas of growth would he or she say you need to focus on?
- Describe yourself as a worker.
- What do your close friends or associates think about your work and career?
- If you were to pick three words to be used to describe you at your retirement party from a career in the restaurant and foodservice industry, what would they be?

WORK ATTITUDE/PERSONALITY INFORMATION

- If you were to receive a package that you wanted sometime in this coming week, what would be in it and who would it be from?
- If you could call one famous person—historical or current—for advice about your career, who would the person be and what would you ask him or her?
- If you won the lottery tomorrow, what would you do with the money—where would you live, what would you do?
- What do you want to tell me about yourself that I have not asked?
- Tell me about one of the biggest mistakes that you ever made at work and what you learned from it.

GENERAL

- Any questions about the job?

T 212 555 0648   sushi-izagaya.com

Activity

Create an Interview Schedule

Suppose your quick-service restaurant is interviewing people for a counter-help position. Your restaurant has had problems with employees not being able to work as scheduled because of transportation, child care, and health issues. As the manager, your main goal is to find someone who is courteous, customer-service oriented, and reliable. You desire these traits more than prior foodservice experience, although experience is a plus.

Create an interview schedule with at least five questions that would be appropriate to ask during a screening interview for this position.

_____

_____

_____

_____

_____

_____

_____

_____

Conducting Job Interviews

There are many types of questions and interview strategies to use in selecting employees. Once an applicant has reached the point of a job interview, you need to choose the types of interview questions and interview formats that are the most productive for your needs. Different types of questions are typically asked in these different formats, which include information gathering/skill interviews, stress interviews, and character/personality interviews.

Many interviews involve one person interviewing another person. (See *Exhibit 4f.*) Group and sometimes successive interview formats are variations on this common one-on-one meeting.

Exhibit 4f

Many interviews are conducted in a one-on-one format.

While you may use any of the interview formats in combination with others, you should use the same interview process and questions for each applicant being considered for the same job. Otherwise, the interview process will not be fair, and your operation will be vulnerable to claims of discrimination.

Questions for Information Gathering/Skill Interviews

An information gathering/skill interview involves asking questions about the person that focus directly on his or her background, work experience, previous employers, and job challenges. It is a way of inviting the person to talk about his or her working situations and successes. Questions often used in this format include:

- Why do you want this job?

- How are you qualified for this job opening?

- What are your greatest strengths?

- What areas of your work skills do you want to improve?

- What do you expect from this job?

- How does this job relate to your last job?

- Tell me what you did on your last job.

- Review your previous employment and discuss the skills you developed in those jobs.

- What are you looking for in this job?

- How do you think this job would be like or unlike your last job?

- How would your colleagues describe your work habits and patterns?

- What three or four phrases would your last supervisor use to describe you?

- What skills are you most proud of?

While you may not use all of these questions or find some of them redundant, they will provide you with a range of questions to ask and may suggest other follow-up questions that you could develop. In this interview format, you should give the applicant plenty of time to answer questions, show your interest by nodding in response to questions, and comment whenever appropriate. Your goal is to put the person at ease so that he or she can tell you as much as possible, thereby enabling you to make a better judgment about this person as a candidate for the job opening.

Think About It...

Do you think there are any negative consequences to stress interviews? Is it a good idea for the manager to be the one who conducts the stress interview? Why or why not?

Questions for Stress Interviews

Stress interviews are designed to put applicants in a difficult and stressful situation to reveal how they handle stress, and therefore, the difficult challenges of the job. In this interview format, you may interrupt the applicant in the middle of a response, ask several questions in a rapid-fire format, or avoid smiling or displaying any reassuring body language. Alternatively, you may want to show no response to any of the person's questions or pause for a long time after the person has answered a question to see what he or she does with the silence. Often, the applicant will keep talking and reveal more information about himself or herself and previous work situations.

In addition to creating stress through interpersonal communication methods, you can ask questions about how the applicant would handle stressful situations. Following are some examples:

- You are the dining room manager, and several customers want to talk to you—one about a problem with a waiter, one to complain about the food, one thinking that the bill is not correct, and one to make reservations for a special party. What would you do first and why? How would you handle each situation?

- As a chef working with your team preparing for dinner service, you find that the fresh fish for your signature dish has gone bad in the walk-in cooler, one of the staff informs you that another chef has cut himself seriously and is being driven to the local hospital emergency room by one of the cooks, and the phone is ringing. What do you do first and how do you handle these challenges?

If you use this interview format, be especially careful to use it equally with all applicants you interview for a job. Do not single out candidates for different treatment or make this format more or less difficult for some candidates. Also, be careful that this format does not become an exercise in hostility.

Questions for Character or Personality Interviews

A character or personality interview is often used when you already know that the person has the basic qualifications to do the job, but you are interested in finding out what he or she is like and whether the person will work well in the pace and culture of your restaurant or foodservice operation. In this type of interview, you are assessing an applicant's aptitude and attitude—what he or she will do or is likely to do.

What you are looking for is the way a person looks at his or her life, what his or her values are, and how this person has handled various life challenges. The assumption behind these interview questions is that the person has a personality or work pattern and attitude that he or she will bring to this work situation.

In this interview format, you might ask questions such as:

- What do you like to do in your free time and why?

- What are you reading these days?

- Why did you choose this career?

- What have you gotten out of your education? (This question is appropriate for all levels of education, since individuals can talk about their schooling, lack of schooling, high school, college, graduate school, or education in the "school of hard knocks.")

- What are your dreams for your life?

- How does this job fit into those dreams or long-range plans?

Group and Successive Interviews

While interviews are conducted in a one-on-one situation in many cases, often a group interview is an effective strategy. In a **group interview,** multiple people from the operation interview one applicant. (See *Exhibit 4g.*) The kinds of questions asked in a group interview are the same as those asked in one-on-one interviews. It is essential for the group of individuals conducting the interview to understand the legal limits of the questions they can ask, to develop a plan for the interview, and to interview all the applicants in a consistent format. Sometimes that plan means the group decides on the questions and assigns them to individual interviewers. Doing this ensures the questions are always asked and everyone gets to hear the answer at the same time. At the end of the interview, each person completes a standard candidate evaluation form. (See *Exhibit 4h.*)

Other times, an applicant goes through a series of interviews as part of the screening process. This serial interviewing process is known as **successive interviewing.** Successive interviewing is used

Exhibit 4g

Group interviews, in which multiple people from the operation talk with a candidate, can be an effective strategy.

Candidate Evaluation Form

SUSHI IZAGAYA
425 West 52nd Street
New York 10019

CANDIDATE EVALUATION FORM

Position — Dining Room Manager
Candidate — Kerry Ramirez
Interviewer — Jean Garneau
Type of Interview — First, Group
Interview Date — 4/2/06

RATING SCALE

1 = Unsatisfactory
2 = Fair
3 = Good
4 = Very Good
5 = Excellent

COMPETENCY — **RATING (CIRCLE ONE)** — **COMMENTS**

Functional Skills
- Depth and breadth of experience in profession
- Position-specific experience
- General business acumen

1 2 3 4 (5) N/A

11 years experience, 3 in BOH as prep cook, dishwasher; 8 in FOH, 2 as DR mgr
Managed 120 seat DR, all shifts
Sales increased 10% in 2 years
Reduced FOH turnover 6%

Restaurant Knowledge
- Front of the house
- Back of the house
- Back office

1 2 3 (4) 5 N/A

Extensive FOH knowledge, good BOH knowledge
Could benefit from more back office knowledge but training can address this

Management Skills
- Leadership and experience
- People management skills

1 2 3 4 (5) N/A

Was able to discuss several successful leadership roles
Good listener
Good responses to stress scenario questions

Project Management Skills
- Results orientation
- Organizational skills
- Budgeting/cost control skills

1 2 3 (4) 5 N/A

Has had successful projects but I'd like to see a little more about experience with cost control projects

Organizational Fit
- Interpersonal skills
- Customer-centric mentallity
- Work ethic
- Congruence with core values
- Success traits

1 2 3 4 (5) N/A

Positive attitude, seemed relaxed and confident

Additional comments — Referred by Yvette Jones & Charles Tsai
Overall Hiring Recommendation — ☐ Hire ☐ Close Out ☒ Continue interviewing
Interviewer Signature — _____ Date 4/2/06

T 212 555 0648   sushi-izagaya.com

primarily for management and other senior positions. These interviews may be conducted by the same person or by different people. For example, in the case of an applicant for the position of dining room manager, the general manager may conduct a job interview and then have the executive chef or purchasing agent also interview the person, often using the same questions. Successive interviewing helps to provide various impressions of an applicant, even when the same person conducts all the interviews. Pooling information from various interviews gives a better picture about the applicant and a glimpse at how well he or she may work out as part of the management team.

Completing a standard interview evaluation form will enable the general manager or human resources professional to collate and analyze those perspectives. Meeting as a group as soon after the interview as possible also enables the analysis of these various perspectives and prepares you for the next step, which is hiring.

Exhibit 4i

Providing a tour of the operation will help a candidate learn more about your restaurant.

Providing a Realistic Job Preview

Another part of the interview process is to provide the applicant with information about the job. The more information you can provide about the job, the work situation, and your restaurant or foodservice operation, the better the applicant can obtain a **realistic job preview**—a realistic expectation for the position and operation. Providing this information helps the applicant understand if your operation is one in which he or she wants to work and will be successful. Giving an applicant information about your restaurant or foodservice operation in the form of a brochure, sample menus, Web site URL, and other documents gives the person a chance to read about your operation. Providing a chance for the applicant to ask questions during the interview serves a similar purpose. Providing a tour as part of the screening and interview process can also be helpful. (See *Exhibit 4i.*)

Conducting Reference Checks

Once you have narrowed your search to the best candidates for a job opening, you should check the references they provided. These references may be personal or professional. Most organizations are less interested in personal references since those individuals cannot speak to the candidate's work skills and experience. Personal references also may be more biased.

Activity

Interviewing for the Sous Chef Position

As the general manager of an elegant white-tablecloth restaurant, you have a reputation for graciousness and a welcoming style. Your restaurant is currently considering a candidate, Gloria Pichardo, for the sous chef position.

A sous chef is the person in charge of a kitchen or shift, who works for the executive chef. For example, at lunch, a sous chef may be in charge of the restaurant; at dinner, he or she may be the chef or the person in charge of the casual restaurant while the chef is in charge of the fine-dining restaurant. Often, the sous chef does the expediting (to coordinate production). The name comes from the French words for "under chef."

How will you prepare to interview Ms. Pichardo for the sous chef position? She has already passed the screening tests, been highly recommended, and impressed the executive chef during a previous interview. You want to find out what she will be like on the job, how well she will fit into your team, and what her future might be in your restaurant. Take a few moments to consider an interview strategy and then plan the interview.

1 What information do you want to gather?

_____

_____

_____

2 What questions will you ask?

_____

_____

_____

3 How and where will you conduct the interview?

_____

_____

_____

Many application forms request names and contact information for references. Sometimes applicants do not complete the application form or apply with a cover letter and résumé. In these cases, you need to request reference information and permission from the applicant before you can contact the references. (See *Exhibit 4j* on the next page.) If the applicant refuses permission, you should factor the refusal into your decision whether to proceed with the individual's application.

Exhibit 4j

Sample Letter Requesting Reference Information

Once you have the reference information, you can contact the persons giving the reference, by letter, email, or phone, and ask questions about the applicant. As with interviews, having a standard list of questions helps you obtain the information you need and ensures that you treat applicants in a fair manner. When requesting information in writing, provide a standard reference letter or checklist. Doing this is very helpful to the people acting as references and increases the chances you will get the information you requested.

The references supplied by the applicant are typically former managers or others who are familiar with the applicant's skills and abilities. These people are unlikely to offer negative comments about an applicant because the applicant selected them as references. In addition, recent lawsuits have discouraged people from saying much about applicants. However, you can learn to look for what is *not* said, as well as what is said.

Some people do not have many professional references, especially if they are still at an early point in their career, or have just come back to the workforce after an absence. In these cases, you may want to consider a wider range of references and learn about the applicant's qualities from their perspective.

If you call an individual's reference to see what that person has to say about an applicant, listen for the way the person talks about the applicant in addition to the content of the message. Often, the pauses, choices of language, and the way in which the person responds to questions can tell you a lot. If you have already conducted an interview, you can use the reference conversation to find out information in an area you are wondering about or about a job situation that you did not understand. Remember that the best predictor of future work habits and accomplishments is past performance.

Some of the common questions used in telephone reference checks are listed below. Many of these questions are also applicable to written reference checks.

- Can you tell me in what context you knew this person?

- What were the person's greatest strengths?

- Describe a situation that he or she handled particularly well.

- What were the person's strongest work characteristics?

- What is his or her potential for growth?

- What did he or she do that was exceptional at work?

- Why did this person leave?

- Would you hire this person again?

- Is there anything else you want to share about the person?

In cases in which the reference does not know the applicant through a work relationship, consider questions such as the following:

- What problems have you seen this person handle? How did he or she handle them?

- In what situations have you had a chance to observe this person interact with persons different from themselves? What did you notice about how he or she responded to the situation?

- What has struck you about how this person conducts himself or herself in a variety of social situations? Can you give me some examples of that behavior?

Summary

Screening is the process of learning more about job applicants to determine how suitable they are for a job opening at your restaurant or foodservice operation. This process includes reviewing initial application documents; conducting screening interviews; administering tests, assessments, or simulations; conducting job interviews; and checking references. Some operations also conduct background checks and require applicants to undergo physical examinations or drug tests, or submit medical records, although these activities when used are usually conducted after a job offer is made. At every stage in the process, applicants are evaluated.

Throughout the screening process, it is critical to comply with employment laws regarding discriminatory language and practices. Avoiding discrimination ensures all applicants have a fair chance for the job and protects your operation from claims of discrimination and lawsuits.

Several types of interviews are used during the screening process. Screening interviews, or preinterviews, are intended to (1) gather information about the person applying for a position, (2) make him or her feel welcome, and (3) build interest in the operation. Job interviews are intended to gather additional information about an applicant and to give the applicant a realistic idea of what the job entails. Different types of job interviews and questions can be used to gather information: information gathering/skill interview questions, stress interview questions, and character/personality interview questions. These formats can be combined so different kinds of questions are asked in the same interview. Other interview formats include group interviews and successive interviews.

Review Your Learning

1 Briefly describe the purpose of each of the phases of the screening process:

A. Reviewing initial application documents

_____

_____

_____

_____

B. Conducting screening interviews

_____

_____

_____

_____

C. Administering tests, assessments, or simulations

_____

_____

_____

_____

D. Conducting job interviews

_____

_____

_____

_____

E. Checking references

_____

_____

_____

_____

2 Which of these is *not* a common technique for checking references?

A. Letter

B. Email

C. Phone call

D. Site visit

3 Which statement best summarizes how to comply with federal laws during the screening process?

A. Use different screening methods for each applicant based on his or her abilities, and focus only on tasks the applicant can perform.

B. Use the same screening methods with every applicant, unless the applicant belongs to a federally protected class.

C. Use the same screening methods with every applicant, and focus on the abilities needed to do the job.

D. Use whatever screening methods make sense at the time, and focus on work done by the applicant on previous jobs.

4 Which question is acceptable to ask in an interview?

A. Where were you born?

B. Where do you live?

C. How tall are you?

D. Are you single?

5 Suppose you need to interview people who have applied for a server position at your casual restaurant. On a separate piece of paper, create an interview plan that defines

A. what you want to learn in the interviews.

B. where and when you will interview people.

C. what interview formats you will use.

D. how much time to allow for each interview.

E. what you will say in the interviews.

Notes

Hiring and Orienting New Employees

5

Inside This Chapter

- The Importance of Orientation
- Hiring and Orientation Activities
- Making a Job Offer
- Notifying Unsuccessful Candidates
- Conducting Final Background Checks
- Processing Hiring-Related Documents
- Planning an Orientation
- Managing the Hiring and Orientation Process
- Evaluating an Orientation

After completing this chapter, you should be able to:

- Explain the importance of orientation.
- List the information that belongs in a job offer.
- Identify documents and methods commonly used to communicate operation policies and practices.
- Describe methods for conducting final background checks.
- Recognize the types of documents that need to be produced or processed as part of hiring a new employee.
- Describe the information that belongs in a personnel file and how this file should be stored.
- Develop a checklist to manage hiring-related documents and the orientation process.
- Identify the tools, documentation, and personnel commonly involved in a successful orientation program.
- Recognize the importance of the contributors who conduct orientation activities.
- Identify a method for evaluating orientation programs.

Test Your Knowledge

1 **True or False:** You should conduct all background checks on a job candidate before making a job offer. *(See pp. 99-100.)*

2 **True or False:** Job offers should never be made orally; they should always be extended in writing. *(See p. 97.)*

3 **True or False:** The employee handbook is a document that explains operation policies, benefits, and other workplace information. *(See p. 98.)*

4 **True or False:** Orientation is the meeting with human resources professionals in which new employees sign all the documents necessary to start a new job. *(See p. 105.)*

5 **True or False:** A personnel file contains an employee's hiring- and employment-related documents. *(See p. 109.)*

Key Terms

Employee handbook

Employment contract

Employment letter

Job offer

Negligent hiring

New hire checklist

Orientation

Orientation buddies

Orientation checklist

Orientation kit

Personnel file

Summary plan documents (SPDs)

Union shop

Introduction

The process of hiring and orienting new employees can be a significant challenge for managers who do not have much experience in screening candidates, making a job offer, or planning and conducting orientation programs. As a manager in a restaurant or foodservice operation, you need to understand the steps involved, so you can add employees to your staff and help them become productive and satisfied members of your team.

Hiring involves making a job offer, following careful steps in processing that offer, conducting final background checks, and preparing an individual for employment. All of these steps are at the crossroads of the legal, moral, and personal aspects of hiring. You want to hire the best person for the job and bring him or her into the organization in a welcoming manner. At the same time, there are a number of administrative and legal processes to attend

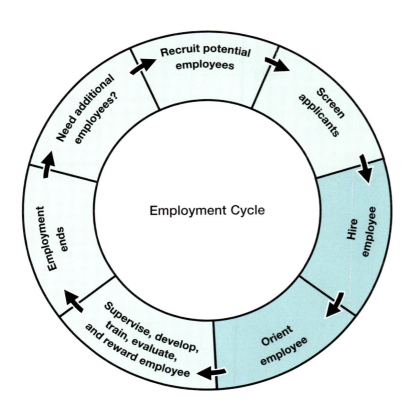

Employment Cycle

- Recruit potential employees
- Screen applicants
- Hire employee
- Orient employee
- Supervise, develop, train, evaluate, and reward employee
- Employment ends
- Need additional employees?

to, so that the new employee gets paid on time and receives the benefits you promised.

Related to hiring, **orientation** is the process of providing an introduction to the organization and the job, so employees know what to do and how to do it. Successful orientation programs help new employees feel welcome in their jobs while they learn the policies, philosophy, and procedures of their new place of employment. Orientation programs also provide employees with an important first impression of their new workplace, which builds a foundation for the employee's attitude. The graphic to the left shows where hiring and orientation occur in the human resources cycle.

In some restaurant and foodservice operations, hiring and orientation tasks are left to the supervisor or manager. In large operations, human resources professionals play a significant role in hiring procedures and the planning and delivery of orientation programs. Whichever model an operation uses, it is important to remember that new employees have lots of questions and significant amounts of anxiety when they start a job. The better the program that welcomes them, the more relaxed they will be, and the quicker they will become effective and productive employees.

The Importance of Orientation

A good orientation program fulfills the needs of both the new employee and the restaurant or foodservice operation. An orientation program has two main purposes: to provide the information that a new employee needs to function effectively at work and to make the employee feel welcome. To do this, orientation programs help set employee expectations for the job and address employees' job questions.

An orientation program demonstrates the hospitality and customer service orientation that you want all employees to adopt and practice. Especially in the hospitality industry, you want your employees to feel comfortable in their jobs, happy in their work, and geared toward customer needs. That means the orientation program should establish a culture of hospitality from the very beginning by welcoming new employees in a careful and thoughtful manner.

Another important function is the guarantee of consistency, something critical to meeting safety and legal obligations. In a formal orientation program, everyone receives the same information, learns the same safety practices, has the same opportunities to learn about the operation, and meets the same key people. This consistency helps ensure that every employee starts with an equal chance at success, which helps you comply with equal opportunity employment laws. A formal orientation program also provides a way to instruct all employees in the fair treatment of customers and employees, as well as meeting the operation's goals for quality, customer service, and safety.

While it is often hard to justify a comprehensive orientation program for employees when there is a high turnover rate, the lack of an orientation program often contributes to more turnover because people do not feel comfortable in their new positions. If new employees do not feel they belong in an operation, they will find another place to work, or they will stay and remain unhappy and unproductive. In the long run, a well-planned orientation program reduces the time and costs needed to help an employee become productive.

Hiring and Orientation Activities

In the human resources cycle, the lines between screening and hiring—and especially between hiring and orientation—can be blurred. (See *Exhibit 5a.*) For example, some operations send tax forms and other documents to a new hire as soon as the job is accepted. Others wait until the employee begins orientation on the first day of work. The order in which many of these steps occur does not matter, as long as they happen within a short time after the employee starts.

Exhibit 5a

Overlap between Hiring and Orientation Activities

Activity	Hiring	Orientation
Make job offer	X	
Send employment letter or contract	X	
Distribute job description	X	X
Distribute employee handbook	X	X
Distribute orientation handbook	X	X
Explain job expectations and probationary period	X	X
Notify unsuccessful candidates	X	
Check background	X	
Check physical abilities	X	
Conduct drug test	X	
Have tax forms completed	X	X
Request proof of eligibility to work	X	X
Request certificates and licenses	X	X
Process job eligibility documents	X	X
Request proof of age	X	X
Request permission for minor/work permit	X	X
Explain benefits and distribute summary plan descriptions	X	X
Complete benefit enrollment forms	X	X
Create and use personnel file	X	X
Create and use new hire checklist	X	X
Explain organizational policies and procedures	X	X
Explain company vision, mission, and history	X	X
Distribute company contact numbers	X	X
Distribute work and payroll schedule	X	X
Introduce employee to staff	X	X
Create and use orientation checklist	X	X
Conduct orientation meeting		X
Provide tour of work area and facilities	X	X
Conduct training		X
Collect feedback		X
Evaluate program effectiveness		X

Screening and hiring activities generally include:

- Making and sometimes negotiating a job offer
- Notifying unsuccessful candidates that the position is filled
- Conducting final background checks
- Managing and processing hiring-related paperwork
- Helping the new employee get oriented to the operation
- Training the new employee how to do the job

In large operations, human resources professionals will be involved in most or all of these steps. Regardless of the size of the operation, as a manager bringing in a new employee, you also will be involved in most or all of the hiring and orientation steps. In addition, you may be involved in the many planning activities that support an employee's hiring and orientation. These include:

- Developing support tools and materials, such as checklists and training guides
- Planning the orientation program and job training
- Preparing employees who will conduct parts of the orientation or job training
- Evaluating the orientation program and job training

Making a Job Offer

Once you have investigated a candidate's references and background and are sure that the individual is the right person for the job, you are ready to make a job offer. A **job offer** is a formal invitation to join an organization as an employee on a certain date to perform a described range of duties for a specific salary or hourly rate and benefits package. If you manage a small operation, you probably will make the job offer yourself. If you work in a large operation in which the human resources department extends the job offer, you most likely will need to file an application or form to have the offer made.

Regardless of the process, as soon as you have made your decision, you or the human resources staff should contact the candidate immediately to make the job offer. The sooner you let the candidate know that you want him or her to join your team, the more likely it is that the candidate will accept your offer.

The actual process of making a job offer will be influenced by the policies of your operation, the culture you have built during

---

Think About It...

- Many experienced food and beverage preparation and service workers are promoted into managerial positions; however, applicants with a bachelor's or an associate's degree in restaurant and institutional foodservice management should have the best job opportunities.

- Most new jobs will arise in foodservice operations as the number of establishments increases along with the population.

- Job opportunities for salaried foodservice managers should be better than for self-employed managers, because more restaurant managers will be employed by larger companies to run multi-outlet establishments.

U.S. Department of Labor's *Bureau of Labor Statistics Occupational Outlook Handbook*, 2004–05 ed.

the recruiting, screening, and interview processes, and sometimes the type of position. Some operations use an initial telephone job offer followed by an employment letter; others use an employment letter or an employee contract directly. An **employment letter** is a letter conveying the job details and starting information to the potential employee. (See *Exhibit 5b.*) An **employment contract,** sometimes called an employment agreement, might be used by some employers. It includes much of the same information as an employment letter. However, an employment contract is a legally binding agreement that includes additional terms of employment, such as termination provisions, and removes an otherwise "employment at will" relationship between the employer and the employee.

Exhibit 5b

Sample Employment Letter

October 28, 2007

Leo Jackson
1320 Green Bay Road
Wauwatosa, WI 53201

Dear Leo:

Thank you for your application for the position of cook and your participation in the search process. Our management staff have met and discussed your experience and background, and evaluated the results of your interviews and cooking demonstration at our restaurant. Consequently, with this letter, I am offering you the position of line cook at Ready Restaurant Row for an annual salary of $45,000, effective November 21. As discussed during the interview process, once you start work, you will be evaluated continuously on your job performance and progress. This offer of employment is contingent on your academic transcripts and references confirming the information on your résumé.

As with all Ready Restaurant Row employees, you will be paid on a biweekly basis and provided with uniforms appropriate to the position. This salaried position offers basic health benefits for yourself, and you have the option of adding your family members to the plan at your expense. As with other employees, your relationship with us will be "employment at will," which means that either of us may terminate the employment relationship at any time for any reason.

I look forward to meeting you on Monday, November 21, at 8:00 a.m.; please arrive in whites and bring a knife kit. We will start with a detailed tour of the facility and some orientation information. Before our meeting, please review closely the enclosed Employee Handbook.

Please sign, date, and return the attached copy of this letter indicating that you accept this position and understand all the conditions. All of us look forward to having you join our team and helping us provide the best ethnic food and quality service in the area.

Cordially,

George Fredricks

George Fredricks
General Manager

When you make a job offer, the information you convey needs to be clear and detailed, so the candidate can make an informed decision. The offer should include:

- **Position information**—Job title, responsibilities, supervisor's name.

- **Compensation information**—Salary in hourly or annual terms, structure of the payments (weekly, biweekly, monthly).

- **Benefit information, as applicable**—Health insurance, retirement plan, details on vacation and other days off, moving and settling benefits.

- **Logistical information**—Start date, contact person, work location (especially important when several facilities exist), hours, scheduled shifts, equipment to bring, uniforms.

- **Employment contingencies, if any**—Results of transcripts, background checks, medical and drug tests.

- **Union information, if applicable**—Whether the operation is a **union shop** (where all employees are required to join the union and pay union dues as a condition of employment).

- **At will statement**—If your operation is located in an "employment at will" state, you should notify the employee that either the employee or the employer can end the employment relationship at any time for any reason.

A job description, employee handbook, or other documents are often included with an employment letter or contract, so that the individual understands the expectations of the operation. An **employee handbook** is a manual or document that contains the policies and procedures for the operation. It can include information on policies relating to dress code and uniforms, vacation, time off, smoking, meal plans, harassment, parking, employment practices, and the workplace environment. In some organizations, the job description and employee handbook are distributed after the new employee accepts the job offer in writing, or as part of orientation.

After you make a job offer, the candidate may need time to consider it. Sometimes, a candidate may want to negotiate elements of the offer, such as the start date or salary. If you are able to come to an agreement that differs from the original offer, the final offer also needs to be documented in another employment letter. In addition, if the person accepts the position verbally, then you should send an employment letter reiterating these details. If you work in a large organization, the human resources department may prepare and send the letter. In any case, two copies of the final letter should be sent, and the person should sign one copy and return it for your files.

In most situations, the new hire will start promptly after accepting the job offer. In other cases, most typically when hiring managers from other operations, there is a period of time between acceptance of the offer and the beginning of employment, since the person may need to give his or her current employer a fair amount of notice.

Activity

Making a Job Offer

Assume you are a manager hiring a new chef. You have reviewed her application, letter, and résumé; studied the results of her cooking test; consulted with others who have interviewed her; and read her interview evaluations. Now you have decided to hire the chef and to call her with a job offer. On a separate sheet of paper, make a list of all the things you need to discuss with her, and then write a script for your telephone call.

Notifying Unsuccessful Candidates

After a job offer has been accepted, you need to let the other candidates know that the position has been filled and thank them for their interest in your operation. For those individuals who you will not be considering for a future position, you can send a simple letter thanking them for their application, indicating the position has been filled and wishing them well in their work or career. If you keep some applicants' letters and résumés on file for other possible positions, then tell them that in your letter. In either case, a positive and encouraging letter contributes to the good image you have with that person and makes it easier to recruit again within the same population and area.

Conducting Final Background Checks

Once you have completed the thorough process of screening applicants and have narrowed it down to the best candidates for the job, you will probably want to conduct a final set of background checks. When conducting background checks, numerous laws come into play, including, for example, the Family Educational Rights and Privacy Act of 1974, the Fair Credit and Reporting Act, and the Americans with Disabilities Act, to name a few. Background checks are used to verify information provided by the applicant, learn more about the applicant's character, and possibly uncover information that the applicant may have withheld. Many of the laws set notice and consent requirements, limit the type or scope of information that can be gathered, and limit the employer's use of the information. While these checks can be done at almost any time in the screening process, they are most often done just after an offer of employment is accepted. Your company should ensure that any background check program it institutes is fully compliant with all applicable laws.

While it may seem odd to do a background check after a job offer is made, operations often do this because they do not want to risk losing their best candidates while they wait for the results of a background check. If a background check turns up a problem, most operations have policies allowing them to dismiss employees who have provided false information or withheld relevant information. In addition, many application forms include a statement for the applicant to sign, which explains that providing false information is grounds for dismissal.

One of the main reasons for conducting a comprehensive background check is to prevent an accusation or legal suit over **negligent hiring**— the failure to ensure, through background checks, that the person is a safe and competent person for the position. To prevent this difficulty, many operations conduct careful background checks in some or all of the areas listed in *Exhibit 5c*.

Exhibit 5c

Types of Background Checks

Area	Common Methods for Background Checks
Work experience	Conduct reference checks or request other documents, such as pay stubs. (See Chapter 4 for more information on conducting reference checks.)
Education	Request that the employee provide school transcripts or copies of certificates, which can take several weeks.
Other preparation and background for the position	Request certificates, licenses, or other documents that can prove a person's preparation or background. The other documents used to help verify a person's background can vary greatly; for example, photos of prepared food or letters of reference.
Criminal background	Hire a firm that conducts criminal background checks; many companies offer this service through the Internet.
Driving record	Hire a firm that conducts background checks; many companies offer this service through the Internet.
Credit record	Buy a credit report from one of the major consumer reporting agencies (Equifax, TransUnion, and Experian). This information can be accessed through the agencies' Web sites. If you check credit records, be careful to comply with all federal and state restrictions on how this must be done.
Physical ability	Request recent health records from the employee or ask the employee to get a physical examination.
Drug use	Request that the employee submit to a drug test.

Drug Testing

Some operations routinely conduct drug tests before a person begins work or as part of the hiring process. When an operation uses drug testing for new hires or job applicants, it must be equally and fairly implemented for all people and not just for selected individuals. For example, if you are going to test applicants for kitchen staff positions, you also need to test all applicants for dining room, administrative, and maintenance positions. Singling out one job category for drug testing is illegal and discriminatory and will open you to possible lawsuits. There may also be legal restrictions on drug testing under either federal or state law. Be sure to understand the applicable laws in your area before proceeding.

Other difficulties with drug testing are the uneven results of various testing systems, the likelihood of false results, and the expense of administering these tests.

Exhibit 5d

Reasonable accommodation for a vision-impaired employee could include magnifying tools or increased lighting.

Health Records and Reasonable Accommodation

The Americans with Disabilities Act (ADA) of 1990 outlaws job discrimination against a disabled person who can perform a job, with or without reasonable accommodation. When an operation offers employment to a candidate who has disclosed that he or she has a disability, the operation typically requests health records or a physical examination to make sure it can reasonably accommodate the new employee. For example, if hiring a person with limited vision, an operation might accommodate the person by increasing the lighting over the station where the person will be working. (See *Exhibit 5d.*) To avoid even the appearance of discrimination, requests for health records or examinations should be made with or after a job offer. According to the U.S. Equal Employment Opportunity Commission, reasonable accommodation may include, but is not limited to:

- Making existing facilities used by employees readily accessible to and usable by persons with disabilities

- Job restructuring, modifying work schedules, reassignment to a vacant position

- Acquiring or modifying equipment or devices, adjusting or modifying examinations, training materials, or policies, and providing qualified readers or interpreters

An employer is required to make a reasonable accommodation to the known disability of a qualified applicant or employee if it would not impose an "undue hardship" on the operation of the employer's business. Undue hardship is defined as an action requiring significant difficulty or expense when considered in light of factors such as an employer's size, financial resources, and the nature and structure of its operation.

Processing Hiring-Related Documents

At some point between when a person accepts a position and the first days on the job, many documents will need to be produced and processed. Exactly when all this paperwork is completed varies by operation. Some can be done before the employee starts, some can be done on the employee's first day, and some can even be done within the employee's first payroll period. For example, before beginning work and being placed on the payroll, the employee must demonstrate that he or she is legally able to work in this country; this proof is documented on an I-9 form. Other documents, such as transcripts and benefit enrollment forms, can wait until the employee starts work. The timing depends on an operation's hiring and orientation practices, which should accommodate payroll and benefit schedules, company policies, and legal requirements. The important thing is that all necessary documents are completed and processed within enough time to do the following:

- Set up the employee on payroll before the first paycheck is due

- Ensure the employee can receive any benefits due on the first day of employment

- Ensure company policies are met, such as having emergency contact information or signed policy agreements on file

- Meet any legal requirements

Hiring-related documents can be grouped into three categories: required employment and payroll documents, benefit enrollment documents, and job and company policy documents. Managers or human resources professionals are responsible for some of these documents, and the new hire is responsible for providing others. When a new hire provides documents, the items usually are needed to prove eligibility to work, as required by I-9 forms, or qualifications for the job, such as a driver's license or sanitation certificate. Whenever an employee provides required documents that need to be returned to the employee, the manager or human resources professional should make a copy of the document to keep on file.

Required Employment and Payroll Documents

The most critical documents that need to be completed or produced are the ones required by law and those that put an employee on the payroll. These documents are usually the first to be completed or shown.

- **W-4 form (Employee's Withholding Allowance Certificate)—**
This federal tax form is provided by the employer and is used for payroll and tax withholding purposes.

Exhibit 5e

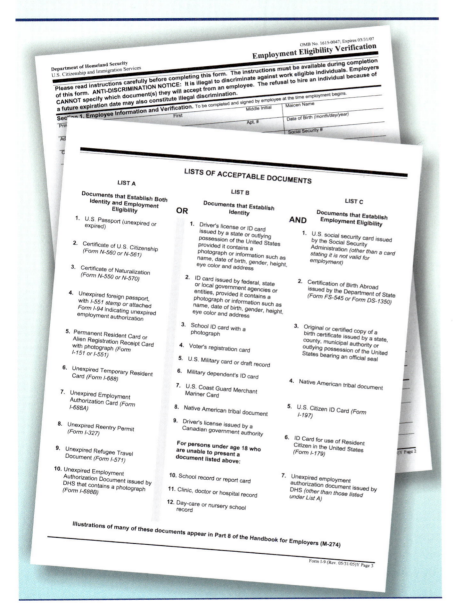

I-9, Employment Eligibility Verification Form

- **State and local tax forms—**The employer provides the necessary state and local tax forms for payroll and tax withholding.

- **I-9 form (Employment Eligibility Verification)—**The employer provides this form, which requires an employee to show specific documents to prove his or her legal right to work in the United States. The required documents are listed on this form. (See *Exhibit 5e*.)

- **Other documents relating to the position—**Depending on the position, its requirements, company policies, or state and local regulations, the employee may need to show or complete some of the following documents:

  ☐ Sanitation certificate

  ☐ Valid driver's license and proof of auto insurance

  ☐ Responsible alcohol service certificate

  ☐ Tip allocation agreement

- **Job eligibility documents, if applicable—**If a person is hired under a governmental program, such as the Work Opportunity Tax Credit (WOTC) Program, additional documents may be required.

■ **Permission documents**—These forms give an employer permission to check the employee's references and background or for the employee to consent to drug testing, if not already covered on the application form.

You also need additional documentation when hiring a minor or hiring someone for a position that involves serving alcohol. First, you need to verify the person is legally old enough to hold the position. Proof of age can be found on many of the other required documents. In addition, in most states, a person younger than eighteen years of age must show written permission from his or her parent or legal guardian to be able to work. Some locations may require a work permit instead. For more information on managing minors, see Chapter 11.

In addition, if the new hire did not complete a standard application form, you should have him or her complete one before starting work. Having all employees complete an application form ensures they are treated equally in this regard. Some forms also provide an acknowledgement of grounds for dismissal.

Benefit Enrollment Documents

Typically, paperwork for enrolling an employee in a benefit plan, such as health or life insurance, is completed on or soon after the employee's first day. While many orientation programs provide presentations on benefit choices, some operations also send the new employee benefit information before employment starts, especially when there is a choice in benefit options. Doing this enables the employee to come prepared to discuss the choices and complete the necessary paperwork, so the employee is included on the benefit plan in a timely manner. If an operation offers retirement benefits, even if the benefits are not available to the employee until after a specific period of time, that information also should be provided. In fact, the federal government requires it in some cases, especially for certain pension and healthcare benefits. Documents called **summary plan documents (SPDs),** which explain plan benefits and participants' rights and responsibilities under a plan, must be provided to employees within ninety days of their participation in a plan. For more benefit notices and disclosures, see Chapter 11.

Job and Company Policy Documents

To ensure new employees understand the job requirements and operation policies, and to protect your operation from potential legal problems, you need to give employees a current job description and the employee handbook. (See *Exhibit 5f.*)

You also should provide a schedule for orientation, information about any probationary period, and other legal documents relevant to your organization. If the employee handbook has been updated since its last publication, you should also distribute these updates and have the new hire sign a document indicating the updates were received.

Exhibit 5f

Sample Employee Handbook Table of Contents

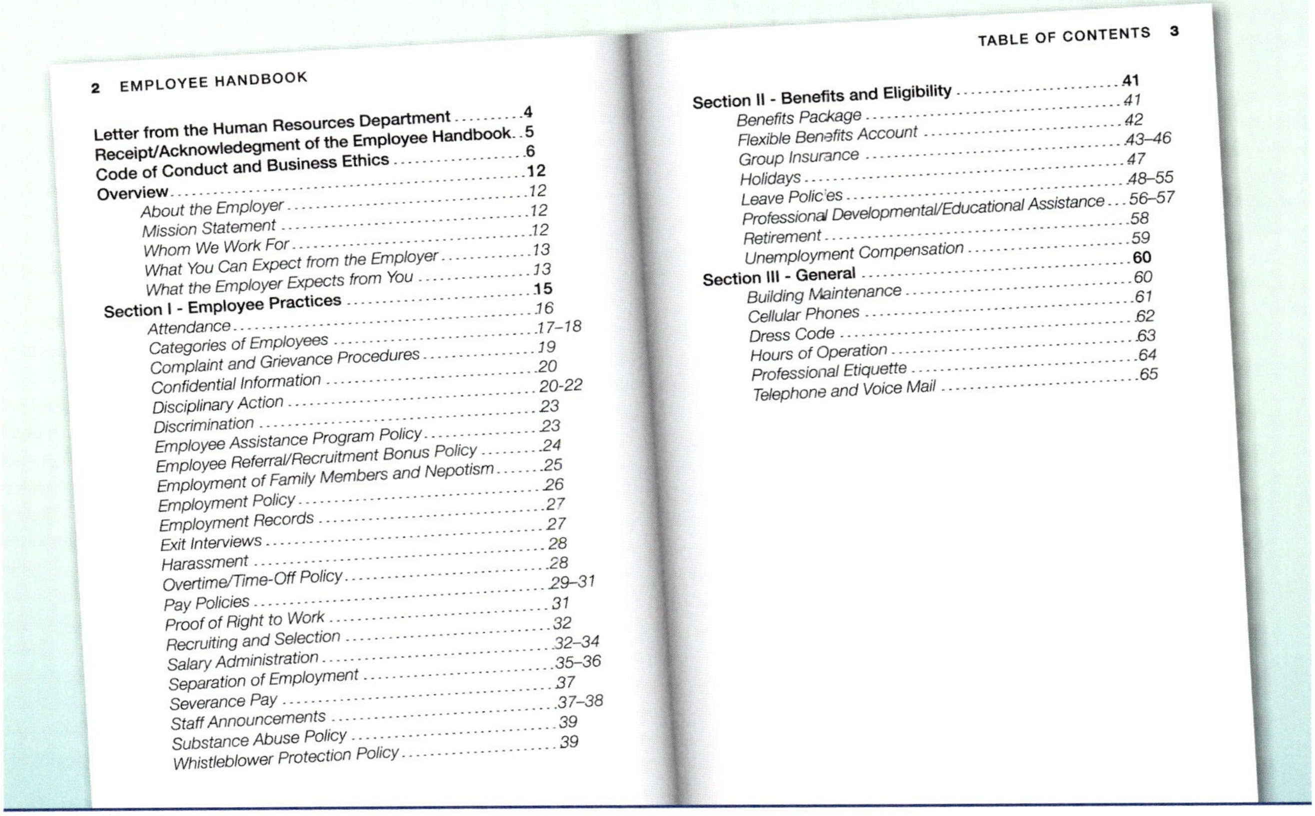

Planning an Orientation

Orientation is much more than a meeting to discuss benefits, fill out forms, make health insurance decisions, and receive an employee handbook. This meeting and its associated technical details are only part of a comprehensive program that involves many components, such as documents, training, and meetings. To coordinate these components and ensure an orientation supports your employees and operation, you need to consider the content that should be included, the structure of the orientation, the materials and resources needed, and the time frame.

Time Frame

Depending on the new employee's position and the size of the operation, an orientation may be as short as several hours or as long as several months. Orientation programs for professional employees and managers can sometimes be as long as three to six months in some organizations because there is so much information to cover. Hourly employees usually have shorter orientations since their time commitment to the restaurant is often shorter, and they do not carry the same responsibility as managers and specialists. In smaller organizations, the orientation period is often even shorter since there is not as much information to convey, and the informal network of employees provides a lot of information. In these situations, managers tend to rely more on documents and one-on-one meetings rather than large group events. (See *Exhibit 5g.*)

Before you can determine a time frame for your orientation, however, you need to consider the information you want to include, sequence of this information, and methods of delivery.

Exhibit 5g

An orientation meeting in a small operation

Content and Structure

Orientation programs are generally comprised of two main areas: information about the operation as a whole and information about the position. In an orientation program that includes a number of new employees, everyone can participate equally in the orientation about the company. Regardless of whether this general orientation is done in a group or on an individual basis, it is typically the first portion of an orientation program and should include the following activities:

- Review of the operation's mission, vision, history, and culture

- Identification of key managers and organizational structure

- Explanation of benefits and benefit schedules, when applicable

- Completion of any outstanding hiring-related paperwork

- Explanation of company policies and procedures

- Distribution of the employee handbook, if not already done

After the general orientation, new employees need to learn about the specific demands of their job, which also may include an overview of how their department fits into the operation. Starting with a job description, the person learns what he or she is expected to do, when it must be done, and what materials are provided. Typically, the direct supervisor conducts this detailed job orientation and provides time for asking questions, although sometimes the job orientation is delegated to others.

At minimum, the job orientation should include:

- Review and distribution of the job description
- Explanation of expectations for the employee's performance in training and on the job
- Training on how to do the job to standards
- Review of the employee's work schedule
- Distribution of contact numbers
- Introduction to coworkers and other staff
- Tour of the work area
- Distribution of any personal equipment or materials supplied by the operation

These last two points cover basic logistics. The tour should include not only the area where the person will be working, but also the offices, break room, time clock, restrooms, parking facility, employee entrance, and storage locations. (See *Exhibit 5h.*) An employee also should receive his or her uniform, nametag, locker information, keys, pager, telephone, or other equipment supplied by the operation.

Longer orientations often include periodic meetings with a supervisor to review how the person is doing on the job and what the person is learning. Often, when a company has a probationary period, the orientation program lasts just as long.

Exhibit 5h

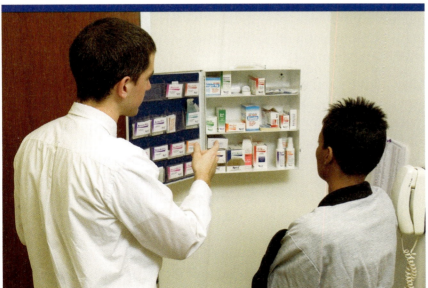

An orientation tour

Materials and Resources

Once you have identified the information and activities that need to be included in an orientation program, you can determine the tools, documentation, and personnel that will help you best accomplish your goals. These resources typically include trainers and other program participants, training materials, and various documents.

In addition to the job description and other hiring-related documents, additional documents used in orientation programs include organization charts, work schedules, copies of menus and promotional materials, and contact information. Of course, there are many other possibilities. To avoid overwhelming new employees with documents, some operations collect and organize these documents in an **orientation kit,** which is given to new hires before or during orientation.

A trainer's guide is an essential tool that helps people prepare for giving an orientation. This guide should include a detailed outline of everything that is covered in the orientation program and all the materials needed to complete the orientation checklist. While it may seem overwhelming, creating a trainer's guide is not as critical as finding and preparing the right person to lead the orientation and supervise the program.

Trainers and Other Contributors

Orientation builds a strong first impression with new employees and provides a foundation for their attitudes, and the people who present the orientation provide new employees with their first real point of contact with the operation. As such, the impressions made here can have long-lasting effects on an employee's attitudes, behavior, and morale.

Many trainers and orientation contributors are chosen for their expertise or their positions in the operation. (See *Exhibit 5i.*) For example, a human resources professional may present information on company policies and benefit information, while a general manager may present information on the operation's vision, mission, and values. The reasoning behind who is chosen to present what information depends on many factors, including the size of the operation, the number of people being oriented, and the availability of the potential contributors. In addition to trainers, some of the roles that orientation contributors may take on include presenters, meeting facilitators, administrators, coaches, and

Exhibit 5i

A general orientation meeting led by orientation contributors

orientation buddies—persons who serve as mentors or guides to new employees during orientation. In small operations, these distinctions may not matter, since the manager or a designee often conducts the entire orientation. Regardless, orientation trainers and contributors need to care about helping people learn the philosophy, polices, and procedures of the operation. To lead an orientation and facilitate these meetings successfully, a person also should be able to present information clearly, with some style or finesse, and handle questions with diplomacy. Ideally, trainers will have at least some of these skills naturally. When they do not, preparing a good trainer's guide for them becomes especially important.

Managing the Hiring and Orientation Process

As the manager in charge of hiring and orienting a new employee, you need to manage the process, as well as prove that certain steps were completed. A good tracking and filing system can help you do this.

Using a Personnel File

Both federal and state employment regulations require that most of the documents processed during the hiring and orientation process be kept on file. These records and other information should be kept securely in an employee's **personnel file,** which is a confidential file that contains documents related to hiring, training, evaluating, promoting, and, if necessary, disciplining an individual. (See *Exhibit 5j* on the next page.) When an employee leaves an operation, information about this separation is also included, such as a resignation letter and an exit interview. The federal government and some state and local governments require that certain records be kept for employees.

Personnel files should be stored in a safe, secure, and private space protected from fire, theft, damage, and curious employees. The files should be kept in a locked cabinet or room, so that unauthorized people cannot access them.

Not all employee records, however, should be kept in personnel files. Medical records, for example, can be kept in separate files.

Exhibit 5j

Information That Should Be Kept in a Personnel File

- Job application
- Cover letter and resume (if applicable)
- Competency or assessment test results
- Interview evaluation forms
- Healthcare forms
- Retirement forms
- Benefits documentation
- Signed employment letter or employment contract
- Job description
- Educational transcripts

- Copies of any certificates
- Letters of reference, or notes of reference checks done by telephone
- Signed W-4 form and state and local tax forms
- Copy of driver's license (if applicable)
- Proof of automobile insurance (if applicable)
- Copy of document proving eligibility to work in the U.S.
- Other internal documents related to employment decisions, such as interview notes and test results from the screening process, and new hire or orientation checklists

Items That Must Be Kept Separately

- Medical information
- I-9
- Work injury records

- ADA accommodations
- FMLA certifications
- Drug test results (if applicable)

Using Checklists

Once you have a method and a place for storing employee records, you can begin to manage the other elements of the hiring and orientation process. Checklists provide an easy way to track and manage the process. A good checklist that is faithfully used will help ensure that you are meeting all the legal, payroll, and policy requirements, as well as ensure that the employee gets off to a good start with no unpleasant surprises.

Two types of checklists are commonly used to help manage hiring and orientation: new hire checklists and orientation checklists.

Given the frequent overlap between hiring and orientation steps, some operations use only one. When an operation uses both, the **new hire checklist** generally focuses on getting the employee and operation ready for the employee's first day on the job, while the **orientation checklist** records what happens on the first day of employment and during follow-up meetings. However, this distinction is relative and depends on the operation.

To ensure all the steps are covered and each new employee is treated equally, checklists should include a way to identify who was responsible for each step and when it was done. Therefore, each step in the checklist should include a place for a name and date. When a step is completed, the person who performed the step or ensured it was done should sign or initial the form and enter the date the step was completed. In this way, especially if employees sign or initial the checklists, the checklists can be used to show that an employee received certain information, such as an insurance policy. Keep completed checklists in employees' personnel files.

New Hire Checklists

A new hire checklist is a form that typically lists all the steps a manager or human resources professional needs to do, or ensure are done, as part of hiring a new employee. (See *Exhibit 5k.*) New hire checklists are particularly valuable for ensuring that all hiring-relating documents are produced or completed. At minimum, a new hire checklist should include steps for verifying the following types of documents were completed or shown:

Exhibit 5k

Sample New Hire Checklist

New Hire Checklist

Name: _Jamie Park_   SSN: _321-54-9876_

Activity or Task	Name	Date
Personnel file created	M. Martinez	9/2/06
Job offer extended in writing	M. Martinez	9/2/06
Job description distributed	M. Martinez	9/2/06
Job offer accepted in writing	M. Martinez	9/6/06
Signed copy of job description received	M. Martinez	9/6/06
Completed job application form on file	M. Martinez	9/2/06
Letter of welcome distributed	C. Kantas	9/7/06
Employee handbook distributed (and signed for)	C. Kantas	9/7/06
Uniform and dress code policy distributed	C. Kantas	9/7/06
Nondiscrimination policy distributed	C. Kantas	9/7/06
Employee referral policy distributed	C. Kantas	9/7/06
Tax forms distributed	C. Kantas	9/7/06
Valid ID shown	C. Kantas	9/7/06
Proof of eligibility shown	C. Kantas	9/7/06
Proof of citizenship shown	C. Kantas	9/7/06
Proof of age shown (or N/A)		
Sanitation certification shown	C. Kantas	9/7/06
Other document shown (please list): RAS cert.	C. Kantas	9/7/06
Other document shown (please list): N/A		
Health benefits plan and form distributed	C. Kantas	9/7/06
Health benefits explained	C. Kantas	9/7/06
Retirement plan and form distributed	C. Kantas	9/7/06
Retirement benefits explained	C. Kantas	9/7/06
New employee gift distributed	C. Kantas	9/7/06
Uniform issued	C. Kantas	9/7/06
Orientation schedule developed		
Orientation schedule distributed		

■ Employment application, job description, proof of employment eligibility, tax forms, proof of age or work permit for minors, and other documents specific to the operation, job, or individual, such as the WOTC Program.

■ Any other documents distributed to the new hire, such as an employee handbook or other company policy documents.

Orientation Checklists

Over the years, operations have developed orientation checklists to ensure that each person has the same orientation experience and a chance to learn all the information associated with the topics in the orientation program. This checklist is a way of guaranteeing equal opportunity to all new employees. It is also a way to monitor each person's progress through the program, such as visiting certain departments or meeting with key supervisors, or managers.

While similar to a new hire checklist, an orientation checklist focuses on a broader range of activities. This checklist should contain the items that need to be covered during orientation, which were previously detailed in the section, "Planning an Orientation." A sample list is shown in *Exhibit 5l*.

In some organizations, the employee must maintain the list. In other organizations, the individual works with another staff member or someone from human resources to ensure all tasks on the list are completed.

Exhibit 5l

Sample Orientation Checklist

Orientation Checklist
Hourly Employees

Name: Terry Blazek   Start date: 03/01/06

Activity or Task	Name	Date
Initial orientation meeting	E. Silverstein	03/01/06
Received health benefits orientation	E. Silverstein	03/01/06
Signed health enrollment form	E. Silverstein	03/01/06
Signed tax form	E. Silverstein	03/01/06
Received retirement orientation	E. Silverstein	03/01/06

Interview with personnel assistant
Interview with general manager
Tour of facility

Received Employee Handbook
Received policy orientation
Received procedures orientation
Received policy of nondiscrimination
Signed equal treatment agreement
Received work schedule
Received job description

Orientation to responsibilities of new job

Initial meeting with trainer
Week 2 meeting with trainer
Week 3 meeting with trainer
Week 4 meeting with trainer

Activity

Create an Orientation Checklist

On a separate sheet of paper, create an orientation checklist for the new hourly employees of a foodservice company that operates a college cafeteria. Include steps for processing hiring-related documents. Consider that new employees need to be familiar with the foodservice operation, its policies, the college environment, and the college's policies for its vendor employees.

Evaluating an Orientation

Managers evaluate orientations for many reasons. First, they want to know if the participants liked the program and felt that it was useful. Second, they want to know if the participants learned anything—if the orientation helped them become more productive, more quickly. (Evaluating training is covered in Chapter 7.) Third, they want to know if the program accomplished its objectives in a cost-effective manner. The ultimate purpose of all this evaluation is to improve the orientation program.

To evaluate an orientation program, managers do several things. They talk to new employees frequently, often on a daily or weekly basis, to see how the orientation is proceeding. From these conversations, the managers can determine how things are going and share this feedback with the person who is running the orientation program. These conversations also support the orientation because the manager can answer questions that are not addressed by it.

In addition, the managers or human resources professionals responsible for orientation often administer evaluation forms at the end of various phases of the orientation program or periodically during the program. *Exhibit 5m* on the next page shows how questions can be posed to rate various aspects of the orientation program and obtain general information. From this evaluation form, human resources professionals or managers can determine whether participants are pleased with the orientation and find it helpful. Evaluations also can be used to get feedback on the trainers' performance or to gauge how well employees feel they are performing after orientation.

Beyond reactions from participants, managers normally ask the trainers or other persons responsible for the orientation program how they think the program is proceeding and what changes need to be made. Combining their insights and the results of evaluation instruments can provide a clear picture of what needs to change to make the orientation more effective.

Exhibit 5m

Sample Orientation Evaluation Form

Orientation Program Evaluation

Start date: _____   Today's date: _____

Please rate the following elements of the orientation program by circling 1 to indicate very poor, and 5 to indicate excellent. Use N/A if item is not applicable, or if you have no opinion due to lack of experience.

Element of the Program   **Ranking**

Element of the Program	Very poor			Excellent		N/A
1 Design of the orientation program	1	2	3	4	5	N/A
2 Usefulness of the information	1	2	3	4	5	N/A
3 Clarity of the presenter(s)	1	2	3	4	5	N/A
4 Clarity of the materials	1	2	3	4	5	N/A
5 Answers to my questions	1	2	3	4	5	N/A
6 Information about the organization	1	2	3	4	5	N/A
7 Chance to meet new employees	1	2	3	4	5	N/A
8 Chance to meet managers	1	2	3	4	5	N/A
9 Interaction with my colleagues	1	2	3	4	5	N/A
10 Individual interviews	1	2	3	4	5	N/A
11 Reading assignments	1	2	3	4	5	N/A
12 Effectiveness of the program so far	1	2	3	4	5	N/A

13 What do you like best about the orientation program so far?

_____

_____

14 What do you like least about the orientation program so far?

_____

_____

In some large operations, human resources professionals or managers evaluate the overall functioning and productivity of the entire orientation program every year. All employees who were new during that year are polled or interviewed to determine how well the orientation program worked. By comparing this information with data collected from other evaluations against the estimated or actual costs of the program, an operation can assess the cost effectiveness of the program. Given the considerable time spent developing and conducting orientation programs, this evaluation time is well spent. In small organizations, an evaluation is done more casually and with fewer cost calculations, since there is often no staff time or resources for a detailed cost-benefit analysis.

Summary

Hiring and orientation affect many aspects of a person's critical first experiences as a new employee. Hiring involves making a job offer, processing that offer, conducting final background checks, and preparing the individual for employment. Orientation involves introducing a new employee to an operation and a job, so that he or she feels comfortable and welcomed. Successful orientation programs offer many benefits, including welcoming new employees, demonstrating hospitality, ensuring consistency, and reducing turnover.

When a job offer is made, it should include details about the position, compensation, and benefits, as well as logistical information and any employment contingencies. If the operation is a union shop, the job offer should mention this. Job offers may be made orally, but the final job offer should always be documented in a letter or employment contract that the employee signs. A job offer may be contingent on the results of a final background check or health examination. Once a position is filled, you should notify the other candidates that they did not get the job.

At some point before or on an employee's first day of work, several documents need to be completed or produced to ensure that the employee can legally work for you and is added to the payroll successfully. Several other documents also need to be distributed or processed within a short time of the start date, including summary plan descriptions. These include benefit documents, such as plans and enrollment forms; job documents, such as a job description; and company policy documents, such as an employee handbook. Benefit, job, and company policy documents also should be explained orally as part of orientation.

Most of these documents need to be stored in the employee's personnel file. This confidential file also should include other employment-related documents. Personnel files should be stored in a safe and secure location.

Successful orientation programs require careful planning and often involve a range of resources. Checklists provide a way to manage the hiring and orientation process, but perhaps the most important resource is the people who will conduct the orientation activities. When an orientation is complete, you should evaluate how successful it was, so that you can make improvements to the program when necessary.

Review Your Learning

1 Which document does *not* need to be shown or completed as part of hiring a new employee?

A. W-4 form
B. Job-related certificates
C. Job application form
D. Tour checklist

2 Which document or set of documents does *not* prove a person's eligibility to work in the United States?

A. U.S. passport
B. Driver's license, along with an ATM card
C. Green card
D. State identification card, shown with another photo identification card

3 Which document does *not* need to be distributed before or soon after an employee starts work?

A. Worker's compensation forms
B. Benefit plans and enrollment forms
C. Job description
D. Employee handbook

4 Which describe the best way to communicate policies and practices?

A. Distribute the employee handbook, and explain the policies and practices orally.
B. Distribute the employee handbook, and tell the employee that raises will be based on whether it is followed.
C. Distribute the employee handbook, and tell the employee to let you know if he or she has any questions.
D. Tell the employee where to find a copy of the employee handbook, and explain the policies and practices orally.

5 Which describe the personnel file?

A. Public file that contains employment-related documents for one employee
B. Confidential file on an operation's employment-related activities and its employees
C. Confidential file that contains employment-related documents for one employee
D. Public file that contains benefit claim forms for one employee

6 Which best identifies the types of materials and resources used in a successful orientation program?

A. Trainers, orientation buddies, meeting facilitators, and human resources personnel
B. Trainers and other program contributors, training materials, job materials, and documents
C. Training guides, handouts, charts, tax forms, and an employee handbook
D. Uniforms, nametags, timecards, keys, and pagers

Supervising and Motivating Employees

Inside This Chapter

- Making the Transition to Supervisor
- What Motivates Employees?
- Planning for Success
- Setting the Right Tone
- Communicating Your Message
- Monitoring Employees and Ensuring Standards
- Disciplining Employees
- Motivating Employees on a Daily Basis
- Creating Recognition and Incentive Programs

After completing this chapter, you should be able to:

- Describe the primary function of a supervisor.
- Recognize needs and factors that affect employee motivation.
- Identify the basis upon which employees should be trained, coached, rewarded, and disciplined.
- List communication techniques for providing feedback to employees.
- Describe techniques for motivating employees on a daily basis.
- Identify the most effective time to recognize or reward good performance.
- Identify the elements of a good employee recognition or incentive program.
- Give examples of rewards given for accomplishment.
- Give examples of incentives that motivate people to change behaviors or improve performance.

Test Your Knowledge

1. **True or False:** Providing feedback to employees helps them improve their performance. *(See p. 132.)*

2. **True or False:** The primary role of a supervisor is to tell employees what to do. *(See pp. 121, 131.)*

3. **True or False:** Greeting every employee every day is a way to motivate employees. *(See p. 135.)*

4. **True or False:** Employees are more likely to follow policies that the supervisor follows. *(See p. 129.)*

5. **True or False:** Incentive programs can encourage employees to uphold standards and improve the operation. *(See p. 140.)*

Key Terms

Coaching	Maslow's hierarchy of needs	Safety needs
Dissatisfiers	Motivation factors	Satisfiers
Ego needs	Motivation-hygiene theory	Self-actualization
Employment at will	Mystery shoppers	Social needs
Esteem needs	Physiological needs	Two-factor theory
Hygiene factors	Primary needs	Wrongful termination
Incentive program	Progressive discipline	
Maintenance factors	Role model	

Introduction

In an industry so dependent on good customer service, many times the difference between a restaurant or foodservice operation that thrives and one that does not is the quality of its supervisors and managers. Good supervisors help their employees be successful, and supervision impacts several areas of the employment cycle. While supervisors are accountable to their own managers, the establishment owners, and customers, helping their employees succeed should be their ultimate goal. Supervisors can only be as successful as the individuals they lead.

To meet this goal, supervisors serve many functions. One is to encourage productivity and quality by creating an environment that makes good use of many tasks and skills. Supervisors plan for success, communicate with individuals and groups, and encourage teamwork. They train and coach employees, monitor and evaluate their work, and discipline them when needed. For good or bad,

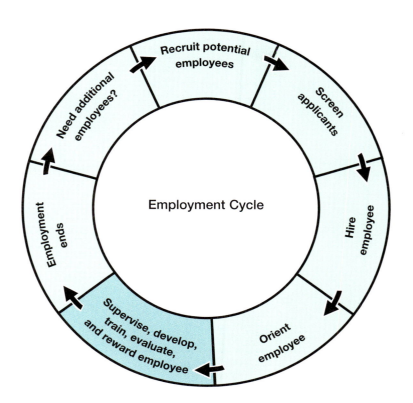

Employment Cycle

- Recruit potential employees
- Screen applicants
- Hire employee
- Orient employee
- Supervise, develop, train, evaluate, and reward employee
- Employment ends
- Need additional employees?

supervisors also set the tone of an operation by the way they treat employees and the behaviors and attitudes they display as a **role model;** that is, supervisors' behavior sets an example that employees will imitate.

Providing the right environment is only part of helping employees be successful. The other main part is motivating them to do the best work they can do. What motivates people varies by individual, so good supervisors should get to know their employees and what motivates them. They should also integrate motivational techniques in their everyday work.

As a new supervisor, your responsibilities may be focused primarily on the "people" aspects of management, although you still will need to plan for your shift and any other responsibilities. As your responsibilities grow, your title may change, and your role may include higher-level monitoring and planning activities. In restaurant and foodservice operations, the title "supervisor" often means the person who manages the hourly employees—those who cook, serve, and clean up after customers. The title "manager" generally means a person who manages supervisors or other managers. However, titles and responsibilities can vary widely among operations. Since both titles imply supervisory responsibilities, this chapter uses the "supervisor" and "manager" titles interchangeably.

Also in this chapter, you will learn about ways to create a productive environment, which includes good communication with employees and planning for performance improvements. You will learn informal and formal ways to help motivate employees, as well as to discipline them. All of this information should help you to be a better manager—one who recognizes the efforts of your employees and who shows them you care not only about their work, but also about them as people. As a foundation for this, you should understand how supervising differs from "doing," which can be a challenge for anyone making the transition from hourly worker to supervisor.

Activity

The Ideal Supervisor

What responsibilities and traits do you think a good supervisor should have?
Be prepared to discuss your answers.

_____

_____

_____

_____

_____

_____

_____

_____

_____

Making the Transition to Supervisor

In the restaurant and foodservice industry, as in many other industries, good employees typically get promoted to supervisory positions on the basis of their performance in a specific job—often based on their ability to perform technical tasks with ease and expertise—and the potential they have to lead others. Restaurant and foodservice operations, like many other organizations, seldom have detailed assessment programs and well-organized orientation programs for new supervisors. People are promoted and provided with support, but they are usually expected to learn the job on the job—to learn how to supervise by supervising. The challenges these new supervisors face are the focus of work efforts and the importance of people and performance.

Changing Your Focus

One of the chronic dilemmas facing many new supervisors is the paradox of working versus leading. As an employee, you can usually see the results of your work in an immediate way: the pots are washed and put away, the guests are happy in the dining room, and the food has been prepped for service. Many people feel a high level of satisfaction from getting specific things done on time and in a visible way. Supervisors, however, can lose that sense of accomplishment and concrete results.

Finding that technical tasks—preparing meals, setting tables, baking bread, or butchering meat—is no longer the focus of work can be intimidating for new supervisors. Recently promoted sous chefs who are now expediting the food at the front of the line, but not preparing it themselves, often get nervous about seemingly not doing any work. New dining room managers who are no longer waiting on tables sometimes find themselves unclear about what they are supposed to do.

In these situations, the new supervisors need to remind themselves that their new job is to set and monitor standards of quality, productivity, and efficiency and to see the larger picture of the entire operation. What they are doing is planning the work of their staff, focusing on the people who will get the work done, motivating the team, and monitoring the performance of the team. The sous chefs focus on the people who prepare and present the food, and the dining room managers focus on the waitstaff who serve the guests. Although the results of your efforts as a supervisor may be less visible than those of an employee's, your work is still important.

As a person coordinating the work of others, you will notice when things are not going well, and you should be ready, willing, and able to pitch in and help. If the plates are backed up in the kitchen, carrying them to tables in the dining room will assist everyone and also show your employees that you are part of the team. If a cook is behind and you are expediting, stepping up to the line and helping him or her may be essential to move forward the orders and prevent a real problem later. The assistance you provide shows that you care about the success of the team and reminds the rest of your employees that you are not above doing the technical work along with them.

As your supervisory experience grows, you may eventually feel too far removed from the actual work. You should know how to do the work of your employees, even if you cannot do it as well as they do. You should also know the standards for this work—how well and how often the work should be done—and the policies everyone must follow. If you do not know these things, your employees will not respect your authority.

While this shift in focus can be hard for new supervisors, the more they consider what they need to plan for and how to build relationships with their employees, the easier it will be for them to reorient their perspective and perform as supervisors.

Building and Managing Employee Relationships

An important aspect of supervision is building relationships with the members of your team—your employees—and their relationships with each other. (See *Exhibit 6a.*) If you were promoted into your position,

Exhibit 6a

An important aspect of supervision is building and maintaining relationships with your team.

you will need to adjust from being one of the group to being the leader of the group. Some of your employees will push you hard to see what decisions you will make and how much they can get away with. As a supervisor, you need to make the right decisions for the right reasons, stand by your decisions, and not be swayed by your relationships with employees.

At the same time, you may find yourself trying to rely on friendships and previous interpersonal relationships to get people to do their work. Unfortunately, when you are a supervisor, these strategies no longer work. You are now their boss and not their colleague, and you need to take charge, make decisions, and remind them of what they have to do, even if this is hard to do. At the same time, it becomes more critical to maintain good relationships with each and every employee and not just the ones that you were friendly with before you became a supervisor. Your work involves everyone, and treating each person fairly and impartially is essential to successfully managing the group.

To build good relationships, you need to be clear about what you say, careful about the implications of your comments, and honest and fair. As a supervisor, you have access to information that employees might not have, and therefore, you often see things from a different perspective. Explaining this perspective and making fair decisions will build positive relationships with your employees. You may end up making decisions that are not popular, but if you make the right decisions for the right reasons, the team members will adjust and work productively with you. In your employees' eyes, your integrity is your most important quality, because they want and need to trust you.

Walking around the operation and talking with employees, listening to their concerns, and sharing your perspective also helps you build new relationships as their supervisor. In addition, you can build these relationships by not taking sides in situations in which you do not need to intervene. In a small organization such as a restaurant, everyone works together and knows each other, and your team wants to know you and trust you as well.

Reflecting on Your Experience

Supervisors get better at their work by reflecting on what they do and its impact on employees and the operation. When mistakes happen, it is important to learn from them so that you can avoid making the same mistakes in the future. When something goes well, it is important to understand why, so you can duplicate or increase your success. While this reflection helps all supervisors, new supervisors especially should examine their work and its effects.

Good supervisors also consider the potential effects of their actions *before* they act. They think before they speak, and they consider their options in every situation. One advantage of thinking before you act is that you can respond to employee requests, guest demands, and institutional pressures from a thoughtful state rather than an emotional one. This behavior also helps supervisors model thoughtful and considerate action to employees.

What Motivates Employees?

The issue of motivation can be a very complex one. In reality, you cannot motivate anyone; motivation must come from within each person. You can direct employees, but if they are not motivated to work, you will not get the responses you want. They may do the work, but not as well, as quickly, or as enthusiastically as you would like. When employees are not motivated to do a good job, customer service, employee morale, work quality, teamwork, and ultimately, profits can all suffer.

While you cannot force employees to feel motivated to do a good job, you can create conditions that employees will find motivating. Yet what motivates one person may not motivate another. People are motivated by different needs—money, social interaction, job satisfaction, or any number of factors—and these needs may change over time. Everyone is different, which is why you as the supervisor need to know your employees and what motivates them as individuals.

Even so, there are situations that commonly motivate people and situations that commonly demotivate people. Some operations develop employee recognition and incentive (reward) programs to try to motivate people. These formal programs are discussed in more detail later in this chapter. However, there is much you can do outside of such programs to help motivate employees, and these techniques are discussed throughout this chapter as well.

Before getting into motivation techniques, it helps to have a better understanding of the needs that motivate people. There are many theories about this. Two of the most widely accepted today are Maslow's hierarchy of needs, and the motivation-hygiene theory.

Maslow's Hierarchy of Needs

Psychologist Abraham Maslow theorized that human beings have five basic needs that arise or evolve in a specific hierarchy, or order. This theory is known as **Maslow's hierarchy of needs.** In this hierarchy, as soon as one need is fulfilled, a person is motivated to fulfill the next higher need. These five needs are depicted by the graphic in *Exhibit 6b.*

Exhibit 6b

Maslow's Hierarchy of Needs

- Self-Actualization
- Esteem
- Social
- Safety
- Physiological

Primary

In this theory, the lowest or most basic needs are **physiological needs.** These needs relate to the body, such as the need for food, water, air, or sleep. In most work environments, employees' physiological needs are met through heating, air conditioning, lighting, meal and rest breaks, and limits on work hours. When physiological needs are not being met, people are motivated to fulfill them. Once these needs are met, people are motivated to fill their needs for the next level, safety.

Safety needs deal with those things that make us feel secure or keep us safe. These things can be physical, such as shelter or a stable income, or they can be emotional, such as a familiar routine or freedom from anxiety. In the workplace, safety needs can be met by fair wages, healthcare and other benefits, safety procedures, standard procedures, protective equipment, and a number of other factors.

The next level, **social needs,** involves people's needs to be with others. Social needs include love, belonging, and friendship. In the workplace, social needs can be met through friendship, teamwork, and a sense of belonging or acceptance, all of which are encouraged by a welcoming atmosphere. Social, safety, and physiological needs are sometimes called **primary needs** (as shown in *Exhibit 6b).* After these are met, people are motivated by the need for esteem.

Esteem needs or **ego needs** focus on how people feel about themselves and how they perceive what others feel about them. These needs are concerned with self-esteem, self-respect, and the esteem and respect of others. Esteem needs in the workplace may be met through recognition, promotions, titles, acknowledgments, appreciation, opportunities, and many other factors.

At the highest level is the need for **self-actualization**—the realization of one's own potential. The need for self-actualization or self-realization drives people to push themselves, to learn new things, to be creative, and to otherwise become the best they can be. In the workplace, this need may motivate people to become the most productive they can be, produce the best quality work they can, or develop themselves for other positions.

While most people have some needs in common, these can vary by individual. For example, the lack of health insurance may cause one person to feel unsafe or insecure while another person may not be bothered by this. Or one person may have a need to be recognized through promotions while another person may not care about job titles. Complicating this for supervisors is that people's needs change, so that what motivated an individual at one time may not motivate him or her later.

Activity

Identify Needs According to Maslow's Hierarchy

Match the activities to the correct level in Maslow's hierarchy of needs.

**Maslow's Hierarchy of Needs
(lowest to highest)**

1. Physiological _____
2. Safety _____
3. Social _____
4. Esteem _____
5. Self-actualization _____

Activities

A. Create new dishes

B. Take a bathroom break

C. Receive training on operating a meat slicer

D. Hear compliments about a good job

E. Have a drink with coworkers after work

Motivation-Hygiene or Two-Factor Theory

Many people assume that the factors that motivate and demotivate people are opposites. For example, people may think that if someone is motivated to work hard to earn vacation time, the same person would not be motivated to work hard if he or she did not get any vacation time. Frederick Herzberg's **motivation-hygiene theory** proposes that this reasoning is not correct. His theory, which is also called the **two-factor theory,** identifies different sets of factors that can motivate and demotivate employees. Factors that motivate employees are called motivation factors and factors that demotivate employees are called hygiene factors, as shown in *Exhibit 6c.*

Exhibit 6c

Motivation and Hygiene Factors

Motivation Factors	Hygiene Factors
■ Esteem	■ Working conditions
■ Accomplishment	■ Company policies
■ Contribution	■ Hours
■ Responsibility	■ Equipment
■ Acknowledgement	■ Fair pay
■ Recognition	■ Health benefits
■ Growth	■ Time off
	■ Working relationships
	■ Supervision style

Motivation Factors

Since motivation is something that comes from within a person, the factors that motivate employees sometimes seem intangible or abstract. According to the motivation-hygiene theory, **motivation factors** include opportunities for esteem, accomplishment, contribution, responsibility, acknowledgement, recognition, and growth. For example, the sense of self-worth (esteem) and accomplishment that comes from completing a project can motivate a person to do a good job on a special project. Motivation factors encourage employees to work harder, go beyond the ordinary, and make a real difference in their workplace. These factors make employees happy about their workplace, which is why they are sometimes called **satisfiers.**

Think About It...

According to psychologist Frederick Herzberg, fair pay is a hygiene factor and does not motivate employees to work harder.

Hygiene Factors

Hygiene factors are work situations that can make employees unhappy and prevent them from doing a good job. These factors can maintain employee satisfaction or make employees unhappy, which is why they are sometimes called **maintenance factors** or **dissatisfiers.** Hygiene factors include working conditions, company policies, hours, equipment, fair pay, health benefits, time off, working relationships, and supervision style, among others. If an employee feels that he or she is not making a living wage, for example, this belief will demotivate the employee, with the possible result that the employee feels justified in doing less than a full day's work.

On the other hand, better hygiene factors *do not* motivate employees to do better work. Satisfactory hygiene factors exist to make sure employees can do their work, and employees expect that certain conditions will be adequate. For example, if you fix the air conditioner in the kitchen, employees initially may feel motivated, but adequate air conditioning does not motivate them in the long run. However, improving hygiene factors still benefits the operation in other ways:

■ Provides the tools, situations, and support employees need to do their work

■ Shows you care about your employees and are interested in their concerns

■ Helps prevent demotivation, poor morale, and turnover

■ Models respectful and caring behavior

Exhibit 6d

Spectrum of Hygiene and Motivation Factors

Fulfillment of motivation factors

- HIGH motivation
- LOW job satisfaction

- HIGH motivation
- HIGH job satisfaction

- LOW motivation
- LOW job satisfaction

- LOW motivation
- HIGH job satisfaction

Fulfillment of hygiene factors

Hygiene factors provide a foundation for the workplace, like the river does for a rowboat. If the water is calm, no one pays it much attention. If the water is rough, it makes people uncomfortable, afraid, and distracted, and the boat becomes harder to row. Motivation factors encourage employees to move the boat faster.

To help their employees be successful, good supervisors do their best to create an environment that encourages success—an environment with satisfactory hygiene factors and some motivating factors. (See *Exhibit 6d.*) An environment like this does not just happen on its own; good supervisors plan for it, develop it, and nurture it.

Planning for Success

Developing a positive, productive work environment involves a range of activities. It begins with creating a clear vision of the kind of workplace that you want and then making plans to get there. Most supervisors' visions include a functional, profitable, and quality based establishment that customers enjoy, but you need to consider other aspects as well. Do you want employees to feel good about their work? How do you want them to feel about their role in your operation? Do you want employees to feel camaraderie with their coworkers? What kind of environment do *you* want to work in? As a supervisor, you need to think about what it is you want to create, and then you need to plan for both the day-to-day work and the future improvements that will support your vision.

An important task of supervision in a restaurant or foodservice operation involves planning and organizing the work of your team. This task can involve organizing the work schedules, planning for regular and special events, and ordering supplies ahead of time to make sure everything runs smoothly. To accomplish this work, you need to know the strengths and weaknesses of each person on your team so you can plan the work accordingly. (Chapter 9 deals with additional day-to-day work that you need to plan.)

The other aspect of planning is preparing for future improvements. A large part of this involves developing the potential of your employees. Employees are the "ingredients" you have to work with to make your operation run profitably, effectively, and smoothly. Therefore, you need to reflect on and develop a plan for developing the potential within each employee. This development includes reviewing their work performance and goals, considering their possible future in the operation, and developing a personalized plan to move an employee toward a goal that you set together. Moving into this form of planning will open up new vistas and will help you see that motivating and developing employees is a full-time job in itself, and one of the most important jobs you have as a supervisor.

There are many ways to help your employees develop. Many of these are covered in more detail in Chapter 7. However, employee development is only one way to help improve employee performance.

Setting the Right Tone

Once you have a clear sense of what you want to happen in your establishment, you will find it easier to communicate your vision to employees. Part of this communication is indirect and sometimes unconscious. As a supervisor, your behavior and attitude set the tone for your operation. Deliberately or not, you are a role model for your employees. If you want people to like each other and care about each other, for example, then getting to know them as individuals and showing that you care about them sets that tone for the rest of the team. If you want to encourage teamwork, then rolling up your sleeves and pitching in when needed demonstrates what you want employees to do. If you want employees to follow the policies of the operation, then you need to follow them yourself, without exception.

Serving as a *good* role model takes a commitment to practice what you believe in all the time. Being a good role model means showing others what you want them to do by practicing it yourself. It means being constantly aware of what you do and what you say because your behavior illustrates the range of acceptable behaviors for others. Although subtle, messages given through this type of modeling can be very powerful and will have a greater impact than any sign or announcement you might make.

While being a role model sets the tone of your operation, inspires employees, and communicates the importance of certain behaviors and attitudes, a supervisor's role also includes more direct methods of communicating with employees.

Think About It...

What do these supervisor behaviors tell employees?

- Picking up a piece of litter in the entryway

- Helping to clear tables during an unusually busy rush

- Staying calm and impartial when reacting to conflict

- Asking employees how they are

- Throwing away food as soon as its holding time has expired

- Listening actively to customer and employee complaints

- Making eye contact with people and smiling

Communicating Your Message

Clear and frequent communication about what you want employees to do and how you want it done makes it easier for them to accomplish your goals and to align their work with your goals. Unfortunately, many supervisors do not take the time to discuss with their employees what they want to happen and how they want it done, or what the employees are doing well and what needs improvement. This lack of information often leaves employees guessing about priorities. In restaurants, customer service is often the clear priority, but food safety, good food, careful and prompt service, cost consciousness, and personal safety are also very important. The clearer you can be about how you want employees to communicate with each other, what needs to be done in what sequence for the shift, and the importance of food sanitation and personal safety, the better the employees can follow your lead.

Exhibit 6e

A common communication method is the preshift meeting.

Communicating with restaurant or foodservice employees can be done through a variety of methods. One of the most common ones is the preshift meeting, a short meeting held in the kitchen before the shift starts or in the dining room before it opens for the guests. (See *Exhibit 6e.*) Other methods include production meetings in which key employees meet with managers to discuss production issues and plans for upcoming events. Although not common in restaurant and foodservice operations, sometimes having a large group meeting with all employees can be a productive way of communicating a lot of information and ensuring everyone hears the same message at the same time. Another way to communicate information to all employees is by posting it on the employee bulletin board. (If you use this method, make sure to change the information regularly to encourage people's continuing interest in the board.)

In large operations, supervisors and key employees also may be part of a management group meeting to talk about an upcoming event or series of events that will take a significant amount of coordination. In these meetings, you will be communicating with a small but important group of employees and involving them in planning for upcoming events. Being part of such a meeting also can motivate employees who participate.

Monitoring Employees and Ensuring Standards

A large part of a supervisor's daily work is monitoring employees, informally evaluating their performance or work, and providing them with feedback. Good supervisors circulate around the operation, noticing and commenting on how things are going and making sure that everything happens as it should. As a supervisor, your presence and involvement help you know what is going on. It also shows that you care about what is happening and enables you to help make the operation a better place to work.

Because there are so many performance expectations in a restaurant or foodservice operation, it is easy to forget to uphold other important and critical standards. As a supervisor, however, enforcing standards is one of your primary responsibilities. To ensure standards are met, you will need to spend time helping employees learn—or relearn, if they forget—the standards of the operation. Part of this learning will come from the feedback and coaching you provide to individuals. In some organizations, coaching is a formal program through which an employee is matched with a coach—an experienced employee or supervisor—who helps the employee achieve career goals or increase skills and knowledge. Coaching also can be done informally and involves observing an employee's behavior and then providing feedback on ways to improve performance. However, for employees whose work meets standards, you need to remember to reinforce their positive performance.

Reinforcing Positive Performance

When employees are following policies and meeting or exceeding standards, you have the chance to recognize superior performance and compliment or reward it. The most powerful reward is saying "good work" and "thank you" to employees when it is deserved. The power of this recognition is magnified if you express your appreciation as soon as you notice the good work rather than waiting until later.

There are, of course, other rewards that you can use for employees, ranging from different work schedules, transfers, cross-training opportunities, educational opportunities, new assignments, bonuses, promotions, and raises. (Formal incentive programs are discussed later in this chapter.) However, the most powerful reward continues to be timely praise and recognition for a job well done and the satisfaction that comes from doing good work and having it recognized.

To help employees who are not meeting standards, you need to provide coaching and feedback. These activities can be part of a formal program or done informally on a day-to-day basis.

Providing Feedback for Improvement

Most employees work hard and want to do well. While feedback given to a group can be helpful, it does not usually have the impact that specific, individual, and deserved feedback has on an employee. Providing comments to someone about what he or she is doing well and what can be improved shows that you notice and appreciate the employee's efforts and hard work. For example, a sous chef might say to a line cook, "Your plates look really good tonight."

Feedback also is one of the most important tools a supervisor has for improving employee performance. The feedback supervisors give can be informal, such as the compliments and suggestions given to employees on a routine basis, or it can be formal, such as through coaching programs (discussed in detail in Chapter 7) or employee evaluations. Here are some points to keep in mind about feedback:

- **It needs to be provided in a timely manner and with specific recommendations about what to do differently.** Of course, compliments should be given immediately, but feedback designed to encourage change is better delivered one-on-one in a private setting. Since there are so many things happening in restaurant and foodservice operations at the same time, good supervisors take notes about things that cannot be addressed at the moment and find a more appropriate time to talk to the individuals involved.

- **Consider using the sandwich method of giving feedback.** In this method, you provide a compliment, point out the problem behavior, give the suggestion for correction, and then end with another positive compliment. Done this way, employees are often more able to hear the corrective feedback. However, in using this method, be careful not to provide so many positive comments relative to the corrective ones that the employee does not hear the message you intended to give.

- **Maintain a professional and positive attitude.** Be sure to focus on the behavior, not the person. If you are frustrated by what is happening, wait to provide the employee with feedback because your emotional state will make it hard for the employee to hear what you really want to say. A good way to start is to ask the employee to describe any difficulties they find in their performance. Doing this provides an indication of the employee's awareness of the problem. Then you can correct their understanding or affirm it and compliment them on their insight. After this, make suggestions for improvements, listen to the employee's response, and ask the employee for input on how to improve the situation.

- **When you see the person improve, compliment him or her as soon as possible to acknowledge the effort and to encourage continuing improvement.** Not acknowledging the change may communicate that you really do not care about the person or the new behavior. If you are asking a person to make many changes or a particularly difficult one, noticing improvement along the way will encourage him or her to keep moving forward. (See *Exhibit 6f.*)

Exhibit 6f

Noticing improvement will encourage an employee to keep moving forward.

Disciplining Employees

In restaurant and foodservice operations, supervisors spend a lot of time training and monitoring the performance of employees to ensure they meet standards. Those who need help should be provided with it immediately by front-line supervisors and peers. When an employee who has had adequate training and help does not learn from feedback and reminders, you are obligated to remind the employee of the basic job expectations and of the possibility of disciplinary action. Using the job description or employee handbook to remind an employee can be a helpful strategy, especially for employees who might say that they did not know any better. However, when employees do not seem willing or able to perform to standards, you may need to discipline them.

The most effective disciplinary system involves **progressive discipline,** a model in which the employee has plenty of warning and support to improve his or her behavior and performance. Progressive discipline begins with feedback to an employee about what he or she is doing well and not doing well. If feedback and additional training do not help the individual improve, then you as a supervisor will need to provide notice about the behaviors that are below standard and remind the individual to improve them by a certain time, or there will be consequences, ranging from reduced hours to reassignment to eventual termination.

A system of progressive discipline requires that you provide an employee with written feedback about what is below standard, the support needed to improve, a timeline for the expected new behavior, and clear consequences. If the employee improves in a timely manner, then the system has succeeded. If not, then you will have to move to a more serious consequence, which can vary depending on the person's job and the nature of the restaurant or foodservice operation but eventually will end with termination.

To prevent **wrongful termination,** in which employees are fired for arbitrary, unproven, or discriminatory reasons, some states under various legal theories require an employer to have a legitimate cause for terminating an employee. However, even in states that adhere entirely to the **employment at will** doctrine, in which employers can fire anyone for any reason, good supervisors use progressive discipline. The progressive discipline process shows all employees that you want them to succeed and helps keep morale high, even when someone has been let go for poor performance. In fact, implementing progressive discipline reminds everyone that you are serious about the policies and standards of your operation, and they will respond accordingly.

Activity

Identifying Needs You Can Fulfill with Communication

Consider the needs or factors that motivate people as defined by Maslow's hierarchy of needs and the motivation-hygiene theory, including the hygiene factors that can dissatisfy people. Which of these needs and factors might a supervisor meet just by communicating (including listening) with employees? List all the factors or needs that apply, and be prepared to discuss your thoughts with the class.

From Maslow's hierarchy of needs:

_____

_____

_____

_____

_____

_____

From motivation-hygiene theory:

_____

_____

_____

_____

_____

_____

Motivating Employees on a Daily Basis

While the fear of termination may motivate some employees to do their jobs, there are much more effective ways to motivate people. When developing a strategy to motivate people, consider that basic communication and employee involvement can fulfill many of the needs or factors that motivate people. For example, a person's need for esteem might be filled by a simple "thank you," or a need to contribute might be filled by asking an employee's opinion of a problem. Being aware of employee needs and using communication and employee involvement as a way to meet these needs are easy, inexpensive, and effective ways to motivate your staff.

Aside from explanations to assuage fears or improve hygiene factors, communication that motivates employees generally falls into a few categories, including:

- Acknowledging people
- Expressing appreciation
- Sharing information
- Expressing interest

Acknowledging People

Routinely acknowledging your employees—showing that you notice them as individuals and care about them along with their work—is an important yet often overlooked aspect of motivating employees. Simple acts, such as saying hello, calling people by name, or making eye contact can make a big difference to employees and help set a positive tone.

A good habit that acknowledges people and has other benefits is greeting your employees every day at the start of the shift. Greet them by name, make eye contact, shake hands (if this comes naturally to you), and smile. These actions communicate to employees that you care about them, and that they are important to you. Conversely, people who never communicate with their manager often feel unappreciated and absorb the message that they are not important. In a restaurant or foodservice operation in which everyone is important, you do not want to give anyone that unintended message.

Saying hello every day also gives you an opportunity to check *in* with employees rather than check *on* them. This daily exchange gives you the chance to ask how they are doing and to see whether everything seems to be going smoothly. It also has value beyond motivation: you can verify the employee is ready for work.

In addition, make a habit of saying goodbye at the end of the shift to acknowledge your employees and their importance to you. Whenever possible, also mention something that went well during the shift, especially any contributions made by the employee. This gesture is always appreciated, even if employees do not show it.

Expressing Appreciation

There are several common motivation strategies that every employee appreciates, and the most common one is a simple and honest thank you for a job well done or for exceptional effort. Besides appreciation expressed in an informal way, there are other methods you can use in combination with this strategy.

- **Extend your personal thanks by placing a positive note in the employee's file (either your file or the official personnel file).** Such a note helps you remember later what the person did that

Think About It...

According to the Gallup Organization, approximately twenty-two million workers are presently "actively disengaged," or extremely negative about their workplace situation. This costs the U.S. economy up to three hundred billion dollars a year in lost productivity—not accounting for absence, illness, and other problems that result when workers are disengaged from their work and their companies.

Gallup Press, July 6, 2004

was special, which is useful when you need to formally evaluate the employee's performance. The disadvantage of this strategy is that the employee will not see the positive note unless you share it with him or her.

■ **Publicly express your appreciation, or that of a guest.** In some operations, when managers hold a large group meeting to review policies, standards, and other operating information, they also use the meeting as an opportunity to publicly thank individuals or the group. Smaller team or shift meetings provide the same opportunity. Likewise, when a guest writes a complimentary letter that mentions an employee's name, share that compliment with your entire staff. Post a copy of the letter, or read it aloud at a shift meeting. (See *Exhibit 6g.*) The power of this recognition for the person being complimented and for the rest of the group cannot be underestimated. Although sometimes this activity can embarrass an employee, normally it makes him or her and the rest of the employees feel good. It also encourages everyone to work harder to get that kind of recognition.

Sharing Information

People like to know what is going on in their operation. This interest is natural because it satisfies a person's need to feel secure, to feel a sense of belonging, to feel valued, and to feel involved. If new things are happening in the operation, tell your employees. If there is a special party coming in, the possibility of an upcoming large event, or new tables, chairs, or linens, tell your employees. Let them share in the information. Too often, managers, especially front-line supervisors who are new to management, are excited to learn this information and forget or are reluctant to share it with employees. You have nothing to lose and a lot to gain by keeping employees informed.

Sharing information also creates a foundation for involving employees in the operation. If you want employees to cooperate with new policies and procedures, for example, they are more likely to do so if they understand why these changes are needed. As you can imagine, sharing information with employees also is the first step in asking for their help in solving a problem. For instance, one of the most successful ways to encourage employees to take care of the glassware and plates is to tell them about the cost of breakage. If they understand how the cost of breakage diverts money away from other things, such as new equipment or bonuses, then they will be motivated to be more careful.

Exhibit 6g

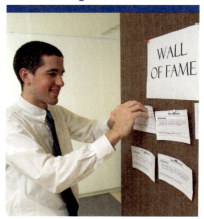

Appreciation motivates people.

Think About It...

Has someone ever asked you a question and then not paid attention to your answer? How did you know they were not interested? How did that make you feel?

Expressing Interest

Expressing interest in your employees is another way to show you care about them both as individuals and as team members. Asking someone, "How are you?" and listening to the answer demonstrates your interest in that person as an individual. Asking "How is it going here?" or "What do you think about that?" shows that you care about their experience at work and are open to hearing their perspectives and suggestions. When you ask a question, *listen* to the answer and show you are interested. If you fail to do this, your questions will be seen as phony, and may very well do more harm than good.

Conversely, be careful not to get too personal in your questions. In an employee's mind, there may be a fine line between harmless interest and harassment, discrimination, or plain nosiness. Avoid asking about any of the topics you would not ask in a job interview, such as marital status, race, ethnicity, religion, sexual preference, or disability, unless the employee brings up any of these topics first. If you are not sure whether it is appropriate to ask a question, then do not ask, but try not to seem indifferent. Keep in mind that differences and life experiences are things to celebrate, and take your cues from the employee.

Involving Employees

Involving employees in the operation can motivate people for many reasons. When you involve employees in planning, problem solving, and decision making, you are recognizing them as valuable individuals and team members, and providing opportunities for responsibility, contribution, creativity, and growth. In addition, soliciting employee suggestions and feedback shows your commitment to the team and to teamwork. Involving employees also produces better plans, resolutions, and decisions than those that do not consider employee input.

You can involve employees in various ways, from informal discussions to formal committees, projects, and programs. Make time to talk to employees and get their ideas—something some of them may be initially reluctant or unused to doing—and consider their input before announcing your priorities. Listen to what they say, and show that you listened by acknowledging what they shared with you, even if you do not use their ideas. Do not criticize their suggestions. If you do not listen to or acknowledge employees' suggestions, or if you criticize them, then employees will stop sharing ideas with you.

When guests complain, share this information with employees and ask for suggestions to solve the problems identified by the guests. Your employees can help you identify patterns, both good and bad, based on guest feedback. In these situations, honest and caring employees who have the best interests of the operation at heart can make very helpful and insightful suggestions and comments.

Whenever you can, involve your employees in the operation. For example, large operations often have several committees in which employees can participate, such as the safety committee, menu and logistical planning committee, banquet committee, and total quality management (TQM) committee. In smaller establishments, this involvement usually takes place through one-on-one conversations or short stand-up meetings while other things are going on. Regardless of the size of an operation, if you know your employees and understand what motivates them, you can ask for their involvement in various areas. *Exhibit 6h* lists examples of areas where you might want to ask for employee feedback or involvement.

Exhibit 6h

Examples of Areas for Employee Involvement

- New food items for the menu
- New beverage items
- Ways to respond to guest complaints
- Suggestions about saving money
- Improving guest satisfaction
- Setting goals for the team

- Improving the overall operation
- Food safety practices
- Fcod storage suggestions
- Marketing ideas
- Promoting the number of covers or house counts

Activity

Acknowledging Suggestions

Consider the following scenarios and how you as the supervisor might respond to each employee. Work in groups of three for this activity. Role-play the supervisor in one of the scenarios and have classmates role-play the other two roles. Switch roles for each scenario, so each person role-plays the supervisor once. After each scenario, discuss how the supervisor did and what he or she might have done better.

Scenario 1

You are the supervisor of a large family-owned restaurant. Kim, the owner, has been pressuring you to reduce costs and has suggested reducing portion sizes. You are worried that both employees and customers might not like this idea, so you ask Pat, one of your most experienced employees, for ideas. Pat suggests some inventory and purchasing changes that sound terrific. Before you get a chance to respond to Pat's ideas, Kim approaches both of you. How will you acknowledge Pat's ideas?

Roles

- The supervisor
- Kim, the owner
- Pat, the employee

Scenario 2

You are the new supervisor of a hospital foodservice department. Patient surveys have suggested that they find your menu dull and outdated. In an informal conversation with two employees, you share this information and ask for suggestions. One of the employees, Jean, is a young new hire with no foodservice or healthcare experience. Jean suggests making the trays more interesting by including candy. The other employee, Jamie, is a jaded worker who has been at the hospital for several years. Jamie laughs at Jean's suggestion and says the nutritionists would never allow it. How will you acknowledge Jean's suggestion?

Roles

- The supervisor
- Jean, the new employee
- Jamie, the long-time employee

Scenario 3

You are a supervisor for a multiunit chain, and you have just been transferred to a new unit in a different city. During your first week on the job, the general manager asks you to take care of the operation's recruiting efforts on an extremely limited budget. Because of your move and the extra hours you have been working your first week, you have not had any time to learn about your new city. However, you have contacted the career placement office of the local technical college and asked for referrals. During a preshift meeting, you ask employees for referrals and for recruiting ideas. One of the employees, Morgan, suggests that you call the local technical college. Sam, another employee, agrees that doing this is a good idea. How will you acknowledge Morgan's suggestion?

Roles

- The supervisor
- Morgan, the employee who made the suggestion
- Sam, another employee

Creating Recognition and Incentive Programs

Some operations use formal employee recognition or incentive programs as additional ways to motivate employees. Recognition programs provide a way for organizations to publicly express appreciation for employees or acknowledge and celebrate them as individuals. **Incentive programs** are designed to entice employees into meeting specified goals by offering some kind of reward. These programs often have an element of competition. However, there is no clear line between recognition programs and incentive programs. Most incentive programs include some public recognition, and for many people, the acknowledgement conferred by recognition programs is an incentive.

In multiunit operations, recognition and incentive programs often are designed by upper management and then implemented in all the units. However, supervisors at the local level and those in independent operations can develop these programs as well. These tools are motivators, and often the supervisors closest to the employees are in the best position to understand what motivates and challenges employees. To develop effective programs, supervisors must plan for them and ensure that certain components are in place.

Planning a Successful Program

Although the range of incentive and reward programs is unlimited, there are several challenges to creating and administering reward and recognition programs that may not be clear at first. They include issues of realism and capability, criteria for winning, length of the program, details of the reward, and expectations of success.

Goals and Parameters

In many incentive programs, employees need to feel that they have a realistic chance to win and that their effort will make a difference in reaching the established goal. That means that you need to set high—but realistic—goals and be very clear about those goals at the beginning of the competition. These goals should identify the tasks to be completed. The parameters of the program also need to be clearly defined, such as the measures of success, the eligible participants, the tracking methods, and the duration of the program.

If the criteria for success are not clear and everyone does not understand them, employees will not participate fully. For example, when you are running a competition to improve guest satisfaction, it is critical to clarify how that will be measured. (See *Exhibit 6i.*)

Exhibit 6i

Determine how to measure success before starting an incentive or recognition program.

If your employees think the program is unattainable or the measurement of success is rigged, then the program loses its impact. Employees must understand what to do to succeed, and they must believe that success is possible.

With complex programs, it can be difficult to determine who will be the winner. If everyone participates in the reduction of accidents and the improvement of safety, for example, you need to determine who will get the reward. This detail has to be worked out before you launch the program, unless everyone gets some personal reward or the reward benefits the team.

Even so, you must determine how to track participants' progress. The method you use will vary drastically depending on what you are trying to measure. For example, if you develop a program to increase sales, you can measure the progress through point-of-sale (POS) system reports. (Additional examples of programs and possible ways to measure progress are discussed on pp. 143-144.)

A program can also lose its impact if the intended behavior is not rewarded quickly enough. If you run a competition for too long, for example, it can lose focus and employees will tire of it. That is why many programs to increase sales of particular wines or menu items often run for only a week, and then someone gets a prize. In this way, employees quickly see the benefit of their efforts and are encouraged to work hard.

However, not all programs need to be short to be effective. In a long, complex, and detailed program that involves lots of effort, you need to periodically report on efforts during the competition. This interim recognition helps to keep employees motivated. Consequently, part of your program should include regular communication with participants. To sustain the employees' motivation, you should keep them informed about their progress and their competitors' progress. Communicate this information at consistent intervals. If you fail to keep employees involved, they may think that the program has been abandoned and may abandon it themselves.

Think About It...

A survey of human resources professionals by the Society for Human Resource Management (SHRM) found that managers are more likely to be rewarded for reaching long-term goals, while nonmanagerial employees were more likely to be rewarded for reaching short-term goals. Common incentives for managers included year-end bonuses and profit sharing. Common incentives for nonmanagerial employees included bonuses for employee referrals and spot bonuses.

Nation's Restaurant News,
April 25, 2005, p.18

Rewards and Celebration

The rewards you set for any program need to reflect the effort employees have to expend. For example, for improving customer comments over the period of a week or two, a cash reward or gift certificate may be sufficient. However, if you are aiming to improve safety records over the period of a quarter, you may want to post the records each week and set a large cash prize.

Celebrating the end of a program and recognizing the winners is another reward. Such a celebration provides a way to publicly recognize not only the winners, but also everyone who participated.

In some operations, some employees do all the work and win all the competitions, which can destroy the best-laid plans for incentive programs. In this situation, you may need to find other methods to encourage and motivate employees. Incentive programs only work when all participants have the same chance to win.

Implementing and Evaluating the Program

After you have planned your recognition and incentive program, you can present it to employees. There are many methods for communicating a new program, but the most common way is announcing it during a meeting. Depending on the complexity and length of the program, you might also post information about it on a bulletin board or distribute a written explanation.

Regardless of the method used, you should clearly explain the parameters of the program. Verify that employees understand the goal of the program, who can participate, how the winner will be selected, how long the program will run, and what the incentive is. Once your program is underway, be sure to provide employees with regular updates on their progress.

Tracking employee progress is important not only for motivating employees, but also for helping to evaluate the success of the program. While employee progress in large part determines whether a program worked or not, there are many other issues to consider:

- Did the program motivate most or all of the intended participants, or only a few?

- Did employees like the program?

- Did the program achieve its goals?

- Were the benefits of the program worth the effort and expense?

- Was there anything about the program plan or implementation that could have been done better?

Considering these questions will help you improve the way you plan and implement your next program. As in so many situations, if you can identify the strengths and weaknesses of the program, you can learn from your mistakes and build on your successes.

Examples of Incentive Programs

To provide the recognition and incentive that most employees appreciate and respond to positively, you may want to create programs that target service, sales, and productivity, customer satisfaction, safety, and longevity. As you can imagine, there are many types of programs. Some of these are described below.

Service Awards

A common incentive and reward program is an employee-of-the-month (or quarter or year) program, most typically designed to provide public recognition of employees who provide extraordinary service. Sometimes, these programs involve peer nominations; sometimes, the winners are nominated only by managers; and typically, there is a significant reward, often a one-time check, gift certificate, or special perk such as a reserved parking space or a public transportation pass (if your operation is in an urban area). To enhance the value of such programs, most restaurant or foodservice operations have a short ceremony in which the person is applauded and recognized, followed by posting the employee's name in a public location, often for customers to see.

However, if you have a program that recognizes individuals for regular effort and you do not have a large number of employees, there may be a common expectation that persons feel they will get the recognition sooner or later—especially when there is an employee-of-the-month program and not many employees in the restaurant or foodservice operation. In this situation, they may not be very motivated to strive for excellent service. In this case, you might want to give an award quarterly or establish that an award will be given only when there have been examples of exceptional service.

Sales and Productivity Awards

Other incentive programs designed to increase sales or productivity might focus on increasing check sales, decreasing food costs, or improving safety records. For example, if you are aiming to increase the average check amount by two dollars, you may want to communicate that broad goal, or you may want to establish more specific goals to help focus employees, such as increased sales of appetizers or upscale wines and liquors. The advent of POS systems makes this type of incentive program easy to track since the records are all stored in the POS system and can be retrieved in any form you need.

Customer Satisfaction

To measure customer satisfaction, you might want to employ **mystery shoppers,** people who visit the establishment as customers and rate employee performance. This strategy can be very helpful if you have the right people as mystery shoppers. Often, to show their usefulness, they think they should focus on what is going wrong, and they neglect what is going right, which can distort the picture of what is happening in the operation. However, measuring actual guest satisfaction can be challenging because you depend on the voluntary feedback of guests. Comment cards and customer letters normally get only the fringe responses—those people very happy with the customer service and those very unhappy.

Safety Awards

Safety awards are often given to employees who have made improvements in their individual safety record or suggestions that have led to overall safety improvements in the operation. The improvements can be tracked using an accident log, which documents each time an employee is injured, and a record of safety in various sections of the operation. Restaurant or foodservice operation safety programs can be organized in these ways:

- Severity of accidents measured by time lost

- Number of accidents in a specific time period

- Type of accidents and frequency

Longevity and Perseverance Awards

Other strategies that motivate employees might include service awards that recognize longevity or perseverance. These honor employees who have been with the operation for a significant period of time. Some restaurants provide birthday bonuses and other gifts. For example, one franchise provides twenty dollars to employees on their birthday and fifty dollars on their service anniversary. Many operations say thank you to all employees by hosting company picnics and annual parties and by giving special gifts or food items at Thanksgiving or during the December holiday period. These special celebrations and gifts are ways to recognize all employees, thank them in a public manner, and build the morale of the entire group.

Activity

Developing an Incentive Program

You are a dining room manager in an independently owned restaurant known for its friendly service, relaxed ambiance, beautiful décor, and great food. Your restaurant is especially famous for its creative menu and well-stocked bar.

Victor, the owner, has asked you to develop an incentive program to help introduce three new appetizers. During weekday dinner shifts, your operation typically serves 120 covers, and during weekend dinner shifts, your operation typically serves 160 covers. On average, approximately 25 percent of your customers order appetizers.

Victor wants to sell at least 150 orders of these new appetizers within the next month. To encourage this, he is offering them at a special introductory price for the first month and has created table tents announcing the new items. Your budget for the incentive program is $100.

For the next month, Victor wants every server to:

- Tell every table about the new appetizers.
- Ask customers who try the new items how they like them.
- Report any customer feedback during preshift meetings.

1 What parameters will you set for the program?

A. Measures of success: _____

_____

_____

B. Tracking methods: _____

_____

C. Eligible participants: _____

_____

D. Program duration: _____

2 How will you introduce the program to participants?

_____

_____

3 How and when do you plan to communicate employees' progress in the program?

_____

_____

4 What rewards and celebrations will you have when the program ends?

_____

_____

Summary

The primary function of a supervisor is to help employees be successful. To fulfill this goal, supervisors encourage productivity and quality by planning for and creating the right environment. As part of this, they set the tone for an operation by the way they treat employees and the behavior they model. They also communicate their goals to employees and what they want employees to do.

When hourly employees are promoted to supervisory positions, they often need to adjust the way they think about their work. This adjustment includes changing their focus away from doing the visible, technical work to managing the people who do this work and building and managing employee relationships. A good habit for all supervisors to develop is to reflect on their management practices. By doing this, they can improve their own performance.

A large part of supervision is monitoring employees and enforcing standards. Supervisors should train, coach, reward, and discipline employees based on standards. To reinforce positive performance, good supervisors express their appreciation to employees. To improve poor performance, good supervisors provide corrective feedback, which should be delivered in a timely, professional, and positive manner. There are many models that can be followed when giving feedback. Some methods are asking the employee to describe any work difficulties, affirming or correcting this understanding, complimenting the employee, making suggestions for improvement, giving the employee an opportunity to respond, and asking for input on how to improve the situation. When training and coaching are not enough to bring an employee's performance up to standards, supervisors use progressive discipline as needed. Ideally, employees will be motivated enough so that this is not needed.

Supervisors are responsible for motivating their employees on a daily basis. Maslow's hierarchy of needs and the motivation-hygiene theory are two theories that explain what motivates people. Informal ways to motivate employees include acknowledging them as individuals; expressing appreciation for good work; sharing information to encourage involvement and belonging; and involving employees in various aspects of planning, problem solving, and decision making. Formal recognition and incentive programs also can motivate employees.

When planning an effective recognition or incentive program, the goals and parameters need to be clearly defined, as well as how and when to communicate results and how to celebrate the end of the program. When the program ends, it should be evaluated so that information learned can be used to improve future programs.

Review Your Learning

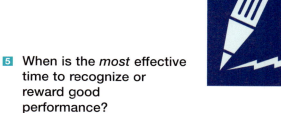

1 Which statement *best* describes the primary goal of supervision?

   A. To set the tone of the operation

   B. To help employees be successful

   C. To motivate employees

   D. To tell employees what to do

2 According to the motivation-hygiene theory, which of these is a motivating factor?

   A. Working conditions

   B. Benefits

   C. Acknowledgement

   D. Fair pay

3 On which basis should employees be trained, coached, rewarded, and disciplined?

   A. Standards

   B. Attendance

   C. Regulations

   D. Motivation

4 Which technique is *not* generally used when providing corrective feedback?

   A. Start with a compliment.

   B. Listen to the employee.

   C. Tell the employee to listen.

   D. Describe the behavior.

5 When is the *most* effective time to recognize or reward good performance?

   A. During a group meeting

   B. When you can talk to the employee alone

   C. During the employee's annual performance review

   D. As soon as it happens

6 Which technique can be used to motivate people?

   A. Expressing appreciation

   B. Expressing doubt

   C. Sharing personal information

   D. Involving customers

7 Which helps to ensure the success of a recognition or incentive program?

   A. Clear goals and parameters

   B. Expensive rewards and parties

   C. Short duration and limited participants

   D. Personalized goals and prizes

Notes

Developing Employees

7

Inside This Chapter

- The Function of Employee Development
- Employee Development Process
- Employee Development Planning Meeting
- Methods of Employee Development
- Coaching Employees

After completing this chapter, you should be able to:

- Explain what employee development is and why it is important in restaurant and foodservice operations.
- Describe the important features of the employee development planning meeting.
- Describe how to set developmental goals for employees.
- List and describe the types of possible employee development methods.
- Discuss the advantages and disadvantages of each employee development method.
- Describe how to set up and implement a cross-training program.
- Describe the coaching process.

Test Your Knowledge

1 **True or False:** Employee development is a training class that restaurant and foodservice operations run to make their employees successful at what they are supposed to do. *(See p. 152.)*

2 **True or False:** Managers are solely responsible for each employee's development. *(See p. 152.)*

3 **True or False:** Coaching is the process of building a team of employees and helping them work together. *(See p. 164.)*

4 **True or False:** There are five different ways to develop employees. *(See pp. 162–163.)*

5 **True or False:** The needs of both the job and the employee should be considered when developing employees. *(See p. 151.)*

Key Terms

Attitudes

Coaching

Cross-training

Developmental goals

Employee development goals

Employee development process

Employee development program

Employee goals

Employee performance goals

Knowledge

Skill gap

Skills

Introduction

As a restaurant or foodservice manager, you do a good job of hiring the best employees available. However, your job is not yet done. An employee seldom has all the skills needed for the present job or future jobs. This is where employee development comes in. In this chapter, you will gain an awareness of the function and importance of employee development, the range of employee development methods, and how to undertake developing your employees.

The Function of Employee Development

Employees are the most critical asset of any restaurant or foodservice operation because the hospitality industry relies so much on individual customer attention and service. Although you have done the best possible job in hiring good employees, every employee has more potential that can be developed. That is why

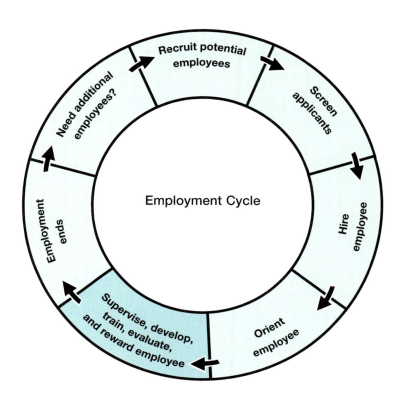

Employment Cycle

- Recruit potential employees
- Screen applicants
- Hire employee
- Orient employee
- Supervise, develop, train, evaluate, and reward employee
- Employment ends
- Need additional employees?

developing the potential within each employee is, and always will be, an essential part of any manager's job.

Why Employees Need Development

There are several reasons why an operation should develop employees' skills, knowledge, and attitudes beyond where they presently are. These reasons might include any combination of the following:

- The employee, when hired, did not have all the skills needed for the job.

- The employee has basic skills, but more advanced skills would improve productivity.

- The employee has been assigned to a new job with different or additional skills.

- Changes have been made in equipment or procedures.

- New requirements have been mandated by upper management or the government.

- The employee wants to qualify for a different job that requires different or additional skills.

These are all different ways of saying that there is a **skill gap**—a gap between the skills the employee presently has and the skills that are needed.

There are several ways that managers can learn about employees' skill gaps:

- Personal observation
- Reports by supervisors
- Reports or complaints by other workers, customers, or vendors
- Routine performance evaluations

Exhibit 7a

Employee development helps employees do the best work possible.

Think About It…

According to the American Society for Training & Development's *2004 State of the Industry Report*, customer service employees received the largest percentage of expenditures on employee development in 2003: 18 percent. Middle managers received the next highest: 11 percent.

Generally, the information from all these sources is assembled into a description of the various skill, knowledge, and attitude gaps for each employee. This information should be used for the employee's development. (See *Exhibit 7a).*

Employee Development Programs

As a manager, it is up to you to implement a program of action that will develop your employees. Such a program is called an **employee development program,** which is any organized series of actions that are intended to reduce a gap in an employee's skills, knowledge, or attitudes. The term is used to refer both to the actions taken for a single employee and the actions that the restaurant or foodservice operation takes to improve employees in general. An employee development program can also be a formal program, much like a performance management program, or it can be an informal program that might be implemented when you observe a performance gap that needs to be addressed.

Whose Responsibility Is Employee Development?

The operation, the immediate supervisor, and the employee all share the responsibility for employee development. They all have different responsibilities, and they will all benefit differently from effective employee development.

■ **The operation** is responsible for providing methods and opportunities for development, including paying for the costs. In return, an employee will function with increased productivity.

■ **The immediate supervisor** is responsible for assessing development needs, recommending development methods, and assessing progress. In return, he or she will benefit from an employee who is easier and more enjoyable to supervise and who can handle more assignments.

■ **The employee** is responsible for making the development happen and achieving the goals that were agreed upon. In return, he or she will receive increased skills and knowledge, which in turn will lead to greater appreciation in the current operation and possible career advancement.

Of the three, the employee carries the most responsibility for his or her development.

Employee Development Process

There is a simple process to develop employees—the **employee development process,** as shown in *Exhibit 7b*. It involves identifying developmental goals, determining how to make improvements, and evaluating the results. These steps apply to both the formal and informal types of employee development.

There are many types of actions that can be used to develop an employee's skills. Prior to deciding which action will work best to bridge a performance gap, you must be clear about the employee's developmental goals. These are determined during an employee development planning meeting.

Employee Development Planning Meeting

When should employee development be planned? An employee development planning meeting is usually held in conjunction with, but separate from, an employee's performance review. However, the two subjects should not be discussed at the same time. Since performance reviews affect employees' pay and employment, most employees would take an adversarial position if they perceive development planning as a criticism of their skills, knowledge, and attitudes. This would be exactly the opposite of what is desired. Employee development planning meetings should be collegial in nature, with the manager helping the employee determine how to grow.

The employee development planning meeting typically goes through a planned sequence of events. (See *Exhibit 7c* on the next page.)

Here are several guidelines for a constructive planning meeting:

- Choose the meeting location carefully.

- Agree on the agenda.

- Allow plenty of time.

- Be prepared.

- Set a relaxed and collegial atmosphere.

- Provide feedback on the employee's skills, knowledge, and attitudes.

- Do not provide feedback or corrections on work performance.

Exhibit 7b

Employee Development Process

- Identify a skill gap.
- Identify time frame for development.
- Set developmental goal(s).
- Determine employee's learning style.
- Select developmental methods.
- Organize developmental plan.
- Implement developmental plan.
- Evaluate behaviors.
- Communicate feedback and progress.
- Developmental goal achieved?
- YES
- NO
- DONE

Exhibit 7c

Development Planning Meeting Process

- Identify time frame for development
- Discuss the needs of the current position
- Discuss corrective improvements needed
- Discuss career goals, steps, and skills needed
- Create list of current developmental goals
- Discuss learning style
- Select developmental methods
- Set completion / review date
- **DONE**

- Listen to the employee's needs and concerns.
- Discuss career options.
- Utilize all sources of information about developmental needs.
- Discuss skill, knowledge, and attitude goals.
- Discuss available methods and actions to develop new or improved skills, knowledge, and attitudes.
- Select a program of action.
- Set review dates.

Meeting Preparation

The best meeting location for a discussion of goals is a quiet, uninterrupted space. (See *Exhibit 7d)*. An office is ideal, but a corner of the dining room can be used between shifts as long as it is quiet and private, and you will not be interrupted.

In preparation for the meeting, establish a clear agenda and length of meeting with the employee ahead of time. Prepare yourself by gathering all data related to the developmental needs of the employee. Write an outline or script of the points you want to cover.

Starting the Meeting

Start the meeting by stating that you want to help the employee improve and be happier in the job. This should help set an informal, relaxed mood. You should specify the time frame for the individual's development. It is important for the employee to know that you want to help him or her improve and to clearly know how long is available to make improvements. An informal chat about the employee's career goals will help both of you relax. Being relaxed is important because this type of interchange can be emotionally charged with a boss-subordinate relationship. The more relaxed the employee, the more likely you are to have an honest and productive discussion about his or her personal development.

Before you start telling the employee what you want to do, listen to the employee's needs and concerns first. Most employees want to do a good job and to advance. You may find that the employee has already figured out what improvements are needed to do this. Even if the employee is mistaken, the fact that you listened first will give you the right to respond and make corrections.

Exhibit 7d

Plan an employee's development during an employee development planning meeting.

Determining Developmental Needs

In discussing the skills, knowledge, and attitudes that might be improved, use all sources of information available to you, such as:

- Employee's own interpretation of skills
- Skills and knowledge needed for other or higher positions
- Your observation of the employee's work
- Reports by supervisors
- Reports or complaints by other workers
- Routine performance evaluations

Other ways of identifying the skills, knowledge, and attitudes in need of improvement could include:

- Providing a checklist of skills and knowledge in the industry
- Using a personality inventory or test
- Encouraging the individual to take a learning style inventory or test
- Sharing your own list of possible goals or a range of personal goals that the individual might consider

You and the employee should agree on which skills, knowledge, and attitudes are adequate and which could be improved.

Setting Developmental Goals

For most activities, it is important to set goals. **Employee development goals,** also known as **developmental goals,** describe the skills, knowledge, and attitudes that need to be gained or improved in order to eliminate or reduce a performance gap.

The goal-setting session is a discussion between the manager and employee to uncover employee goals. During this session, the following items are discussed:

- Current work assignment and the skills and knowledge needed for it
- Current skills and knowledge of the employee, based on input the manager has received and the employee's own observations
- Any corrective action needed
- Employee's career aspirations and the skills and knowledge required to reach those goals

Types of Developmental Goals

There are two kinds of developmental goals:

■ Attainment of a certain skill or item of knowledge

■ Improvement in a skill or attitude

For example, a baker might have the goal of preparing and baking an angel food cake to certain specifications (an attainment goal). A short-order cook might have the goal of lessening tensions between himself and the waitstaff (an improvement goal).

In addition, employee development goals can address three areas:

■ **Skills**—Intellectual or physical actions that help accomplish a goal, such as baking a cake or planning a menu

■ **Knowledge**—Information stored in a person's mind, such as facts, concepts, rules, and procedures

■ **Attitudes**—Feelings about facts or situations that influence behaviors, such as liking to help people or disliking being interrupted

Together, the two types of goals and the three objects of goals result in six categories of goals for employee development as shown in *Exhibit 7e.*

Exhibit 7e

Categories of Goals for Employee Development

	Skill	**Knowledge**	**Attitude**
Attainment	Attainment of a new skill	Attainment of new knowledge	Attainment of a new attitude
Improvement	Improvement of a skill	Improvement in an area of knowledge	Improvement in an attitude

Setting the Goals

Most of the time, each employee's developmental goals will be unique because each person has a unique set of skills, experiences, and gaps. (See *Exhibit 7f*). Developmental goals should support the overall goals for an operation; in other words, the operation should not be expected to provide development in skills unrelated to the employee's work. Developmental goals, for example, may include any of the following types of outcomes:

■ Improving speed, efficiency, or quantity

■ Learning a new set of recipes, a new cuisine, or a new set of cooking skills

■ Learning intellectual skills such as a foreign language, financial analysis, or wine selection

Exhibit 7f

Each employee will have unique aspirations.

In each case, as a manager, you will establish these developmental goals with the employee. In a formal program, the goals would be written down and perhaps signed by both the manager and employee. In an informal program, a verbal statement and agreement would be sufficient.

Employee goals are different from an organization's performance goals for an employee. **Employee goals** focus on an employee's issues beyond job performance, such as getting a certification, moving ahead in life, finding a better job, or improving a personal situation, whereas an **employee's performance goals** focus on the tasks that an employee must be able to perform as part of their job. As a manager, you are responsible for setting the employees' performance goals, but you can also help your employees clarify their personal developmental goals and align the two types of goals in a mutually advantageous manner. For example, if a person wants to gain new skills and move ahead in a restaurant, you can help him or her identify the positions to prepare for, the knowledge and skills needed, and the resources involved. Initially, you may have to work carefully while assisting an employee to include personal goals, since he or she may not be used to thinking about personal goals or sharing them with a manager.

Use your knowledge about the operation, existing development opportunities with the company or community, and other positions that the employee can plan to grow into. Help the employee understand what skills and knowledge are needed for advancement to higher positions. In the discussion about career development options, you should share information about the career ladder in your operation. If there is no formal career ladder, share stories about how people got promoted, and which position would normally lead to another position. These conversations will encourage employees to think about expanding their skills and moving up in the organization.

Determining Developmental Opportunities

You also should provide employees with information about developmental opportunities that are available both inside the organization and in the community.

Generally, you as the manager should be the one who uncovers the opportunities inside the organization. These include:

- Developmental opportunities you set up within your own operation

- Cross-training opportunities that you organize between yourself and another manager

- Programs available from the training department or human resources

You also should be able to discuss how your employees can take advantage of these opportunities within the scope of their jobs.

Either you or the employee can research developmental opportunities available in the outside community. Possible sources include:

- Local community college or four-year institution programs

- Trade school programs

- Trade or professional association opportunities and materials

- Books, videos, and computer-based training that can be purchased or obtained from the library

- Educational materials available on the Internet

For outside opportunities, there may be costs involved, although some will be free. As a manager, you must be ready to explain what the organization will sponsor and what the employee should pay for.

Activity

Discovering Developmental Goals

Working with a classmate, hold a developmental goal-setting session in which you uncover each other's developmental goals. One person plays the part of the restaurant or foodservice manager; the other person plays the part of the employee. The manager should make sure that all elements of the goal-setting session are covered and should base feedback on his or her own work experience. The employee should respond based on his or her background, work experience, and career aspirations. Take ten minutes for the session, then switch roles and conduct a goal-setting session for the other person. Afterward, share your developmental goals with the rest of the class. You may use the following space for notes.

Dealing with Personal Problems

If you discover that an employee's development is affected by a personal problem, you can refer him or her to an employee assistance program, if your operation offers one. In addition, if the employee is affected by a family situation, such as a birth/adoption or a serious illness, the employee may be entitled to unpaid time off under the Family and Medical Leave Act. These situations are covered more thoroughly in Chapter 12.

Establishing the Developmental Plan

Taking all of the above into account, you and the employee must agree on the developmental plan. This is a relatively short statement of:

- Time frame of the plan

- Goals of the plan

- Method or methods that will be used for development

- How the development will be measured

- When progress check meetings will be held

Implementing the Developmental Program

After the developmental program planning meeting, be sure to follow up on any questions or concerns the employee expressed in your discussions. Get back to the employee with your responses as soon as possible. Timely follow-up shows the employee that he or she is important to you, and that you are dedicated to helping the employee develop.

Once you and the employee have agreed upon a developmental program, it is up to the employee to complete it. Throughout the time frame of the program, you and the employee should meet to discuss progress and how to overcome any obstacles or problems. This is essentially a coaching session about the employee's development. During the implementation period, you should be:

- Observing the employee's new (and existing) behaviors

- Communicating feedback about what you have observed and your satisfaction with it

- Communicating your estimation of progress on the developmental plan and your satisfaction with it

Methods of Employee Development

Restaurant and foodservice operations can help their employees grow both personally and professionally through many types of individual and group activities. The table shown in *Exhibit 7g* on pp. 162–163 summarizes many of these methods, including the advantages and disadvantages listed in the "Pros and Cons" column.

Creating Development Opportunities

Once you are familiar with some of the methods available to help your employees grow, you can create development opportunities for your employees. Some of the developmental methods are entirely up to you to plan and execute; only your creativity and the resources of your operation limit the range of methods you can use. Other developmental methods use in-company or in-community programs; either you or the employee can investigate what is available.

One or more of the developmental methods should be selected and assembled into a program for the employee. The sequence of methods might have to be considered when preparing the developmental program. Methods in which the work depends on prior knowledge or skills must take place after that knowledge or skills have been mastered. For example, a special project in menu planning would depend on the employee knowing about nutrition, allergens, and food preparation, to name a few.

Two of the strongest developmental methods that do not require the employee to be away from the job are cross-training and coaching. These developmental programs are cheap and easy to set up; they are well within the means of even the smallest restaurant or foodservice operation.

Organizing a Cross-Training Program

Cross-training is a method through which employees learn a job related to their own, often one that is "upstream" or "downstream" in a process. For example, a busser might learn a dishwasher's job. Cross-training has many benefits and only a few disadvantages (see *Exhibit 7g* on p. 162), and good management can control the disadvantages. As a result, most restaurant and foodservice operations would benefit from setting up an effective cross-training program. It is fairly easy to do.

1. **Prepare a list of the skills in each job, including the subskills that are important.** For example, a baker would have major skills in bread baking, cake baking, and cookie baking. A baker would also have subskills of measuring flour, measuring liquids, kneading bread, preparing pans, operating mixers, and assessing doneness; these subskills enable the major skills. If you have a

new hire training plan, job analysis, or job descriptions, you can use them as a starting point for your list, which forms the foundation of your cross-training plan.

2 **Identify the employees who will be cross-trained.** If you are using cross-training as a general development opportunity for everyone, such as to improve teamwork or morale, then you need to make sure that everyone has an equal opportunity to participate in cross-training. Providing equal access in this situation is important for building morale and complying with equal opportunity laws.

On the other hand, if you are using cross-training as a way to develop a person for a different position, then you do not need to offer cross-training to everyone. However, the same equal opportunity guidelines that apply to screening during the recruitment process also apply when you are promoting from within or moving an employee into a different position.

When considering candidates for cross-training, you need to observe employees in order to identify their missing skills and their work attitudes. Look for employees who are self-starters with organizational skills. Also look for personality compatibilities because the relationship between trainer and trainee is a very close one.

3 **Implement cross-training opportunities.** Look at work schedules and find the slack times in the operation's daily schedule. You also need to support the cross-training program in these ways:

☐ Be understanding of lowered productivity when a person is being cross-trained.

☐ Encourage both the trainer and trainee that they can complete the cross-training.

☐ Teach the trainer how to tutor the trainee and to be patient while the trainee learns.

When setting up an individual cross-training plan for an employee, start with any previous training plan that the employee had. The cross-training plan should include time frames, skills and knowledge to be gained, how many attempts at gaining a skill will be provided, how to measure whether the skills and knowledge were attained, which jobs in the program will provide these skills and knowledge, who will provide one-on-one training, and what special considerations the trainer will receive for this assignment. If the trainee does not master the skills intended to be taught through cross-training, or if new developmental needs arise, you can modify the original training plan accordingly.

Exhibit 7g

Employee Development Methods

Method	Description	Pros and Cons
Apprenticeship	A form of training in which a master craftsperson assumes responsibility for the total development of a person new to the field. The result after many years is another master craftsperson.	**Pro:** Thorough training under a master. **Con:** Takes years and can accommodate only a limited number of students.
Coaching	A manager or other supervisor helps an employee select areas for improvement and develops strategies to carry out the improvement. In a coaching relationship, the coach takes charge of the process rather than the employee. Compare coaching to mentoring. (For more information on coaching, see the "Coaching Employees" section.)	**Pro:** Individual attention for employee; utilizes coach's experiences. **Con:** Takes a lot of coach's time; success depends on the coaching skills.
Cross-training	Employees learn parts of another job, typically through the buddy system. The employee is cross-trained on the important parts of an adjacent job in the restaurant or foodservice operation. Cross-training benefits the organization more than the individual, so that employee absences and sudden surges in demand can be met with available staff.	**Pro:** Develops backups for operation; lets employees discover different interests and career goals; aids in scheduling; reduces overtime and turnover; boosts teamwork and morale. **Con:** Skills may never be used and can be forgotten if not used.
Informal learning	Employees learn how to do their jobs from their colleagues and through trial and error. This is unstructured development that may or may not result in the proper skills being learned.	**Pro:** Cheap and easy to initiate. **Con:** No guarantee that right things will be learned; great risk that wrong methods will be learned.
Job rotation	An employee is assigned to another job in the organization and one or more methods are utilized to learn the new job. This results in broadening the employee's understanding of the original job, the organization as a whole, and how all the parts of the organization work together. Job rotation can be a formal system in which the sequence of jobs is planned for all employees, or it can be more impromptu. Job rotation differs from temporary assignment because it involves the intentional changing of jobs on a regular basis until all or most jobs have been learned.	**Pro:** Develops well-rounded employees who know the "big picture." **Con:** Relies on existing employees to train person being rotated; can build resentment in those who train others, but are not selected for rotation.

Method	Description	Pros and Cons
Mentoring	A manager or colleague helps an employee sort out his or her goals, develop strategies to reach those goals, and pursue ways of growing in the organization. In a mentoring relationship, the employee takes charge of the process and approaches the mentor with goals and issues. Compare mentoring to coaching.	***Pro:*** Individual attention for employee; utilizes mentor's experiences. ***Con:*** Takes a lot of mentor's time; success depends on person's mentoring skills.
On-the-job training (OJT)	Traditionally the most prevalent form of employee development, OJT involves learning something new by doing it under the supervision and guidance of an expert. OJT differs from Informal Learning by being more formal and organized. In OJT, the trainee is assigned to the expert, and the expert is directed to teach the trainee specific things.	***Pro:*** Teaches employee how to do the job; quick and easy to set up. ***Con:*** No guarantee that right methods will be learned; great risk that wrong methods will be learned.
Outside training and education	The employee is sent to college courses, commercial classes, or the company school for formal training and education. Classes can be attended instead of regular work (e.g., a weeklong cooking workshop), or on the employee's own time (e.g., evening classes at a local college).	***Pro:*** Usually thorough and effective; covers topics the operation is not equipped to handle. ***Con:*** Takes time away from the job or personal life; can be expensive.
Self-study	The employee studies one or more forms of individualized materials on the topics to be learned. Materials can take many forms, from print workbooks to e-learning. For more information, see Chapter 8.	***Pro:*** Usually thorough and effective; covers topics an organization is not equipped to handle; relatively cheap. ***Con:*** The student must be well disciplined.
Special project	The employee is given a special work project that is somewhat outside his or her skill set, but within reach. For example, a cook might be assigned to develop a new menu from concept through printing. Additional self-study and research are usually necessary to successfully complete the project. Other employees are also available to help or advise the employee.	***Pro:*** Broadens skills well; produces usable results. ***Con:*** Relies on individual research and other employees.
Temporary assignment	The employee is temporarily assigned to another job with the purpose of learning that job. For example, a pastry chef might be assigned to work in the salad department. Temporary assignment differs from job rotation in that it is typically a one-time situation, not an overall plan to rotate through a series of jobs.	***Pro:*** Develops new skill set; easy to set up. ***Con:*** Relies on other employees to train the temporary employee.

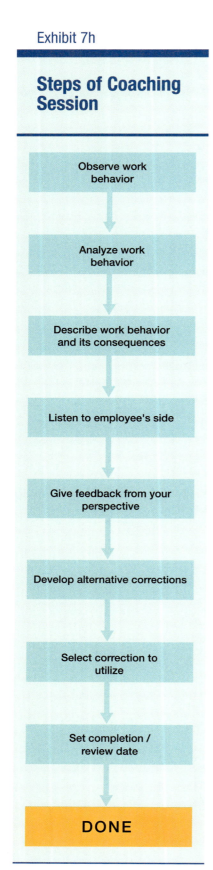

Exhibit 7h

Steps of Coaching Session

- Observe work behavior
- Analyze work behavior
- Describe work behavior and its consequences
- Listen to employee's side
- Give feedback from your perspective
- Develop alternative corrections
- Select correction to utilize
- Set completion / review date

DONE

An effective cross-training program can be inexpensive, yet very effective. However, no employee development program can be maximally effective without follow-up, evaluation, and possible retraining. This is where coaching comes in—it is the best method for handling these areas.

Coaching Employees

One of the most empowering and effective ways to help your employees grow is through coaching. For years, managers have been helping their employees grow by providing advice and feedback on an individual basis. Now, this practice has become enhanced and codified through the method known as **coaching.** The steps of a coaching session are shown in *Exhibit 7h*.

Managers who play the role of coaches commit to helping their employees grow while the employees drive their own development. It takes considerable listening skills, patience, and focus to serve as a coach, but good coaching will help an employee develop as a person and a professional.

The Coaching Process

There are many variations on the basic coaching process shown in *Exhibit 7h*. They all consist of describing behaviors rather than personality traits, getting all sides of a situation, looking for a variety of solutions, agreeing to a solution and time frame for implementation, and having regular progress reviews.

Normally, restaurant and foodservice operations reserve coaching time and energy for supervisory employees or those who might become supervisors. Hourly employees receive feedback and comments, but not the full approach, in part because it takes a great deal of time and commitment from the coach, and many hourly employees are transitory. However, more time should be spent coaching hourly employees; by strengthening their skills, knowledge, and attitudes, great improvements in productivity can be realized.

The role of the coach is to provide feedback and make suggestions for changes, provide reaction to the employee's ideas and responses, and help the employee plan how to improve. Acting in this way is totally different than the way a manager normally acts toward an employee—giving orders and criticizing mistakes. Many managers cannot be effective coaches because they find it difficult to change roles from boss to coach.

Coaching is not a one-time activity; it involves a commitment to help an employee grow over time and an interest in helping the employee determine how to accomplish this. The function of the coach is to think about feedback for employees and how to help employees solve their own problems.

Continuous Coaching

Seldom does a single event or even a single developmental program move an employee all the way to his or her final goal. Typically, several feedback and planning sessions are interspersed among multiple improvement periods. In other words, the coach must routinely monitor the employee's development and determine to what degree the current performance meets the developmental goal. The coach should arrange a meeting with the employee and provide feedback on what was observed. Any performance problems should be identified and the causes discussed. Then the coach and the employee should agree on modified improvement goals and methods to achieve those goals. This cycle will be repeated continuously.

It is important to realize when planning an employee developmental program or using coaching and feedback that training or retraining may or may not improve the employee's skills.

1. Training is good only for improving skills and knowledge. Training can have a small effect on attitudes, but other work factors have a much greater effect and will overcome whatever effect training has.

2. Training cannot totally counteract an employee's physical capabilities and aptitudes. Some people are faster, have better eyesight, or are naturally friendly, to name just a few characteristics that training cannot correct.

3. Some people cannot learn certain things. These things might be beyond their capabilities, interests, or aptitudes, and no reasonable amount of training would make a difference.

4. You cannot apply retraining to something that was not learned in the first place. You would have to start from where the employee is at the present time. For example, you cannot retrain a person to make a variety of salads without the person first having the skills of correctly and efficiently cutting up vegetables.

You as the manager must analyze whether retraining is going to solve a particular problem.

Think About It...

Seventy percent of restaurants that offer table service provide regular, formal training to hourly employees (as well as formal job descriptions and an employee handbook), while 80 percent provide ongoing training beyond the entry-level employment training that all employees receive.

National Restaurant Association's *State of the Restaurant Industry Workforce 2003: An Overview*

Summary

Employee development is an important part of every restaurant and foodservice manager's job. It is the primary method of turning adequate employees into outstanding employees. Employee development addresses both the acquisition of new skills, knowledge, and attitudes, and the improvement of existing ones. The employee's own goals should also be considered. The manager can help the employee determine his or her goals for improvement, but it is the employee's responsibility to make those improvements. A simple but effective process for developing employees is available.

There are many methods for developing employees. It is up to the manager and the employee to select the appropriate method(s) in light of what is available and what works best for the employee.

Employee development planning is a one-on-one situation that should be handled in privacy. Regular progress reviews and adjustments are also part of the process.

Activity

Preparing for an Employee Development Planning Meeting

You are the night supervisor for Chez Parisienne, an upper-middle quality dining establishment in the heart of Des Moines, Iowa. Susan Clancy is a waitress with one year's experience at Chez Parisienne and three years additional experience, mostly at a local coffee shop. She is doing an adequate job, but she is still transitioning up to your level of customer service, menu knowledge, and dining protocol. You have scheduled a meeting with Susan to discuss her development program for the upcoming year.

As preparation for that meeting, think about and write down answers to the following questions. Each person will first develop his or her own list, and then in small groups, each person will share the list. Use this sharing of ideas to see what others think and to expand your list so that you can use it in the future when you become a manager.

1 How will you start the meeting?

_____

_____

_____

2 What questions will you ask during the meeting?

_____

_____

_____

3 What information do you need to go into the meeting?

_____

_____

_____

4 Where will you hold the meeting?

_____

5 How long do you plan for the meeting to take?

_____

6 What do you want to have accomplished by the end of the meeting?

_____

_____

_____

Review Your Learning

1 Employee development in foodservice operations can best be defined as

A. a special training class employees take to help their social and cultural development.

B. taking college courses on foodservice topics.

C. a series of coaching sessions that improves the employee's skills, knowledge, and attitudes.

D. actions taken to acquire skills needed in the present and future jobs.

2 Employee development is important in foodservice because

A. an employee seldom has all the skills needed for the present and future jobs.

B. foodservice operations rely so much on individual customer attention and service.

C. it gives foodservice managers another way to control their employees.

D. there are few college programs devoted to foodservice skills.

3 What is the primary advantage of coaching as a development method?

A. Individual attention for the employee

B. Takes little time on the manager's part

C. Most effective of all the methods

D. Guaranteed to produce results

4 What is a disadvantage of on-the-job training?

A. Takes time away from productive work

B. Produces resentment of the teacher by the trainee

C. Risk that wrong methods will be learned

D. Takes a lot of discipline on the part of the student

5 What are the steps in the employee development process?

A. Identify a time frame, set goals, determine learning style, select methods, organize program, implement program, evaluate behaviors, and communicate feedback and progress.

B. Identify a time frame; discuss current needs; discuss corrective improvements; discuss career goals, steps, and skills; list goals; discuss learning style; select methods; and set completion and review dates.

C. Observe work behaviors, analyze work behaviors, describe work behaviors and consequences, listen to the employee's side, provide feedback, develop alternative corrections, select correction to utilize, and set completion and review dates.

D. None of the above

6 What are the steps in setting developmental goals for employees?

A. Identify a time frame, set goals, determine learning style, select methods, organize program, implement program, evaluate behaviors, and communicate feedback and progress.

B. Identify a time frame; discuss current needs; discuss corrective improvements; discuss career goals, steps, and skills; list goals; discuss learning style; select methods; and set completion and review dates.

C. Observe work behaviors, analyze work behaviors, describe work behaviors and consequences, listen to the employee's side, provide feedback, develop alternative corrections, select correction to utilize, and set completion and review dates.

D. None of the above

7 **What is a disadvantage of informal learning?**

A. Can build resentment in those who train but are not selected

B. Takes much time away from the job or personal life

C. Skills may never be used and can be forgotten if not used

D. No guarantee that right things will be learned

8 **What are the steps of the employee development planning meeting?**

A. Identify a time frame, set goals, determine learning style, select methods, organize program, implement program, evaluate behaviors, and communicate feedback and progress.

B. Identify a time frame; discuss current needs; discuss corrective improvements; discuss career goals, steps, and skills; list goals; discuss learning style; select methods; and set completion and review dates.

C. Observe work behaviors, analyze work behaviors, describe work behaviors and consequences, listen to the employee's side, provide feedback, develop alternative corrections, select correction to utilize, and set completion and review dates.

D. None of the above

9 **Cross-training programs are**

A. large and complicated developmental efforts used only by large companies.

B. well within the means of even the smallest foodservice operation.

C. used only by foodservice chains to move people around from restaurant to restaurant.

D. available primarily through the Internet.

10 **What are the steps of a coaching session?**

A. Identify a time frame, set goals, determine learning style, select methods, organize program, implement program, evaluate behaviors, and communicate feedback and progress.

B. Identify a time frame; discuss current needs; discuss corrective improvements; discuss career goals, steps, and skills; list goals; discuss learning style; select methods; and set completion and review dates.

C. Observe work behaviors, analyze work behaviors, describe work behaviors and consequences, listen to the employee's side, provide feedback, develop alternative corrections, select correction to utilize, and set completion and review dates.

D. None of the above

11 **When should coaching be done?**

A. Continuously

B. Once a month

C. Once a quarter

D. Once a year, around the time of annual performance reviews

Notes

Training Employees

8

After completing this chapter, you should be able to:

- Explain ways in which training can help an organization.

- Differentiate between training and education.

- Identify the elements of a successful training program.

- Explain the content that training materials should include.

- List and describe the steps of the ADDIE model of training development.

- Describe the steps of a thorough evaluation of training activity.

Test Your Knowledge

1 **True or False:** Training is not an important function in restaurants, since you can simply hire people who know what to do. *(See pp. 173–175.)*

2 **True or False:** The best training involves preparation, presentation, practice, and performance. *(See pp. 184–186.)*

3 **True or False:** Designing training only requires setting the goals for the event, selecting a good trainer, and ensuring follow-up. *(See pp. 193–194.)*

4 **True or False:** Obtaining trainee evaluations at the end of training provides all the information you need to know about evaluating the effectiveness of that activity. *(See pp. 195–197.)*

5 **True or False:** Training and education are really the same concept in different settings. *(See pp. 177–179.)*

Key Terms

ADDIE

Chunk

Classical model of training

Design document

Four P approach (or four Ps)

Four-step training method

Instructional design

Integrative practice

Job instruction training

Learning objectives

Needs assessment

Negligent training

Task analysis

Validation

Introduction

Training activities can be fun and educational, and a powerful tool for developing employees. Training is not the only tool for developing employees, as you have read in Chapter 7, but it is, in essence, distilled and concentrated experience. The effect of training is to take the experience of an expert and impart it in a concentrated form to the trainee. Employees will become productive much more quickly with training as it enables learners to achieve large gains in skills, knowledge, and attitudes in a relatively short time—markedly less than would be required using any other form of development. *Exhibit 8a* represents the difference in productivity between training and informal learning.

Achieving this level of effectiveness can be relatively expensive. Training is the most costly method per hour for developing employees. You pay for the development of the training, and then you pay for the employees to attend classes or seminars away from work. However, training can end up being the least costly method overall to achieve the desired gain in skills, knowledge, and attitudes.

Training is really an investment, not an expense. This is because the benefits for training your employees are paid back over a period of time following the training. This is similar to buying a better oven; it will pay back dividends over its lifetime of use. Therefore, although training is expensive, it will pay back dividends for a long time, usually much more than its initial cost.

To use training effectively and get a good return on investment, you have to know when and how to use it. This chapter provides an understanding of the benefits of training, the structure of good training, the different types of training, and the ways to ensure quality training in a restaurant or foodservice operation.

Exhibit 8a

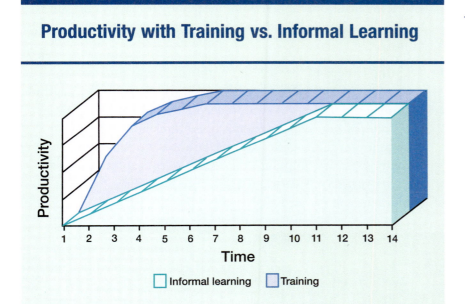

Productivity with Training vs. Informal Learning

Productivity

Time

1 2 3 4 5 6 7 8 9 10 11 12 13 14

☐ Informal learning ☐ Training

Benefits of Training

Training has a specific function: to improve the skill, knowledge, and attitude of employees for their jobs. When training is focused and done well, great improvements can be realized. Effective training improves the quality of employee work, promotes employee growth, keeps employees challenged and satisfied in the organization, and creates talent to help the organization grow.

Although it is sometimes unappreciated and is often the first area to receive budget reductions, effective training is essential to the productive functioning of an operation. Detractors of training, and those seeking to diminish or eliminate it, point to the low return on investment from training. Although it is true that some types of training are not worth the time and money, effective training is a worthwhile investment. Why is it important in restaurant and foodservice operations? There are several reasons.

Job Skill Reasons for Training

No matter how large or small a restaurant or foodservice operation, employees need to be trained—when they start as new employees, when they move to new positions, when they meet a roadblock and their skills stagnate, and when new programs and new equipment are added to an operation.

■ **Training supplies basic foodservice skills.** Employees in the restaurant and foodservice industry are often first-time, entry-level, or unskilled workers. Or sometimes employees have transferred from other industries and lack basic foodservice skills. Often, there is no choice but to train them in the skills they need to have. (See *Exhibit 8b.*)

■ **Training prepares employees for new assignments.** When an employee is moved from one assignment to another in an operation, training is the quickest way to get the person up to speed with the best skills and knowledge. The alternative would be for the employee to muddle through and learn by trial and error. Your operation could have many unhappy customers by the time an employee became productive through this way of learning.

■ **Training is needed for new or complicated equipment.** As computers and software programs increase in complexity and become integral parts of equipment such as ovens, refrigerators, and point-of-sale (POS) systems, operations need to use training for employees to function effectively in this environment. Sometimes basic computer skills and concepts will be needed. At other times, only concepts and procedures for specific equipment will be needed.

Exhibit 8b

Training improves job skills.

■ **Training is needed for new procedures.** New recipes and new procedures for food preparation are constantly introduced into restaurant and foodservice operations. If the change is large enough or important enough, you will want to use training to expedite the transition. Training teaches all employees to do things the right way from the start and reduces errors, waste, and rework. Training can make a real difference between doing something right on a consistent basis and not being able to launch a new procedure.

Think About It...

The average amount of money spent on training employees in U.S. corporations in 2003 was $1,745 per employee, and the range was from $298 to $5,665 per employee. In terms of percentage of payroll, the average was 3.97 percent. The employee group that received the highest percentage of training funds was management—from executives to first-line supervisors (28 percent)—and the second-highest group was customer service (18 percent).

Training and Development
(March 2005): 18

■ **Training increases job proficiency.** Restaurant and foodservice operations rely heavily on skilled employees to provide a hospitable and successful dining experience. Training increases job skills and knowledge and improves job attitudes. These qualities will ensure that your operation will offer improved, effective, and efficient customer service.

■ **Training increases sales and profitability.** Well-trained employees tend to sell more and work more efficiently than employees who are not as well trained. Think of the last time you were in a restaurant and the waiter told you about the specials with knowledge and excitement, explaining all the details that you wanted to hear without having to read notes or check with the kitchen. Were you not tempted to order those specials, even if they cost more? Such knowledge and attitudes are the result of good training.

Other Reasons for Training

The primary purpose of training is to teach employees how to do their jobs well. Additionally, training serves many other purposes and offers other benefits.

■ **Training helps non-English speaking employees.** Training is an effective tool to compensate for lack of education or experience in employees with poor English skills. Many organizations have found that some employees have difficulty reading and writing English, so they have developed in-house programs to ensure a minimum level of literacy. Other organizations have brought in literacy training experts or sent employees to literacy training classes.

■ **Training transfers values.** Training can indoctrinate employees with the mission, vision, and values of an operation and encourage employees to adopt them. Training materials and activities should support and reinforce these concepts.

■ **Training creates consistency.** Training all employees to the same standards creates consistency in products and service. Following the same standards creates consistency of look, feel, and taste across a brand or between two or more locations. Brand consistency is important for single restaurants, but especially for chains and franchises.

■ **Training increases employee morale and confidence.** Training helps employees do their jobs better. Then they can be confident that they are working the right way, and that they are appreciated by management. This confidence boosts morale, motivation, and commitment to an operation.

■ **Training combats turnover.** Everyone knows that employee turnover is high in the restaurant and foodservice industry. When you replace an employee, the new employee usually starts at a skill and knowledge level that is lower than a fully productive employee. Rather than waiting for the slow process of informal learning to show results, you should train the employee quickly and reap productivity benefits, as shown previously in *Exhibit 8a* on page 173. Also, training is one way to demonstrate to employees that they are appreciated; it may help increase job satisfaction and commitment to an organization, which in turn can help reduce turnover.

■ **Training reduces legal liabilities.** Providing equal opportunity for employment and promotion is the cornerstone of equal opportunity laws. Since training is both an opportunity and a vehicle for other opportunities, having all employees in the same role participate in the same training ensures equal treatment. Providing the same training opportunities to all employees helps ensure that all of them have an equal chance at success and promotion.

Exhibit 8c

Training increases safety.

■ **Training increases safety.** Training employees to properly handle food, as well as potentially hazardous equipment, materials, and situations, reduces safety risks to both employees and guests. (See *Exhibit 8c.*) For example, a common training topic for restaurant and foodservice employees is avoiding slips, trips, and falls. The costs of accidents far outweigh the costs of properly training employees on safety procedures. Good training not only makes the workplace safer, but also reduces the risk of liability even if an accident or other unsafe situation should occur. This is because, with proper safety training and record keeping, a foodservice operation will be able to demonstrate that an accident was due to employees not following procedures they were trained to do.

■ **Training increases guest satisfaction and profitability.** Most restaurant and foodservice professionals recognize that customers are not usually lost through high prices, but through poor service. Customer retention and repeat business are the mainstays of a successful restaurant. Well-trained kitchen and waitstaff are able to provide the level and quality of service that you want to offer and that customers want to receive. As a manager, you can either spend a lot of money regaining lost customers, or you can spend less money training your staff properly.

Inadequate Training

Recently, **negligent training,** which is a lack of training or inadequate training, has received a lot of national attention. This attention has grown because many customers have sued companies for poor service or other problems and placed the blame on the company's lack of good staff training. Some ways to prevent these claims of negligence include providing employees with overt and frequent invitations for training, and creating equal training opportunities for all employees.

Especially concerning the topics of food safety, equipment care and use, and personal safety and security, every employee should receive adequate training and regular retraining. In addition, as a manager, you should keep a good record of all the training invitations issued, the training received by each employee, and documentation of what each training course covered. For some subjects such as material safety, the law requires these records.

To avoid negligent training and reap the benefits of good training, you need to understand more about what makes training effective. Part of that understanding is knowing the differences between training and education.

Differences between Training and Education

People who do not know much about training often confuse education and training, assuming they are one and the same. But there are significant differences between them. While many people think that education is what happens in school or college and training involves on-the-job learning, the distinction between these two activities is far broader and covers several categories such as goals, applications, and time frames. (See *Exhibit 8d* on the next page.)

Exhibit 8d

Differences between Training and Education

	Training	Education
Goal	To improve job skills and employee performance	To improve knowledge; not necessarily related to a specific job or task
Focus	Teaches how to do something	Teaches concepts and broadens knowledge
Conducted by	Managers and trainers	Teachers and a variety of other people
Time frame	Short-term or immediate application of learning	Long-term or no direct application of learning; timeless

■ **Goals**—Training aims to improve specific job skills and performance, while education aims to improve knowledge of a subject or topic and is not connected to a specific task or job. Education is a way to broaden people's perspectives. It enhances their view of the world, builds their intellectual strength, and improves their mental ability. Even when education is related to a particular job, it focuses on conceptual learning and expanding people's knowledge of a particular area.

■ **Applications**—Training and education are used differently. Training is about learning "how," and education is about learning "what." For example, if you are training a prep cook to make several salads, the goal is to teach him or her to make specific salads in a particular way. Your goal is to provide the trainee with detailed information to ensure that he or she can do the job regularly and consistently to your standards. In contrast, if you were educating the prep cook about salads, you would teach him or her the concept of salads, their history, their nutritional information, the variety of ingredients used to make them, the range of dressings that can be used, the differences between hot and cold salads, and the plating choices available. After being educated, the prep cook has not learned how to make a specific salad, and might not be good at making salads, but he or she knows a lot about salads in general. Where or whether the prep cook applies this information is not a consideration in the educational process.

■ **Time frame**—Training is concerned with the short-term or even immediate application of job skills, while education aims at long-term learning with distant or no future application to job or life situations. Because there is a short-term expectation, training is usually conducted just before an employee needs to use this information or skill. Education, on the other hand, means helping employees learn information—about different cultures, about world cuisines, about politics, art, or history—that they may never apply to their jobs. Education is a timeless activity that is not meant to be applied to any specific function, although it may help with career development.

While the distinctions between education and training are important to understand, they can be blurry because people participating in training often learn new ideas as well, and college students often pick up skills in addition to new ideas and perspectives. Nevertheless, the skill orientation, job specificity, and immediate application that are characteristic of training demand that a focused method be used to develop good training programs.

Forms of Training

There are different ways to train employees (see *Exhibit 8e* for one example), and each one has advantages and disadvantages, as summarized in *Exhibit 8f* on pp. 180–182.

Exhibit 8e

Instructor-led training can be effective because employees apply and practice concepts with immediate feedback.

Exhibit 8f

Forms of Training

Method	Description	Pros and Cons
Buddy method	Informal, on-the-job training in which a trainee is paired with another employee, or "buddy," who shows the trainee how to do the work. This method is less formal than one-on-one training.	**Pro:** Teaches employee how to do the job; quick and easy to set up. **Con:** No guarantee that right things will be learned; great danger that wrong methods will be learned.
Computer–based training (CBT)	(See e-Learning below.)	(See e-Learning below.)
Distance learning	Occurs when the trainer and the trainees are not in the same location, and they communicate through a computer network (such as the Internet); video conferencing; or other form of telecommunications technology.	**Pro:** Everyone included at same time; trainer available to answer questions and adjust for learners' needs. **Con:** Requires special hardware and software; visuals are small and available only through video; not suitable for practice or classroom-style open exchange; more presentation than actual training.
e-Learning	Delivered to an individual through a computer (the "e" stands for "electronic"). The two prevalent forms are computer-based training (CBT) and Web-based training (WBT). Both CBT and WBT deliver content via text and pictures in a sequence with occasional interactions such as quiz questions. With CBT, the learning materials are stored on a CD-ROM or hard drive. With WBT, the learning materials are accessed through a centralized, Internet-based computer.	**Pro:** Can teach a wide variety of subjects in different styles, from knowledge to concepts to problem solving; individual can learn at own pace or can learn a different subject than others; can be very engaging and interesting if done well. **Con:** Very expensive to produce, so is not often updated; expensive to do well, so usually does not live up to capabilities (most e-learning is simple "page turning"); requires computer and perhaps Internet connection; unable to handle interpersonal skills or manual skills; difficult for CBT to collect and analyze student results.
Mediated learning	Any group or individual training that uses audio-visual media—slides, overhead, film, videos, audiotapes—to convey information. Sometimes the audio-visual media are the only teacher.	**Pro:** Adds graphics, pictures, motion, and/or sound to increase communication and understanding; accommodates a variety of learning styles. **Con:** Extra preparation work and cost; requires audio-visual equipment and a screen.

Method	Description	Pros and Cons
Experiential learning	Individuals are not trained, but learn their jobs from colleagues and through trial and error.	**Pro:** Cheap and easy to initiate. **Con:** No guarantee that right things will be learned; great danger that wrong methods will be learned.
Individualized paper-based training	Books and workbooks that employees complete primarily on their own, although can be combined with feedback from a trainer or teacher. Sometimes called self-study or self-paced learning, individualized training can involve individual assignments and reading.	**Pro:** Cheap and easy to initiate; enables learner to work at own pace; covers subjects a foodservice operation is not equipped to handle. **Con:** Requires great discipline to continue and finish; does not provide practice with expert advice (except sometimes afterward, by conference or mail).
Instructor-led group training	The most common form of training. Includes lectures, demonstrations, simulations, seminars, conferences, clinics, and other events that involve multiple trainees, usually from the same company. Most often, group training means events conducted by a trainer or manager, although a local expert from the foodservice crew can be the instructor. This method usually includes time and facilities for practice under the instructor's guidance.	**Pro:** Instructor is present to adjust training to needs of class, answer questions, and advise the learners during practice. **Con:** Expensive to assemble a group together; takes employees away from their jobs; must be taught so the slowest person can learn, and thus is often too slow for others in class; requires large presentation space, large practice space, and equipment.
Laboratory training	Hands-on practice in a realistic setting. Similar to a simulation but not job-real. Practice assignments can be simple or elaborate and are given to individuals or groups to complete under an expert's supervision. The expert usually provides coaching and feedback both during and after the assignment. Usually done in conjunction with instructor-led group training.	**Pro:** Hands-on practice with advice from an expert. **Con:** Requires an equipped laboratory that can handle most or all of the class at one time; requires consumable supplies.
Web-based training (WBT)	(See e-Learning.)	(See e-Learning.)
One-on-one training (also known as tutoring)	Type of on-the-job training in which a trainer, manager, or experienced employee teaches another employee new tasks through a defined, four-step process: preparation, presentation, practice, and performance (four Ps).	**Pro:** Teaches employee how to do the job; quick and easy to set up. **Con:** No guarantee that right things will be learned; great danger that wrong methods will be learned.

continued on next page

continued from previous page

Method	Description	Pros and Cons
On-the-job training (OJT)	Traditionally the most prevalent form of employee development, OJT involves learning something new by doing it under the supervision and guidance of an expert. The trainee is assigned to the expert, and the expert is directed to teach the trainee specific things. There are several ways OJT can be done: ■ One-on-one training—the most common form of OJT ■ Buddy method ■ Apprenticeship training ■ Job rotation	**Pro:** Teaches employee how to do the job; quick and easy to set up. **Con:** No guarantee that right things will be learned; great risk that wrong methods will be learned.
Outside training and education	Employee is sent to college courses, commercial classes, or the company school. Classes can be attended instead of regular work (e.g., a week-long cooking workshop), or on the employee's own time (e.g., evening classes at a local college). Various names are given to these offerings: workshops, seminars, course, programs.	**Pro:** Usually as thorough and effective as internal training or education; covers topics the organization is not equipped to handle; exposes trainee to other companies' values and procedures. **Con:** Takes time away from the job or personal life; can be expensive.
Simulation, or vestibule training	Training provided on equipment or in a situation similar to the actual one in which the skills will be regularly performed; similar to Laboratory Training, but more job-real (e.g., training in a complete test kitchen instead of a working restaurant).	**Pro:** Cheaper and safer than training in a live situation; very effective; high transfer back to the job. **Con:** Very expensive to produce and manage; time-consuming to conduct.

Elements of Good Training

Good training programs have certain elements in common: to focus the training on the needs of a specific job or group of employees, and to cause the training to be effective and efficient. The most effective training includes the following:

■ Only those things that are relevant to the job

■ Only those things not presently in the skill set of the employees

■ Much hands-on work to reinforce the learning

In addition, effective training is organized to maximize learning. As a result, it may not be organized in the way an expert in the subject would think about it. To maximize learning, good training incorporates the following elements:

- Content based on established job guidelines

- Clearly stated learning objectives

- Solidly designed learning methods and sequence

- Thoroughly prepared materials

- Qualified and thoroughly prepared trainers

- Sufficient practice

- Effective learning evaluation

Content Based on Established Job Guidelines

Since training is meant to impart learning about a specific job, the guidelines, standards, procedures, and practices of that job must be the foundation for the training. If the training is about part of a job—such as setting a table, baking a kind of bread, or preparing a type of salad—then only the job essentials for that part are needed.

Clearly Stated Learning Objectives

The skills, knowledge, and attitudes to be learned should be clearly stated as **learning objectives.** These thorough descriptions are used both to guide the preparation of the learning and as the basis for the evaluation of the learning. It is important that learning objectives are stated in terms of what the learner will be able to do, not what the instructor will do or hopes to accomplish. Only learner-based objectives are useful for designing, developing, and evaluating the learning. There are many resources available that give guidance on writing good learning objectives. To help employees subconsciously prepare for learning new content, the objectives are usually made known to the employees at the beginning of training or the start of each training method.

Learning objectives often contain four parts:

1. **Performance**—What the trainee will be able to do

2. **Conditions**—Under what situations the trainee will be able to do it

3. **Standards**—How well the trainee will be able to do it

4. **Repetition**—How often or how long the trainee will be able to do it

Here is an example of a learning objective:

"Prepare and bake six loaves of French bread during off-hours in the restaurant kitchen, given that all necessary ingredients, tools, and equipment are available, so that the bread meets all standards for doneness, firmness, texture, and taste as judged by the master baker. This process must be completed within the standard time allotment for this recipe."

Solidly Designed Learning Methods and Sequence

Much research has gone into determining good learning methods and sequences. In fact, there is a professional specialty in this area called **instructional design**—a systematic process of developing instruction based on adult learning principles. Nevertheless, the basics of solid design are relatively simple:

- Break the learning into manageable **chunks** or modules. For example, in baking bread, the chunks might be:

  - Ⓐ Measuring and mixing
  - Ⓒ Rising and rekneading
  - Ⓑ Kneading
  - Ⓓ Panning and baking

- Teach each chunk following the classic model of training.

Classic Model of Training

The **classic model of training** is also known as the **four-step training method** or **job instruction training.** In this method, each chunk goes through four steps:

- **1** Preparation
- **3** Practice
- **2** Presentation
- **4** Performance

Because all these steps start with the letter "p," this method is also called the **four P approach** (or **four Ps**). This model is costly in terms of time and human energy, but it is the most effective way to make sure that a person learns the content of each chunk well. To ensure success, the trainer needs to have thorough knowledge and skill about how to accomplish the task, an interest in helping the trainee learn, patience with the process, and a commitment to honor all four steps of the process. Each of the steps is explained below.

1. Preparation

Preparation is about preparing the trainee to learn. The first part of preparation is motivating the trainee to pay attention and learn the content. This usually involves relating the content to the person's job and his or her personal success at the job. The next parts of preparation serve as advance organizers. You should communicate your expectations for learning by clearly conveying the learning objectives, and orient the trainee to the content by previewing the concepts and procedures at a high level.

To use the bread-baking example, the preparation for Chunk A, Measuring and Mixing, might include discussing who is responsible for bread baking, why proper measuring and mixing are important, and looking at the recipe to see what the measuring and mixing tasks are.

2. Presentation

Presentation is the part of the training process in which you convey the new information and demonstrate the skills you want the employee to learn. It usually involves showing the task, explaining what you are doing, and giving tips about the most critical aspects of the job.

Whenever possible, provide pictures, diagrams, and handouts that reinforce the information you demonstrate, so the employee has a better chance of remembering what you taught. Most people learn best by watching and doing, as opposed to simply reading or listening, so demonstration and audio-visual aids are central to success in one-on-one training. Additionally, you might encourage the employee to take notes during the presentation. Allow plenty of time for questions and answers since you want the employee to be an active learner.

Using the bread-baking example, the presentation for Chunk A, Measuring and Mixing, might include demonstrating the proper way to measure the ingredients and then the proper way to mix them.

3. Practice

After you have shown the employee what to do and explained the key points, give him or her a chance to practice the task while you observe and advise. (See *Exhibit 8g.*) This situation gives you a chance to immediately correct any error or misunderstanding, and to review or demonstrate again how to accomplish the task the way you want it done. During this step, the trainee will realize what he or she learned from the demonstration and presentation—what looked simple during the demonstration might become more complicated in the actual

Exhibit 8g

Practice is part of the classic model of training.

doing. By being there, you can answer questions, correct behavior, and help shape the employee's work habits.

Returning to the bread-baking example, the practice for Chunk A, Measuring and Mixing, could have the trainees measuring the ingredients and then mixing them, with observation and correction by the instructor.

4. Performance

Performance refers to on-the-job performance of the new skill. When a trainer has explained the task, demonstrated it, and observed the employee practice it once, most managers—and some trainers—think the training function is over. However, the performance step of observing and following up on the routine performance of the task is the most critical. Ongoing observation and feedback help the employee learn the task correctly. The lack of feedback and correction in the critical time just after training can lead the employee to develop bad habits and sloppy work, even if unintended.

Returning to the bread-baking example, the performance for Chunk A, Measuring and Mixing, might have the trainees measuring the ingredients and then mixing them, without correction by the instructor.

Integrative Practice

There is usually an integrative practice at the end of several chunks belonging together. In the **integrative practice,** there is no new content; rather, the learner is helped and then expected to integrate the prior chunks into a useful whole.

Returning to the bread-baking example, there could be an integrative practice at the end, in which the trainee takes a different bread recipe and prepares it from start to finish.

Exhibit 8h

Pattern of Training

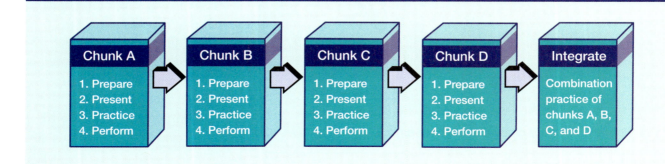

Chunk A	Chunk B	Chunk C	Chunk D	Integrate
1. Prepare 2. Present 3. Practice 4. Perform	1. Prepare 2. Present 3. Practice 4. Perform	1. Prepare 2. Present 3. Practice 4. Perform	1. Prepare 2. Present 3. Practice 4. Perform	Combination practice of chunks A, B, C, and D

While the bread-baking example and *Exhibit 8h* both have four chunks of instruction, there can be any number of chunks before the final step of integrative practice. For example, training on how to use a dishwasher might include three chunks: loading the machine, operating the machine, and unloading the machine. The number of chunks should depend on the complexity of the material; the more complex the material, the greater the number of chunks before integrative practice. However, with even the simplest material, the best practice is to limit the number of chunks to no more than seven.

Activity

Using the Classic Model of Training

Use the four-step training method to train one of your classmates on a task. When possible, choose a task from your own workplace, such as taking an order, setting a table, or making a salad. If it is not possible or practical to choose such a task, then select some other activity that you can train someone else to do. Some examples are how to do a dance move, repot a plant, or play a simple game. For tasks that require special equipment, bring props or equipment when possible, or just pretend they exist. As you think about how to train someone to do your task, keep in mind the elements of good training as well as how to use the four steps.

Thoroughly Prepared Materials

Good training has materials that comprehensively cover all the content of the training and provide primary and backup content as well as instructions for conducting the training in a repeatable manner. These resources should identify the duties, responsibilities, and tasks to be taught, and also include the following information:

- Tools and equipment needed
- Safety and sanitation issues
- Impact on customers
- Impact on operation functions and employees

As you can see, considerable thought, planning, and development goes into good training materials. How to create these materials will be explained later in this chapter.

Exhibit 8i

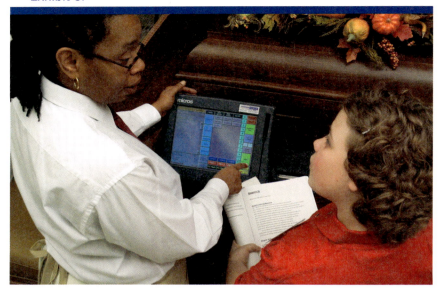

Effective trainers are experts in their subjects and comfortable with training others.

Qualified and Thoroughly Prepared Trainers

For training to have the desired effect, the trainer must be a qualified expert in the subject, and should also be good at training others. (See *Exhibit 8i.*) If you define training as "causing the intended learning to occur," the trainer must be able to do this well. Training and simply giving a presentation differ greatly. There is a tremendous difference between giving a presentation, lecture, or demonstration on a subject or skill, and enabling other people to learn a subject or skill. The latter involves understanding what it takes to start with a novice and go through the steps to make that person proficient. Important skills for training include:

- Motivating the learner
- Setting the stage and providing advance organizers (previews of what is to come)
- Chunking the subject or skill into manageable pieces
- Letting the learner try and make mistakes without interference
- Giving constructive feedback
- Observing the extent of understanding and learning
- Adjusting or expanding on topics or procedures based on the extent of learning
- Helping the learner transfer the learning back to the job

Sufficient Practice

People learn by doing, and the more doing, the more learning and retention. Watching and listening involve very little mental exercise, but actually doing something involves a tremendous amount of mental exercise as well as physical learning. In good training, between 33 and 90 percent of training time should be spent on practice by the trainees, with the average being somewhere around 50 percent.

Effective Learning Evaluation

Another element of training is evaluating the learning that took place. It would be advantageous to the operation for the trainee to know and be able to do all that he or she was trained to do, so the evaluation of learning should cover all of the training. Typically in training, the evaluation of learning covers every major objective and many of the sub-objectives, and thus can take a lot of time.

To use the bread-baking example again, a training-style evaluation of learning would be the Performance step. In this step, the trainee performs all the previous steps under the instructor's observation. The instructor would use a written checklist so notes could be made about each part of the trainee's bread baking. This checklist could then be shared with the trainee, who would benefit from the detailed feedback. Also, the checklist could be used to certify the trainee as a bread baker.

Validation of training is important to ensure that the training teaches what is actually needed. **Validation** means that someone has compared the content of the training and its evaluation methods to the actual job of a master performer in order to determine whether they are in sync. If they are, then the training is validated.

There are several ways that would enable training and its evaluation methods to be validated:

- Paper comparison with the work procedures and standards, if they are thorough enough

- Independent analysis of the job's skills and knowledge as compared to what was taught in the training class

- Statistical analysis and comparison of the trainees who passed, those who did not pass, those who were successful at the job, and those who were not successful at the job

The training and its evaluation methods can also be used to certify trainers as "authorized" trainers of a subject. Remember that part of the requirement of a qualified trainer is thorough knowledge and skills in the content of the training. Another way to certify a trainer is to review the person's actual job performance in the subject being taught. The job performance of the trainer should receive a rating in the highest category available.

There is much involved in good training and good training materials. A later section will discuss the standard methods for ensuring that these elements are achieved.

Industry-Recognized Training

Before you go to the expense of developing your own training, however, you should consider using training outside your organization that is already available. Developing good in-house training can be costly, and you do not want to waste valuable resources reinventing the wheel. There is a lot of good training available on an "off-the-shelf" basis. Some of it is training that you buy and bring into your operation, and some is training to which you send your employees.

To best use training provided by another organization, you must have a clear sense of the objectives that need to be met and the skill level and preparation of the intended trainees. It is critical to analyze your operation's training needs and consider the training program's design, so you can find training that meets the needs of your operation and employees and is actually effective. If you choose a program just because it looks good, but it makes your employees fit into a prepackaged, standard mode, you will be wasting time and money. With careful analysis based on an understanding of what makes good training, you can make use of the many good training resources outside your operation.

There are many sources of external training:

Exhibit 8j

External training can meet an operation's needs.

- The Internet can be useful in finding good sources for WBT and CBT. Use a search engine to help locate the training you need.

- Workshops offered by a variety of training companies can be helpful for training on general topics such as interpersonal skills, team building, customer service, or financial statements. (See *Exhibit 8j.*) These programs provide training at relatively low cost with minimal travel expenses. They would be appropriate if you have an individual or two who would benefit from learning more about these topics.

Think About It…

According to the National Restaurant Association, it typically costs 1.5 times an employee's salary to replace him or her. Since the cost of replacing employees is so high, keeping people can make a real difference in the bottom line.

■ Training opportunities for your employees are also provided by professional organizations such as the American Culinary Federation, the National Restaurant Association, the Club Managers Association of America, among others. These organizations provide workshops as part of their annual conferences, and some offer classes at locations around the country.

■ Local colleges often have workshops in their continuing education or business development programs. These resources can expand what you are able to offer to your employees and provide a private place for them to learn new things.

■ For employees experiencing difficulty with literacy, the Literacy Volunteers of America and other social service organizations provide one-on-one tutoring and assistance in learning English. Other local organizations may also offer education in areas such as harassment, diversity training, payroll systems, teamwork, and customer service. The chamber of commerce and community colleges are also good local resources.

Activity

Finding External Training Resources

Find at least one resource for each of the following types of external training

1 Local literacy assistance course or program

_____

2 Local English as a Second Language (ESL) course or program

_____

3 Workshop, course, conference, or other training sponsored by a hospitality, restaurant, foodservice, or culinary professional organization

_____

4 WBT or CBT course or program relating to hospitality, foodservice, human resources management, or general management (such as marketing for small businesses, purchasing, or bookkeeping)

_____

5 Workshop, course, conference or other training offered by a training company and relating to hospitality, foodservice, human resources management, or general management

_____

6 Workshop or other training event offered by a local college and relating to hospitality, foodservice, human resources management, or general management

_____

Five-Step Training Development Model (ADDIE)

Restaurant and foodservice operations today have many choices when it comes to training employees—from using traditional one-on-one training to developing formal group training to buying training programs. As a manager, you need to ensure that your training efforts get the best results possible; therefore, you need to understand what it takes to develop good training. This section explains how this is done and how you could do this yourself.

There are many good models, or established processes, for creating successful training programs. While different training models offer different steps and may use different terminology, they have many elements in common. Described in this section is a standard model for training development.

To ensure that all the necessary issues in designing and developing training have been considered, experts in designing training usually follow some variant of a five-step model commonly referred to by its acronym, **ADDIE:**

1. Analyze
2. Design
3. Develop
4. Implement
5. Evaluate

These steps can be used to create a wide range of training programs—from short training meetings to multimedia programs to long-term, company-wide training and employee development programs. In small operations in which the manager or key worker is responsible for developing the training, this model should be used to create instructor-led training.

1. Analyze

Analyze, the first stage, is often the one most neglected by people unfamiliar with good training development. However, this stage is actually the most important because a good analysis ensures the training is directly job related.

Typically, managers see what they think is a problem, then either ask for or design training to solve the problem, only to find themselves disappointed because the problem is still not solved. However, becoming aware of a problem is only the first step; you must determine the real cause of it. For example, suppose you want to create training to solve the problem of food arriving cold to the table, and you believe the problem lies with the waitstaff. If you design training to help the waitstaff set priorities and move quickly to deliver food from the kitchen, but their behavior was not the cause of the cold food, you will not solve the problem. An analysis might uncover that the problem was actually due to cold plates, a cold dining room, a long distance to the tables, or several other causes.

Therefore, the problem should be carefully analyzed to see whether training is the solution and who should be trained. Once you have determined who should be trained and the duties, responsibilities, or tasks that they should learn, then you should determine the proper or best way to perform these duties. This is called a **task analysis** and it usually involves observing and interviewing experts. The analysis results in a thorough description of all the elements of the job or work, including tools and equipment, cultural and historical impact, safety and sanitation, and impact on customers and other parts of the operation. All of this information should be included in the training materials to be developed later.

For the group to be trained, you should administer a **needs assessment** of the participants to ascertain their readiness for training and their existing skills and knowledge. Determining the needs of the possible trainees and comparing them to the ideal employee helps you see what the gaps are. Needs assessments also uncover a great deal of useful information about the participants, what the training should cover, and how the training should be conducted. For example, poor English reading and listening skills might be uncovered in a needs assessment.

2. Design

The second step, design, involves creating the objectives for the training event and organizing the chunks and sequence of training as previously described. Typically, these objectives provide clarity to participants about what they will learn and what they will be able to do after the training event or activity. Getting clear about the goals and overall structure of the training—time, length, location—sets the groundwork for detailed planning of the training.

Regardless of the development strategy you use as a manager or trainer, you should ensure that the sequence of activities is designed to motivate and focus your participants and that the content is aligned with the training objectives. Also, the design should include sufficient practice time to help trainees thoroughly acquire the knowledge and skills being taught.

The detailed plan should be written in a report format called a **design document.** This detailed planning work can be complex and fun for some people, while others find it very difficult and painstaking.

The design step also includes writing the learning evaluation. This might be a written and practical test, a checklist, or some other form. The evaluation is written at this point, before the content of the training is written, so that it reflects the learning objectives and not the extra details that might be added to the training materials. Another reason for doing it first is that the actual evaluation tool is an excellent target for the writer of the materials. If at any time the materials do not lead to one or more evaluation questions, then they are off-target and should be discarded. Working this way helps keep the training focused.

Another kind of evaluation for the training itself should be planned and written at this point. This involves developing the evaluation instruments to assess how effective the training is on several levels. Preparing these instruments now will help you focus on the training objectives, the ways in which you want to gather information on how well the event went, and how you will use those comments to improve the training activity in the future. Later in this chapter, evaluation will be covered in more detail.

3. Develop

Most of the time in creating training is spent on developing the specifics of the training. These include the instructor guide, trainee materials, CBT or WBT pages, media, activities and exercises, and job transition materials. Note that, contrary to what many people think, this is not the only work required when developing a training course.

In large organizations, there is often a reservoir of modules and media to use or borrow when developing training. In small organizations, you may have to develop the training materials yourself.

Once you have developed the training materials in the appropriate form for the type of training you have planned, you are ready to implement the training.

4. Implement

Implementing the training means doing the following:

- Arranging for the training space, either individual or group
- Scheduling the trainers, if any
- Inviting the participants and arranging for their participation
- Preparing the participants to attend the training
- Practicing the delivery of the training
- Duplicating the training materials and evaluation forms

As you lead the event, you may realize that changes could be made to improve it or that the training objectives are not clear. Collecting that information will help you to improve the next training event.

5. Evaluate

Evaluation determines whether the training addressed the right areas and made a difference. As a manager or trainer, you should do the following things to obtain feedback on the comprehensiveness and effectiveness of the training:

- Create a checklist that includes all tasks and subtasks, and then verify with your employees that all of these were covered and actually learned.

- Create an evaluation form for training classes called a reaction form (see the "Reaction Evaluation" section on the next page).

- Check in with the trainer and trainees after each day of training to informally evaluate progress.

- Create an evaluation process for trainees to ensure their performance has incorporated the new learning and to receive feedback about the trainer.

- Make adjustments and modifications to your training materials and process as needed.

This kind of thorough evaluation of training is a critical step that is often ignored by most organizations. Instead, trainers or managers hand out simple reaction forms to participants at the end of the training that collect the participants' ratings and comments on the subject, the training, and the trainer. These so-called "smile sheets" are only a small part of evaluating the value and effectiveness of the training.

There are four levels of evaluation that can be applied to most training programs (see *Exhibit 8k*):

1. **Reaction level**—How well the trainees liked the training and the trainer

2. **Learning level**—Whether the trainees gained the knowledge and skills during the training class

3. **Job behavior level**—Whether the trainees applied the knowledge and skills on the job, and whether there was support by the trainees' supervisor for these new skills

4. **Organizational impact level**—Whether the newly applied knowledge and skills made the work more effective and profits greater

Exhibit 8k

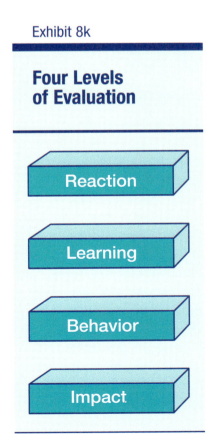

Four Levels of Evaluation

Reaction

Learning

Behavior

Impact

In some situations, organizations also analyze costs and benefits to determine if the dollar value of the benefits from training is greater than the costs of developing and delivering it. Although it is difficult to calculate these benefits in dollars, the cost-benefit ratio—or return on investment (ROI)—calculations provide a careful analysis of whether the training is making a difference and producing a desired effect.

Reaction Evaluation

At the first level of evaluation, reaction, trainers typically collect comments from participants to determine how the participants felt about the training event and what went well. This initial information provides trainers with reactions so that they can make improvements to the training, the skills learned, the materials, the facilitators, the design, and the situation (room set-up, audio-visuals, handouts, temperature, timing) in which the training was conducted. The purpose of the evaluation at this level is to make any immediate corrections before the training activity is conducted again. Using a tool to collect feedback such as a post-training reaction form (PTRF) can provide insights and comments for changes that can be made before the next session, thereby adapting to the participants' needs. *Exhibit 8l* shows a sample PTRF.

Learning Evaluation

The second level of evaluation, learning, gathers data about what the participants have learned during the training. Evaluation of learning during the training is usually done by impartial testing or by expert assessment. The last two steps of the four Ps method, practice and performance, can satisfy this level of evaluation; alternatively, a written test can be given for certain kinds of learning, namely knowledge. For example, to evaluate how well an employee learned the menu, you might provide a written test.

Exhibit 8l

Sample Post–Training Reaction Form (PTRF)

Post–Training Reaction Form

Date _____

Topics _____

I would rate today as (circle all that apply):

Productive	Exciting	Boring	Useful	Tiring	Too Loose
Overwhelming	Wonderful	Intimidating	Insightful	Too Structured	Relevent

Today, I expected that _____

What I found was _____

The best thing(s) about the training event was (were) _____

The worst thing(s) about the training event was (were) _____

Job Behavior Evaluation

Although the training might have been successful at transferring skills and knowledge to the trainees, that is not enough. Remember, the function of training is to change how the job is actually performed. You must determine whether the training was actually implemented on the job and to what extent. The third level of evaluation, job behavior, involves collecting information from both the trainees and their supervisors to help you understand how well the training was transferred to the job and what needs to be done to improve the degree of transfer. Gathering information about what behavior has changed, what behavior has not, and how well the trainees have implemented what they have learned is the goal of this level of evaluation.

Much can happen between the training class and returning to the job. Obstacles to the trainees using their new knowledge and skills, other than the possible ineffectiveness of the training, may include:

- Lack of opportunity (e.g., the need to bake bread has not occurred yet)
- Equipment or tool problems or shortage
- Scheduling difficulties
- Supervisory resistance to change
- Coworker jealousy
- Delays in implementing the new program, policy, or procedure

Often the trainees will not show significant improvements in performance until these obstacles have been removed. Therefore, the job behavior evaluation should be done at least six weeks after the training.

Organizational Impact Evaluation

The fourth level of evaluation, organizational impact, involves assessing the overall impact of the training on the organization. To gather useful and appropriate information for this level, you will need to interview supervisors and collect information about productivity improvements, costs, and benefits.

Sometimes the evaluation will indicate that everything went well and the training is having the desired impact on the job performance of the trainees. Other times, the evaluation will indicate that changes need to be made to the training or post-training support. In still other situations, the evaluation will indicate that both the training and the post-training systems are working correctly, and that the problem lies with the employee.

197

Retraining Employees

When employees demonstrate real difficulties in consistently performing to the standards expected in a restaurant or foodservice operation, you may need to retrain them to provide them with accurate and clear details of what you want done and how to do it.

Before you go to the expense of retraining, however, go through the coaching process to eliminate other possible causes of deficient behavior. You should:

- Gather useful information about employees' work behavior by monitoring their behavior over time.

- Determine what the source of the problems might be—equipment, directions, other employees, or the employee.

- Find out whether the employee's behavior is the core issue and, if so, provide the employee with specific, detailed feedback about what he or she is doing wrong and what needs to be done differently.

While good recruitment, selection, hiring, orientation, and initial training can prevent most of these difficulties, often employees are not originally taught the correct way to do things and have to be retrained. (See *Exhibit 8m.*) Especially if the employee teaching the tasks did not fully understand them, or if you, as a manager, followed only three parts of the four P approach, new employees can learn a wrong, inefficient, or sometimes harmful way of performing tasks. In that case, retraining is probably the answer.

Exhibit 8m

Retraining may be needed.

When retraining is needed to correct performance, start by modifying the original training. As with any training, determine what the employee already knows, then modify the original training to address deficiencies. After retraining, continue coaching the employee to ensure that the retraining adequately addressed the performance problems. This includes routinely monitoring the employee's performance and providing feedback. Evaluate the results of the retraining and then adjust it, or the employee's development plan, as needed.

The need for retraining is not always due to performance problems with an individual. Sometimes the need for retraining comes from changes in the organization, such as the introduction of a new style of service in the dining room, the addition of a self-serve buffet in the foodservice operation, or the implementation of tableside food preparation. In these cases, the employee's performance may currently be appropriate, but he or she needs to learn new ways of doing things to keep up with the changes. Since change happens often in the restaurant and foodservice industry, managers often use employee training and retraining strategies to ensure excellent customer service in their restaurant or foodservice operation.

Summary

Training is a powerful way of improving employees' skills, knowledge, and attitudes, as long as training is what is needed to correct a performance deficiency, the training actually addresses the skill knowledge gap of the employees, and an effective and affordable type of training is used. If this is not the case, then training will not be effective. Training gives an operation many benefits, such as improving skills, productivity, cohesiveness, and loyalty. It is much easier to do nothing or to provide education, but these tactics will not provide the benefits that training does. Although it takes time and money to analyze actual training needs, design good training, and develop good training, the payoff of this investment can be great.

The analysis stage is critical for aligning the training with the needs of the job and the trainees. Designing good training by following the four Ps of preparation, presentation, practice, and performance results in the most effective type of training. For instructor-led training, using a trainer who is an expert in both the subject and in enabling learning causes the training to be the most effective possible.

Training developed in-house is not the only source of good training. In fact, there is a lot of good training available from commercial companies, professional associations, and institutions of higher education.

Activity

Mamma Mia Restaurant

You are the manager of a one-hundred seat restaurant called Mamma Mia located in Kansas City; you have owned and operated this successful restaurant for over twenty years. Your Italian cuisine ranges from mainstream dishes popular with families to a few unusual house specialties for those with more refined tastes.

A couple of months ago, you invested in some capital improvements. You installed new landscaping, remodeled the bathrooms, and put in a new automated stove.

Recently, you noticed that your featured dishes are not selling as well as they used to, and you are considering training the waitstaff about the features and benefits of these dishes. However, your son just came back from a seminar on training in the foodservice industry with some new ideas. Before you go ahead with the training, he wants you to answer the following questions.

1 What other causes of poor sales could there be?

_____

_____

_____

2 How can you find out which of these is the main cause of poor sales?

_____

_____

_____

3 If the cause turns out to be poor preparation of the dishes by the chef, what should you do next?

_____

_____

_____

4 If the cause of poor preparation by the chef turns out to be the new automated stove you just installed, what should you do?

_____

_____

_____

5 After you do this, what should you do next?

_____

_____

_____

Review Your Learning

1 The most effective training

A. contains many role-playing activities.

B. is firmly linked to the job.

C. is done by colleges and universities.

D. has excellent reaction form results.

2 Which is *not* a characteristic of good training?

A. It includes a thorough review of the trainees' present knowledge.

B. It includes only those things not presently in the trainees' skill sets.

C. It utilizes the four Ps of preparation, presentation, practice, and performance.

D. It was implemented after a thorough analysis of performance deficiencies.

3 Which is *not* true about training?

A. It is costly to prepare.

B. It is an investment.

C. It is concentrated experience transferred in a short time.

D. It is the most effective way to change all behaviors.

4 Which is *not* true about training in restaurant and foodservice operations?

A. Training supplies basic foodservice skills.

B. Training increases turnover.

C. Training prepares employees for new assignments.

D. Training is needed for new equipment.

5 Which is *not* one of the four levels of evaluation?

A. Learning

B. Impact

C. Relevance

D. Reaction

6 Which is *not* a source of good outside training?

A. Professional organizations

B. Literacy Volunteers of America

C. Commercially available CBT and WBT

D. Food suppliers

7 What does ADDIE stand for?

A. Assess Deficiencies in Development of Individual Effectiveness

B. Analyze, Design, Develop, Implement, Evaluate

C. Acquire, Deliver, Demonstrate, Investigate, Eliminate

D. Adjust Different Duties for Individual Effectiveness

8 When might retraining of employees be needed?

A. When work practices have changed

B. When so many people needed training that it was held multiple times

C. When an employee was absent during the training

D. When other employees have difficulty with an employee

9 Which information typically is *not* included in thoroughly prepared training materials?

A. Tools and equipment needed to perform the duties, responsibilities, and tasks

B. Statistics on performance evaluations related to the duties, responsibilities, and tasks

C. Safety and sanitation related to the duties, responsibilities, and tasks

D. Impact of duties, responsibilities, and tasks on customers and the operation

Notes

Managing Shifts to Ensure a Quality Operation

9

Inside This Chapter

- Setting the Standards of Service and Quality
- Setting Shift Goals
- Planning for Your Shift
- Scheduling Staff
- Using Checklists to Ensure Quality
- Using Opening and Preshift Checklists
- Conducting Preshift Meetings
- Additional Opening Activities
- Using Midshift Checklists

- Using Shift-End and Closing Checklists
- Additional Closing Activities
- Evaluating Shift Performance
- Using Communication Logs
- Recording Information in Communication Logs
- Coordinating and Communicating During Shift Change
- Conducting Postshift Meetings
- Other Operational Challenges

After completing this chapter, you should be able to:

- Identify the purpose of using checklists in a restaurant or foodservice operation.
- Discuss the importance of planning for a shift and developing shift goals.
- Identify typical areas that should be included in longer-term goals for the operation.
- Explain why managers should inspect operating areas before a shift starts.
- Describe the purpose of communication logs.
- Identify information that is typically included in communication logs.
- Identify information that should *not* be included in communication logs.
- Recognize critical incidents.

Test Your Knowledge

1 **True or False:** Physical checklists are unnecessary for most restaurant or foodservice operations because everyone knows to pick up and clean up around themselves. *(See p. 219.)*

2 **True or False:** Communication logs contain information for planning, for remembering, and for helping the next shift do the right things. *(See p. 233.)*

3 **True or False:** Preshift checklists are for employees and not for managers. *(See p. 219.)*

4 **True or False:** Communication logs are places to record all the information about accidents and emergencies. *(See p. 237.)*

5 **True or False:** Communication logs are private documents, and therefore, not able to be subpoenaed. *(See pp. 206-207.)*

Key Terms

Banquet and catering log

Bleeding the register

Cash drop

Chef's communication log

Communication log

Covers

Critical incident

Day part

Dining room log

Dining room manager's communication log

Fiduciary

Labor chart

Manager's communication log

Manager's report

Operating standards

Point-of-sale (POS) system

Postshift meeting

Postshift review

Preshift meeting

Production sheet

Reservation log

Service period

Side work

Staffing chart

Staggered schedule

Standard operating procedures (SOPs)

Standards

Subpoenaed

Work schedule

Z report

Introduction

The quality of a restaurant or foodservice operation depends on its established standards and the smoothness with which they are implemented. The smooth operation of each shift depends on the coordination of many people doing many specific jobs and meeting the quality standards. This coordination ensures that guests have a successful experience.

To guarantee this coordination and consistent success with customers, operations have developed standards and routine procedures, oftentimes by setting shift goals. Operations also have developed various tools, such as checklists and communication aids, for ensuring the following:

- Standards are met.

- Shift transitions are seamless.

- Business patterns are tracked, and therefore, can be forecasted.

- Potentially litigious situations are documented.

Standard Operating Procedures and Standards

Before checklists and logs can be created, restaurant and foodservice operations need to establish standard operating procedures (SOPs) and standards for how to do things. **Standard operating procedures** define what steps people should take in certain circumstances. Although SOPs can be used to handle unusual situations, they are often thought of as the routine procedures that people do on a day-to-day basis. For example, operations have regular ways of handling the tasks associated with opening and closing. In each circumstance, these tasks are often done in a specified order. When employees know what they are supposed to do and what they can expect coworkers to do, there are fewer surprises to deal with, and work gets done in a well-coordinated way.

Standards indicate the level of quality, speed, food safety, or hospitality that employees are expected to demonstrate while completing their work. When an operation sets and follows clear standards, customers receive a consistently good experience with every visit. Standards also help the staff know how to do a particular task—how well, how often, how quickly, to what degree, etc. Standards identify equipment settings, measurements, frequencies, and other criteria of good and safe foodservice. For example, an operation will have a standard way of setting a table, a standard procedure by which certain dishes are prepared, and a standard ratio for mixing sanitizing solution and water. Standards exist in all areas of an operation, from the back of the house to the front of the house. Both SOPs and standards may be written or passed on by word of mouth.

Once routine procedures and standards are established, an operation can develop tools for ensuring these procedures are completed and standards are met.

Exhibit 9a

Checklists remind people what to do.

Checklists and Communication Logs

To help people remember and manage routine procedures and standards, many operations have developed various tools, such as checklists and communication logs. Checklists help staff remember and complete all of the tasks necessary for a successful operation. Using different checklists for different shifts and areas or roles helps ensure that everyone is doing the tasks they are supposed to do. (See *Exhibit 9a.*) Since there are so many areas to consider—physical (inside and outside), fiduciary/financial, food safety, equipment, and staffing—checklists can help employees remember exactly what to do each day and remind them to anticipate unusual events.

Communication logs are documents in which managers record information about what happens on a particular shift for the purpose of sharing information with the managers of the next shift and future shifts. Sometimes paperwork systems can get very complicated and detract from your ability to respond to customers. Other times, they can keep you from being blindsided by a situation you were not expecting.

Other Common Logs and Checklists

In addition to checklists and communication logs, there are many similar documents that are commonly used in restaurant and foodservice operations:

- Hazard Analysis and Critical Control Point (HACCP) logs are used to record ongoing monitoring and corrective actions in operations that use a HACCP system to manage their food safety practices.

- Par stock level checklists are used to ensure that stock is at or above the par (minimum) level.

- Inventory checklists are used to assess levels of ingredients and supplies and to track property.

- Receiving checklists are used to verify receipt of goods and their condition as received.

- *Mise en place* checklists serve as a task list for chefs to ensure that preliminary food preparation has been completed.

- Bar stock checklists are used to ensure that sufficient liquor and bar supplies are on hand.

These logs and checklists have many purposes:

- Remind staff to cover all the tasks in a timely and comprehensive manner.

- Ensure both quality operations and consistent record keeping.

- Provide a way to record information for accounting and planning purposes.

In addition, there are legal and risk management reasons for some lists; for example, HACCP logs can help protect you and the operation in the case of a suspected foodborne-illness outbreak. Finally, all of these logs and lists support standards for service and quality.

Setting the Standards of Service and Quality

One of the more important areas in which managers ensure a high-quality operation is establishing, communicating, and reinforcing **operating standards**—ways of doing things correctly and in the manner that management wants them done. By being clear about the standards, managers provide employees with information about what they need to do and how they need to do it. Operating standards refer to a wide range of requirements in such areas as:

- Beverage
- Customer greeting
- Customer relations
- Food costing
- Food presentation
- Food safety
- Portion sizes
- Record keeping
- Service styles
- Table setup
- Teamwork

A comprehensive set of standards provides the foundation for good checklists and sometimes for setting shift goals. An example of a set of service standards for a restaurant is given in *Exhibit 9b* on the following pages. As you can see, there are many types of standards that can be identified, and this example only covers *service*.

Exhibit 9b

Example of Restaurant Service Standards

SERVICE STANDARDS

Introduction

The following standards have been designed to ensure the service level in the restaurant remains at the high level to which we aspire. They also help guarantee that the level of service is not dependent on who the server is.

Our service standards are based on principles that we feel are necessary to maintain the desired level of service. The intention is to create a framework within which you should feel comfortable to operate. We do not attempt to address every possible situation, but rather set examples to act as a guideline for your own decisions.

Many of the service staff are familiar with most, if not all, of these standards. Approach those you know as a reminder and these that are new as an opportunity to increase your knowledge. In addition, please remember that all standards are to be followed within reason. If you have to inconvenience the guest to follow the standards, you are replacing good guest service and friendly hospitality—which are also priorities of this restaurant—with rigidly following standards.

Dining Room Floor Plan

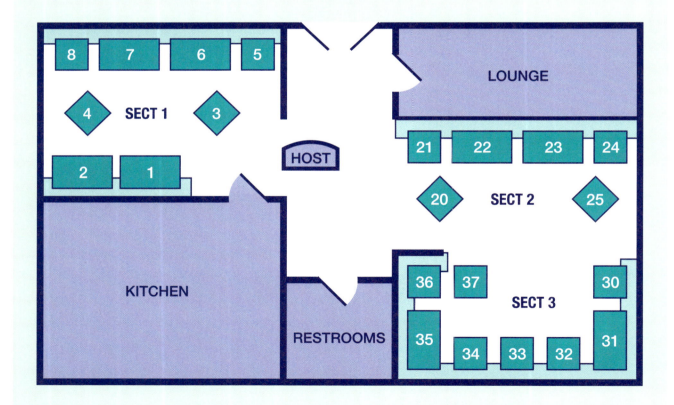

Adapted with permission from David R. Wightman, CEC

Table Setup Standards—Lunch

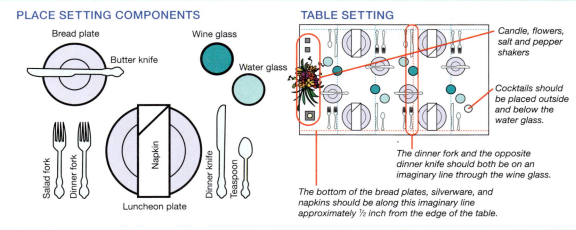

PLACE SETTING COMPONENTS

Bread plate
Butter knife
Wine glass
Water glass
Salad fork
Dinner fork
Napkin
Dinner knife
Teaspoon
Luncheon plate

TABLE SETTING

Candle, flowers, salt and pepper shakers

Cocktails should be placed outside and below the water glass.

The dinner fork and the opposite dinner knife should both be on an imaginary line through the wine glass.

The bottom of the bread plates, silverware, and napkins should be along this imaginary line approximately ½ inch from the edge of the table.

- Silverware: dinner knife, dinner fork, salad fork, teaspoon, and butter knife.
- The coffee cup should be placed in the same position as the wine glass if ordered with the meal. Remove the wine glass.
- Candle, flowers, and salt and pepper shakers should always be on the other side of the table from the entrance of the room. Exception: end tables, table 25, and table 36, as shown on p. 208.
- Align the tables and the wine and water glasses on the tables.

Table Setup Standards—Dinner

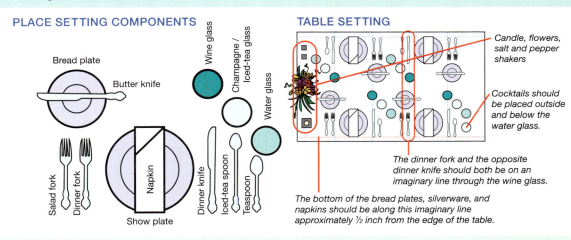

PLACE SETTING COMPONENTS

Bread plate
Butter knife
Wine glass
Champagne / Iced-tea glass
Water glass
Salad fork
Dinner fork
Napkin
Dinner knife
Iced-tea spoon
Teaspoon
Show plate

TABLE SETTING

Candle, flowers, salt and pepper shakers

Cocktails should be placed outside and below the water glass.

The dinner fork and the opposite dinner knife should both be on an imaginary line through the wine glass.

The bottom of the bread plates, silverware, and napkins should be along this imaginary line approximately ½ inch from the edge of the table.

- Silverware: dinner knife, dinner fork, salad fork, teaspoon, and butter knife.
- The iced-tea glass should be placed in the same position as the champagne glass in the above illustration. The iced-tea spoon should be placed outside the dinner knife. The chance that someone will order both champagne and iced tea is minimal.
- The coffee cup should be placed in the same position as the wine glass if ordered with the meal. Remove the wine glass.
- Candle, flowers, and salt and pepper shakers should always be on the other side of the table from the entrance of the room. Exception: end tables, table 25, and table 36, as shown on p. 208.
- Align the tables and the wine and water glasses on the tables.

continued on next page

Example of Restaurant Service Standards *continued from previous page*

General Service Standards

- Serve water and bread within one minute.

- Follow the guidelines as to where different glasses go on the table (see "Table Setup Standards" in the previous illustrations for the meal period in question).

- Set silverware for all courses (except dessert) prior to serving the appetizer. Place first course silverware farthest away from the show plate, entrée silverware closest to the snow plate, and second course (if ordered) in between.

- When bringing new silverware to a table, use a plate with a folded napkin on it. When busy, two pieces of silverware can be carried on a napkin.

- Always avoid touching the tops of the forks and the knife blades with your hands.

- Keep the tabletop neat at all times (remove glasses, cups, and silverware that are not being used).

- Never remove empty plates before all guests at the table are finished, except when a guest asks you to do so. Do not use a beverage tray when clearing plates.

- When clearing tables, please do so as follows: If you can get all plates, including bread and butter plates, plus all silverware in one turn, go ahead and start with the largest plates. Otherwise, any side order and butter plates go first, then bread plates, then dinner plates.

- Never walk through the dining room empty-handed.

Dining Room Service Standards

- Follow all general service standards.

- Greet guests within three minutes of being seated. You are encouraged to use the guest's name if it is known.

- When upselling a guest, keep in mind that you want the guest to return for all special occasions. If the guest leaves the restaurant with the feeling it was too expensive, the guest will not return. It is a skill to evaluate how far to go; if you push it too far, future business will be lost and, most likely, you will have lost a tip.

- Serve all poured beverages from a tray *(no exceptions)*. Never carry a glass in your hand. When serving beverages in stemware, always hold the stem. Other glasses should be touched only at the bottom of the glass.

- When serving beer, gently pour the beer down the side of the glass, and then place the bottle on the table with the label facing the guest.

- Always serve beverages before serving the food.

- Never let water or coffee levels go below half full. Avoid lifting the water glasses from the table unless absolutely necessary.

- Keep bread service going until the entrée is finished or the guest declines.

- Serve women before men and older people before younger people.

- Always offer freshly ground pepper with cream soups, salads, and pasta.

- Never "auction" food at the table (by asking the guests who gets what food item); make sure you know the correct position on the table for each item before you leave the kitchen.

- Check back with the guests after they have eaten two bites, giving them time to try the food.

- Remove salt and pepper shakers before dessert is served.

- Never have your hands in your pockets when in the guests' view.
- Never lean on anything.
- Take a moment to organize and prioritize your thoughts and actions.
- Treat all coworkers with respect at all times.

Dinner Closing Standards

- Always reset tables up to 10:00 p.m. (11:00 p.m. on Friday and Saturday).
- The earliest time to close a section is 9:00 p.m. (10:00 p.m. on Friday and Saturday).
- If Section 1 or 2 is closed early, always leave candles, flowers, and salt and pepper shakers on the tables until 10:00 p.m. (11:00 p.m. on Friday and Saturday). Wait until 9.30 p.m. (10.30 p.m. on Friday and Saturday) to set coffee cups and spoons; just leave the knife and fork with the napkin between them on the table.

These standards are designed to ensure that your guests feel welcome whether they arrive ten minutes before closing or at 7:00 p.m.

Host Opening and Closing Standards

Setup Duties

- Check the waitstaff schedule to see who is working.
- Check supplies: pencils (sharpened), pens, grease pencils, and message pads.
- Retrieve the reservation book from the bartender and transfer the phone to the host station.
- Turn music on and set to correct level (appropriate music is classical or jazz, no vocals).
- Ensure the lights are at the correct level (and dimmed at 5.30 p.m.).
- Ensure the light in the bus station is dimmed.
- Check for cleanliness of hostess area, foyer, and restaurant; pay special attention to the floor.
- Ensure all empty coat hangers are to one side.
- Check glass in entrance door and doors to kitchen; clean as needed.
- Ensure the hostess stand looks neat and orderly.
- Instruct the servers of any special table setup.
- Check the reservation book five days ahead to see whether there are any special situations that need to be communicated to the kitchen or a manager.

Closing Duties

- Count the number of covers (number of people fed during a meal period).
- Remove all personal belongings from the host stand.
- The bar staff is here until midnight.
- If you are leaving after lunch, transfer the phone to the bar and bring the reservation book and a sharp pencil to the bartender.

continued on next page

Example of Restaurant Service Standards *continued from previous page*

Bar and Lounge Service Standards

- Follow all general service standards.

- Greet guests within two minutes of their being seated. Use the guest's name if it is known.

- Know your liquors so you can easily suggest a brand name to substitute for well liquors.

- Keep the bar top and tabletop neat at all times (remove glasses, cups, and silverware that are not being used).

- Never remove empty plates before all guests at the table are finished, except when a guest asks you to do so.

- Never walk through the bar or lounge empty-handed. Try to bring a tray at all times.

Reservation Standards

When taking reservations:

- Always use a pencil.

- Write neatly and legibly. Stay within the lines.

- Be sure that you get all the information requested on the reservation sheet.

- If a guest is reluctant to give you a phone number, inform him or her that it is used for confirmation and is always useful if the guest inadvertently leaves something behind, such as a credit card.

- If a guest leaves a phone number from out of town, inquire whether there is a local phone number or hotel name. Because staff do not confirm reservations until the day of the reservation, the out-of-town home phone number may not be of help that day.

- Ask whether there is a special occasion that day. If the answer is yes, ask them whether they would like to order a cake.

- For parties of five or more, always circle the number to draw attention to the larger parties. With the small dining room, there is limited space for large groups, and therefore, group size will need to be monitored closely.

- Inform the guest that for parties of six or more, you will only present one check at the table and that a 15 percent gratuity will be added.

- It is appropriate to ask the guest to call prior to arrival if there is a change in the number of guests. Always make this request in December.

Handling Guest Complaints

On occasion, you will have guests complaining about food or service. Sometimes it is due to the staff not living up to the standards, and sometimes it is due to the guest's expectations being different from the establishment's standards. Never make a guest uncomfortable for bringing a complaint to the attention of staff. All service establishments make mistakes. Oftentimes, what differentiates one place from another is how such situations are handled. Following are procedures for those types of situations.

Preparation of the Food

If a guest complains about the preparation of the food:

- Immediately bring the food back to the kitchen to be prepared according to the guest's preferences.

- Inform a manager.

Taste of the Food

If a guest complains about the taste of the food:

- Never argue with his or her opinion, but kindly inquire what he or she disliked about the dish.

- If less than half the portion has been consumed, immediately take the plate off the table and ask whether the guest would like anything else instead; inform a manager.

- If more than half the serving has been consumed, apologize to the guest and immediately inform a manager so that appropriate compensation, if any, can be applied.

- *This is why it is so important to check back with the guests after they have eaten a few bites!*

Taste of the Wine

If a guest complains about the taste of the wine:

- If the wine is bad, take it off the table and inquire whether the guest would like to try another bottle of the same kind or see the wine list again.

- If you recommended the wine, discuss with a manager what, if any, action should be taken.

- If the guest chose the wine, take no action; remember, guests taste the wine to determine that the wine has not gone bad, not to see whether they like the wine (exception: wine by the glass).

Taste of Any Other Beverage

If a guest complains about the taste of any other beverage, then follow these standards:

- Nonalcoholic beverages are exchanged without question.

- Follow the rules for food when it comes to mixed drinks.

Refusing Alcohol Service to a Guest

Unfortunately, there are times when staff must refuse the service of alcohol to a guest. Here are some tips on how to do it while minimizing the possibility of a scene at the same time:

Where to Tell the Guest

- If the guest is standing up, try to get him or her away from his or her party while explaining the situation.

- If the guest is seated, try to tell him or her in a manner so that the rest of the party cannot hear what you are saying.

- If none of the above is possible, ask the guest to come aside with you so you can explain the situation.

continued on next page

Example of Restaurant Service Standards *continued from previous page*

Refusing Alcohol Service to a Guest

What to Say to the Guest

■ "I'm sorry, but I cannot serve more alcohol to you right now. I'd be happy to bring you a coffee or a soda." You may suggest bringing something nonalcoholic that is served in the same kind of glass and with the same garnish as his or her current drink, if possible. Examples of that would be a nonalcoholic beer poured at the bar instead of bringing the bottle to the table, virgin drinks, and plain soda in a bucket glass with a lemon slice or berry, if appropriate.

■ Create a "bond" with the guest by blaming the decision on your manager. "I'm sorry, but my manager told me I cannot serve more alcohol to you. If I do, I will be in trouble." Then suggest the same solution as in the previous paragraph. You should always inform your manager when you decide to "stop service" and when you are using this approach. The guest may ask to speak with the manager.

How to Tell the Guest

■ The less authority in your voice and posture, the more successful you will be.

■ A nuance of pleading in your voice often works to your advantage. If you can make it sound as if the guest is doing you a personal favor by going along with your suggestions, he or she will respond favorably.

■ Always remain respectful towards the guest even if he or she is being difficult.

Why Do It This Way?

■ A guest that has "lost face" has nothing left to lose. You are less likely to have a situation on your hands if you allow the guest to keep his or her dignity.

What Do I Do if the Guest Causes a Scene?

■ It is a good idea to always inform security prior to approaching a guest.

■ Get your manager as quickly as possible.

■ If a guest becomes rude, walk away. If you think the person may listen, try the following: "We aspire to a high level of service here. However, that does not mean I have to listen to offensive or rude language. I encourage you to change your attitude, or I will have to ask you to leave."

■ If a guest becomes physically threatening, get a manager. The manager will escort the guest off the premises.

Handling Foodborne-Illness Complaints

If a guest calls and complains about foodborne illness, the procedures are very simple:

■ Do not discuss the matter with the guest but forward the phone call to a manager. Before doing so, ask for his or her name and phone number and assure the guest that you will follow up on the situation with a manager. Be very sympathetic with his or her situation.

■ Under no circumstances should you agree with the guest that your restaurant could be responsible.

■ Do not share with the guest whether you have had previous calls of the same nature.

Setting Shift Goals

As a manager, you will develop or will have been given goals for your restaurant or foodservice operation. In addition, you will probably create specific goals for each shift. Setting shift goals can help you focus your efforts and keep a clear sense of direction during the shift, even in the face of many demands and challenges.

In many situations, the goals will come from observation and analysis of the previous shift. Sometimes, the goals will come from other sources of information, such as the communication log that you review on a daily basis. The log may alert you to a challenge created by the previous shift or an unforeseen event—like a large private party booked just that day—and these immediate goals will take precedence over more long-standing goals that you have established.

Often, your goals for a shift might simply be reinforcing the standards for quality that have already been established, some of which might be slipping. For example, the goals of a shift could include:

- Ensuring quality service
- Reducing breakage of china and glassware
- Increasing sales of specials
- Decreasing the amount of customer complaints
- Improving the speed with which staff responds to customers
- Reducing food costs
- Improving employee teamwork

Whatever they are, sharing shift goals with your employees will help them contribute to what you are trying to accomplish. This means being clear about what the goals are and reminding employees whenever they seem to need it. Writing down these goals will help you to focus on them even more than you might otherwise and will help you to communicate them to your team. Often, this type of communication takes place during a preshift meeting, which is discussed in more detail later in this chapter.

Planning for Your Shift

Since there are always unplanned and unforeseen happenings in the restaurant and foodservice industry, you do not want to spend your time haphazardly reacting to crisis after crisis or "putting out fires." If you plan ahead and anticipate possible difficulties, you can then spend your time improving the quality of the food and service, the efficiency of the operation, and the teamwork among staff.

Often, additional or unusual situations alter the course of a regular shift. In planning for a shift, you will want to know what is normal for that shift and what will be different. When creating or following an operational plan for a shift, some of the questions you should ask include:

- Is there anything new or different in today's shift?

- Are there any special meals (breakfasts, lunches, or dinners)?

- Was the room booked correctly or overbooked?

- At what times do we expect the highest demand, and are we prepared for that time period?

- Will the timing of reservations jam up the kitchen?

If you as a manager do not pay close attention or plan more carefully, the challenges to a smooth operation may increase dramatically. Anticipating these unusual events will allow you to prevent difficulties and ensure that you are accommodating unusual events as much as you can. The more "surprises" that you can prepare for, the easier it will be to avoid crises among the employees and problems in providing quality food and service to your customers. Once you have a general plan for your shift, you can schedule staff or adjust the schedule to support your plan.

Scheduling Staff

Planning a staff work schedule—a listing of who reports for what shift on what days for what duty—for any shift means determining what staff you need for the front and back of the house and at what time. That means considering the entire day in one-hour modules—sometimes even smaller units—as you develop a schedule. Most managers break the full day into hourly segments and then determine how many people are needed for each hour. However, before developing a schedule, you need to consider a variety of information, such as:

- Forecasted covers (number of people fed during a meal period)

- Actual reservations

- Historical pattern of cover counts, reservations, and walk-ins

- Potential for bad weather

- Other unusual situations that might affect the number of patrons in the restaurant or foodservice operation

Developing a weekly work schedule or staffing pattern for the operation involves using information on customer demand and peak business hours to create a **staggered schedule,** through which staff members start and stop at varying, overlapping times as needed. For example, most restaurants serving dinner plan for low numbers of waitstaff at 5:00 p.m. and then add staff as the evening progresses. At the peak time, you want all the skilled staff necessary to make the operation run smoothly. In these situations, some waitstaff will do their **side work**—work in addition to the main job of serving customers, such as stocking stations, and filling salt and pepper shakers. Side work can be accomplished before, during, or at the end of the shift, depending on customers' demands. The same scheduling pattern should be used for bussers and bartenders. However, you do not want too many people on duty when they are not needed. Consequently, employees who come in early are scheduled to leave early so that the schedule maximizes benefits for the guests and minimizes costs to the operation.

Using a staggered schedule is also beneficial when planning for kitchen staff. Depending on the size and volume of the restaurant, some cooks come in early to receive products, start stocks, make soups, and prep food for the day. They may work a full day but leave before the dinner service is finished or has even started. The exact timing depends on the hours they have been there, the details of that daily production and staffing schedule, and the planned customer demand. A similar scheduling dynamic works with dishwashers, one of whom may come in during the morning to clean, with more coming in later in the day as the demand for their services picks up. Those who work the last shift will be responsible for closing duties, such as mopping the kitchen, hauling out trash, and closing down the relevant equipment.

While these scheduling principles are true in all settings, the application may change depending on the size of the restaurant, the nature of its menu (and how labor intensive it is), and its patterns. **Labor charts** (also called **staffing charts**) are to help you calculate the number of hours for which individual employees are scheduled. Such charts help managers to ensure people are getting the right number of hours at the right times and that busy times are covered by better-trained or more experienced employees.

Labor charts are sometimes developed on software purchased by the operation or are sometimes handwritten. These schedules should be developed at least one week ahead and openly displayed so that employees know when they are scheduled to work. (See *Exhibit 9c.*)

Although developed a week or more before the events, schedules are often adjusted on a daily basis or even during the day. Changes in weather, unexpected crowds, or other out-of-the-ordinary events might call for rearranging a schedule quickly.

Exhibit 9c

Schedules should be displayed at least a week ahead of time.

Activity

Planning for a Shift and Setting Shift Goals

You are the dining room manager for a casual chain restaurant in a shopping district. You typically work the night shift on weekends, which includes closing the restaurant. Some of the restaurant's most experienced dining room staff work your shift, and most of the time, they get along and work well together. However, lately things have been strained between the waitstaff and the kitchen staff because a beloved line cook left and her replacement is still getting up to speed. Since the new line cook started, orders are slower to come up, portions are smaller, and regular customers are noticing. The waitstaff are aggravated by the complaints and worried about their tips. To try to help the servers, two of your three bartenders have become overly generous with drink portions. You also have noticed that one of your assistant managers, John, suddenly seems to be tired and sad all the time. Other employees have noticed a change in him, too, but so far, John has hidden his bad mood from the customers. You worry that he might be looking for another job.

On a typical weekend shift at this time of year, your team serves 150 to 170 covers with an average check of $32.50, which, until recently, met the goals set by the corporate office. Corporate has recently increased the average check goal for your operation to $34.00. Corporate also has set a goal for an 8 percent increase in the overall profit (the money left over after expenses) of your operation. Your operation has six months to meet these goals. A new television advertising campaign is supposed to help; however, you know the advertising alone will not be enough.

The management staff have informally discussed various ways of meeting these goals, but the general manager has not yet communicated a formal strategy. Until then, you are supposed to use your own strategies for increasing revenue, decreasing costs, or doing both.

When you arrive at the restaurant to start your shift at 4:00 p.m., the general manager tells you one of your bussers called in sick, but one of the day shift bussers can stay for three extra hours. You review the dining room manager's communication log, which mentions an unusually high cover count and a large reservation that was booked earlier in the day. When you check the reservations log, which shows a higher than average number of reservations—not counting the large party booked that day—you discover that you will be short-handed if you do not find at least one more server and another busser to work that night. You also suspect that, based on the large increase in business that day, you may even need an additional server for your peak hours, between 6:00 p.m. and 9:00 p.m.

You have thirty minutes before your preshift meeting to plan for your shift. What goals will you set, and what will you do to help ensure they are met? Be prepared to discuss your strategy with the class.

_____

_____

_____

_____

_____

_____

_____

_____

Using Checklists to Ensure Quality

Checklists are used for ensuring that both standards and routine procedures are met or performed consistently throughout and across shifts. There are many types of checklists used in restaurant and foodservice operations, and they have many purposes. Some are designed to remind staff to cover all the necessary tasks in a timely and comprehensive manner. Others are used to ensure both quality operations and consistent record keeping. However, checklists are typically designed for specific times and areas or roles of the operation. For example, an opening checklist for the back of the house might include such things as turning on ovens, checking cooler temperatures, and ensuring stations are clean and ready to use. An opening checklist for a manager might include preparing cash register tills, verifying all employees have arrived and are dressed appropriately, and checking the heating or air conditioning. Regardless of the shift, area, or role, at minimum, checklists should include items relating to financial or fiduciary checks, front-of-the-house and service-readiness checks, back-of-the-house and sanitation checks, and facility checks.

As you consider the example checklist items presented in this chapter, keep in mind that they are designed to accommodate a wide range of operations, from fine dining to quick service to institutional foodservice. Therefore, the combination of checklist items may seem unusual, such as checking linens and self-service stations.

In any type of operation, as checklists are routinely followed, employees develop good habits. These habits include patterns of taking care of the operation and noticing equipment or facility items that may need to be monitored for maintenance or replacement. As a result, checking on all parts of the operation becomes a regular part of daily work and ensures a consistent approach to taking care of customers and the facilities.

Using Opening and Preshift Checklists

Opening and preshift checklists are used to ensure that everything has been prepared appropriately before a shift starts. These checklists make sure your operation is ready to receive customers and fill orders as soon as the doors open or the shift begins. While employees and managers may use different checklists, just before shift start or opening, each area manager should conduct a walk-through to ensure that all items on the appropriate checklists have been satisfactorily completed.

219

Think About It...

When you first enter a new restaurant, how do you judge the quality of the establishment?

In addition, each manager needs to ensure that each employee has come to work on time, is prepared to work, and is dressed appropriately. Making a practice of greeting employees (and vendors) as they enter the establishment helps managers track who has come in and sets the appropriate tone for a hospitality business. For front-of-the-house employees, there is an additional inspection just before the doors are opened for service, but most managers check on the appearance of front-of-the-house staff at the start of each shift.

Opening and Preshift Checks for the Facility

Monitoring the interior and exterior of the restaurant or foodservice operation involves making sure it is clean, safe, and presentable. The exterior and interior appearance of your establishment may be the most important factor in whether a customer chooses to patronize your establishment. A customer's initial impression of your operation is based on the physical appearance of your facility, and this initial impression can influence everything about the customer's experience.

Making a good first impression is reason enough to routinely monitor your operation's facility, but there are other benefits as well. Monitoring the facility helps you identify current and future maintenance issues. For example, when inspecting the facility on a rainy day, you might notice water leaking from the seams of a downspout. There could be various reasons for this problem, such as the seams deteriorating or a blockage causing the water to back up. Initially, a problem like this is not urgent to repair, but if left alone, it could cause other, more expensive problems, such as water damage to the foundation or ice damage to the roof and gutters. If you or an employee uses the checklist every day, you are more likely to notice such problems while they are small and less expensive to repair. You also are more likely to anticipate the need for major improvements, like exterior sign repair, landscaping, or paving, and can plan for them before they become urgent.

Ensuring security and preventing safety hazards is a huge benefit of performing routine facility checks. Following a checklist can help you to identify safety hazards such as debris on your walkway that could cause someone to trip, wasp nests near the front door, large icicles hanging over the entrance, or loose handrails on your stairway. Checklists also remind people to look for potential security problems, such as broken windows, improperly working doors, and malfunctioning security cameras.

Facility Exterior and Approach

Before an operation opens, someone from the staff should examine the approach to the operation and prepare it for guests. Using a checklist for this purpose will ensure that the employee does not overlook anything. In addition, a checklist gives the employee a chance to record any areas that will need attention in the future, such as landscaping, repaving, or rebuilding the steps.

A common mistake of most managers is entering and exiting the restaurant from the back or the loading dock and not checking on the front of the restaurant where the guests arrive. If this is the case, then using the checklist and assigning an employee to review and prepare the entrance each day becomes even more important. (See *Exhibit 9d.*)

Opening and preshift checklists typically contain items for checking the facility, which include activities for checking the approach to the operation, such as the following:

Exhibit 9d

First impressions are critical.

- Checking for litter and debris in front of the restaurant and around the property

- Checking on light bulbs (especially on signs or directional lights from the parking lot to the front door)

- Sweeping and vacuuming entryways as necessary

- Wiping or cleaning everything to make sure that the front door and access to the operation are inviting to guests

- Checking all secure areas and security doors to ensure there was no security breach and nothing was stolen

- Checking the loading dock to make sure it is clean and free of debris

Even if you have only an internal entrance to your restaurant or foodservice operation, checking the facility exterior every day is critical.

Facility Interior

The rest of the facility checks include monitoring the interior of the building. Opening and preshift checklists include items such as:

■ Ensuring the restrooms are clean, well stocked, and ready for guests

■ Ensuring the floor is clean and free of hazards, such as tears or wrinkles in the carpet or standing water

■ Watering plants and making sure they are free of debris and dripping water

■ Checking that furniture is clean

■ Identifying and replacing burned-out light bulbs

■ Cleaning or dusting handrails, menu boards, decorative objects, and artwork

■ Ensuring the receiving and storage areas are clean and free of debris

■ Ensuring the trash was taken out and recycling bins were emptied

Because the interior of the facility encompasses the dining room and the kitchen, sometimes the division between checks for the facility interior and other areas may be blurred. Managers' checklists may include several areas and contain some of the same items as their employees. For example, both the front-of-the-house employees' and the dining room manager's checklists might contain an item for checking that side stations are clean and stocked. The distinctions between checklists are not important, as long as all the activities happen. *Exhibit 9e* shows an example preshift checklist for a supervisor.

Opening and Preshift Checks for the Front of the House

Opening or preshift checklists for the front of the house include:

■ Ensuring all tables are set and ready for guests

■ Ensuring the linens are clean

■ Ensuring the menus or menu boards are clean and presentable

■ Turning on the music and adjusting the lighting as needed

■ Ensuring the soda guns, coffee machines, and other beverage dispensers are clean and ready to use

■ Ensuring the side stations are stocked and ready to use

■ Ensuring the self-serve sections are fully stocked, cleaned, and adequately labeled

■ Ensuring the trash is taken out and any self-service trays, dinnerware, and utensils are collected

Exhibit 9e

Sample Supervisor's Preshift Checklist

ALUMNI HOUSE

Exterior of Building
- ☐ Parking lot is clean and free of debris
- ☐ Front walk is clean and free of debris
- ☐ Loading dock is clean and free of boxes, garbage, etc.
- ☐ Dumpster and recycling receptacles are clean and picked up
- ☐ Exterior lights are working
- ☐ Patio is ready for service

Kitchen
- ☐ All staff members are present according to schedule
- ☐ All product has been received, with temperatures recorded and dated, put away, and rotated
- ☐ All refrigeration equipment is holding temperature
- ☐ Line is clean and free of debris
- ☐ All kitchen equipment is working properly
- ☐ Equipment is cleaned
- ☐ Cooks are checking the temperatures of food for cooking, heating, and cooling
- ☐ Reach-ins are neat and organized, with food stored properly
- ☐ Floors are clean of spills, water, and other slip/trip hazards
- ☐ Lights are working

Dish Area
- ☐ Dish machine is at correct temperature
- ☐ Titration of soap and sanitizer is correct
- ☐ Tray of machine is free of clutter
- ☐ Walls, floors, and machine are free of build up and clean
- ☐ Machine is delimed

Front of the House
- ☐ Coffee station is clean and organized
- ☐ Messages have been checked
- ☐ Reservations have been plotted
- ☐ Servers' reach-in is clean and organized
- ☐ Opening checklist is being followed
- ☐ Side work is completed
- ☐ Cash handling procedures are being followed

Service
- ☐ Kitchen is ready
- ☐ Specials are posted
- ☐ Preshift staff meeting held, specials discussed, uniforms checked
- ☐ Bar is ready
- ☐ Lights are set
- ☐ Music is set
- ☐ Dining room has been inspected and tables, chairs, lights, floor, and menus are clean and ready for service
- ☐ Inventories have been taken as scheduled
- ☐ Orders are placed as needed
- ☐ Schedules are posted

Adapted with permission from David R. Wightman, CEC

Opening and Preshift Checks for the Back of the House

Because the head chef or the sous chef is the manager of the kitchen, he or she is responsible for determining that the kitchen is ready to prepare and serve food to patrons. An opening or preshift checklist for the back of the house commonly ensures the following areas have been checked:

- All equipment is clean, sanitized, and ready to be used.

- Refrigeration equipment is working properly.

- Equipment, such as ovens and deep fryers, is ready to be turned on as needed.

- Ingredients are taken out of storage or refrigerators and moved to the low boys (refrigerators under the counter), on counters, or to other appropriate areas.

- The *mise en place*—a French term for having all ingredients prepared and ready to combine and cook—is ready.

- Specials are entered into the computer system.

- The **production sheet,** which explains what food will be prepared for that shift, is prepared and posted or explained.

Opening and Preshift Checks for Fiduciary Tasks

Fiduciary activities are those that deal with managing income—cash, checks, gift certificates, and credit card receipts—in a way that ensures no income is lost or stolen. Good fiduciary practices include checks and balances, so each person who handles funds has someone to double-check his or her calculations or counts.

Good fiduciary practices also extend to activities beyond just the physical handling of funds. For example, income also is affected by accuracy of the **point-of-sale (POS) system,** a computer-based system for recording orders, sending them to the kitchen, printing bills, and recording information for management reports. When opening, the manager should verify that any changes to the POS system are complete and accurate, such as pricing changes or daily specials.

Another opening and preshift activity is addressing any employee issues relating to fiduciary activities. As a manager, you need to closely monitor how employees handle income. When problems occur, you should talk with employees to determine the cause, and then take immediate action to correct the problem. This action may include ensuring employees are adequately prepared for and trained in accounting for the funds or taking disciplinary action when warranted.

Examples of fiduciary items on a preshift checklist include:

- Counting the cash on hand

- Double-checking the change in the drawer, so it is ready to open for service with enough quarters, dollars, etc.

- Reviewing the POS system to ensure the prices for the daily specials have been accurately entered

- Issuing serial-numbered guest checks and recording the numbers assigned to each server when handwritten checks are used.

Activity

Create a Checklist from the Field

Go to a restaurant as a customer and make a checklist of all the things that a general manager or dining room manager might have on a checklist to ensure that:

1 The facility is prepared for customers.

2 The dining room is ready for customers.

Conducting Preshift Meetings

Often, before a restaurant or foodservice operation opens for a **service period** or **day part**—breakfast, lunch, or dinner—the manager holds a **preshift meeting,** a gathering of the shift crew to verify readiness and communicate important information. This meeting helps ensure that everything and everyone are prepared and ready for the shift or opening. These meetings are an excellent way to communicate shift goals, specials, and any other information that can help people prepare for the shift. They also provide a way for the manager to clarify common misunderstandings that affect performance and assess employee readiness.

During preshift meetings for front-of-the-house employees, the general manager or dining room manager verifies employee readiness:

- Have employees completed their opening or preshift work (whether or not they use checklists)?

- Are employees wearing the proper uniforms?

■ Can the waitstaff explain the specials, both food and beverage?

■ Are the employees aware of important information about VIPs, special guests, unusual scheduling patterns, etc. (e.g., a high number of reservations at 7:00 p.m., but then none until 9:30 p.m.)?

■ Do the waitstaff know about reservations for disabled persons, people who need a special diet, and other special reservations?

Sometimes, a back-of-the-house preshift meeting is held to give directions for food preparation, alert staff to preparation of the specials, and communicate other important matters. For more information on the roles of these managers, see *Exhibit 9f*.

Exhibit 9f

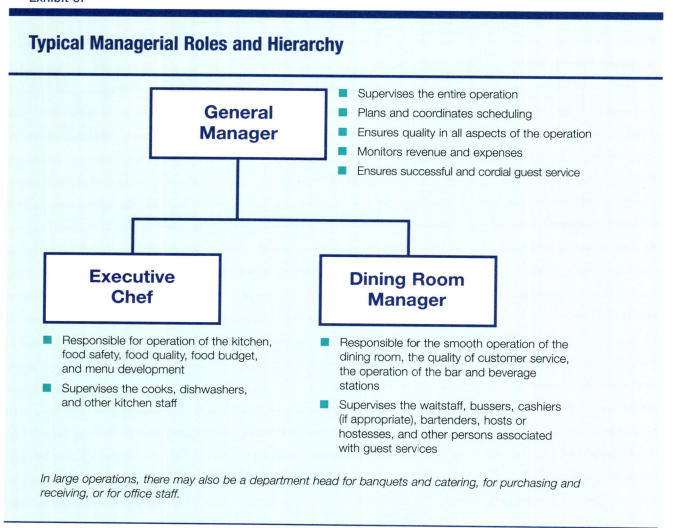

Typical Managerial Roles and Hierarchy

General Manager

■ Supervises the entire operation
■ Plans and coordinates scheduling
■ Ensures quality in all aspects of the operation
■ Monitors revenue and expenses
■ Ensures successful and cordial guest service

Executive Chef

■ Responsible for operation of the kitchen, food safety, food quality, food budget, and menu development
■ Supervises the cooks, dishwashers, and other kitchen staff

Dining Room Manager

■ Responsible for the smooth operation of the dining room, the quality of customer service, the operation of the bar and beverage stations
■ Supervises the waitstaff, bussers, cashiers (if appropriate), bartenders, hosts or hostesses, and other persons associated with guest services

In large operations, there may also be a department head for banquets and catering, for purchasing and receiving, or for office staff.

Additional Opening Activities

Turning on outdoor signs, changing the open/closed sign, and unlocking the guest entrances may be part of the preshift or opening activities (although technically not activities that happen *before* an operation opens). As obvious as these activities seem, they are easy to overlook. How many times have you walked by a business and could not tell whether it was open or closed?

Using Midshift Checklists

During a shift, the general manager reviews the operation of the various stations and positions in the restaurant—both the front of the house and the back of the house—to ensure that staff are doing their work in an effective and efficient manner. In addition, the general manager checks on the physical facilities to ensure that the other managers have done their work of making sure the kitchen is ready, the dining room is ready, and the place looks welcoming. Occasionally, a dining room manager or executive chef reviews the pace of the meal period and adjusts staffing by sending someone home or calling in other workers.

With so many things to keep track of, managers often find that using a midshift checklist is a good way to remind them of critical activities. However, these checklists are only reminders; following a checklist periodically during a shift is no substitute for continuous monitoring.

Midshift Checks for the Front of the House

In the front of the house, the dining room manager should continuously monitor the courtesy of waitstaff, the speed with which meals are being delivered, the attentiveness that waitstaff bring to their tables, the resetting of tables, and the happiness of the guests. Checklist items during the shift should remind managers and others to look for situations that might be forgotten or neglected, such as:

- Side stations continue to be restocked.
- Salt and pepper shakers are filled, and condiment containers are clean and full.
- Self-serve sections are fully stocked, clean, and adequately labeled.
- Music, lighting, and room temperature are at appropriate levels.
- Menus and menu boards are clean and presentable.

- Soda guns, coffee machines, and other beverage dispensers are working well.

- The trash is taken out, and any self-service trays, dinnerware, and utensils are collected.

- Tables are reset as guests leave.

- Specials information is updated as needed on the menus and menu boards.

- The status of orders, number of covers, and other information in the POS system are being monitored.

Midshift Checks for the Back of the House

In the back of the house during the shift, the chef or another manager monitors food preparation, safety, staffing, and food inventory. The chef or manager should continuously monitor the speed with which food is prepared, the extent to which people are busy and prepared, the effectiveness of their work, the teamwork of the staff, the preparation of food, and the operation of equipment. Ultimately, the chef or manager is responsible for ensuring that quality and safety standards are being met.

Food safety is a significant aspect of this managerial role. To ensure food safety and sanitation, the chef or manager periodically must check that employees have been:

- Keeping their work stations clean and safe from cross-contamination

- Following the practice of sanitizing as they work

- Monitoring refrigerators and freezers (walk-ins, reach-ins, and low boys) to ensure they are holding the proper temperatures (See *Exhibit 9g.*)

- Completing any HACCP logs

Other common mid-shift tasks for the back of the house relate to production:

- Ensuring par stock of ingredients are on the line or in easy-to-reach locations so that once service is started, food can be prepared quickly and efficiently

- Reordering food as needed

- Updating production sheets

Exhibit 9g

Monitoring refrigerators and freezers ensures food safety.

Midshift Checks for Fiduciary Tasks

Throughout the shift, managers should monitor how employees write orders, process credit cards, and handle funds, including cash, personal checks, credit card receipts, coupons, and gift certificates.

Periodically during the shift, however, the manager should review and check the cash inventory by completing a **cash drop**—counting all the cash and depositing some of it in the safe. This practice is also known as **bleeding the register.** How often a cash drop should be done varies, based on the operation's policies, the number of cash registers, and the amount of business the operation has done during a shift. Completing a cash drop provides the dual benefits of verifying the accuracy of the cash amount and reducing the amount of cash in the drawer.

In addition to completing cash drops, a midshift checklist for fiduciary tasks might include making sure you have enough change for the shift or day.

Using Shift-End and Closing Checklists

When a shift is ending or an operation is closing, many activities need to be done to ensure the operation is ready for the next shift and the appropriate records have been entered. Many of the same areas that were checked before the shift or opening need to be checked at shift-end or closing. With good checklists and reliable employees, these tasks happen automatically. It is still important for you as the manager to verify these tasks occurred, and problems are avoided.

Shift-End and Closing Checks for the Front of the House

At the end of the shift, there are front-of-the-house tasks that need to be completed before you let the staff go home. A checklist for these tasks might include:

- All side work is completed and side stands are clean and restocked.

- The soda guns, coffee machines, and other beverage dispensers are broken down and clean.

- Back-up carbonated water canisters and beer kegs are ready if needed.

- The bar is restocked and clean.

- Tables are reset for the next meal, depending on the nature of the restaurant or foodservice operation.

- The floor is clean.

- The music is off and the lighting is adjusted or turned off.

- The trash receptacles are empty.

- All dirty linens are placed in the right containers.

- The menu boards are clear.

- Self-serve sections are clean and stocked.

Shift-End and Closing Checks for the Back of the House

In the kitchen, employees should have cleaned the work area at each station, put things away properly, and left everything sanitized and clean for the next shift. In addition, the chef needs to ensure that the quantities on the production sheets used for group dinners and front-of-the-house counts (covers) correspond to each other. Doing this lets the chef know whether the production lists are accurate or need to be revised. (If the next shift is coming in immediately, completing all these tasks may not be needed or possible, depending on operational procedures and how busy the operation is.)

A shift-end or closing checklist for the back of the house might contain the following items:

- Production sheets are completed.

- Production sheets are compared to the actual quantity sold and discrepancies are noted.

- All food is wrapped, labeled, and dated.

- All appropriate equipment—such as ovens, ranges, hoods, and dishwashers—is turned off.

- All food is cooled and stored properly.

- Refrigerators (reach-ins, walk-ins, and freezers) are secured.

- Closing checklists for each station in the kitchen are completed.

- The floor is clean.

- The trash is taken out.

Exhibit 9h

Fiduciary reports should be completed at shift-end or closing.

Shift-End and Closing Checks for Fiduciary Tasks

Fiduciary tasks done at shift-end or closing encompass both front-of-the-house and back-of-the-house activities. A shift-end or closing checklist for fiduciary tasks might include:

- Are the cashiering-out forms completed?

- Has someone double-checked the change so there are enough quarters, dollars, etc., for the next shift?

- If closing, have all the funds been collected and secured or prepared for a night deposit?

- Have the credit card slips been reconciled?

- Have tips been recorded?

- Have you matched the POS system printout or cash register receipts against sales and cover counts?

- Have you completed the **Z report**—a report generated after zeroing out a register or cash drawer (see *Exhibit 9h*)—and the **manager's report**—a detailed report of all financial transactions for the day?

- Has someone collected and accounted for all the serial-numbered guest checks (when handwritten checks are used)?

Shift-End and Closing Checks for the Facility

Shift-end and closing checklists typically consist of items for checking both the inside and outside of the facility. Checklist items for the interior of the facility might include:

- Cleaning and stocking restrooms

- Cleaning or dusting decorative objects and artwork

- Storing menus and menu boards

- Cleaning the receiving and storage areas

- Taking out the trash and emptying recycling bins

- Turning off the lights, outdoor signs, and changing the open/closed sign

- Locking doors and setting alarms (if you are the last one out of the facility)

Checklist items for the outside of the facility might include some of the same checks that are done before opening. Other items that may need to be checked at shift-end or closing include:

■ Checking the loading dock to make sure it is clean and free of debris

■ Ensuring lids of outdoor trash receptacles and enclosure gates are closed

Additional Closing Activities

While probably not included in the closing checklists, there are various practices and policies your operation has to ensure the safety of employees and the security of the operation during this time. These include policies on when and how to make or schedule bank deposits, the minimum number of employees that need to be present at all times, procedures for securing the building at closing, and procedures for how to exit the building after closing.

Evaluating Shift Performance

Near the end of each shift when things are slowing down, as a manager, you should spend some time reviewing the shift. This includes making notes of what happened, reviewing the security system cameras and system functioning (if appropriate), and recording key incidents or information into one or more communication logs. As part of evaluating shift performance, consider the following:

■ Looking at situations more objectively outside of the often frantic pace of the shift

■ Reviewing your performance, the performance of the various employees, and the implications of any decisions

■ Starting a "to-do" list for the next day or shift and trying to resolve problems that occurred during this shift

■ Assessing employees and making notes of any recurring problems that might indicate a need for training, coaching, or discipline; or notes of especially good performance or attitude

■ Reviewing the status of equipment and facilities and considering any possible long-term needs for repair or maintenance

■ Assessing the extent to which the shift goals were met: attendance, financial, check average, amount of breakage, sales of specials, number of complaints, and number of compliments

Routinely evaluating shift performance can make a crucial difference in your ability to manage the operation and your employees.

Using Communication Logs

Communication logs are used to record what happens during a shift. While there are various types of logs, they all provide these benefits:

- They help people communicate across shifts, so the operation runs smoothly; this is the main value of using logs.

- They capture information that can help show patterns—both good and bad—and identify problems, something critical to improving the operation.

- They capture information that can help protect the operation from liabilities.

Establishing the importance of using communication logs as part of the daily work can be a challenge since there is so much paperwork involved in any manager's workday. However, general managers should show other managers and key employees how the log can help them in their daily work. Also, each manager should understand that his or her shift is not done until the log is completed—something often found in the job descriptions of managers. In extraordinary cases, if a manager fails to record something important, he or she may be disciplined for not noticing what happened and writing the facts in the communication log.

The important benefits of communication logs can be realized only when they are used consistently and appropriately. To use these logs appropriately, you need to know what information should be recorded in them and when. Most restaurant or foodservice operations maintain a series of communication logs, which may include the following:

- Chef's communication log

- Dining room manager's communication log

- Banquet and catering log

- Manager's communication log

Exhibit 9i

Communication logs help people communicate across shifts.

Chef's Communication Log

The chef's communication log provides a place for the chef to record information about covers, recipe ideas, customer reactions to specials, allergic reactions, unusual equipment performance, and reminders for the next shift. This log may also be used to record notes about the efficiency and effectiveness of the back-of-the-house staff. This log provides a repository of good information for future reference. (See *Exhibit 9i.*)

Dining Room Manager's Communication Log

The **dining room manager's communication log,** also called the **reservation log** or **dining room log,** is a place to record information about:

- Weather
- Customer service patterns
- Dramatic changes in cover counts
- Balance between reservations and walk-ins
- Guest complaints (and responses if noteworthy or unusual)
- Anything that affected business during that shift

This log also may be used to record things that the staff especially worked on during that shift, such as accommodating late reservations or responding to an unexpected crowd, and any difficulties encountered. It also should contain information that dining room staff members on the next shift need to know as part of their planning and preshift work.

Banquet and Catering Log

The **banquet and catering log** is kept by banquet or catering staff when the operation provides such services. It is used to record information about:

- Guest counts
- Special needs for a banquet or catered event
- Information about equipment needs
- Problems that have been resolved
- Changes that have been requested by the customer
- Staffing requirements

Manager's Communication Log

The master log, or **manager's communication log,** contains information that affects the operation in general, although it also may contain some of the same information recorded in other types of logs. The manager's communication log should include:

- Dramatic increases or decreases in sales or cover counts
- Unusual events or incidents
- Reports of possible foodborne illness

- Incidents of unusual employee interaction
- Weather and other business-related information that you may need to refer to at a later time
- Information the managers of following shifts need to know
- Communication problems on the shift
- Teamwork or team performance
- Employee tardiness, attendance, and absenteeism
- Future challenges that may need to be addressed
- Any critical incidents

Modifications for Smaller Operations

Large restaurant and foodservice operations need to track so much information that they need to use all these various types of communication logs. However, in smaller restaurant and foodservice operations, these communication logs may be combined in a variety of ways. For example, the reservation log may serve as the manager's log and record catering information. The chef's log may be combined with the dining room manager's log, so everyone uses the same source of information and consults it regularly. For restaurant and foodservice operations that have very little catering business, the banquet and catering information is often added to the dining room manager's log, or it can be found on a clipboard posted in the kitchen area.

Recording Information in Communication Logs

The main purpose of communication logs is to share information among managers and some key employees to help ensure smooth operations in the short term. However, other information also needs to be recorded to help the operation in the long term. Because of these purposes, the communication logs must be accessible to various people. Consequently, when adding information to the logs, remember that the information is relatively public. In addition, when there is a potential legal or other complaint, the logs can be subpoenaed—legally required to be produced in a court of law. Therefore, it is important to eliminate judgmental comments, personal comments, and other entries that cannot be supported by facts and that are likely to be misinterpreted. You should only include information that can be defended and explained if required by lawyers or a court, and you should always follow your operation's guidelines for making log entries.

The types of information that should be recorded in a log fall into two main categories: operational information and critical incidents.

Recording Operational Information in Communication Logs

Most of the information that goes into a communication log will be about events or situations that have affected or will affect the day-to-day operations. This operational information may have either a positive or negative effect on the business, and includes both routine and unusual situations. (See *Exhibit 9j*.)

While these example entries include statements about staffing, information about a person's individual performance, attitudes, and disciplinary actions should not be included in communication logs. Personnel information should not be part of a public record. If personnel issues occur, record them in personnel files, other files, or private logs that are kept in a locked drawer or other secure location. Follow your operation's guidelines for recording these situations.

Exhibit 9j

Sample Communication Log

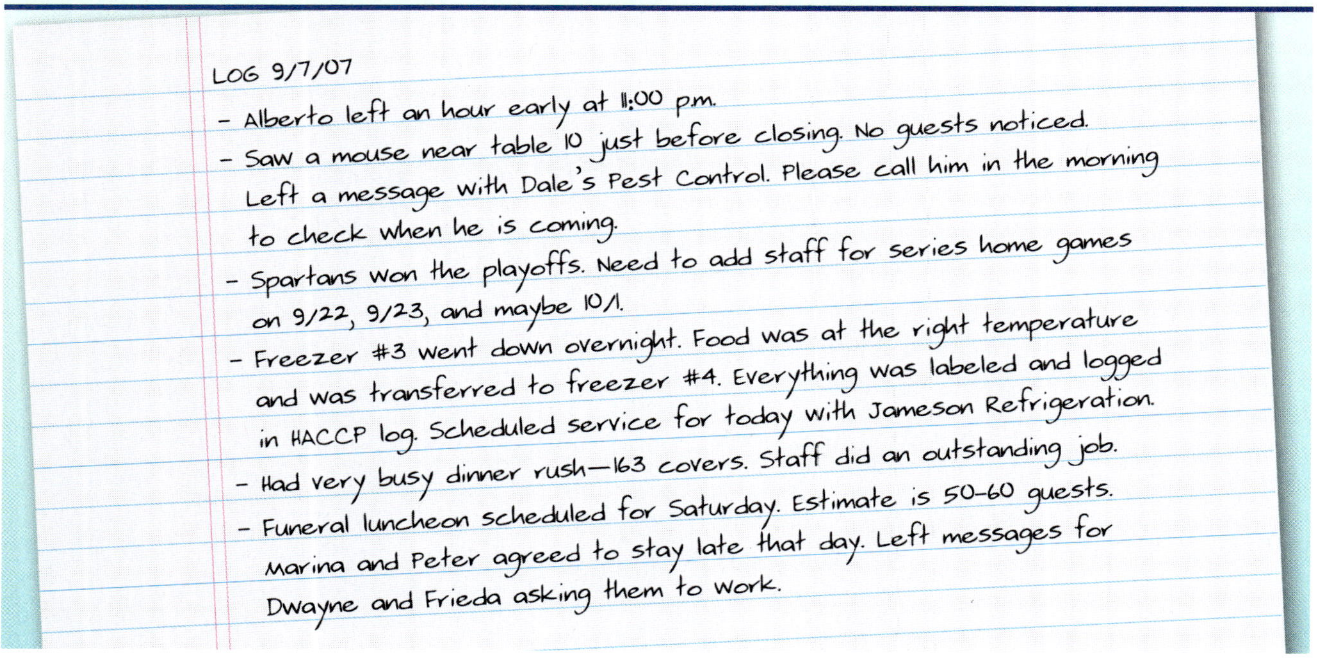

LOG 9/7/07

- Alberto left an hour early at 11:00 pm.
- Saw a mouse near table 10 just before closing. No guests noticed. Left a message with Dale's Pest Control. Please call him in the morning to check when he is coming.
- Spartans won the playoffs. Need to add staff for series home games on 9/22, 9/23, and maybe 10/1.
- Freezer #3 went down overnight. Food was at the right temperature and was transferred to freezer #4. Everything was labeled and logged in HACCP log. Scheduled service for today with Jameson Refrigeration.
- Had very busy dinner rush—163 covers. Staff did an outstanding job.
- Funeral luncheon scheduled for Saturday. Estimate is 50–60 guests. Marina and Peter agreed to stay late that day. Left messages for Dwayne and Frieda asking them to work.

These are examples of typical communication log entries for operational information.

Recording Critical Incidents in Communication Logs

One purpose of the manager's log is to record critical incidents—events that need to be recorded for historical purposes in case of a potential claim or lawsuit. These events include, but are not limited to, anything having to do with food safety, security, police, or emergency personnel.

There are four main categories of critical incidents:

1 **Accidents**—Slips, falls, or other mishaps involving injury or the potential for injury, even when no injuries are visible and the persons involved say they are unhurt

2 **Incidents**—Situations in which a person or persons become involved in inappropriate behavior in the facility or on the property; for example, two patrons striking each other, employees hitting each other, or an intoxicated guest causing a disturbance

3 **Emergencies**—Situations that involve urgent medical or security threats; for example, a patron who collapsed or a robbery, and may or may not include rescue squads, 911 calls, similar emergency calls, and hospital visits

4 **Reports of food problems**—Reports or occurrences of possible allergic reactions, foodborne illness, or foreign materials in food

The facts relating to critical incidents need to be recorded in detail at the time of the incident. However, this detail is not usually included in communication logs. Instead, the incident is recorded in a general way in a communication log and then the details are recorded on other documents or kept in private files. Sometimes, the communication log entry directs readers to the documents or files that contain the details. Examples of communication log entries for critical incidents follow:

- Ten-year-old boy ran into lobby door and bruised forehead, 4:50 p.m. Checked on forehead and it seemed to be fine. Boy was soon up and running around. Gave him and his eight-year-old sister each a few promotional helium balloons.

- Altercation in the break room, 10 a.m., between Yolanda and Jean

- Man choked on roast beef sandwich, 11:20 a.m., table 7. His companion performed Heimlich maneuver. Man is okay. See incident report.

- Customer found piece of plastic in her salad. Talked with guest; she was fine. Gave her a new salad. Checked back at the end of the meal and brought her and her friend dessert. For more info, see incident report.

Recording Critical Incident Details

Each operation should have its own guidelines for managing and recording critical incidents. Many operations use a form, commonly called a critical incident form, to record the details of critical incidents. (See *Exhibit 9k.*) Critical incidents that involve unacceptable or exemplary employee behavior also may be recorded in other private logs or in personnel files. Always follow your operation's guidelines for managing, recording, and reporting critical incidents.

Regardless of the operation and the documents used, the following details should be recorded for each critical incident:

- Description of the situation and people involved, including names, date, and time

- Names and contact information of witnesses

- Any other relevant information, such as employees following or not following normal procedures

- In the case of police officers coming to the scene, their names and badge numbers

- When someone is sent to the hospital, the name of the hospital, the name of the ambulance company, and the names of the persons who operated the ambulance (however, it is *not* necessary to record all the information that may be necessary on hospital, insurance, or other legal forms)

All of this detailed information should be collected and placed in a confidential file that will *not* be read by other employees and managers.

Coordinating and Communicating during Shift Change

As part of the transition from one meal period or day part to another, managers on the shift that is ending should spend time reviewing what happened and how things have been operating during the shift. They should enter this information into the communication logs so the next shift gets that information. These activities help you, as a manager, focus on what information to pass on to the next shift.

Just before the shift change, managers from both shifts should meet to discuss anything that might affect the operation of the next shift. (See *Exhibit 9l.*) If that is not possible, then the manager coming in should read the log carefully. Typically, the general manager shares relevant information with both the incoming chef and the dining room manager. However, depending on the operation, the outgoing dining

Exhibit 9k

Sample Critical Incident Form

Critical Incident Form

Instructions: In any emergency, accident, or situation that may lead to liability, please gather all of this information and print it clearly. If in doubt about what to record, put down as much information as you can, and consult the operation's policies as soon as you can.

If you need room to write, attach additional pages to this form. Also attach any copies of related documents created by others, such as reports.

1. **Has an accident happened?** If so, what was the nature of the incident? What happened? When did it happen? What else was going on at the same time? (Be as detailed—accident, persons, date, day, and time—and factual as you can.)

2. **Was there any medical attention needed and given?** Yes ___ No ___ (If yes, what happened? What professionals were involved? What did they do? Who was taken where? To what emergency room or to what hospital? What are their names, addresses, phone numbers, and email addresses?)

3. **Were there any witnesses?** Yes ___ No ___ (If yes, write down their names, addresses, phone numbers, and email addresses.)

4. **What did they see happen?** (Ask them to tell you or write down what they saw.)

5. **Was security or the police called?** Yes ___ No ___ (If so, find out and write down their name, badge, and office, township or jurisdiction they are from, their organization, badge number, etc.)

Critical Incident Form

6. **What actions were taken?** (Describe the actions that you or others took in response to the incident.)

7. **Were there any unusual conditions?** Yes ___ No ___ (If so, describe the weather, floor, equipment, temperature, and any other element that may have influenced what happened.)

8. **What was the nature of the accident?** (Was there any faulty equipment, improper use of equipment, poorly trained employees, ignorance of safety procedures, employee negligence?)

9. **Was any work lost?** Yes ___ No ___ (If yes, explain if there was any faulty equipment, improper use of equipment, poorly trained employees, ignorance of safety procedures, employee negligence.)

10. **Were any insurance claims filed?** Yes ___ No ___ (If so, indicate what companies were used and any relevant information about the claims.)

11. **Were any workers' compensation claims filed, or do you think they will be filed?** Yes ___ No ___ (Are there any possible permanent injuries? If so, what are they and to whom?)

12. **Record your name as the person who completed this report and the date.**

Name _____ Date _____

Exhibit 9l

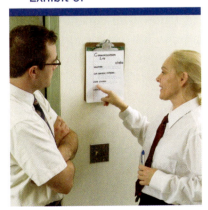

At shift change, managers of both shifts should discuss things that may affect the next shift.

room managers and chefs may meet with their counterparts on the next shift. Once a shift is underway, there is less time for such discussion because the staff are busy responding to customers. This is another reason why communication logs are so important. When verbal communication at shift change is inadequate, nonexistent, or forgotten, the communication log provides a solid record of important information.

Conducting Postshift Meetings

At the end of the shift, some managers hold a short **postshift meeting,** a gathering of shift personnel to discuss what happened during the shift. Sometimes these meetings are held with all employees, and sometimes they are held for only front-of-the-house or back-of-the-house staff. These meetings also provide a time to say goodbye and thank you to the staff.

While most employees are tired and do not respond well to **postshift reviews**—feedback about accomplishments, failures, and behaviors—these can be helpful if short and to the point. Most managers hold this feedback until the next day, when the employees can hear it more carefully and immediately apply what they have just learned. Sometimes, however, it is important to promptly talk to employees about problems or their excellent efforts, and to thank them for making a tough shift work out well for guests. If more extensive or corrective feedback and coaching are needed, make an appointment with the employee to talk about it the next day.

Other Operational Challenges

Besides monitoring differences among shifts, managing shifts, and ensuring standards, managers also play a significant role in thinking about and working to improve the overall functioning of the restaurant or foodservice operation. That means thinking about:

- Expanding marketing programs
- Building the business through new strategies
- Finding new employees
- Assessing employee productivity and staffing needs
- Developing current employees
- Improving controls
- Reducing expenses
- Improving teamwork

These goals go beyond the focus on each shift and raise larger concerns that are critical to the growth of the organization. Consequently, managers typically develop long-term agendas that include monthly and quarterly goals for the operation, and they often create their own systems to focus on those goals. The systems that a manager implements to achieve those goals may include weekly, biweekly, and monthly management activities. While people focus on these larger goals, regardless of the frequency of these activities, these systems should ensure that standards are still being met and goals are being supported by good management practices. These practices include:

- Using several techniques for communicating with coworkers and improving employee performance

- Creating and using checklists for managing the support areas of the operation, such as reservations, marketing, audits, preventive maintenance, purchasing and receiving, labor activity, and routine team meetings

Activity

Communicating Across Shifts

You are the general manager of a foodservice department at a small liberal arts college. Your department operates the student cafeteria, the faculty and staff dining room, and a snack bar. It also provides catering for special campus events.

During your shift, you had a minor equipment problem that seems to be resolved. You also had a late produce delivery, which caused the salad bar to open a few minutes late. Finally, you contacted the work-study coordinator to request two more student workers for next semester.

Of course, other routine events happened as well. Overall, your day was pretty typical for a Wednesday, although the students have been increasingly rambunctious since it snowed two days ago and winter break starts next week.

During your shift, you logged the following items in the manager's communication log:

■ Main kitchen east exhaust fan was making rattling noise, 7:22 a.m. Turned off fan and called maintenance. John tightened bolts at 8:30 a.m., and fan seems to be fine.

■ Lori called in sick at 8:30 a.m. Jorge came in at 10:30 a.m. to cover, but he has to leave by 5:30 p.m. and would like to leave earlier, if possible.

■ Tri-City Produce delivery was two hours late (10:30 a.m.). This delayed salad bar opening to 11:10 a.m.

■ Jeffrey gave notice that he is not coming back next semester.

■ Short on trays again. Ordered six dozen trays from Quality Restaurant Supply for delivery Friday.

■ Emailed Ray to request two additional student workers for next semester.

■ Dr. Benoit dropped off request form for sheet cake; needs it on Monday at 10:00 a.m.

■ Started to clean out walk-in this morning but did not finish the right side.

■ Snack bar lunch shift volume was unusually low.

You are finishing your shift and the evening dining room manager, snack bar manager, and chef are present and getting ready to start their shift. Have three classmates role-play these other manager roles and hold a brief preshift meeting with your managers. Discuss the items that you think they should know before they start their shift.

Summary

Shift management is all about managing for quality. Without constant attention throughout every shift, quality suffers. Quality is about achieving the standards that the restaurant or foodservice operation has set. These standards are documented in the form of policy statements and checklists. There are three primary times in a shift when quality reviews are made using checklists: (1) opening or pre-shift, (2) mid-shift, and (3) shift-end or closing. At each of these times, there are checks made in many areas: facility interior and exterior, front of the house and back of the house, and fiduciary tasks.

Of course, you cannot achieve the quality level you want without having a plan and goals for each shift. An important part of shift goals is having enough staff on hand, so scheduling staff is an important part of shift management.

Shifts do not exist in a vacuum. What happens on one shift will affect the next shift and perhaps many future shifts. In order to transfer information about what happened and what was done on a shift, managers keep communication logs to record information relevant to a specific area.

Review Your Learning

1 **Which identifies the main reasons for using checklists in a restaurant or foodservice operation?**

A. To ensure that standards are met and routine procedures are done consistently

B. To ensure employees meet their annual performance goals and managers notice employee performance

C. To ensure shift goals are met and staffing needs are correctly forecasted

D. To ensure the operation is clean and sanitation guidelines are being followed

2 **Which objective typically is *not* included in an operation's long-term goals?**

A. Reducing expenses

B. Developing current employees

C. Increasing managers' raises

D. Expanding marketing programs

3 **Why should managers inspect all operating areas before shifts start?**

A. To verify everything is clean and food is handled safely

B. To verify all the employees are there and in uniform

C. To verify the operation is ready to serve customers

D. To verify the operation can be profitable during that shift

4 **What is the main purpose of a communication log?**

A. To record details of critical incidents to help with insurance claims

B. To record information to help managers and key employees plan better

C. To record information that might be subpoenaed for a trial or legal proceeding

D. To record details of staff behavior to help managers deal better with employees

5 **Which type of information is typically included in a communication log? Circle all that apply.**

A. Individual employee performance issues

B. Customer service/business patterns

C. Inventory needs

D. Teamwork or team performance

E. Critical incidents

F. Vendor contact information

G. Descriptions of unusual guests

H. Unusual events

I. HACCP records

J. Problems and resolutions

K. Staffing and labor chart locations

L. Par stock levels

M. Staffing information

N. POS system procedures

O. Names of underage guests who tried to order alcohol

P. Computer passwords

Q. Information that should be kept private

R. Customer reactions to specials

6 **Which situation is a critical incident?**

A. A customer says she saw a rat by the trash bins.

B. An employee gets in an argument over the phone with his mother.

C. An employee comes to work with a bad sunburn and says her uniform is aggravating the pain.

D. A customer trips and falls but says he is okay.

Notes

Managing Voluntary Terminations

10

Inside This Chapter

- Using Termination Checklists
- Purpose of Exit Interviews
- Information to Gather
- Exit Interview Methods and Formats
- Conducting Face-to-Face Exit Interviews
- Evaluating Exit Interview Information
- Using Exit Interview Information

After completing this chapter, you should be able to:

- Describe the purpose of an employee termination checklist.
- Explain the benefits of exit interviews.
- Identify information that should be included in an exit interview.
- List advantages and disadvantages of different exit interview methods.
- Identify the qualities a person needs to successfully conduct an exit interview.
- Recognize the best time and place to conduct a face-to-face exit interview.
- Describe how to analyze information gathered during exit interviews.
- Prioritize the issues identified through an exit interview.
- Use information learned through exit interviews to develop action plans.

Test Your Knowledge

1 **True or False:** Exit interviews can provide managers with information about whether the employee who is leaving will sue the restaurant or foodservice operation. *(See pp. 249–250.)*

2 **True or False:** Exit interviews should be conducted on the last day of employment. *(See p. 256.)*

3 **True or False:** The best person to conduct the exit interview is the employee's direct supervisor since that person knows the employee the best. *(See p. 257.)*

4 **True or False:** Exit interviews do not have value for the employees who are leaving. *(See pp. 249–250.)*

5 **True or False:** The best exit interview method for most restaurant or foodservice operations is the computer-based exit interview. *(See p. 251.)*

Key Terms

Consolidated Omnibus
   Budget Reconciliation Act
   (COBRA)

Exit interview

Involuntary termination

Open-ended questions

Structured interview

Termination checklist

Unstructured interview

Voluntary termination

Introduction

Given all the energy and attention that managers and human resources professionals devote to recruiting, selecting, hiring, orienting, and training employees, it can be difficult to accept when an effective employee announces that he or she will be leaving your operation. After all, you have made a significant investment in that employee and finding another employee can be a challenging and time-consuming process.

On the other hand, sometimes it is a relief that an employee has decided to leave your restaurant or foodservice operation and take a position elsewhere. If the person has not been particularly productive or successful in your organization (or perhaps disruptive), there can be a sigh of relief, often marred by the daunting challenge of hiring a replacement.

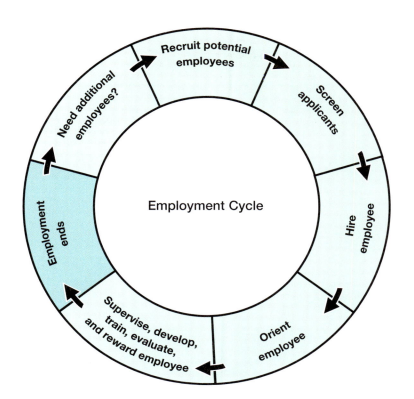

Employment Cycle

- Recruit potential employees
- Screen applicants
- Hire employee
- Orient employee
- Supervise, develop, train, evaluate, and reward employee
- Employment ends
- Need additional employees?

On the bright side, when an employee leaves the organization—regardless of whether the termination is **voluntary** (he or she decided to leave) or **involuntary** (the operation asked the employee to leave)—you have an opportunity to obtain some information that might otherwise be hidden from you. That chance comes in the form of an **exit interview**— an interview with the employee who is leaving to determine what things about the restaurant or foodservice operation could be improved— and for voluntary terminations, why the employee is leaving. The exit interview is an essential part of the termination process.

The two major components to managing the termination process are:

1 Having employees return all company items

2 Conducting an exit interview

Using Termination Checklists

There are many essential tasks in the termination process to ensure a complete exit with no "loose ends." These tasks are often recorded in an employee **termination checklist**—a document that lists all the termination requirements and has space for the appropriate manager to sign when these tasks have been completed. (See *Exhibit 10a* on the next page.)

Exhibit 10a

Sample Employee Termination Checklist

Rusty's Restaurant

Employee Termination Checklist

Employee's name _____ Job _____

Employee's immediate supervisor _____

Reason for termination _____

Last day of work _____

Items to complete prior to or on last day of work   **Mgr. initials**

1 Uniforms returned . . . . _____

2 Equipment returned (listed below) . . . . _____

   _____   _____

   _____   _____

3 Employee handbook returned . . . . _____

4 Keys returned . . . . _____

5 Parking sticker removed/destroyed . . . . _____

6 Outstanding work completed . . . . _____

7 All unfinished projects reviewed with supervisor (listed below) . . . . _____

   _____

8 If a supervisor, all paperwork and evaluations of subordinates submitted . . . . . _____

9 Exit interview completed . . . . _____

10 Insurance termination forms or COBRA forms completed or submitted . . . . _____

11 All loans or salary advances repaid . . . . _____

12 Mailing address for final paycheck provided . . . . _____

13 Personal tools and other possessions removed . . . . _____

14 Locker cleared out . . . . _____

_____   Date _____
Approved by Personnel

The items on an employee termination checklist normally include:

- Returning items that belong to the operation

- Completing **Consolidated Omnibus Budget Reconciliation Act (COBRA)** forms to continue group health insurance coverage or health insurance termination forms to end health insurance coverage (COBRA is explained in more detail in Chapter 11.)

- Completing any outstanding work and/or reviewing the status of any projects not finished

- Repaying any loans or salary advances made by the organization to the employee

- Completing any special paperwork or procedures for the final paycheck

- Delivering the employee's final paycheck as required by state law or company policy, if different from normal payments

- Reporting on subordinates (if the employee leaving was a front-line supervisor or manager); for example, problem employees, evaluations for all employees up to the date of termination, etc.

- Removing the employee's user ID from computer systems

- Collecting keys or uniforms

Completing all these tasks and getting the appropriate signatures of all the persons involved in supervising these areas can be a complicated process for some employees. However, it usually helps to ensure a smooth termination.

Purpose of Exit Interviews

The other main component of managing the termination process is conducting an exit interview. Exit interviews are conducted as part of the normal termination process for employees who are leaving the operation, both voluntarily and involuntarily. There are many reasons for conducting exit interviews:

- They serve as an acknowledgement of the end of the person's work at the establishment.

- They provide the operation with some information about how the managerial and human resources functions have been handled.

- They provide information that can be used to understand why there is either high or low retention of employees in a job; this information can be used to improve supervisory practices and provide training, as appropriate.

■ They provide information about job satisfaction, not only pertaining to the person who is leaving, but also for everyone in that job group and perhaps other job groups with which the employee interacts.

■ They gather information on what employees think of an operation's practices, so management can consider making changes or improvements.

■ They provide an occasion for both the employee and the supervisor or manager to reflect on the experience of working at the establishment. (See *Exhibit 10b.*)

■ The employee who is leaving can, if he or she is honest and thoughtful, provide a lot of useful insights about the operation.

■ The employee gets a chance to say goodbye in a formal way to his or her relationship with the operation.

Exhibit 10b

Exit interviews provide both the employee and the supervisor with the opportunity to reflect on working at the establishment.

■ The interviewer can ascertain whether the employee is angry about leaving and is likely to sue the operation.

Information to Gather

The information you aim to gather during an exit interview will vary depending on your purpose for having the interview. Regardless of the goals, exit interviews typically follow a format prescribed by the human resources department or a standard format adopted by the general manager. Often, a form is used to record basic employment and interview facts as well as broader topics that typically involve some conversation or explanation. The minimum basic information that should be collected includes:

■ Employee's name

■ Current position or job in the restaurant or foodservice operation

■ Initial date of hire or length of employment

■ Date of the exit interview

■ Name of the exit interviewer

Additional basic information may include the employee's permanent address, as you may need to send him or her future information and forms; the employee's initial position or job when hired; and sometimes equal employment opportunity (EEO) information, such as gender and race. (Present any EEO questions as optional.)

Depending on the goals of the exit interview, broader topics might include:

■ Reason for leaving

■ Areas of satisfaction and dissatisfaction

■ Effectiveness of the orientation and initial training process

■ Stages of employment the person has gone through and an evaluation of each stage

■ Adequacy and appropriate support for the employee's professional development

■ Nature and style of supervision

■ For employees you would rather not see leave, anything the operation could have done (or could do) to keep the employee

Exit Interview Methods and Formats

The information to be gathered when a person leaves an operation may be collected using various methods. Exit interviews may be conducted in person, by telephone, in writing, or by computer (although written and computer-based forms act more as surveys than actual interviews). These four methods all have advantages and disadvantages, as shown in *Exhibit 10c* on the following pages.

To encourage the most honest responses from employees, some organizations use paper or computer-based forms or arrange for people outside the operation (consultants) to conduct the interview. However, for many operations, these choices are not practical because of limited computer access or computer competency, English-literacy issues in the employee population, or the effort and expense required for outside consultants. For most restaurant and foodservice operations, the best and most common method is the in-person or face-to-face interview conducted by someone from the operation.

Exhibit 10c

Pros and Cons of Exit Interview Methods

Method	Description	Pros
Face-to-face	Interviewer and employee meet in person.	■ Interviewer can see employee's facial expressions and nonverbal behavior, which helps with communication ■ Enables follow-up questions to be asked ■ Most personable method; most likely to leave employee feeling good about the interview and the operation ■ Easy and inexpensive to implement
Telephone	Interviewer and employee talk on the phone.	■ Puts physical and visual distance between interviewer and employee, so some employees may be more honest and open ■ Enables follow-up questions to be asked ■ Helps individuals who are not comfortable in a formal office interview format ■ Not as personable as the face-to-face interview method, but still likely to leave employee feeling good about the interview and the operation ■ Protects the employee's privacy more than interviews done on-site ■ Easy and inexpensive to implement
Computer-based (online)	Employee completes a survey or form on a computer.	■ Automatically captures data so it does not need to be entered into a database ■ Can provide a structured format that makes comparisons and analysis easier than face-to-face and phone interviews ■ Employee can take as much time as needed to complete form ■ May allow the employee to complete the interview form off-site; information is less likely to be subjectively interpreted ■ Fastest method for aggregating and analyzing data (assuming a program was written for doing this)
Paper	Employee completes a paper form.	■ Easiest and cheapest method to use ■ Can provide a structured format that makes comparisons and analysis easier than face-to-face and phone interviews ■ Employee can take as much time as needed to complete form ■ Allows the employee to complete the interview form off-site ■ Information is less likely to be subjectively interpreted

Cons

- Employee may be uncomfortable with interviewer, and therefore, reluctant to tell the truth
- More involved to set up than some other interview methods
- Interview may be constrained by interviewer's time or availability of an appropriate location
- Interviewer needs some training and skills to conduct an effective interview

- Puts physical and visual distance between interviewer and employee, which means the interviewer cannot see nonverbal cues
- Employee may be reluctant to tell the truth for fear of interviewer's response
- Employee may lie or misrepresent information because of anger or resentment against interviewer
- Less involved to set up than face-to-face interviews
- May be constrained by interviewer's time

- Can be costly and time-consuming to implement
- Employees may not be comfortable using a computer, and therefore, may not use it effectively
- Not a good method for asking open-ended questions; if these are used, employees are less likely to complete them than with other methods because of the typing and composition involved
- Generally, does not allow for follow-up questions; some questions may be programmed, but this would be an additional expense
- Information may not be clear or complete
- Impersonal; may leave the employee with bad feelings about the operation
- More time-consuming for employees than verbal methods

- Does not allow for follow-up questions
- Information may not be clear or complete
- Impersonal; may leave the employee with bad feelings about the operation
- If open-ended questions are used, employees are less likely to complete them than they would be in a verbal interview because of the writing involved
- More time-consuming for employees than verbal methods
- Literacy problems may cause miscommunication or omissions

Think About It...

Why does it matter how the employee feels about the operation he or she is leaving? What possible business benefits or consequences might occur because of how the employee feels?

Face-to-Face Interviews

Face-to-face interviews are an effective method for several reasons. First, the interviewer can see the employee's facial expressions and nonverbal cues. This visual information helps the interviewer to be more attuned to any hidden meaning in what an employee says or does not say. It also helps the interviewer to ask relevant follow-up questions. In addition, if the employee has language difficulties, a face-to-face interview can help break down this barrier. Finally, depending on the skill of the interviewer and the relationship between the interviewer and the employee, a face-to-face interview can provide the best opportunity for the employee to leave with a feeling of finality or "closure," and leave feeling good, or at least neutral, about the operation.

Structured and Unstructured Formats

Regardless of the method used for an exit interview, its format may be structured or unstructured. **Structured interviews** are designed to collect specific information. Typically, a form is used during these interviews to ensure that the topics established ahead of time are covered adequately. *Exhibit 10d* shows an example exit interview form that is completed by an interviewer during a structured, face-to-face exit interview. When used consistently, structured interviews and forms make it easier to compare the responses of different employees, even when they were interviewed by different people.

On the other hand, **unstructured interviews** provide an opportunity for the employee to bring up a wide range of subjects—whatever the employee wishes to address or whatever topics just naturally come up during the interview. This format often provides a lot of information about the employee being interviewed, but it makes comparing and analyzing exit interviews difficult. Also, this format is not practical for computer-based or written methods, although these methods may use **open-ended questions** that enable the employee to provide answers in an unstructured way. The form in *Exhibit 10d* is designed for structured interviews but shows examples of open-ended questions.

Exhibit 10d

Sample Exit Interview Form

Rusty's Restaurant

Exit Interview Form

_____

Employee's name   Date

_____

Title of current position

_____

Title of initial position   Date of initial hire

_____

Reasons for leaving

1   In what ways was your orientation effective or not effective in helping you learn the policies, procedures, and standards of the organization?

2   In what ways was your orientation effective or not effective in helping you learn your job?

3   How could the orientation be improved?

4   Were the sanitation and quality standards of the restaurant or foodservice operation clear? If no, please explain.

5   Were you supported in upholding those standards?

6   What did you do for your professional development?

7   Did you have support for your professional development?

8   How would you describe the practices of your supervisor?

9   Were you satisfied with your supervision? Please explain.

10 What changes would you like to see in the restaurant or foodservice operation?

_____

Employee Signature   Date

Interviewer's Name

Conducting Face-to-Face Exit Interviews

Gathering exit interview information can be a difficult task, depending on the individual employee being interviewed. Even the most positive employee can find leaving difficult and be reluctant to share information. Consequently, it takes considerable planning and skill to interview employees who are leaving. You need to consider a range of issues including where and when to conduct the interview and who should conduct the interview.

When to Conduct the Interview

An employee's last day at work can be one of his or her most difficult days. Often, employees feel emotional because they are leaving people they care about and making a change in their life that can be scary (even when going to a better job). Also, employees often have a lot of last-minute things to attend to that make it difficult for them to make time for an interview.

If a face-to-face exit interview is scheduled on an employee's last day and the employee misses the interview, there is little or no chance to reschedule it after the employee leaves. In addition, if you learn information in the exit interview that you want to investigate further, there may not be enough time to do so.

Therefore, whenever possible, face-to-face exit interviews should be conducted on a day near the employee's last day of employment but not the very last day. When scheduling an exit interview, be sure to allow plenty of time, so the interviewer can ask the employee as many follow-up questions as needed.

Where to Conduct the Interview

Exit interviews should be conducted in a private place free from distractions. The quieter and less public the space, the less likely you are to be interrupted, and the more likely you will acquire the information you want. (See *Exhibit 10e.*) Ideally, no one outside the interview should be able to see or hear any part of it. Such a location helps protect the employee from coworkers overhearing and ensures the interviewer can listen closely.

Conduct exit interviews in a quiet place with no distractions.

Who Should Conduct the Interview

Face-to-face and phone exit interviews may be conducted by a variety of different people, depending on the employee leaving the operation. Ideally, the person conducting the interview should be a neutral party who does not have a direct relationship with the employee. Also, this person should be skilled in conducting interviews.

Relationship Between the Interviewer and the Employee

Exit interviewers should be trained in interview methods and should not have a direct reporting relationship with the employee who is leaving. Outside consultants fit this description and are considered by some to be the best choice. However, as previously mentioned, using an outside consultant is not practical for many operations. In this case, a general manager or professional from the human resources department, if there is one, should conduct the interview (see *Exhibit 10f*), especially when the employee leaving is a skilled professional or manager. When the general manager or HR professional is not available, the next best choice is the manager above the employee's immediate supervisor.

When none of these choices is possible, having the employee's direct supervisor conduct the interview is still better than not doing the interview at all. In some cases, the direct supervisor may even be the most likely person to elicit honest responses because of the employee's comfort level with the supervisor. However, because employees often leave due to issues with their supervisors—such as distrust, conflict, and lack of support—the supervisor is often the least likely person to obtain accurate information.

Possible Interviewers, From Best to Worst Choice

1 Outside consultant

2 Human resources staff person (in a large organization) or general manager (if no human resources person is available)

3 Manager to whom the employee's immediate supervisor reports

4 Employee's immediate supervisor

Activity

Pros and Cons of Possible Interviewers

List the benefits and disadvantages of each possible interviewer listed below. Compare your responses with your classmates and see what conclusions you can draw from these pros and cons.

1 Outside consultant

_____

_____

2 Human resources staff member or general manager

_____

_____

3 Manager to whom the employee's supervisor reports

_____

_____

4 Employee's immediate supervisor

_____

_____

Think About It...

How would you determine whether a person would be good at conducting an exit interview? What questions would you ask him or her? Why?

Exit Interview Skills

Remember that the primary purpose of the exit interview is collecting information from the employee about a range of management and human resources practices, such as the hiring process, orientation, training, professional development, support, and supervision. Therefore, as a manager, you need to make sure that you or the person you designate to conduct the interview has experience in conducting interviews and demonstrates the following abilities:

- Communication skills, including listening skills

- Question-asking skills

- Recording skills

- Patience to conduct a careful interview

In addition, the interviewer should be capable of setting an appropriate tone for the interview.

Tone of the Interview

The interviewer should establish a relaxed, professional, and private tone, so the employee feels safe sharing honest reactions to the operation, its practices, and its management. Unfortunately, some employees fear reprisals to themselves or their friends and colleagues in the operation if they provide honest comments. As a result, employees often hide their real reasons for leaving. (If the employee talks to several people about leaving, you will often find the employee giving different reasons for leaving to different individuals.) Therefore, it is critical to establish an atmosphere of trust and confidentiality, so employees realize the information they share will not be used against anyone, including themselves.

Establishing the appropriate tone from the beginning of the interview increases the likelihood of gaining useful information. The interviewer should begin by explaining the purpose of the interview and how the information will be used.

Evaluating Exit Interview Information

Since the major reason for conducting exit interviews is to determine how well the human resources practices are working both for employees and for the operation, you need to make sure that you or the person conducting the interview listens carefully for any information about those areas. After an exit interview has been conducted, you need to analyze the information gathered during the interview. To do this, you should review and categorize the interview information, gather any additional information that might be needed, and then analyze the information to identify patterns.

1. Review and Categorize Information

When an exit interview is complete, the interviewer or the person responsible for analyzing exit interview information should start by reviewing the exit information and then categorizing it. Categorizing makes it easier to compare information gathered from different interviews, identify patterns, and then improve the operation based on those patterns.

Information can be categorized in many ways. Categorizing information by job, job group, or department is important for identifying patterns—both good and bad—within certain areas of the operation. If your operation collects equal employment opportunity data, that information should also be categorized by protected class to identify any patterns of illegal discrimination. Categorizing information in other ways helps identify specific issues within areas, issues that cross departments, and issues within the entire operation. (See *Exhibit 10g* on the next page.) While the main focus of exit interviews is learning about problems, the interview also may uncover things that work well in your operation.

Exhibit 10g

Sample Categories for Exit Interview Information

- Reason for leaving

- Satisfaction with training

- Satisfaction with orientation

- Satisfaction with professional development opportunities

- Satisfaction with compensation and benefits

- Satisfaction with management support

- Impressions of employee morale

- Impressions of teamwork

- Impressions of organization's culture

- Impressions of standards and policies

When first reviewing exit interview information, start by looking for events or information regarding sanitation, safety, security, discrimination, harassment, or anything that might lead to a legal problem. If you find any of these issues, you should immediately investigate the employee's claims. If you can corroborate the information, follow your operation's guidelines for dealing with these matters. If you cannot corroborate the information, you still may be looking at the first signs of trouble. Do not ignore or discard this information. Even if you believe the employee's claims are false, make sure you record the allegations and report them to the appropriate authority.

Next, begin categorizing the information and recording it in a way that will help you compare it to information from other exit interviews. In addition to reasons for leaving an operation, such as compensation issues, scheduling problems, or management problems, you might have categories for training, orientation, workplace morale, incentive programs, benefits, and other areas that might not be given as reasons for leaving.

2. Gather Additional Information

As you review and categorize the exit information, you may find that you need to clarify some of the information mentioned in the interview. Sometimes this may mean talking with the employee again, if possible, or observing other employees' performance or behavior more closely. Other times, it may mean talking with the employee's immediate supervisor or coworkers, looking up employee records, or reviewing other documents and data. For example, if an employee complains about being penalized for not knowing how to do certain procedures despite having followed what he or she was trained to do, you might want to check the employee's personnel file for training records, performance reviews, and any disciplinary actions, and you may even want to check the contents of the training materials.

Extensive investigations of every issue mentioned in an exit interview are not always practical or necessary. Before you go to such lengths for issues that are not immediate, or do not present any potential legal issues, you may want to consider whether the issue is part of a pattern that needs further investigation.

3. Look for Patterns

When you start to analyze the interview data, look at it in light of other exit interviews to identify any patterns, especially in the areas of standards regarding food safety, security, harassment, teamwork,

Think About It...

What benefits or consequences might there be to making immediate changes in an operation based on information from a single exit interview?

and professionalism. You need to look for patterns because a single interviewee may be disgruntled, or have unusual and inaccurate perceptions of the workplace. However, when you see patterns emerge from multiple interviews, you have clearer evidence that something is actually there.

Also, consider whether the employee was a good fit for the job in the first place. Sometimes during an exit interview, you can learn more about the employee and whether you hired the right person than you can about other areas to improve in your operation. The information that employees share regarding what they have noticed about the policies and standards, their ability to answer questions, and their willingness to help the organization improve may indicate a lot about their knowledge and their attitude. If you find that the person who is leaving was not a good fit for the job, you need to analyze the selection process to determine how to improve it.

To identify patterns, total and compare the responses from persons who had the same job or same level of responsibility, as shown in *Exhibit 10h*. For example, if assistant managers have similar complaints, there may be something for the manager to examine more fully and address. However, if only one waitstaff person out of the three who left in the last year mentions difficulty with the coffee equipment, then you have an isolated or idiosyncratic response. Also compare responses across job groups, departments, and the entire operation. Once you identify a pattern, you know what needs to be investigated further and possibly changed.

Exhibit 10h

Reasons Cited for Leaving by Nonmanagerial Employees

Reason Cited	Front of the House			Back of the House			Total by Category
	Servers	Bussers	Assistant managers	Dishwashers	Prep cooks	Chefs	
Safety	0	0	0	0	0	0	0
Security	0	0	0	0	0	0	0
Sexual harassment	1	0	0	0	0	0	1
Discrimination/unfair treatment	0	0	0	0	0	0	0
Low compensation	1	2	1	2	2	1	9
Scheduling problems	5	3	1	0	0	0	9
Management difficulties	0	1	0	1	0	0	2
Lack of opportunities	1	0	0	1	0	0	2
Career change (new industry)	1	1	1	2	0	0	5
Temporary/seasonal employment	0	1	0	0	0	0	1
Other	1	0	0	0	1	0	2
Total by Position	**10**	**8**	**3**	**6**	**3**	**1**	**31**

Activity

Identifying Patterns

1 What patterns do you see in the information in *Exhibit 10h?*

_____

_____

_____

_____

_____

_____

2 Are there any patterns as to why people are leaving particular jobs, particular areas (front of the house or back of the house), or the operation?

_____

_____

_____

_____

_____

_____

_____

Using Exit Interview Information

At this point, you have gone through a lot of effort and expense to gather and analyze exit information. But do not stop here, as many people do—take action to make things better.

Once you have identified patterns, you can prioritize which issues to work on first. One way to begin prioritizing is to rank information within the different categories. Doing this helps you learn which items your employees see as your operation's biggest weaknesses and which ones as strengths. Because the reasons employees leave your operation often illustrate what they think are the most extreme problems, prioritizing reasons for turnover is a good place to start. For example, you might prioritize the problems of unfair treatment, low compensation, scheduling, and management issues based on the reasons people give for leaving. After you know which problems are seen as the worst, you can begin working on solutions for these items. However, you may need to consider other factors that can affect the priorities, as in the following examples:

■ **Problems that may result in legal claims or lawsuits—**
A significant number of minority employees leave your company
because of lack of opportunity, but this reason is not given by
white employees. This situation may reveal a discrimination
problem in your operation, even if no discrimination claims have
been made.

■ **Policies or business plans that may dictate priorities—**
A large number of employees give low compensation as the
reason for leaving, but your company policy dictates the same
pay structure for all its units across the country, and your unit is
in an area with a high cost of living. In this case, you probably
will not be able to change the compensation structure at your
establishment—at least not right away. (However, you can make
a case with the corporate office for raising compensation.)

■ **Return on investment (time, cost, and effort versus benefits)—**
Many employees express dissatisfaction with your operation's
retirement plan, but this dissatisfaction is not usually the primary
reason people give for leaving. In this case, the cost of improving
the retirement plan might far outweigh the benefits that your
operation would gain.

After you determine which issues are the highest priorities, you need
to investigate the issues in more depth to understand their root
causes. For example, if you have learned that people did not feel they
were fully oriented when they first started with the operation, asking
some supervisors and managers about how they think orientation is
being conducted and received by the employees will provide you
with useful information. If the managers see no problems or areas of
improvement, but the employees leaving have mentioned this topic
consistently, then you probably have a problem with the skills or
quality of supervision. More investigation is needed in this area.

By carefully analyzing exit interview information, you can establish
plans to make appropriate changes and work with individual
supervisors or employees as needed. Planning for those changes and
enlisting the help of others to implement the changes will yield a
higher success rate than just operating alone. In addition, bringing
your concerns to other supervisors and managers will produce
useful discussion about changes that need to be made, and the result
normally will be a more efficient, better focused, more welcoming,
and more profitable operation.

Activity

Evaluating and Applying Exit Interview Information

One year ago, Joe and Betty bought Erle's Grill, a large, independently owned restaurant in Denver, Colorado. They believed most areas of the operation were in good shape, so they only made minor changes to the operational policies and procedures and the employee benefits when they first took over. However, the operation had a very high turnover rate, which averaged around 110 percent a year. Therefore, one of their most immediate goals was to reduce the turnover rate. To do this, and to learn more about other issues in their new operation, they began conducting exit interviews.

In the meantime, Joe and Betty also increased their recruiting and hiring efforts. Before changing ownership, Erle's Grill generally recruited people through newspaper ads and employee referrals, and the general manager personally screened and hired every employee. As soon as Joe and Betty took over in the first quarter of last year, they also began running help wanted ads much more frequently and recruiting through local school career placement offices and the state unemployment office. These extra efforts produced many more qualified applicants. To handle the large increase in applicants, Joe and Betty decided, with input from various managers, that the executive chef and dining room manager would screen and hire their own people.

Another area that Joe and Betty immediately addressed in that first quarter was employee training. They developed a formal orientation program that involved various individuals and helped to standardize the training that new employees received. They also developed ongoing training events for experienced employees. Initial feedback from employees and managers indicated the new programs were successful.

Joe and Betty were also fortunate enough to keep all of the managers during the first several months of their ownership. However, near the end of the second quarter, one of their best assistant dining room managers moved out of state. To fill the position, they promoted a senior waitstaff member. Unfortunately, this decision angered another staff member who had expected the promotion and subsequently quit in the fourth quarter. Also in the fourth quarter, one of the sous chefs left to take an executive chef position at another restaurant. For this position, Joe and Betty brought in a chef they knew from another operation.

On a separate piece of paper, answer the questions that follow based on data that Joe and Betty collected from exit interviews, which are shown on the following pages. These numbers are based on a total count of sixty employees, with thirty-one in the front of the house (FOH) and twenty-seven in the back of the house (BOH). (When considering the average figures, keep in mind the number of responses for that category.)

This chart shows the primary reasons employees gave for leaving. The total by job number indicates how many employees left in each quarter.

Reason Cited	First Quarter			Second Quarter			Third Quarter			Fourth Quarter			Annual Total by Reason	% Annual Turnover by Reason[1]
	FOH	BOH	Subtotal	FOH	BOH	Subtotal	FOH	BOH	Subtotal	FOH	BOH	Subtotal		
Career change (new industry)	4	4	8	3	2	5	1		1		1	1	15	25%
Discrimination/ unfair treatment														
Lack of opportunities				1	1	2				1	1	2	4	7%
Low compensation	1	1	2										2	3%
Management difficulties	1	1	2		1	1	4	1	5	6		6	14	23%
Safety														
Scheduling problems	2	1	3	1		1	1	1	2				6	10%
Security														
Sexual harassment														
Temporary/ seasonal employment							1	1	2				2	3%
Other	1		1	1	1	2				1		1	4	7%
Total by Job	9	7	16	6	5	11	7	3	10	8	2	10	47	78%
% Turnover by Area[1]	116	104	107	77	74	73	90	44	67	103	30	67		

[1] Percentages are rounded to the nearest whole number.

continued on next page

Evaluating and Applying Exit Interview Information *continued from previous page*

This chart shows the scores that employees gave during exit interviews to various areas of the operation.

1 = poor, 3 = average, 5 = excellent

Category measured	First Quarter			Second Quarter			Third Quarter			Fourth Quarter			Annual average
	FOH	BOH	All areas	FOH	BOH	All areas	FOH	BOH	All areas	FOH	BOH	All areas	
Orientation and training	1.7	1.9	1.8	2.0	2.2	2.1	3.7	3.3	3.5	4.1	4.0	4.1	2.9
Professional development opportunities	3.3	3.7	3.5	1.0	1.0	1.0	3.3	3.6	3.5	1.0	2.0	1.5	2.4
Compensation and benefits	2.7	2.6	2.7	3.6	3.2	3.4	3.6	2.6	3.1	3.5	3.5	3.5	3.2
Organization's culture	3.9	3.0	3.5	3.7	3.6	3.7	2.6	3.6	3.1	2.6	3.5	3.1	3.3
Standards and policies	3.0	2.8	2.9	3.5	3.6	3.6	2.3	3.6	3.0	2.0	3.5	2.8	3.0
Management support	3.7	3.0	3.4	3.7	3.2	3.5	1.6	3.7	2.7	1.3	4.0	2.7	3.0
Number of employees who responded	**9**	**7**	**16**	**6**	**5**	**11**	**7**	**3**	**10**	**8**	**2**	**10**	

1 What does the data show for reasons why front of the house (FOH) employees left? (Are there any patterns?)

2 What additional information do the scores that FOH employees gave various areas tell you?

3 What might these patterns in the front of the house mean?

4 What patterns do the data show for reasons why back of the house (BOH) employees left?

5 What additional information do the scores that BOH employees gave various areas tell you?

6 What might these patterns in the back of the house mean?

7 Which three areas should Joe and Betty try to resolve first and in which order?

8 What should their action plan be?

Summary

The voluntary termination of a valued employee can be a sad and costly event, but it can lead to improvement in the operation if handled well. By conducting a good exit interview, you can learn more about the effects of the policies, practices, working conditions, and management of the operation. You can then use this information to improve the operation by addressing problem areas or capitalizing on the employee's insight about a better way of doing things. Besides assisting management in making improvements, exit interviews can benefit the employee leaving by providing closure to the employment experience and a formal way to say goodbye.

The information to be gathered during an exit interview will vary depending on your purpose for having the interview and will typically follow a format prescribed by the operation. Exit interviews may be conducted in person, by telephone, in writing, or by computer. The best and most common method is the face-to-face interview conducted by someone from the operation. These interviews may be structured or unstructured.

When planning for a face-to-face exit interview, schedule it on a day near the employee's last day of employment and conduct the interview in a private place where there are no distractions. The person interviewing the employee should not be the employee's immediate supervisor, unless all other options have been exhausted. Ideally, the exit interviewer should have interviewing experience and communication skills (including listening), question-asking skills, recording skills, and patience. The interviewer also should be able to establish the right tone.

After an exit interview, analyze the information collected. To do this, review and categorize the interview information, gather any additional information needed, and then compare the information to identify patterns. Follow your operation's guidelines for investigating and dealing with issues that could lead to legal problems.

Once you have analyzed the exit information, prioritize which issues to address. Rank information within the different categories to find out which areas need the most improvement, according to your former employees. Then consider other factors that can affect the priorities, such as legal problems that may arise, policies or business plans that may dictate priorities, and potential return on investment.

In addition to conducting an exit interview, you need to manage the termination process, so everything that needs to be done before the employee leaves is taken care of. Using an employee termination checklist helps ensure nothing in this process is forgotten.

Review Your Learning

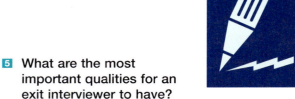

1 **What is the purpose of using an employee termination checklist?**

A. To fulfill the equal employment opportunity (EEO) laws that require these checklists for all employees

B. To ensure everything that needs to be done on or before an employee's last day actually happens

C. To ensure managerial employees say goodbye to the employees on their last day of work

D. To make sure the employee is interviewed to find out why he or she is leaving

2 **Which is *not* a benefit of exit interviews?**

A. Providing an opportunity to reflect on the work experience

B. Providing valuable information about the operation

C. Helping to identify recurring reasons for turnover

D. Helping to ensure that all loose ends are addressed

3 **A good exit interview determines all these types of information *except***

A. rejected career choices.

B. effectiveness of training.

C. nature and style of supervision.

D. reason for leaving.

4 **Which location is the best place to conduct an exit interview?**

A. Employee's normal workstation

B. Employee's home

C. Manager's office

D. Dining room

5 **What are the most important qualities for an exit interviewer to have?**

A. Communication skills, question-asking skills, recording skills, and patience

B. Communication skills, question-writing skills, computer skills, and tolerance

C. Listening skills, nonverbal communication skills, reading skills, and friendliness

D. Facilitation skills, organizational skills, managerial skills, and persuasiveness

6 **When should the exit interview be conducted?**

A. The employee's last day at work

B. A day near the employee's last day

C. The day after the employee gives notice

D. The day the employee gives notice

7 **Where is the best place to conduct an exit interview?**

A. Quiet place where you can hear well

B. Public place in case the employee gets mad

C. Private place free from distractions

D. Relaxing place where the employee feels comfortable

8 **List at least two advantages and two disadvantages of each interview method:**

A. Face-to-face interview

Advantages:

_____

_____

Disadvantages:

_____

_____

B. Telephone interview

Advantages:

_____

_____

Disadvantages:

_____

_____

C. Computer-based form

Advantages:

_____

_____

Disadvantages:

_____

_____

D. Paper form

Advantages:

_____

_____

Disadvantages:

_____

_____

Notes

Ensuring a Lawful Workplace

11

Inside This Chapter

- Impact of Laws on Restaurant and Foodservice Operations
- Providing Safe Food
- Serving Alcohol Responsibly
- Ensuring a Fair Workplace
- Balancing Needs for Food Safety, Employee Rights, and Legal Compliance
- Communicating Workplace Hazards to Employees

- Protecting Younger Workers
- Ensuring Adequate Breaks
- Working with Unions
- Providing Adequate Notice of Closings and Layoffs
- General Guidelines for Complying with Laws

After completing this chapter, you should be able to:

- Identify labor laws that affect restaurant and foodservice operations.
- Recognize a manager's responsibilities in complying with sanitation laws.
- Recognize a manager's responsibilities in complying with alcohol service laws.
- Describe the impact of antidiscrimination laws on restaurant and foodservice operations.
- Define sexual harassment.
- Describe ways to respond when an employee discloses an illness.
- Identify the principles of OSHA's Hazard Communication Standard as they relate to restaurant and foodservice operations.
- Identify the impact of child labor laws on restaurant and foodservice operations.
- Recognize the impact of unions on the manager-employee relationship.
- Describe general guidelines for complying with workplace laws.

Test Your Knowledge

1 **True or False:** Hazardous chemicals must be labeled to comply with safety regulations. *(See p. 296.)*

2 **True or False:** An employee's work must be negatively affected before a situation may be considered sexual harassment. *(See p. 283.)*

3 **True or False:** You may not ask an employee who seems ill if he or she has a disability. *(See p. 291.)*

4 **True or False:** Dram shop laws hold operations and servers responsible for any damages caused by intoxicated patrons. *(See p. 282.)*

5 **True or False:** A sixteen-year-old who gets good grades may work as a pizza delivery driver. *(See pp. 298–299.)*

Key Terms

Active managerial control

Americans with Disabilities Act Accessibility Guidelines for Buildings and Facilities (ADAAG)

Arbitrator

Bargain in good faith

Bloodborne Pathogens Standard

Child labor laws

Collective bargaining

Designated first-aid provider

Dram shop law

First aider

Flow of food

Food Code

Food safety management system

Foodborne illness

Grievances

Hazard Communication Standard (HCS)

Health code

High-risk population

Hostile environment

Labor contract

Layoffs

Material Safety Data Sheet (MSDS)

Mediator

Minors

Occupational Safety and Health Administration (OSHA)

Potable water

Quid pro quo

Reasonable care defense

Sexual harassment

State dislocated worker units

Strike

Union dues

Union steward

Unions

Whistleblowers

Zero tolerance policy

Introduction

As a manager for a restaurant or foodservice operation, you need to know the legal and regulatory environment in which you operate. Knowing the applicable laws is important because you, as a manager, must ensure that the operation complies.

Fortunately, the policies and procedures of most operations closely follow the laws. Therefore, you may not need to understand the details of every law that affects your operation, but you do need to understand the intent of the laws and the details that directly affect your workplace. You also need to know what you do *not* know, so you can recognize when to get additional information or defer issues to specialists, such as a human resources or legal professional.

Not knowing or following the laws puts you and your operation at risk for complaints, fines, and lawsuits. Restaurant and foodservice operations, especially large corporate ones, often must deal with lawsuits that arise from not understanding or following corporate policies or applicable laws and regulations. In worst-case scenarios, breaking these laws can result in criminal charges and jail time for managers, executives, and sometimes, even employees.

Since laws and regulations vary from state to state and may be amended, one of your responsibilities as a manager is to keep abreast of the changing laws. If your operation has a human resources professional, he or she can keep you informed of applicable changes in the laws. If not, you will need to develop your own resources for doing this. This chapter will give you a basic understanding of the federal laws as well as variations in practices from state to state, but it is your responsibility to find out the latest developments in these areas. These laws impact all areas of an operation, and understanding them is an important aspect of your job as a manager.

Impact of Laws on Restaurant and Foodservice Operations

In the restaurant and foodservice industry, there are numerous laws and regulations governing what can and cannot happen and what should and should not happen in the workplace. Many of these laws protect employees from discriminatory, unsafe, unfair, or unethical treatment. However, some of these laws also protect customers and the community from unsanitary foodservice practices, discriminatory practices, and irresponsible alcohol service. Laws affect all areas of the employment cycle (see *Exhibit 11a* on the next page) and other areas as well.

Exhibit 11a

Employment Cycle

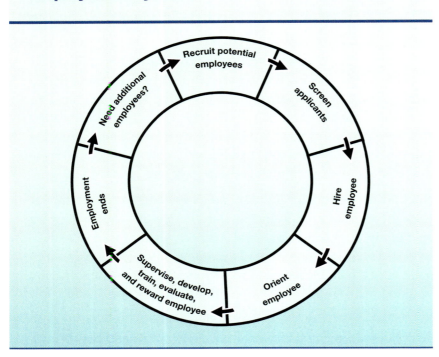

As you have learned in previous chapters, antidiscrimination laws can impact many aspects of daily operations, including job descriptions, recruiting, screening, hiring, employee development, training, and promotions. Most company policies enforce these laws and contain zero tolerance statements for discrimination of any kind. Additional areas that are impacted by laws include:

- **Sanitation and alcohol service**—Sanitation and alcohol service laws require safe sanitation and foodhandling practices and responsible alcohol service.

- **Scheduling and work assignments**—Federal, state, and local laws restrict the work assignments and hours that minors can work; state and local laws define the minimum breaks required for various schedules; and alcohol service laws restrict the tasks that servers younger than twenty-one years of age can handle.

- **Workplace safety**—Federal and sometimes state laws mandate certain safety standards for restaurant and foodservice operations.

- **Union relations**—Federal laws restrict how employers and unions can attempt to influence an employee's decision to join or not join a union. In addition, the labor contracts negotiated by unions affect how managers can interact with employees as well as other aspects of employment.

- **Wages and payroll**—Federal laws establish the minimum hourly wage you must pay certain employees, when you must pay them overtime, and various aspects of payroll administration. In addition, antidiscrimination laws make it illegal to pay employees different amounts of money for essentially the same work based on certain immutable characteristics. (For more information, see Chapter 12.)

■ **Employee benefits**—Federal and state laws require the employee benefits that must be offered in some situations and how many types of employee benefits must be administered. (For more information, see Chapter 12.)

Exhibit 11b

Costs of a Foodborne Illness versus the Benefits of Safe Foodhandling

Costs of a Foodborne Illness	Benefits of Safe Foodhandling
■ Loss of customers and sales	■ Higher profits
■ Negative public relations	■ Repeat business
■ Loss of prestige and reputation	■ Better food quality
■ Embarrassment	■ Reduced health code violations
■ Possibility of lawsuits and lawyer and court fees	■ Reduced chance of lawsuits
■ Increased insurance premiums	■ Reduced or minimized insurance costs
■ Need for retraining employees	■ Reduced food waste
■ Lowered employee morale	■ Increased job satisfaction
■ Employee absenteeism	

Providing Safe Food

As a manager, your most important food safety responsibilities are to serve customers safe food and to train employees in safe foodhandling practices. Safe foodhandling helps your operation avoid causing a **foodborne illness,** a disease carried or transmitted to people by food. Serving safe food also helps you comply with **health codes,** local laws designed to ensure food safety. As *Exhibit 11b* shows, there are many reasons to do this. Essentially, to stay in business, your operation must comply with applicable health or sanitation codes.

Food Sanitation Laws

Government control of food in the U.S. is exercised at the federal, state, and local levels. At the federal level, the government agencies directly involved in the inspection process are the U.S. Department of Agriculture (USDA) and the Food and Drug Administration (FDA). Among other responsibilities, these two agencies regulate food businesses that operate in two or more states.

The FDA also writes the **Food Code,** the federal government's recommendations for foodservice regulations to prevent foodborne illnesses. Currently, these recommendations are updated every two years to reflect developments in the restaurant and foodservice industry and the field of food safety. Operations that are inspected by the FDA or USDA must follow the Food Code. Other operations need to follow their state or local health department regulations instead.

Many state and local regulations are based on the Food Code, but these governments adopt and interpret the Food Code recommendations differently. Consequently, health codes may vary widely from one state to another, or in some cases, from one locality to another.

However, most health codes contain provisions for the following areas:

- Food safety
- Personal hygiene
- Sanitary facilities
- Equipment and utensils
- Safe operating practices
- Training
- Enforcement procedures

State and local governments may also differ in the recommended frequency of inspection. To find out what regulations apply to your operation, consult your local health department.

Understanding Your Responsibilities

Regardless of the inspection frequency for your operation, it is your responsibility as a manager to keep food safe and wholesome throughout the operation at all times. In fact, the FDA recommends that local and state health departments hold the person in charge of a restaurant or foodservice operation responsible for knowing and demonstrating the following information:

- Rights, responsibilities, and authorities the local code assigns to employees, managers, and the local health department
- Diseases carried or transmitted by food and their symptoms
- Points in the **flow of food**—the path food takes through your operation (see *Exhibit 11c*)—where hazards can be prevented, eliminated, or reduced, and how these procedures meet the requirements of the local code
- Relationship between personal hygiene and the spread of disease, especially concerning cross-contamination, hand contact with ready-to-eat food, and handwashing
- How to keep injured or ill employees from contaminating food or food-contact surfaces
- The need to control the length of time that potentially hazardous food remains at temperatures in which disease-causing microorganisms can grow
- Hazards involved in the consumption of raw or undercooked meat, poultry, eggs, and fish

Exhibit 11c

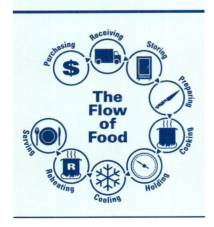

The Flow of Food

- Safe cooking temperatures and times for potentially hazardous food items, such as meat, poultry, eggs, and fish

- Safe temperatures and times for storing, holding, cooling, and reheating potentially hazardous food

- Correct procedures for cleaning and sanitizing utensils and food-contact surfaces of equipment

- Types of toxic materials used in the operation, and how to safely store, dispense, use, and dispose of them

- The need for equipment that is sufficient in number and capacity to handle food safely and is properly designed, constructed, located, installed, operated, maintained, and cleaned

- Approved sources of potable water—water that is safe to drink or use as an ingredient in food—and the importance of keeping it clean and safe

- Principles of active managerial control or a HACCP-based food safety system (discussed in the next section)

As a manager, you need to know this information, and you need to make sure that all your employees know how to safely handle food.

Ensuring Food Safety

Serving safe food is vital to your operation's success. The best way to protect your operation, your employees, and your customers from the negative effects of poor sanitation is to develop and maintain a sound food safety management system and ensure all employees follow this system.

Developing and Maintaining a Food Safety Management System

A food safety management system is a group of programs and procedures designed to control hazards throughout the flow of food. A strong food safety management system incorporates the principles of active managerial control and Hazard Analysis and Critical Control Point (HACCP).

- Active managerial control is a proactive approach to addressing common risk factors responsible for foodborne illness. It requires you to continuously monitor your employees to ensure they are following policies and procedures.

- A HACCP (pronounced *HASS-ip*) system focuses on identifying specific points within the flow of food that are essential to prevent, eliminate, or reduce a biological, chemical, or physical hazard to safe levels. To be effective, a HACCP system must be

Exhibit 11d

Managers must ensure sanitation policies and procedures are being followed.

based on a written plan that is specific to an establishment's menu, customers, equipment, processes, and operations.

You also should keep a copy of your local or state sanitation regulations and be familiar with them. Regularly compare the code to procedures at your operation and adjust your food safety management system as needed. Remember, however, that code requirements are only minimum standards to keep food safe.

Providing Adequate Training

A food safety management system provides a foundation for safe foodhandling, but it is your responsibility as a manager to ensure that everyone in your operation follows this system. (See *Exhibit 11d.*) As part of this, you must ensure all employees are properly trained in food safety as it relates to their jobs. A food safety training program should consist of the following:

- Components for both new and experienced employees

- Assessment tools to identify the need for ongoing food safety training

- A selection of resources to support training, such as books, videos, posters, and technology-based materials

- Records documenting that employees have completed their training

Performing Self-Inspections

In addition to training employees on food safety, your operation should continuously perform self-inspections to ensure your food safety management system is working and food is safe. Operations with high sanitation and food safety standards consider health department inspections as only a supplement to their self-inspection programs. A good self-inspection program provides many benefits, including:

- Safer food

- Improved food quality

- A clean environment

- Higher health department inspection scores

Your customers also will notice your commitment to providing them with a safe, sanitary dining experience.

Activity

Evaluating André's Training

André, a restaurant manager, has been on the job for five months at the Charter Café. In his first two weeks, ten new employees joined his team of twenty-five. To his credit, most of the thirty-five employees are still with the operation.

André knew from his management training program that food safety training was important to the success of his restaurant. With that in mind, he made sure all of his employees went through a four-hour food safety training session that he presented himself. André tried his best to impart the knowledge that he learned in his training to his employees. He used a flip chart, posters, and overhead slides to illustrate his points, and he passed out food safety pamphlets he got from the local health department. André even had employees take a quiz he created.

Four months after André conducted his training, he found himself responding to a foodborne-illness complaint and a failing health inspection score. Because all of his employees had been trained in food safety, he was puzzled as to what could have gone wrong.

1 What did André do right?

_____

_____

_____

2 What did André do wrong?

_____

_____

_____

3 What should André do differently in the future?

_____

_____

_____

Protecting Your Operation Against Legal Action

Despite the best intentions of restaurant and foodservice operations, customers today are likely to file a lawsuit to obtain compensation for injuries that they feel they have suffered as a result of the food they were served. If you have a quality food safety management system in place, however, you can use a reasonable care defense against a food-related lawsuit. A **reasonable care defense** is one that requires proof your establishment did everything that could be reasonably expected to ensure the food served was safe. The keys to this defense are documented standards, training practices and procedures such as a HACCP plan, and positive inspection results. Since decisions in these suits follow the law in their respective states, you should check applicable state laws to determine the appropriate defense in any action.

Serving Alcohol Responsibly

Just as businesses that serve food have legal responsibilities to ensure food safety, so do restaurant and foodservice operations that serve alcohol. As a manager of such an operation, you must understand the responsibilities that you, your operation, and your servers all have in complying with alcohol service laws. You must ensure that your employees understand their own responsibilities and the risks that breaking these laws pose to them, the operation, and the community. If someone in your operation breaks the law, you, the server, and the operation could face serious consequences—from lawsuits to criminal charges, including fines or even imprisonment. In addition, your operation could lose its liquor license, leading to a significant loss in sales that could force the operation to close. When it comes to serving alcohol, you must ensure that all employees understand and comply with the applicable laws.

Each state's liquor board or liquor authority develops and enforces its own regulations for alcohol service. In addition, these agencies are responsible for issuing and monitoring liquor licenses, issuing citations for violations, and holding hearings for violators of the liquor code. (See *Exhibit 11e.*)

Since the laws pertaining to the sale and service of alcohol vary widely, you must become familiar with the ones that apply to your establishment. These may include:

■ **Legal age to drink**—In all fifty states, a person must be twenty-one years old to purchase alcohol. In some states, it is currently legal for a parent or legal guardian to purchase alcohol and serve it to a minor child.

Exhibit 11e

A liquor authority violation can result in the suspension or revocation of an operation's liquor license.

Think About It...

A new law in New Mexico went into effect on July 1, 2004, making it a felony to purchase, give, or sell alcohol to anyone under the age of twenty-one. Each violation could result in eighteen months in jail and a five-thousand-dollar fine. This is the first law in the U.S. that imposes felony charges on those who provide alcohol to a minor.

■ **Legal age to serve**—In general, a person must be twenty-one years old to serve alcohol. However, this law can vary. For example, some states allow underage servers to bring alcohol to the table but not to pour it. Others allow underage servers to take the order and payment for the drink but not to serve it. Some states require an underage server to apply to the liquor authority for permission to serve alcoholic beverages. In all cases, persons who are younger than twenty-one and serve alcohol must be supervised by someone older.

■ **Legal age to enter the establishment**—In some areas, the law does not allow minors to enter a tavern or restaurant bar area. Some establishments may require guests to be older than the legal age in order to enter the bar.

■ **Serving intoxicated guests**—It is illegal to serve a guest who is intoxicated or who shows signs of intoxication.

■ **Serving a pregnant guest**—It is illegal to deny alcohol service to a woman because she is pregnant. Doing this would be considered sex discrimination. Many states, however, require establishments to post signs warning of the effects of alcohol on a fetus.

■ **Hours and type of service**—Local liquor authorities control the hours for the legal sale and service of alcohol and the type of alcohol that may be sold or served, such as hard liquor or carryouts. These laws must be strictly followed.

■ **Happy hours and other drink promotions**—Some states, counties, and municipalities restrict or forbid "happy hours" and other drink promotions. These laws may prohibit serving a guest any of the following:

☐ Two or more drinks at a time

☐ An unlimited number of drinks for a fixed price

☐ Reduced-price drinks for a specified period of time

☐ Drinks containing additional alcohol without an increase in price

☐ Drinks as a prize for a game or contest conducted at the establishment

■ **Certification to serve**—Some states, counties, and municipalities require that people who serve alcohol be certified in safe alcohol service practices. These certifications may be earned through local educational institutions and other organizations, such as the ServSafe Alcohol Certification offered by the National Restaurant Association Educational Foundation.

Another factor that affects alcohol service is the **dram shop law,** a regulation that varies from state to state but which holds the server—and the restaurant or foodservice operation—liable for serving liquor to an already intoxicated person or someone who is underage. The penalties and liabilities for violating these laws differ by state. These laws and the insurance premiums required for serving liquor have led many managers to establish detailed training for employees who make cocktails, tend bars, and serve liquor. Understanding your local dram shop law is essential to you as a manager—whether you are a general manager, dining room manager, or executive chef—in training *all* your employees and supporting them if they have to address potentially awkward situations.

Activity

Liquor Laws in Your Municipality

Research the following information for the location where you work or live.

The city/town and state where I work or live is _____

The local liquor authority for this location is _____

1 How old must servers be to do the following?

   A. Serve alcohol   _____

   B. Pour alcohol   _____

   C. Take a drink order   _____

2 How old must a guest be to enter a tavern or bar area in a restaurant? _____

3 Are operations that serve alcohol required to post warning signs about the effects of alcohol on a fetus?

_____

4 If your workplace serves alcohol:

   A. During what hours can alcohol be served?   _____

   B. What kinds of alcohol can your operation serve or sell?   _____

5 If your operation does not serve alcohol, during what hours can operations in your municipality serve alcohol?

_____

6 What, if any, drink promotions are restricted?

_____

_____

_____

Exhibit 11f

Federal Antidiscrimination Laws

- Equal Pay Act of 1963

- Age Discrimination in Employment Act of 1967 (ADEA)

- Title I of the Americans with Disabilities Act of 1990 (ADA)

- Title VII of the Civil Rights Act of 1964

- Pregnancy Discrimination Act

- Immigration Reform and Control Act of 1986 (IRCA)

- Uniformed Services Employment and Reemployment Rights Act (USERRA)

Ensuring a Fair Workplace

As you have been learning throughout this book, there are many laws that prohibit discrimination against employees, customers, and vendors based on certain characteristics. (See *Exhibit 11f.*) These laws are intended to provide equal opportunities for all people, regardless of race, color, religion, sex, national origin, age (forty or older), disability, military service, or other traits. Some of these laws warrant further discussion. One of them, Title VII of the Civil Rights Act of 1964, prohibits sexual harassment as a form of sex discrimination.

Preventing Sexual Harassment

Sexual harassment is an issue of particular concern in the restaurant and foodservice industry. Under Title VII of the Civil Rights Act, employers have a legal obligation to protect their employees from sexual harassment. This obligation means that you need to protect your employees not only from harassment by coworkers, but also by anyone who comes into the workplace, including customers, salespeople, vendors, and suppliers. Likewise, you also need to protect these people from being harassed by your employees.

While the law mandates your responsibilities in this area, protecting employees from sexual harassment is also a good business practice. As you learned in Chapter 1, creating a welcoming environment in which employees feel valued has many benefits. Ensuring that people can both work free from harassment and know that any problems will be resolved fairly goes a long way toward building an environment where morale is good, turnover is low, and employee referrals are high. To be able to provide such an environment, you need to understand what sexual harassment is, how to prevent it, and how to respond when it is reported.

Sexual harassment is unwelcome behavior of a sexual nature that has the effect of interfering with the employee's job performance. The victim of such behavior, not the person who displays the behavior, determines what is considered "offensive or unwelcome." Given this definition, the issue of sexual harassment is a complex one because what one person might regard as simple teasing might be considered harassment by another.

However, the law recognizes two types of sexual harassment:

- **Quid pro quo**—From the Latin phrase meaning "this for that," quid pro quo harassment is when one person asks for or expects an action of a sexual nature from another person as a condition of that person's employment or advancement. Such conditions include hirings, firings, raises, scheduling, or promotions.

For example, a supervisor promises a raise in return for a sexual favor.

■ **Hostile environment**—An atmosphere that is sexually demeaning or intimidating in which a person is treated poorly or feels uncomfortable; for example, when people tell offensive jokes of a sexual nature, call others by demeaning names, display sexually explicit or offensive pictures or other materials, or otherwise behave in ways that are threatening or offensive.

Although sexual harassment laws originally were intended to protect women from inappropriate advances or intimidation from men, the context has changed. Now sexual harassment includes men harassing women, women harassing men, men harassing men, and women harassing women.

Because sexual harassment can be a confusing topic, some people may overcompensate in their behavior to avoid accusations of harassment. However, as a manager, you want to encourage normal, friendly interactions and other social behaviors that help create a welcoming environment and foster good morale. Therefore, it is helpful to understand what is *not* considered to be sexual harassment, such as the following behaviors:

■ Normal, friendly interaction

■ Non-offensive joking

■ Being polite or nice

■ Socializing and being friendly

■ Any behavior that would not offend a reasonable person

Sexual Harassment Policies

To help people understand and avoid sexual harassment, most operations have a zero tolerance policy against sexual harassment. A basic **zero tolerance policy** is a policy that includes the following types of statements:

■ The operation does not tolerate harassment in any form by any person.

■ All persons are responsible for stopping harassment whenever it occurs.

■ Harassment should be reported.

The procedures for stopping and reporting sexual harassment vary from one operation to another depending on the location, size, and structure (such as independently owned, corporate ownership, or a franchise).

Activity

Your Experience with Sexual Harassment

What sexual harassment experiences have you faced or witnessed at work? What were the operation's policies and procedures for dealing with sexual harassment? What did the managers do or not do in these situations? If you were the manager, how would you have handled these situations?

_____

_____

_____

_____

_____

_____

Think About It...

As a manager, what does your behavior say to employees when you participate in teasing someone or ignore harassment?

Preventing a Hostile Environment

As a manager, you are responsible for following and enforcing your company's policies on sexual harassment. However, preventing a hostile environment in your operation encompasses more than just enforcing policies. You also need to:

- **Help employees understand what sexual harassment is, how to avoid it, and how to deal with it.** Educate employees about sexual harassment, and train them to follow your company's policies and procedures. Ensure the training teaches people how to say no and communicate their discomfort, so that others can understand when their behavior is unwanted or offensive.

- **Encourage open communication.** Help employees feel comfortable bringing issues to your attention. Listen to what they say and take their concerns seriously.

- **Set a good example for your employees by following company policies and demonstrating appropriate behavior.** Let your employees know through your words and deeds that harassment is not acceptable, and show them positive ways to interact with people.

- **Actively look for signs of harassment in your operation.** Get rid of any items that might offend people, such as cartoons or pictures of a sexual nature, and observe how people interact. Stop inappropriate behavior whenever you see it.

If you see signs of harassment, promptly enforce your operation's sexual harassment policies in a fair and equitable manner. If you do not consistently enforce these policies in all cases and with all affected employees, you will create confusion and resentment, and you will put your operation at risk for claims of discrimination. Conversely, whenever you enforce sexual harassment policies or correct someone's behavior, you show that you are serious about protecting employees' rights, and most people will behave accordingly.

Activity

Watching for a Hostile Environment

When visiting a restaurant or foodservice operation, what would you look for to see if it provides a hostile or nonhostile working environment?

_____

_____

_____

_____

Think About It...

If a harassment complaint is made, often the best defense against possible legal claims is to address the issue promptly in a thorough and professional manner. Doing this goes a long way toward protecting your company if you can show you responded to the incident promptly, wrote down what happened and kept records, and treated all employees equally and fairly.

Responding to Reports of Harassment

Despite your best efforts to provide a welcoming environment, sexual harassment and other forms of discriminatory harassment may occur. If someone reports harassment in your operation, do you know what to do? While your company policies should help guide you, there are also general guidelines you can follow to protect the victim and your operation. These guidelines vary based on whether an employee or someone else is accused of harassment.

Reports of an Employee Harassing Someone

If an employee harasses another employee or anyone else, address the issue promptly and follow these guidelines (unless they conflict with company policy):

- Discuss the complaint with the person who reported it to learn more about the situation.

- Try to collect any evidence of the harassment, such as notes or letters.

- Assure the person who reported the harassment that everything will be kept as confidential as possible and that the operation will not allow any retaliation for reporting the situation.

- Inform senior management or your human resources department of the complaint.

- If necessary, change the work schedule for either party so that they do not have to work together.

- Find out if there were any witnesses and interview them. However, do not lead them with any information you might already know. Let them tell their version of the situation in their own words.

- Interview the accused with a witness present. Always include a third person in the interview—either a manager or supervisor—to witness everything that is said and done. Explain the accusation, and ask the accused what he or she believes happened. After this discussion, you may need to talk again to the complaining party or witnesses to clarify the situation further.

After the investigation is complete, consult with your manager, human resources department, or legal counsel, and take whatever action is reasonable for the circumstances uncovered during the investigation. Each case is different, so if harassment is found, the action taken by the company should be reasonably related to the severity of the situation.

Reports of a Nonemployee Harassing Someone in Your Operation

When dealing with reports of harassment initiated by someone who is not an employee, such as a vendor, supplier, or customer, promptly explain your policy for harassment to the accused. Also explain that everyone who comes to your establishment needs to follow this policy. During this discussion, remain professional and do not get personally involved or trade insults. Focus on the behavior and not the personalities of the people involved.

Complying with the Pregnancy Discrimination Act

Although Title VII of the Civil Rights Act prohibited sex discrimination, female employees still experienced various forms of discrimination if they became pregnant. This is why Congress passed an amendment to Title VII to specifically protect the rights of pregnant women in the workplace. The Pregnancy Discrimination Act of 1978 prohibits employers from discriminating against women on the basis of pregnancy, childbirth, or related medical conditions. (See *Exhibit 11g.*) This law states that women affected by these conditions "shall be treated the same for all employment-related

Exhibit 11g

Discrimination based on pregnancy, childbirth, or a related condition is illegal.

purposes, including receipt of benefits under fringe benefit programs, as other persons" who have similar abilities or limitations to work.

According to the Equal Employment Opportunity Commission (EEOC), this law in practice means you:

■ Cannot "refuse to hire a woman because of a pregnancy-related condition as long as she is able to perform the major functions of her job"

■ Cannot "single out pregnancy-related conditions for special procedures to determine an employee's ability to work"

■ Cannot require an employee who is pregnant to go on leave or remain on a leave until the baby's birth

■ Cannot prohibit an employee from returning to work for a predetermined length of time after childbirth

■ Must treat an employee who is temporarily unable to perform her job due to pregnancy the same as any other temporarily disabled employee. (At this point, the pregnant employee may also be eligible for time off under the Family and Medical Leave Act—see Chapter 12.)

■ Must allow pregnant employees to work as long as they are able to do their jobs

In addition, this law affects the healthcare coverage that employers must provide. Healthcare plans must cover the expenses for pregnancy-related conditions on the same basis as the costs for other medical conditions and should offer the same level of coverage to the spouses of both female and male employees. Any pregnancy-related benefits must be given to all pregnant employees, whether or not they are married.

While the issue of sex discrimination is important, it is not the only area where people need to treat each other fairly. One area that many people do not understand well is discrimination against people with disabilities and how to comply with the ADA.

Ensuring the Rights of Disabled People

It is illegal under the Americans with Disabilities Act to discriminate against anyone in the workplace because of a disability. When a disabled job applicant or employee can perform the essential functions of a job with or without reasonable accommodation, the ADA prohibits discrimination in screening, selection, hiring, training, compensation, promotion, termination, and other terms, conditions, and privileges of employment. These provisions are written in Title I of the ADA.

Think About It...

The EEOC enforces Title I of the ADA and may fine employers who are charged with disability discrimination. The EEOC reports that it "received 15,376 charges of disability discrimination [and] … recovered $47.7 million in monetary benefits" in fiscal year 2004 on behalf of those who filed discrimination claims with the EEOC and other aggrieved individuals.

Exhibit 11h

Major Life Activities under the ADA

- Walking
- Seeing
- Hearing
- Breathing
- Sitting
- Standing
- Lifting
- Learning
- Thinking
- Caring for oneself
- Performing manual tasks
- Interacting with others

Other sections of the ADA prohibit discrimination against disabled people in other ways. Title III is the other section you most need to be familiar with because it requires disabled people—including customers—to have equal access to buildings and public services. In learning more about how these sections of the law affect your operation, you first need to understand who is covered under the law.

Coverage under Title I of the ADA

As a manager, you need to understand if your operation must comply with Title I of the ADA and which employees may be entitled to protection under this law. This understanding will help you protect the rights of both disabled employees and the operation. If your operation has fifteen or more employees on each workday during twenty or more weeks in the current or preceding year, it must comply with Title I. According to the EEOC, employees are considered disabled, and therefore covered under the law, if they:

- **Have a physical or mental impairment that substantially limits one or more of the major life activities of such an individual.** (See *Exhibit 11h.*) According to the EEOC, conditions such as epilepsy, paralysis, HIV infection, AIDS, a substantial hearing or visual impairment, mental retardation, or a specific learning disability qualify as an impairment, but an individual with a minor, nonchronic condition of short duration, such as a sprain, broken limb, or the flu, generally would not be covered.

- **Have a record of such an impairment.** This definition covers people who had a disability, such as cancer or heart disease, but have recovered from it.

- **May be regarded as having such an impairment.** This definition covers people who do not actually have an impairment but may be discriminated against as though they are impaired; for example, a person with a facial disfigurement who is denied a front-of-the-house position because the employer fears negative reactions from customers.

An employee only needs to meet one of these conditions to be considered disabled. In contrast, temporary impairments caused by alcoholism and illegal drug use are not covered under the ADA. However, permanent impairments caused by illegal drug use or alcoholism, such as liver damage that limits a person's ability to work, are covered as long as the person is in treatment or has stopped drinking or using drugs.

Access for Disabled People under Title III

The ADA affects more than an operation's employment practices. Another section of the act, Title III, is designed to break down barriers that can isolate disabled people—employees, customers, and others. As described under Title III, these include architectural, transportation, and communication barriers. It means that your operation must be physically accessible to people with disabilities, such as providing wide restroom stalls for people in wheelchairs. You also may need to provide alternate ways of communicating with disabled people. For example, you might provide a braille menu or offer to read the menu to visually impaired customers.

The U.S. Department of Justice, which enforces Title III of the ADA, has developed certain standards to help employers comply with this section. The **Americans with Disabilities Act Accessibility Guidelines for Buildings and Facilities (ADAAG)** publication covers a wide range of areas, from kitchen design to parking facilities, and is designed to help architects, business owners, and other interested parties understand and comply with Title III. These guidelines are complex and are changed periodically. You should consult with an ADA specialist or other appropriate professional to determine any actions your operation needs to take to comply with Title III.

Balancing Needs for Food Safety, Employee Rights, and Legal Compliance

When an employee appears to be sick or discloses that he or she has an illness or disability, the challenge you face is to balance the rights of the employee, the responsibilities of your operation to provide safe food and comply with applicable laws, and the rights of your operation to protect its own interests. The laws that apply in this situation will vary. Depending on the illness, symptoms, or employee disclosure, the Food Code or local health codes could apply, or the ADA could apply. In rare cases where an illness covered by the health code develops into a disability, both the health code and the ADA could apply. Therefore, you need to be clear about your responsibilities as a manager under these regulations and your company's policies for handling these situations. *Exhibit 11i* provides guidelines for responding to various situations involving employee illness and disability.

Although you may be restricted from asking certain questions in certain situations, it is still legal and appropriate to express concern when an employee first tells you he or she is ill or has a disability.

Exhibit 11i

Guidelines for Responding to an Employee Illness or Disability

Situation	Response	Applicable Law
Employee appears to be sick but has not said anything about his or her health.	■ Ask if the employee has any health conditions that may affect his or her ability to safely handle food. ■ Do *not* ask about symptoms that are not related to safe foodhandling (see below) or specific diseases.	Health code ADA
Employee has a sore throat with fever.	■ If your operation primarily serves a high-risk population (people susceptible to illness because of age or a medical condition), exclude the employee from the establishment. ■ If your operation does not primarily serve a high-risk population, restrict the employee from working with or around food.	Health code
Employee has one or more of the following symptoms: ■ Vomiting ■ Diarrhea ■ Jaundice	■ Exclude the employee from the establishment. ■ Do not allow the person to return to work until he or she has been symptom-free for twenty-four hours or has obtained a written release from a medical practitioner (particularly for jaundice).	Health code
Employee has been diagnosed with a foodborne illness caused by one of these pathogens: ■ Salmonella typhi ■ *Shigella* spp. ■ Shiga toxin-producing *E. coli* ■ Hepatitis A virus ■ Norovirus	■ Exclude the employee from the establishment and notify the local regulatory agency. ■ Work with the local regulatory agency to determine when the employee can safely return to work.	Health code
Employee discloses that he or she has a disability (as defined by the ADA).	■ Keep this information confidential unless the employee also has disclosed it to others. ■ Do ask questions about work restrictions to determine what, if any, accommodations are needed. ■ Do *not* ask for a diagnosis or condition. ■ Document any accommodations made, any accommodations denied and why, or that there were none requested at all.	ADA
Employee (or job applicant) requests reasonable accommodation under the ADA.	■ Document the request, the process used to consider it, and your operation's response and reasoning. ■ Keep the information confidential unless the employee has disclosed it to others. (Some disabilities and reasonable accommodation will be apparent.)	ADA

Activity

Using Resources to Answer Questions about the ADA

The EEOC publishes many resources that employers can use to learn about Title I of the ADA. Research the EEOC Web site at *www.eeoc.gov* to answer the following questions.

1 If a disabled employee behaves in a way that would normally result in discipline (including termination) and says the conduct was caused by the disability, does the operation have to excuse the behavior?

_____

2 Can a restaurant or foodservice operation automatically reject a request to use a service animal?

_____

3 If a person with a disability asks for help in applying for a job, does the operation have to provide the help?

_____

4 Does a disabled employee need to say the words "reasonable accommodation" in order for a request to be considered a legitimate request for reasonable accommodation?

_____

Managing Situations Involving a Communicable Disease

In recent years, the public has expressed concern over serious, communicable diseases that can be spread through intimate contact, bodily fluids, or exposure to blood and blood products. In recent years, diseases such as HIV, AIDS, hepatitis B and C, and tuberculosis have provoked particularly fearful and sometimes discriminatory responses. When an employee is ill or disabled because of such a disease, it can be especially challenging to balance the rights, responsibilities, and needs of everyone involved. If your operation employs someone who has a communicable disease, follow your operation's policies and procedures and keep these points in mind:

■ You must maintain the confidentiality of employees who disclose health information, even if an employee reports a foodborne illness. In this case only, you are allowed to notify other employees that they have been exposed to the illness and may need to be tested (in addition to reporting it to the local regulatory agency). Under no circumstances can you divulge the name of the employee who reported the illness.

■ HIV, AIDS, hepatitis B and C, and tuberculosis are considered disabilities under the ADA. Consequently, you may need to provide reasonable accommodation and comply with other aspects of this law. You also have a right to obtain medical information relating to the employee's capability.

■ HIV, AIDS, hepatitis B and C, and tuberculosis cannot be spread through food or casual contact. Therefore, you cannot remove an employee from a foodhandling position on this basis alone.

■ Normal precautions for safe foodhandling, sanitation, and first aid should protect employees, customers, and other visitors from the possible transmission of these diseases.

At times, you also may need to deal with customer concerns over employees they know or suspect may have a communicable disease. In these cases, educate your customers about the steps your operation takes to ensure food is safe and the steps you are required to take to protect everyone's rights. Remind them that you follow local health codes and federal guidelines for dealing with these situations. One set of guidelines you may need to follow is determined by the Occupational Safety and Health Administration (OSHA).

The Role of the Occupational Safety and Health Administration (OSHA)

In response to the number and range of accidents in the workplace, the U.S. Congress enacted the Occupational Safety and Health Act (OSH Act) of 1970 to ensure safe working conditions and prevent workplace injuries. This act also created the **Occupational Safety and Health Administration (OSHA),** an agency within the Department of Labor that enforces the OSH Act and develops detailed regulations and standards. Many states also have created their own occupational safety and health laws and agencies. The state laws are often more stringent than federal laws.

OSHA and state regulations affect many aspects of running a business. They cover nearly every potential danger an employee might encounter and require preventive and protective measures. These regulations are numerous, specific, and cover a wide range of areas. As a manager of a restaurant or foodservice operation, you do not need to know all of these regulations, but you do need to know that safety for employees and customers is a key priority and that failure to provide a safe environment can result in fines, penalties, lawsuits, and imprisonment.

Exhibit 11j

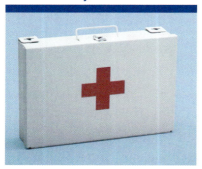

OSHA may require
first-aid providers.

Following OSHA's Bloodborne Pathogens Standard

Given that employees in kitchens work with sharp knives and equipment all the time and may cut themselves, and the perceptions some people have about bloodborne diseases, knowing what to do about blood is essential for you as a manager. To protect people who may have such exposure in the workplace, OSHA has developed a standard for minimizing these risks called the **Bloodborne Pathogens Standard.** While this standard is intended primarily for people who work in healthcare, other organizations also are required to comply if they have a designated first-aid provider. (See *Exhibit 11j.*)

A **designated first-aid provider,** or **first aider,** is an employee appointed to provide first aid; this responsibility should be included in the employee's job description but is not part of the employee's main work. For example, a sous chef could be a designated first aider, but a company nurse could not be. A designated first aider is sometimes required by local law or if certain severe injuries or illnesses can be anticipated in your operation.

If your operation is required to have a designated first aider, it must also follow the Bloodborne Pathogens Standard. Even if your operation is not required by OSHA to follow this standard, voluntarily following it can go a long way toward reducing exposure risks, creating good will with employees, and reducing liability risks. Although the Bloodborne Pathogens Standard sometimes specifies regulations only for designated first aiders, you may want to treat any employee who receives first-aid training according to this standard.

The Bloodborne Pathogens Standard requires the following preventive measures:

- **Exposure plan**—You must provide documented operating procedures to eliminate or minimize employees' exposure to another's blood or other potentially infectious materials. This plan must include provisions for training, annual reviews, and updates.

- **Training**—You must teach designated first aiders how to safely handle this responsibility. Possible training topics include first-aid techniques and certification; ways to avoid or minimize exposure; handling and removal of gloves, clothing, bandages, and laundry; handwashing; emergency phone numbers; cleaning procedures; ways in which bloodborne diseases are transmitted; and how to report an exposure incident.

■ **Personal protective equipment**—You should supply personal protective equipment, such as gloves, waterproof aprons, eye protection, and disposable CPR devices, to covered employees.

If an employee is exposed to another employee's blood in the workplace, the Bloodborne Pathogens Standard requires you to take the following actions:

■ **Hepatitis B vaccination**—Within twenty-four hours after an employee is exposed to potentially infectious materials, counsel the exposed employee and offer to provide a free post-exposure vaccination against hepatitis B. Although this action is only required for designated first aiders, you may wish to consider offering it to any exposed employee.

■ **Medical evaluation**—Arrange for the employee to have a confidential medical evaluation.

■ **Record keeping**—Maintain a record of each occupational exposure to blood.

Activity

Responding to Disclosures of an Employee Illness

Choose an option for completing this activity.

■ Work in threes to role-play the scenarios. For each scenario, one person plays the supervisor, one plays the employee, and one observes and provides feedback. Each person should play each role once.

■ On a separate sheet of paper, describe how you would respond to each of these scenarios to comply with applicable laws. Discuss your answers with the class.

Assume you are the manager of the foodservice department for an assisted living center, where elderly and disabled people live with help from aides and others.

Scenario 1: Lisette, one of your prep cooks, has just cut her finger and dripped blood on her worktable. You are trained in first aid, and the two of you find the first-aid kit so you can help her dress the wound. While you are putting on protective gloves, she tells you to be especially careful because she is HIV positive. How should you respond?

Scenario 2: Victor, one of your servers, calls in before his shift to tell you he has a sore throat and fever. He says he thinks he will feel better later on, but he is calling to tell you because that is company policy. He wants to know if he can come in to work. How should you respond?

Scenario 3: Elena, one of your servers, has called in sick for the third day in a row. During this morning's call, she tells you she was diagnosed with *Salmonella* spp. yesterday. How should you respond?

Exhibit 11k

Top Ten OSHA Violations at Eating and Drinking Places

1 Hazard Communication

2 Personal Protective Equipment, General Requirements

3 Electrical, Wiring Methods, Components and Equipment

4 Portable Fire Extinguishers

5 Walking-Working Surfaces, General Requirements

6 Electrical Systems Design, General Requirements

7 Medical Services and First Aid

8 Sanitation

9 Electrical, Wiring Design and Protection

10 Means of Egress, General

U.S. Department of Labor, Occupational Safety & Health Administration: *"Standards Cited for SIC 5800; All sizes; Federal,"* October 2004–September 2005

Communicating Workplace Hazards to Employees

The Bloodborne Pathogens Standard may be optional for some operations, but all operations must comply with OSHA's standard for communicating information about workplace hazards. The **Hazard Communication Standard (HCS)** is designed to protect employees from both physical hazards, such as explosions, and health hazards, such as medical conditions caused by exposure to chemicals. While you might think a restaurant or foodservice operation is safe from these types of hazards, a violation of the HCS is the most common problem cited by OSHA for eating and drinking places. (See *Exhibit 11k.*)

To comply with the HCS, employers must communicate information about any potential hazards to employees, which involves:

■ Training employees on how to avoid potential hazards

■ Making sure hazardous materials are appropriately labeled

■ Making available the Material Safety Data Sheet (MSDS) for any hazardous material

A **Material Safety Data Sheet (MSDS)** is a document that provides information about the chemical content of a material, instructions for its safe handling, and emergency information on treating someone who has been exposed. (See *Exhibit 11l.*) By law, the manufacturers of potentially hazardous materials must provide MSDSs to their customers, and the customers must make these documents available to their employees. As a manager, you must ensure your suppliers provide your operation with MSDSs when appropriate. You also must ensure that employees know where these documents are, have free access to them, and are trained in how to safely use any hazardous materials.

Not all chemicals used in a restaurant or foodservice operation are considered hazardous materials. OSHA excludes most consumer products, such as window cleaner or toilet bowl cleaner, if the material is used as intended and employees are not exposed to it more frequently than someone using the product in a home environment. If you are not sure whether you need an MSDS for a product, ask the supplier or check with OSHA.

Exhibit 11I

Sample Material Safety Data Sheet

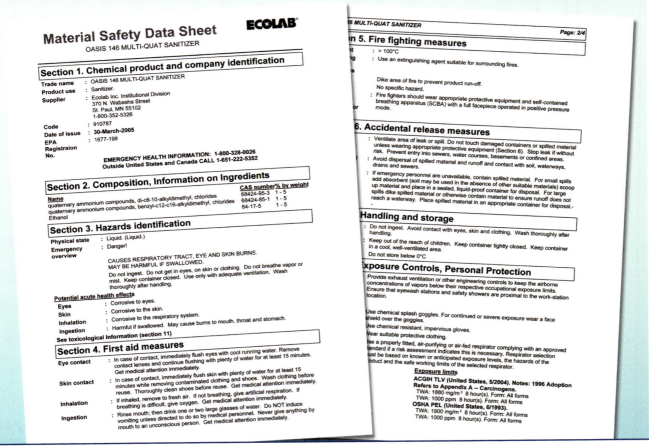

Courtesy of Ecolab, Inc.

Protecting Younger Workers

While OSHA strives to protect all workers, special laws, called **child labor laws,** offer additional protections for children and youth. Unfortunately, **minors**—people younger than eighteen years of age—are much more likely than older workers to be injured in the workplace. To protect minors from unsafe conditions in the workplace and from work schedules that may interfere with their

Exhibit 11m

Risks of Illegally Using Child Labor

- Injuries to youths
- Negative publicity
- Lowered employee morale
- Higher turnover
- Loss of sales
- Fines and imprisonment
- Lawsuits and lawyer and court fees
- Higher insurance costs

education or affect their well-being, various child labor laws have been enacted. The Fair Labor Standards Act (FLSA) of 1938, as amended, established various occupational protections primarily related to wages, but it also established provisions for child labor. Various state and local laws were built on this federal law to offer further protections for minors.

Generally, child labor laws restrict the hours young employees can work and the type of work they can do. Employers who break child labor laws may be fined or even imprisoned. For example, the Department of Labor may impose a fine as high as eleven thousand dollars for each minor illegally employed under the youth employment provisions of the FLSA. Willful violators may even face criminal charges, additional fines, and jail sentences.

As a manager, you have an obligation to provide a safe and legal workplace. In particular, if you break child labor laws, you are risking the health, well-being, and future of your most vulnerable employees—as well as the future of your operation. (See *Exhibit 11m.*)

Job Restrictions for Youth

Under the FLSA, minors cannot be employed in jobs or use equipment deemed hazardous by the Department of Labor. While the restaurant and foodservice industry is not considered hazardous, the FLSA restricts the tasks that minors can perform in restaurant and foodservice operations.

Generally, according to the Department of Labor, sixteen- and seventeen-year-olds can work in front-of-the-house positions but are restricted in the back of the house. Under the FLSA, they cannot operate, feed, set up, adjust, repair, or clean any equipment declared hazardous, such as:

- Power-driven meat processing machines, including meat slicers (even if used to slice cheese or vegetables), meat saws, patty-forming machines, meat grinders, and meat choppers

- Commercial mixers, such as vertical dough and batter mixers, including most countertop models

- Certain power-driven bakery machines, such as dough rollers and dough sheeters

Federal law also prohibits minors from most driving jobs. Sixteen-year-olds cannot drive on the job at all, and seventeen-year-olds are severely restricted in this area. No employee under eighteen years of age is allowed to drive on public roads unless it is only incidental to the job.

Think About It...

According to a survey of states conducted by the Child Labor Coalition, "food preparation (cooking, slicers, bakery machines)" is one of the top five violations of child labor laws related to minors performing prohibited tasks.

If they are at least seventeen and have a valid driver's license, they may drive occasionally with restrictions, such as:

- Cannot make time-sensitive deliveries

- Cannot drive at night

- Cannot ride on a motor vehicle outside the cab

Although fourteen- and fifteen-year-olds also can work in front-of-the-house positions, the work they are allowed to do in other areas is more restricted. According to the Department of Labor, in addition to the restrictions for sixteen- and seventeen-year-olds, fourteen- and fifteen-year-olds cannot:

- Perform any baking tasks, not even weighing ingredients or finishing baked goods

- Operate NEICO broilers, fryolators, rotisseries, or pressure cookers

- Operate, set up, adjust, clean, oil, or repair power-driven food slicers and grinders, food choppers and cutters, and bakery-type mixers

- Work in freezers or meat coolers

However, fourteen- and fifteen-year-olds may:

- Cook with electric and gas grills that do not involve open flames

- Use deep-fat fryers equipped with devices that automatically raise and lower baskets

- Perform kitchen work and other work involved in preparing and serving food and beverages

- Use equipment to do such work, including dishwashers, toasters, dumbwaiters, popcorn poppers, milkshake blenders, coffee grinders, warmers, steam tables, heat lamps, and microwave ovens (if used only to warm prepared food to temperatures at or below 140°F [60°C])

- Clean kitchen surfaces and non-power-driven kitchen equipment when the surfaces and equipment temperatures are not hotter than 100°F (38°C)

- Filter, transport, and dispose of oil and grease when the oil or grease temperature is not hotter than 100°F (38°C)

Generally, child labor laws prohibit children younger than fourteen from any type of work, with some exceptions. Younger children may work in agriculture, which has its own set of child labor law restrictions. In nonagricultural work, they may work for:

- Their parents' business, unless the work involves manufacturing or mining or is classified as a hazardous occupation

- Employers not covered under the laws, such as private homes that hire youths for occasional chores or babysitting

State laws may further restrict the tasks that minors can do or the equipment they can use. However, once a person turns eighteen, the child labor laws no longer apply.

Time Restrictions for Youth

The FLSA and many state laws also restrict the hours that minors can work. According to a Department of Labor survey of child labor compliance by restaurants and grocery stores, violations of these time restrictions accounted for the majority of compliance problems.

Under the FLSA, fourteen- and fifteen-year-olds may work outside school hours for limited periods. *Exhibit 11n* shows these restrictions. The federal government does not limit the hours of sixteen- and seventeen-year-olds. They may even work overtime, and employers must pay them overtime wages the same as they would for anyone else. However, state and local laws may preempt the FLSA in these areas. Check with your state and local departments of labor or seek professional advice.

Exhibit 11n

Federal Restrictions on Hours for Fourteen- and Fifteen-Year-Olds in Nonagricultural Employment

Limits	When School Is in Session	When School Is *Not* in Session
Total hours	Not more than three hours per school day (including Friday) and eighteen hours per week	Not more than eight hours per day and forty hours per week
Time of day	From the day after Labor Day to May 31: not before 7 a.m. or after 7 p.m.	From June 1 to Labor Day: not before 7 a.m. or after 9 p.m.

You also should know if there are other regulations or restrictions that affect the employment of minors. For example, most states require that minors provide employers with a work permit or age certificate as a condition of employment. Depending on the state, these documents may be issued by the local school district or a government labor department.

Ensuring Adequate Breaks

Another occupational area that is controlled by the states is the frequency and length of breaks. Breaks allow employees a brief period of rest to help them remain focused in their work. They also show that employers care about and respect employees' needs. Although most state labor laws require employers to give employees breaks after working a certain length of time, many restaurant and foodservice operations provide for more generous breaks. A common arrangement in the industry is:

- Fifteen-minute break for every four hours of work

- Thirty-minute break for a six-hour shift

- Two fifteen-minute breaks and a thirty-minute meal break for an eight-hour shift

As a manager, you should be familiar with the breaks required by law in your community and thoroughly understand your operation's break policy. This knowledge will help you ensure that employees receive the breaks they need to stay productive and that the break policy is not abused. In addition, since most operations pay their employees while they are on break, you should keep both your operation's break policy and meal policy in mind when you create work schedules. If you schedule work to minimize breaks and meals—while following applicable policies and laws—you can reduce your operation's costs.

Working with Unions

Over the course of the last century, unions have heavily influenced regulations for breaks and most other fair labor practices in this country. Originally created to win basic rights and protections from powerful employers, **unions** are organizations designated by employees to negotiate their employment terms, such as wages, benefits, discipline, and job security. In the restaurant and foodservice industry, the percentage of employees who belong to unions is smaller than the national average. (See *Exhibit 11o* on the next page.)

Exhibit 11o

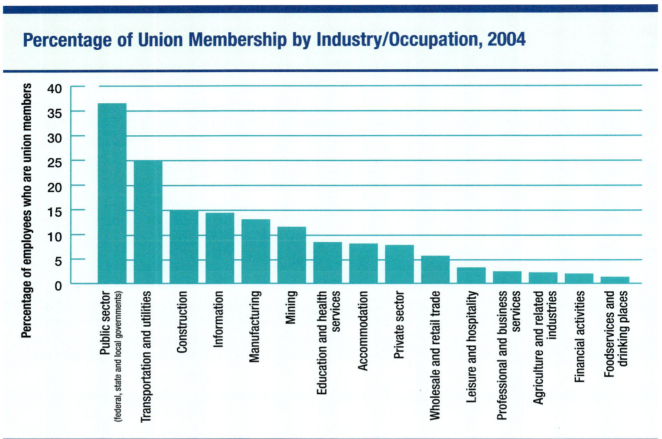

Percentage of Union Membership by Industry/Occupation, 2004

Source: Bureau of Labor Statistics *www.bls.gov*

The Role of Unions

In operations that have unions, employees may be required to join the union, depending on the agreement between the union and the employer. Workplaces where employees must join the union are known as union shops. Employees who join unions must pay **union dues**—fees to help pay for the administration of the union. They also are entitled to elect their union representatives.

The terms of employment that a union negotiates for its members are written into an employment agreement or **labor contract** with the employer. Labor contracts are written for a specific time period, typically two or more years. When a labor contract is set to expire, union and company representatives often renegotiate the terms of the contract; this process is called **collective bargaining.** Once a new contract is written, the union members must vote to approve or reject it. Ironically, in some establishments, the employment terms negotiated for union members automatically apply to some nonunion members. For example, the wages, benefits, and other terms of a labor contract negotiated for union dishwashers and bussers will also apply to nonunion dishwashers and bussers.

If a contract is rejected, the union may call a **strike**—an order to all union members at one or more locations to stop working. Strikes also may be called at other times to protest other situations or conditions, which often begin as grievances.

Grievances are complaints filed against an employer for breaking the terms of the labor contract. They may be filed by an individual and escalated as needed by the union or filed by the union on behalf of all its members. When an individual files a grievance, the complaint is handled through a process defined by the labor contract. Often the first step is for the employee, the employee's supervisor, and a union representative called a **union steward** to meet and try to resolve the grievance. If the grievance cannot be resolved at this level, the issue is escalated to higher levels of management and union representation. Unresolved grievances are eventually escalated to a third party called an **arbitrator** or **mediator** who settles the problem.

Understanding Your Responsibilities and Limits

Given the problems that can result from grievances, managers in union operations need to fully understand their employees' labor contracts and the laws that control union-employer relations. If you are one of these managers, you need to understand in detail how the labor contract affects the way you deal with employees. The terms of a labor contract are usually broad. In your day-to-day interactions with union employees, the contract may determine, for example, the schedules you create, the way you train employees, the promotions you make, the way you communicate job postings and other information, the way you discipline or terminate employees, and other aspects of how you interact with employees.

Regardless of the procedures you must follow to comply with the labor contract, you will want to build good relationships with your employees, whether they are supervisors, union leaders, or regular employees. Make sure these relationships include open communication—something especially important with union leaders. The better the relationships you can create with all employees, the more effective you will be as a manager.

You also need to understand the laws that affect how you and your operation interact with union employees and representatives. One of the oldest and most important acts that legislates union and employer interactions is the National Labor Relations Act (NLRA) of 1935. This act, which is also known the Wagner Act, established the National Labor Relations Board to enforce its provisions, including:

Exhibit 11p

Employees can choose to join a union.

- The right of employees to join—or not join—a union

- The right of employees to have their union negotiate a labor contract on their behalf

- The requirement that employers and unions **bargain in good faith**—make a genuine attempt to reach agreement during negotiations

To comply with the NLRA, employers cannot prevent employees from joining or forming unions or engaging in a group activity to change working conditions. (See *Exhibit 11p.*) Employers cannot use threats, coercion, or discriminatory work practices to try to dissuade employees from union activity. They also cannot attempt to influence union operations, such as by bribing union leaders. Finally, as with many employment laws, employers cannot punish or discriminate against employees who exercise their rights or file charges under the law.

Within twelve years of passing the NLRA, the U.S. Congress amended it with the Labor-Management Relations Act of 1947, also known as the Taft-Hartley Act. This act provides certain rights to employers and employees when dealing with unions and puts limits on union actions. Among its many provisions, the act prohibits unions from requiring job applicants to join the union as a condition of employment, unless the union has this arrangement in their labor contract, and prohibits unions from coercing employees to join the union. The act allows managers to talk to employees about the pros and cons of union membership but does not allow managers to threaten or bribe employees to influence their decision to join a union.

Providing Adequate Notice of Closings and Layoffs

Another labor law that was influenced by unions is the Worker Adjustment and Retraining Notification Act (WARN) of 1988. This law was enacted to provide time for workers and communities to prepare themselves for plant closings or mass **layoffs**—terminations due to economic factors or reasons other than performance. Generally, the law requires private sector employers with one hundred or more employees to provide employees and certain government officials with sixty days' notice if they are planning to close the business or lay off a large number of employees. This number may vary based on an employer's total number of employees and the time frame for the layoffs.

Advance notice must be given to:

- All hourly employees or, if applicable, their union representatives

- Supervisors and managers

- The local chief elected official, such as the mayor or county supervisor

- State dislocated worker unit

State dislocated worker units are state government agencies created by Title III of the Job Training Partnership Act. When there are layoffs or closings that affect many workers, these agencies step in to help workers with job retraining and placement services.

General Guidelines for Complying with Laws

Although federal, state, and local laws deal with many aspects of employment, many of them have several rules in common. To protect your operation from liability and to ensure employees' rights, you should comply with these general guidelines:

- **Follow your operation's policies and practices.** The policies and practices of most companies are based on applicable laws.

- **Keep current on workplace laws.** Laws and regulations vary by location, and they change. Keep your knowledge of workplace laws up-to-date by working with your human resources department or developing your own resources.

- **Monitor employees for compliance.** As a manager, you are responsible for what your employees do on the job. Watch what they do to ensure they follow all policies, procedures, and applicable laws.

- **Provide an "open door" for employees.** Make sure employees know they can come to you with their issues, and when they do, respond in a timely and professional manner.

- **Allow employees to exercise their rights.** Many laws contain provisions to ensure that employees are protected when they:

  - Request or exercise their rights under a law

  - Report a violation or possible violation (these employees are commonly called **whistleblowers**)

  - Complain about behavior or practices that may be illegal

Exhibit 11q

Federal Agencies and Acts That Require Posters

- Equal Employment Opportunity Commission (EEOC)

- Occupational Safety & Health Administration (OSHA)

- Employee Polygraph Protection Act (EPPA)

- Fair Labor Standards Act (FLSA)

- Family and Medical Leave Act (FMLA)

- Uniformed Services Employment and Reemployment Rights Act (USERRA)

☐ May be a witness to a violation

☐ May be a family member or friend of a person who reported a violation or who is a possible witness

- **Post required notices.** Several federal and many state laws require you to post notices in the workplace (see *Exhibit 11q*). Some of these laws have already been discussed; others will be discussed in more detail in Chapter 12. If a large number of your employees speak another language, you may need to display posters in that language as well.

- **Keep accurate records.** Keep records required by law and documents that may reduce your operation's risks of liability. For example, keep new hire paperwork, disciplinary action records, performance reviews, and timecards.

Summary

Laws impact every area of a restaurant or foodservice operation, from the safety and accessibility of the physical environment to the way you treat every person and most products that come into your operation. Given this broad impact and the importance of complying with laws, you as a manager need to have a clear understanding of how the laws affect your operation. Fortunately, the policies and procedures of most operations closely follow the laws. To reduce the possibility of legal problems, you should follow your operation's policies and procedures and keep abreast of changes in the law.

One of your most important responsibilities is to ensure that the food your operation serves is safe to eat. As part of this, you need to thoroughly understand food sanitation laws and your responsibility as a manager to develop and maintain a food safety management system, provide adequate training for employees, and routinely perform self-inspections to ensure your products are safe.
In addition, if you have a quality food and safety system in place, you will be more able to defend your operation in case of a food-related lawsuit.

You also need to ensure that your operation complies with local alcohol service regulations and employees are clear on their own responsibilities under these laws. Employees who serve alcohol should know how to do this responsibly, and all employees should know what to do if a customer becomes intoxicated. These responsibilities are essential for protecting the customers, the community, and your operation.

Other protections are offered to employees through various antidiscrimination laws. Title VII of the Civil Rights Act prohibits sexual harassment, the Pregnancy Discrimination Act protects the rights of pregnant women, and the Americans with Disabilities Act prohibits discrimination based on a disability. If someone in your operation tells you they are being harassed, you need to take prompt action to correct the situation and enforce your operation's policies.

When an employee reports an illness or disability, or is injured at work, this situation can be complex. The local health code, the ADA, and possibly OSHA's Bloodborne Pathogens Standard may cover a particular situation, so you need to understand how to handle it. If employees are exposed to blood in the workplace, you need to ensure not only that the injured employee receives adequate first aid, but also that first-aid providers and other employees know how to safely handle blood.

OSHA has many standards to protect employees on the job. One of these is the Hazard Communication Standard, which requires employers to communicate information about any potential hazards to employees, to label hazardous chemicals, and to make Material Safety Data Sheets available to employees. This OSHA standard is the one most often violated in the restaurant and foodservice industry.

Special workplace protections are required for employees who are minors. Child labor laws restrict the tasks and hours for minors. You should be familiar with these restrictions for your area.

State laws also require that you give breaks to all employees if they work a certain amount of time. These requirements vary, but certain break practices are common in the restaurant and foodservice industry.

Union labor contracts also may specify break times and other workplace practices and conditions. If your operation has union employees, you need to thoroughly understand the labor contracts in your establishment to avoid causing any grievances. You also should have a general understanding of the laws that restrict employers and unions when employees are deciding whether to become union members. However, in union shops, employees must become union members within a certain period after they are hired.

General guidelines for complying with laws include following your operation's policies and practices, keeping current on workplace laws, monitoring employees for compliance, providing an "open door" for employees, allowing employees to exercise their rights, keeping accurate records, and posting required notices.

Review Your Learning

1 **Which statement best describes a manager's main responsibility regarding alcohol service?**

A. Monitor bar tabs to identify guests who should no longer be served.

B. Check that bartenders adequately control drink portions.

C. Have intoxicated guests sign a waiver before they leave.

D. Ensure that employees understand their responsibilities under the law.

2 **Which statement is an example of sexual harassment?**

A. An employee asks a coworker to meet after work for a drink.

B. An employee opens a door for another employee.

C. An employee tells off-color jokes after being asked not to.

D. A customer repeatedly compliments an employee on his or her good service.

3 **Which statement best describes how to comply with OSHA's Hazard Communication Standard?**

A. Ensure that only consumer-grade chemicals are used at work and Material Data Safety Sheets are posted where employees will see them.

B. Ensure that chemicals are properly labeled and Material Data Safety Sheets are available to employees.

C. Ensure that vendors supply the required Material Data Safety Sheets and inventory records for hazardous chemicals are kept on file.

D. Ensure that employees know how to properly store chemicals around food and hazardous chemicals are not used in food preparation areas.

4 **In what areas do child labor laws affect restaurant and foodservice operations?**

A. Wages and breaks

B. Scheduling and work assignments

C. Age discrimination policies and employee benefits

D. Employee morale and payroll

5 **Which areas in restaurant and foodservice operations are most affected by the Americans with Disabilities Act?**

A. Medical leaves of absence and undue hardship

B. Reasonable access if requested and procedures for handling blood

C. All employment decisions and access to the building and services

D. Reasonable accommodation and equal access to promotions and employee benefits

6 **What is the purpose of the Worker Adjustment and Retraining Notification Act?**

A. To give employees, communities, and state agencies notice of mass layoffs or business closings, so employees can prepare for and find new jobs

B. To adjust and retrain employees who lose their jobs through mass layoffs or business closings, so they can warn their new employers

C. To warn surrounding communities and state agencies of mass layoffs or business closings, so other businesses can prepare recruiting plans

D. To comply with labor contracts in companies that have unions

7 **Which action is the best way to prevent sexual harassment?**

A. Make sure employees do not go out together after work.

B. Post a notice stating that no sexual harassment claims are allowed.

C. Stop any flirting or joking you see and document the incident.

D. Monitor the environment for inappropriate interactions and postings.

8 **What is the best way to avoid a union grievance?**

A. Follow the labor contract in all situations.

B. Do not coerce employees into rejecting union membership.

C. Only communicate with employees through their union leaders.

D. Provide sixty days notice of layoffs.

9 **Which is *not* a general guideline for complying with workplace laws?**

A. Monitor employees for compliance.

B. Keep accurate records.

C. Avoid asking about possible violations.

D. Follow your operation's policies and practices.

Notes

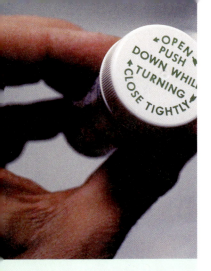

Ensuring Employee Benefits and Compensation

12

Inside This Chapter

- Basics of Employee Benefit Plans
- Types of Employee Benefits
- Common Voluntary Benefits
- Complying with Retirement and Health Benefit Laws
- Ensuring Mandatory Benefits
- Keeping Current on Benefits and Related Laws
- Ensuring Legal Wages
- Ensuring Accurate Compensation
- Controlling Labor Costs

After completing this chapter, you should be able to:

- List and explain voluntary employee benefits common in the restaurant and foodservice industry.

- Give examples of ways to manage the costs of meal and uniform benefits.

- Recognize employer and plan administrator actions to comply with ERISA.

- Recognize employer and plan administrator actions to comply with COBRA.

- Recognize plan administrator actions to comply with HIPAA.

- List and explain mandatory employee benefits.

- Recognize employer actions to comply with FMLA.

- Recognize employer actions to comply with USERRA.

- Describe the tip credit provision of the FLSA.

- Describe ways to manage payroll administration.

- Describe ways to investigate wages paid in your labor market.

- Explain several strategies for controlling overtime in a restaurant or foodservice operation.

Test Your Knowledge

1 **True or False:** An employee's healthcare benefits always end on the employee's last day of work. *(See p. 329.)*

2 **True or False:** Employees can take an unpaid leave of absence for a serious medical condition and still keep their jobs. *(See pp. 339–340.)*

3 **True or False:** The federal and state governments require employers to offer certain benefits. *(See p. 336.)*

4 **True or False:** An employee assistance program is like a company-sponsored savings and loan company just for employees. *(See p. 323.)*

5 **True or False:** Unemployment insurance is a form of long-term aid for people who are chronically unemployed. *(See p. 337.)*

Key Terms

Annuities

Beneficiary

Certificate of creditable coverage

Compensation package

Consolidated Omnibus Budget Reconciliation Act (COBRA)

Conventional indemnity plans

Deductible

Defined benefit (DB)

Defined contribution (DC)

Employee assistance programs (EAPs)

Employee benefit plan

Employee Retirement Income Security Act of 1974 (ERISA)

Enrollment

Exclusion period

Family and Medical Leave Act (FMLA)

Fee-for-service plans

Flexible spending accounts (FSAs)

Garnishments

Group plan

Health Insurance Portability and Accountability Act (HIPAA)

Health maintenance organizations (HMOs)

Health savings accounts (HSAs)

Individual plan

Leave of absence

Levies

Life events

Look-back period

Mandated

Medicare

Open enrollment period

Overtime

Participant

Payroll administrator

Payroll system

Pensions

Person hour

Plan administrator

Plan provider

Preexisting condition

Preferred provider organizations (PPOs)

Premium

Primary care physicians

Qualified beneficiary

Qualified plan

Self-insured

Serious medical condition

Service

Social Security

Special enrollment
  periods

Subminimum wage

Summary annual report

Summary of material
  modification (SMM)

Summary plan description
  (SPD)

Tax deferred

Tip allocation

Tipped employees

Tipped employees' minimum
  wage

Traditional health insurance

Unemployment insurance

Uniformed Services
  Employment and
  Reemployment Rights Act

Vested

Workers' compensation

Youth minimum wage

Introduction

In the past, it was common that cooks and dining room staff did not have healthcare benefits, retirement benefits, or paid vacation. That has all changed as the industry has grown, and finding and keeping good employees has become increasingly more difficult. A good compensation package—a combination of benefits, wages, and incentives—can be a powerful way to encourage people to apply for work at a restaurant or foodservice operation and, if offered a job, to join an operation.

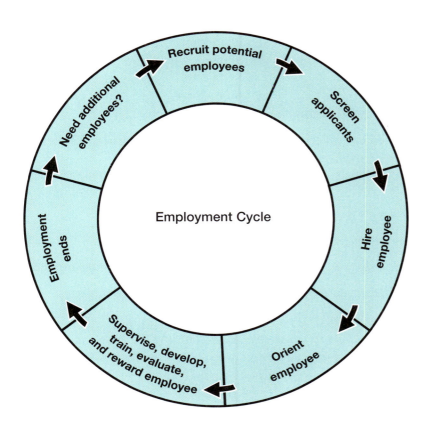

Good benefits, in particular, also make a big difference in the way that potential applicants and current employees perceive their employer. Offering benefits shows that you care about the employees and want them to be happy and focused at work. (For more information about factors that motivate employees, see Chapter 6.)

While good benefits can help recruit and win over new employees, the administration of benefits can impact several areas in the employment cycle, as shown in the graphic on the left. Once a new employee is hired, your operation has a responsibility to explain the benefits and provide written plan information to the new hire. Throughout an employee's time at your operation, the operation is responsible for continuing to communicate certain information about some types of benefits and helping the employee take advantage of the benefits. When an employee temporarily or permanently leaves an operation, he or she may be entitled by law to certain benefits in some situations.

The administration of employee benefits and compensation can be very complex. In many operations, especially larger ones, the human resources department administers the benefits and helps management comply with applicable laws, and the payroll department administers the payroll. In smaller operations that do not have these departments, consultants, contractors, or outside agencies may provide these services, or owners or managers may fill these roles themselves.

Regardless of the support your operation may provide, as a manager, you need to understand your operation's payroll procedures, the benefits offered by your operation, and the federal, state, and local laws and company policies that affect the payroll and benefits. This understanding enables you to comply with the laws and company policies, help employees take advantage of their benefits, and manage the payroll and benefits in a cost-effective, fair manner.

Because of these important roles, you need to be familiar with your company's specific benefit plans and payroll procedures. You also should know the company policies and legal requirements for these areas. For each type of benefit plan your operation offers, you should be able to answer the following questions:

- What does the plan cover?

- Who is eligible for the plan?

- When can an employee enroll in the plan or choose different plan options?

- How does an employee enroll in the plan or make changes to it?

- How much does the plan cost an employee?

- For what period does the plan stay in effect?

- How does an employee obtain benefits when they are needed?

- What are an employee's responsibilities under the plan?

While the benefits offered at different operations will vary, many plans have traits in common. Understanding the basics of employee benefit plans, particularly the terminology, will help you better understand your own operation's benefits.

Basics of Employee Benefit Plans

An **employee benefit plan,** or plan for short, is a program that describes the non-wage compensation or services an employee is eligible to receive and the circumstances under which the employee will receive them. For example, a retirement plan provides a certain monetary benefit to an employee in exchange for a certain length of **service**—days or time spent at work.

When an employee signs up for a benefit plan, this is called **enrollment.** Employees often are entitled to enroll in benefit plans as soon as they are hired. After that, the **plan provider**—the company offering the benefit, such as an insurance company—limits the times during which employees can change their plan or their coverage under a plan. This limited time is known as an **open enrollment period,** and it varies by provider, plan, and employer. During open enrollment, some of the options for an employee are changing plans, changing coverage, and adding or removing family members. For healthcare plans, federal law requires that plan providers allow people to make changes when certain **life events**—events that change a family—occur, such as birth, adoption, marriage, divorce, or death.

Depending on the benefit and the plan, the people who receive the benefit may be employees or former employees, or their family members, former spouses, or friends. For example, an employee who retires is a former employee who may receive a benefit in the form of a pension. Similarly, if a retiree who has a pension dies, his or her spouse may be entitled to continue receiving the pension. To distinguish among the people who have an interest in a benefit plan, two main terms are used:

- A **participant** is someone who is a member of a plan.

- A **beneficiary** is someone who is entitled to receive a benefit under a plan.

In general, a beneficiary is entitled to receive a benefit because of his or her relationship with a participant. (See *Exhibit 12a.*) For example, an employee may be a participant in a healthcare plan, while his or her child may be a beneficiary in the plan. Or a beneficiary may be someone designated to receive a benefit if the participant dies. For example, for retirement plans, life insurance plans, and other plans where the benefit is money, the beneficiary will usually receive the money that the participant is entitled to if the participant dies before getting the entire benefit. Depending on the plan, the participant may name the beneficiary, such as a family member or friend, or the plan may specify the beneficiary, such as a spouse.

Exhibit 12a

A beneficiary may be a family member.

315

As you may realize, there are many categories of employee benefit plans, and within each of these categories, there are more variations. One way to categorize plans is by the number of people in the plan. A **group plan** provides essentially the same benefit to multiple people, such as a life insurance plan offered to all employees in a company, or a healthcare plan offered to all employees in a union. Most employee and union benefit plans are group plans.

An **individual plan** provides a benefit for one person or one family. Most plans purchased outside of the workplace are individual plans. For example, an individual might buy a life insurance policy from an independent insurance agent who is not affiliated with an employer or union. Generally, individual plans cost more to join than group plans. The difference between group and individual plans is important to understand primarily in discussions on healthcare plans, where the costs and administration requirements can differ greatly based on this distinction.

Because understanding such distinctions has legal implications, it takes a lot of specialized knowledge to administer plans. Therefore, for most types of plans, federal law requires a designated person or entity to be responsible for handling the administrative tasks for a plan, such as processing forms and communicating notices. This person or group of people is known as the **plan administrator.** A plan administrator may be a person, a department, or a company. For example, in some operations, the human resources department or specific employees are the plan administrators. In other operations, the insurance company that provides the plan or a third-party firm is the plan administrator. This arrangement is the most common situation in small operations. In other cases, the employer may be considered the plan administrator, even though only certain individuals within the company handle the paperwork.

Types of Employee Benefits

As a manager who needs to help employees understand their benefits, you may find it helpful to have a general understanding of various benefits, even those not offered by your operation. Knowing the different types of benefits provides a foundation for understanding your own operation's benefits and for helping to clarify benefits for your employees, especially those who may confuse information on your operation's benefits with information they have learned elsewhere.

All employers who meet certain conditions are **mandated** or required by the federal and state governments to provide certain benefits, such as Social Security. However, many employers in the restaurant and foodservice industry also voluntarily offer other benefits, which can vary widely from operation to operation.

Even within the same operation, the benefits voluntarily given to employees can vary based on whether the employees are exempt or nonexempt, part-time or full-time, or other factors. *Exhibit 12b* lists the types of benefits that companies may offer their employees and indicates with an asterisk (*) the benefits that are mandated by the federal and state governments.

Exhibit 12b

Descriptions of Employee Benefits

Type of Benefit	Description
Bonuses	Extra pay is given to employees in the form of a lump sum, usually awarded annually or periodically. Bonuses are often tied to incentive programs and given as rewards for good individual or company performance.
Child and dependent care	Some employers provide daycare facilities or establish flexible spending accounts (see below) that employees can use to pay for child or dependent care costs.
Death benefits	Death benefits may include life insurance and can also consist of a small payment to help with funeral costs for an employee or other compensation for the employees' beneficiaries.
Dental insurance	This insurance pays for the cost of some or most dental care. Orthodontic work and other specialized coverage may or may not be included.
Disability benefits	Disability benefits vary widely and have different labels: short-term disability, long-term disability, and disability. These benefits provide a basic—usually reduced—level of income when the employee cannot work because of a medical condition. See Workers' compensation on p. 319.
Educational and professional development support	This benefit includes such things as tuition and training reimbursement, apprenticeship programs, and professional organization membership dues. This benefit is often associated with a formal educational course or degree program. Some companies require that employees obtain a passing grade of C or better to be eligible for this benefit.
Employee assistance programs (EAPs)	These programs are designed to help employees deal with mental health issues and personal problems, such as substance abuse, emotional difficulties, and financial problems. Large companies may have an in-house staff that provides this assistance, while smaller companies may contract with outside services or provide referrals. A later section contains more information on these programs.
Family and medical leave*	Employees are entitled to take an unpaid leave of absence and return to the same or similar job if the leave is taken for certain medical reasons or family situations. The circumstances, duration of the leave, and job protection are defined under the Family Medical Leave Act (FMLA), which is discussed in more detail in a later section.
Flexible spending accounts (FSAs)	Flexible spending accounts (FSAs) are special savings accounts set up by employers and owned by employees. FSAs enable employees to contribute pretax income to these accounts, which can only be used to pay for healthcare costs not covered by health insurance, or for child or dependent care (depending on the type of FSA). These accounts are discussed in more detail in a later section.

continued on next page

*Government mandated benefit

continued from previous page

Type of Benefit	Description
Funeral or bereavement leave	Employees may be given paid time off to make funeral arrangements for an immediate family member or to attend the funeral.
Health savings accounts (HSAs)	Health savings accounts (HSAs) are special savings accounts set up by employers and owned by employees who have healthcare plans with large deductibles. HSAs enable employees to contribute pretax income to these accounts, which can be used only to pay for healthcare costs not covered by a health plan. These accounts are discussed in more detail in a later section.
Healthcare coverage after termination*	The Consolidated Omnibus Budget Reconciliation Act (COBRA) requires optional healthcare coverage to be offered to some employees after employment ends. More information on this act follows.
Healthcare plans	Healthcare plans pay for some medical expenses. Typically, employers pay for some of the monthly cost or premium for this benefit, and employees pay the rest. Healthcare plans and the situations they cover vary widely. More information on these plans is given in a later section.
Life insurance	Life insurance provides money to a deceased employee's beneficiaries to help replace the income the employee would have earned if he or she were alive. Claim amounts are often based on the employee's earnings; for example, a life insurance policy with a claim worth two years of earnings.
Long-term care insurance	Long-term care insurance pays for long-term nursing care or at-home healthcare when employees are not able to take care of themselves.
Meals	Most restaurant and foodservice operations provide free or discounted meals to employees as a fringe benefit. Some companies in other industries also provide this benefit.
Mental health insurance	Mental health insurance covers the costs of psychotherapy, psychiatric treatment, family and couples counseling, and other costs related to mental healthcare.
Military leave*	Employees are entitled to take an unpaid leave of absence and return to the same or similar job, including benefits and anticipated promotions, if the leave is taken to fulfill military service obligations. The circumstances, duration of the leave, and job protection are defined under the Uniformed Services Employment and Reemployment Rights Act (USERRA), which is discussed in more detail in a later section.
Paid holidays	Some companies pay employees for workdays that fall on holidays during which the operation is closed. This practice is not common for restaurant and foodservice operations because many are open on major holidays. However, some employers pay higher wages for working on holidays, such as paying time and a half, as a reward for working or to fulfill union contracts.
Paid vacation	Many companies offer paid time off for vacations. Usually, vacation time accrues, or accumulates, based on how long an employee has worked for the company and how much vacation time he or she is entitled to receive. For example, if an employee were allowed ten paid days of vacation per year, the vacation time would accrue at the rate of .83 days per month. Often, after working a certain number of years, employees are given additional vacation time.

*Government-mandated benefit

Type of Benefit	Description
Pension and retirement plans	Pension and retirement plans ensure that an employee has income other than Social Security when he or she retires because of old age or a permanent disability. These plans are discussed in more detail in a later section.
Personal time off	Like vacation time, personal time off, frequently called personal days, often accrues based on how long an employee has worked for a company. Personal time off is becoming more common, replacing other specific types of paid time off, such as funeral leave or religious holidays.
Profit-sharing plans	Profit-sharing plans are programs that provide special payments to an individual employee's profit-sharing account. The employer contributes a set amount to each employee's account; usually, the amount is a percentage of the company's annual profits. The money is typically distributed to an employee at retirement, year-end, or termination. However, in some plans, an employee can make an early withdrawal under certain circumstances.
Religious holidays	Some organizations allow employees to take days off to observe a religious holiday. However, it is more common for employees to use their vacation or personal days for religious holidays.
Social Security*	Social Security is a federal pension program designed to ensure a minimum level of income for retirees and disabled people. Employers and employees fund this program through payroll taxes. There is more information about this in a later section.
Stock option plans	Stock option plans are offers made by an employer to sell company stock to employees at a certain price in the future. This offer gives employees the chance to buy company stock at a reduced rate. For example, if a plan offers employees the chance to buy stock at five dollars a share within the next ten years, and the actual stock price rises to twelve dollars a share during that time, the employee can still buy shares for five dollars each.
Unemployment insurance*	Unemployment insurance is a federal requirement to make sure that employees who lose their jobs under certain circumstances still receive some income. The amount paid for an unemployment claim is based on the employee's former salary. More information on this program follows.
Uniforms	Operations that require uniforms or have dress codes that require specialized clothing often provide uniforms or reimburse employees in part or in full for this cost. More information on this benefit follows.
Vision care	Vision or eye care is sometimes included in healthcare coverage or can be chosen by the employee at an extra cost.
Workers' compensation*	Workers' compensation insurance pays a set benefit and medical expenses to an employee who becomes injured or disabled while working. This insurance varies by state, and most states also require workers' compensation to cover any diseases an employee develops because of a work environment. More information on this benefit follows.

*Government-mandated benefit

Common Voluntary Benefits

In the restaurant and foodservice industry, some of the more common voluntary benefits offered by employers include uniforms, meals, healthcare plans, employee assistance programs, and retirement benefits.

Exhibit 12c

Uniforms can provide a professional appearance.

Uniform Benefits

In an industry that relies heavily on customer impressions of service, ambience, and cleanliness, uniforms and dress codes provide a professional look. (See *Exhibit 12c*.) Therefore, operations often provide full or partial uniforms for their employees or reimburse them for purchasing their own uniforms.

Uniform benefits vary by operation and job. For example, some operations supply their cooks with jackets, but the cooks buy their own pants and shoes. In other cases, the operation provides the shoes or shares the cost of the shoes with employees. Front-of-the-house employees often are expected to supply their own black pants, skirts, or other appropriate wear while the restaurant provides the shirts, ties, vests, coats, or polo shirts, depending on the nature of the operation. To ensure a clean, crisp, and uniform look in employee attire, some operations also provide laundry service for employee uniforms.

As a manager, you should understand your company's dress code and uniform benefit policies. You should be able to explain the dress code and uniform benefits, tell employees why the dress code and uniforms are important, and identify when employee dress is not up to code.

While uniform benefits can be costly, the positive customer impressions they provide can far outweigh the costs. In addition, uniforms may provide some measure of personal protection. In the back of the house, for example, closed-toe shoes protect feet from dropped knives, hot liquids, and other dangers, while shortened jacket sleeves without cuffs help protect people from setting their sleeves on fire, snagging them on hot cookware and moving equipment, or trapping hot spills next to their skin. Even when employees are expected to buy uniforms that comply with a dress code, sometimes it is less costly to provide the uniforms than to pay for the consequences of even one serious workplace accident. When an employee is seriously injured at work, the employer not only loses that employee's valuable labor, but also may have to pay a workers' compensation claim, including medical costs, and report the accident to the government. There is also the possibility that an injured employee could sue the employer.

Even so, the day-to-day costs of uniform benefits can add up, and you should be aware of these costs and look for ways to reduce them. For example, you might periodically take bids on the uniform and laundry contracts to ensure you are receiving the best value.

Meal Benefits

In addition to uniforms, most restaurant and foodservice operations provide meal benefits to at least some of their employees. Company meal benefits can differ widely. Some operations provide meals to employees as part of the job; others charge them for meals, often at a subsidized rate; and others provide no meals at all. Meal benefits are often restricted to specific positions. For example, kitchen and dining room employees are usually fed, while receiving, cleaning, reservations, and office staff members are not. In other situations, the size of the operation or a union contract determines the meal policy.

As a manager, it is your responsibility to learn the meal policy, enforce it, and be able to explain it clearly to employees. Enforcing the meal policy helps to control costs. Other ways to reduce or control costs associated with meal benefits include:

- Setting a budget for the person providing the meals

- Providing a meal allowance for employees

- Managing the schedule to reduce the number of people eligible for meals

Exhibit 12d

Healthcare benefits may cover various medical costs.

Healthcare Plans

While not as common in the restaurant and foodservice industry as meal plans or uniforms, healthcare plans are offered by many employers to attract and keep employees. These healthcare plans can vary greatly. They can include (or exclude) routine examinations, medical tests, radiological services, surgery, hospital and emergency care, physical therapy, preventive care, vision care, mental healthcare, dental care, and prescriptions. (See *Exhibit 12d*.) Typically, employers offer two or more group healthcare plans from which their employees can choose, and both employers and employees share the cost of the **premium,** or monthly fee. An employee's portion of the healthcare costs can vary drastically based on the plan, coverage options, location, and employer's contribution.

When healthcare benefits are offered, they are generally one of these types of plans:

- **Fee-for-service plans**—These plans are administered by insurance companies that directly pay service providers (physicians, hospitals, etc.) or reimburse the plan participants.

321

These plans are also known as **traditional health insurance** or **conventional indemnity plans.** In this type of plan, participants choose their own service providers and are not limited to certain service providers. The plan pays for any covered service performed by any qualified service provider. Participants usually have higher out-of-pocket costs—the amount they pay for each service—than with other types of plans.

■ **Preferred provider organizations (PPOs)**—PPO plans are managed care plans in which service providers discount the cost of their service in exchange for more patients and timely payment. Participants are given financial incentives for choosing service providers who are part of their PPO plan network. As long as the service providers are part of the network, participants' out-of-pocket costs are usually lower with PPO plans than with fee-for-service plans.

■ **Health maintenance organizations (HMOs)**—The cost of healthcare through an HMO is almost entirely prepaid through premiums, and service providers are part of the HMO. Typically, participants must choose HMO service providers or pay for all or a large part of the service themselves. Before seeing a physician who is a specialist, such as an allergist or dermatologist, HMOs usually require that participants go through their **primary care physicians,** who typically are general practitioners or internists, to get a referral. However, service provided by HMO service providers is often fully covered, so participants usually have minimal out-of-pocket expenses.

With these plans, employers pay a fee to the insurance company, HMO, or PPO, and the employers share the healthcare costs covered under the plan with the plan provider. However, some employers are **self-insured,** meaning they insure their employees and pay all of the covered healthcare costs. Self-insurance is more common in large companies than it is in smaller companies. Some self-insured companies also pay a third party to process the claims and other paperwork.

In most companies that offer healthcare benefits, employees can choose from two or more types of plans. The offered plans usually cost different amounts and provide different types of coverage. In addition, employees often can add family members to their plan at extra cost.

To help employees cover their portion of medical costs and encourage employees to use their healthcare benefits wisely, some companies offer optional savings plans, such as **Flexible Spending Accounts (FSAs)** or **Health Savings Accounts (HSAs).** These special accounts allow employees to contribute a certain amount of income before taxes to their individual account, which can be used only to pay for certain medical expenses that are not covered by the employee's healthcare plan. (FSAs can be set up to pay for child or dependent care, too.) Sometimes employers also contribute to these accounts. With an FSA, any money not used by the end of the year is lost. With an HSA, any money not used by the end of the year carries forward or rolls over to the next year, but an HSA can be used only with plans that have high **deductibles**—minimum out-of-pocket expenses.

Employee Assistance Programs (EAPs)

To encourage employees to adopt healthy lifestyles and prevent the need for serious medical care (among other advantages), more and more restaurant and foodservice operations are offering employee assistance programs.

One of the difficult situations that many managers face is how to help employees who are coping with personal problems. Sometimes, providing support for them and giving them a chance to talk about things can help; other times, they need the professional help that only employee assistance programs are designed to provide. **Employee assistance programs (EAPs)**—also known as referral programs—provide counseling and other services to individuals and families to help them deal with a wide range of problems that impede their ability to function effectively at work. (See *Exhibit 12e.*) These programs address a range of employee problems, including but not limited to:

- Alcohol dependency or abuse

- Chemical dependency or abuse

- Domestic violence

- Emotional issues, such as depression, low self-esteem, and personal problems

- Financial problems

- Gambling dependency or abuse

- Legal problems

- Literacy issues

- Marital, family, or relationship problems

- Stress from any source

- Tobacco dependency or abuse

Exhibit 12e

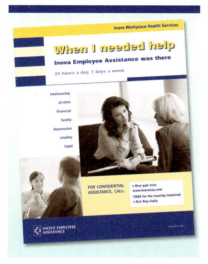

Employee assistance programs are designed to help employees with a wide range of issues.

Think About It...

According to the U.S. Department of Labor, studies show that hospitality industry employees have "some of the highest rates of alcohol and drug abuse."

EAP services can be provided in-house using staff members employed by the organization or contracted out to agencies with expertise in this area. Small employers normally contract out since they do not have the budget or the personnel to operate an EAP; larger operations sometimes have their own staff.

To help make employees aware of the range of assistance they can find in these programs, many operations post signs about EAPs with telephone numbers and reminders that calling and getting help is always kept confidential. Some restaurant and foodservice operations mention these programs in meetings, attach notices to paychecks, send out periodic notices in newsletters (whether print or electronic), hand out cards, or distribute other reminders. This information also should be provided in the employee handbook.

Typically, when a person decides to seek help through an EAP, he or she simply calls the employee assistance number and makes an appointment. However, as a manager, you should be familiar with this program and able to provide the phone number to employees who ask for your help.

Alternatively, you might recommend the program to an employee who, for example, cannot control his or her anger or has a drug problem. However, if a manager requires an employee to change his or her behavior as a condition of employment and recommends the EAP, then the EAP staff members will typically provide some form of proof that the employee showed up for appointments or meetings. Because any information an employee shares within an EAP is confidential, the employee can choose whether or not to share this proof of attendance with the manager. In any case, recommendations that are given to the employee are not shared with the employer.

Exhibit 12f

Retirement benefits support people who retire due to age.

Retirement Benefits

Another common benefit offered in the restaurant and foodservice industry is retirement benefits. Like healthcare benefits, retirement benefits vary widely from operation to operation. Retirement benefits provide regular payments to employees who retire because of age. (See *Exhibit 12f*.) Some plans provide **pensions,** which are regular payments that continue until the retiree dies, and some plans provide **annuities,** which are regular payments that continue for a specified period of time. The retirement benefits that an employer may offer generally fall into two categories: defined benefits and defined contributions.

Defined Benefits

A **defined benefit (DB)** is a retirement benefit in which the employee is guaranteed certain payments upon retirement; the payout, or final value of the benefit, is defined. Defined benefits are traditional pension plans. They are completely paid for by the employer, and consequently, are becoming less common.

Some companies have multiple defined benefit retirement plans. While employees typically enroll in these plans when they are first hired, they cannot choose among the plans because they usually apply to certain types of positions. For example, there often are different plans for exempt and nonexempt employees, and union and nonunion employees. If an employee's position changes, for example, if an employee is promoted from a nonexempt to an exempt position, the pension plan will be changed for the employee as well.

Generally, when an employee is first hired and enrolls in the plan, the employer contributes funds for the employee and all other eligible employees into a common **trust,** an account or series of accounts owned by the employer or plan administrator.

When an employee or former employee is ready to begin receiving a pension or annuity, the employee must notify the plan administrator. Procedures vary, but generally, the employee must give notice within a certain time period to allow for the final benefit to be calculated and for all the paperwork that must be exchanged between the pension administrator and the retiring employee to be processed.

Defined Contributions

Compared to defined benefit plans, defined contribution plans are relatively new, but they have been increasing in popularity. A **defined contribution (DC)** is a benefit that guarantees certain payments will be made into an account owned by an individual employee; that is, the employer's or employee's contribution is defined. This type of benefit can be set up for retirement plans, incentive plans, or other purposes. Perhaps the best-known DC plan offered as a retirement benefit is the 401(k) plan. However, there are many other types of DC retirement plans, such as Keogh plans, individual retirement accounts (IRAs), and 403(b) plans. (The names "401(k)" and "403(b)" come from the Internal Revenue Code.) Small employers may offer contributions to an IRA or Keogh plan instead of a 401(k) account.

With these types of retirement benefits, employees typically contribute a percentage of their pretax income to their own account, and their employers match a portion or all of the employee's contribution. For example, you might contribute 10 percent of your income to your retirement account, and your employer might match half of your contribution. In this example, the total contributions to your account would be 15 percent of your pretax income. When you contribute income before taxes, you do not pay any tax on that amount until you withdraw money from the account. *Exhibit 12g* shows an example of such a **tax-deferred** contribution. The amount that can be contributed to these retirement accounts is limited by the Internal Revenue Service (IRS) and can vary widely based on the type of account, the employee's income, and other factors.

Exhibit 12g

The Value of Tax Deferral

Maria makes $38,000 a year and is able to save $2,000 a year. She wants to put this money toward her retirement.

The following comparison shows approximately how much money she would keep after taxes in one year if she put her money in a qualified tax-deferred account, such as a 401(k) plan, versus an account that is not qualified for tax deferral, such as a regular savings account. On her tax returns, Maria takes the standard deduction allowed by the IRS for a single person with no dependents.

Contribution to Nonqualified Account			**Contribution to Qualified Tax-Deferred Account**		
Gross (total) income	38,000	38,000	**Gross (total) income**	38,000	38,000
Standard tax deduction*	− 7,950		**Standard tax deduction***	− 7,950	
			Tax-deferred contribution to savings	− 2,000	
Taxable income	= 30,050		**Taxable income**	= 28,050	
Taxes paid based on taxable income		− 4,240	**Taxes paid based on taxable income**		− 3,850
Contribution to savings after taxes		− 2,000			
Income left		= 31,760	**Income left**		= 32,150

If Maria puts her money into a tax-deferred account, she will save $390 in taxes that year. However, she cannot withdraw the money before retirement without paying the original taxes plus penalties, except in a few special situations.

*This amount is an estimate based on the 2004 tax table. Standard deduction amounts vary by personal situation and income and may change from year to year.

Normally, with a defined contribution retirement account, the funds are invested in securities such as stocks and bonds, so the value of the account ultimately depends on how well these investments perform. Some employers offer different options for investing retirement money, such as high-risk or low-risk mutual funds. Unlike defined benefits, the value of these benefits at retirement is not guaranteed. (It is even possible for an account to lose value.)

With defined contribution accounts, the employee can close the account within a certain period after leaving the company. If the employee is not old enough to retire under the plan, the money must be kept in another **qualified plan** or account—the former employer's plan if this is allowed, a current employer's plan, or a qualified tax-sheltered retirement account, such as an IRA. If the money is not kept in a qualified plan or account—retirement plans or accounts that have tax advantages and follow certain IRS rules for contributions and withdrawals—the IRS levies substantial fines for early withdrawals.

Although the IRS imposes stiff penalties if an employee withdraws money before retirement, it allows exceptions for certain withdrawals, such as buying a first home or paying major medical expenses. In general, when money is withdrawn, the employee pays the tax at that time on the amount withdrawn.

Common Elements

Both types of retirement plans have certain things in common. First, both have rules for eligibility. Usually, an employee must work a certain number of hours or days per year for a certain number of years (often five) to become fully **vested,** or entitled to the benefit. To determine the value of the benefit—whether it is a contribution to an individual account, or a specific pension or annuity amount—both types of plans use a formula. These formulas usually are based on the employee's salary and how long the employee has worked for the company or how many hours the employee has put in. Formulas differ by plan.

Once an employee is vested in a plan, the benefit belongs to the employee and cannot be revoked, even if the employee leaves the company before retirement. For example, suppose that early in your career you worked for ten years at a company, became vested in that company's retirement plan, and then left for another job. When you retire, you still get the benefit you earned during those ten years. This guaranty and many other elements of these plans are legislated by federal law.

Think About It...

The value of a DB pension or contribution to a DC retirement account is often calculated in part on the amount of time and sometimes the number of hours an employee has worked for a company. Sometimes, working one day in one month or even in one year can make that entire period count toward the benefit. To learn how a benefit is calculated, read the summary plan description for the plan.

Complying with Retirement and Health Benefit Laws

When an organization offers retirement and healthcare benefits, it must also follow the numerous federal, state, and local laws that govern aspects of these plans. Although the plan administrator is ultimately responsible for ensuring these laws are followed, you as a manager also need to do your part. In many cases, your operation will have an arrangement with the plan administrator to have managers or others communicate certain information to employees and the plan administrator. For example, you might be required to provide certain documents to employees or notify the plan administrator when an employee leaves. Most of the time, your company policy and procedures will guide you in your responsibilities. However, to be most effective in this area, you need to understand the laws that affect retirement and health benefits. Three federal laws are particularly important for you to understand:

- Employee Retirement Income Security Act of 1974 (ERISA)

- Consolidated Omnibus Budget Reconciliation Act (COBRA)

- Health Insurance Portability and Accountability Act (HIPAA)

Complying with ERISA

The **Employee Retirement Income Security Act of 1974 (ERISA)** is designed to protect employee pensions and healthcare plans from incompetent, unethical, and unfair administration. ERISA was enacted to ensure that the benefits promised to employees would actually be there when the employees need them. ERISA specifies certain conditions for reporting, membership, payout, and pension administrator conduct. One of these conditions is having a designated plan administrator for the benefit plan. In addition, the plan administrator must provide employees with certain documents related to their plans. The communication aspect of this law is probably the most important part that you need to understand as a manager.

When an employee or plan participant is first enrolled in a retirement plan or healthcare plan, the plan administrator is required to provide the participant with a **summary plan description (SPD).** (See *Exhibit 12h.*) This document explains the plan benefits, identifies the plan administrator, and describes participants' rights and responsibilities under the plan. Many operations provide summary plan descriptions before the employee's first day of work or during orientation. In addition, if a participant requests an SPD at any time, the plan administrator

Exhibit 12h

Sample SPD

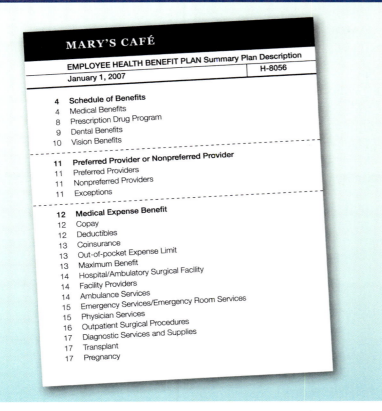

MARY'S CAFÉ

EMPLOYEE HEALTH BENEFIT PLAN Summary Plan Description

January 1, 2007 — H-8056

4 Schedule of Benefits
4   Medical Benefits
8   Prescription Drug Program
9   Dental Benefits
10 Vision Benefits

11 Preferred Provider or Nonpreferred Provider
11 Preferred Providers
11 Nonpreferred Providers
11 Exceptions

12 Medical Expense Benefit
12 Copay
12 Deductibles
13 Coinsurance
13 Out-of-pocket Expense Limit
13 Maximum Benefit
14 Hospital/Ambulatory Surgical Facility
14 Facility Providers
14 Ambulance Services
15 Emergency Services/Emergency Room Services
15 Physician Services
16 Outpatient Surgical Procedures
17 Diagnostic Services and Supplies
17 Transplant
17 Pregnancy

Plan participants are entitled to receive a summary plan description.

must provide it. Depending on your operation's policies and procedures, you as a manager may be responsible for distributing this document, especially to new hires. Given the legal requirements for doing this, using an orientation checklist or other document that proves the SPD was distributed is a good way to show your operation complied with the law.

ERISA also requires other communication to plan participants. As a manager, you are not likely to be involved with these notifications, but you may receive them as a plan participant. When a plan or the SPD is changed, the plan administrator must provide participants with a document called a **summary of material modification (SMM),** which explains the changes. In addition, the administrators of some plans must file an annual report with the government. If an annual report is filed, the administrator also must provide participants and beneficiaries with a **summary annual report,** which summarizes the annual report that was filed with the government.

Complying with COBRA

ERISA was an enormous step in protecting employee pension and healthcare benefits, but an amendment to ERISA, the **Consolidated Omnibus Budget Reconciliation Act (COBRA),** offers further protection. The primary purpose of COBRA is to extend healthcare coverage for people who would otherwise lose their healthcare insurance. Under COBRA, healthcare benefits do not automatically end when an employee or covered family member is no longer eligible for a plan. In some situations, employers must offer to continue healthcare benefits.

COBRA generally requires employers who have twenty or more employees and a group healthcare plan to offer this continued coverage to eligible plan participants. According to the U.S. Department of Labor, Employee Benefits Security Administration (EBSA), an employee, former employee, or family member generally is eligible to continue healthcare benefits under COBRA if he or she was "covered under a group healthcare plan on the day before the event that causes a loss of coverage." These events are shown in *Exhibit 12i*. During a period of COBRA continuation coverage, any child born to a covered employee or placed for adoption with a covered employee also is eligible for coverage. In discussions on COBRA, a person entitled to COBRA continuation coverage is known as a **qualified beneficiary.**

Exhibit 12i

Qualifying Events for Continuation of Coverage under COBRA

Qualifying events for a covered employee if they cause the covered employee to lose coverage

- Termination of the covered employee's employment for any reason other than "gross misconduct"
- Reduction in the covered employee's hours of employment

Qualifying events for a spouse and dependent child of a covered employee if they cause the spouse or dependent child to lose coverage

- Termination of the covered employee's employment for any reason other than "gross misconduct"
- Reduction in hours worked by the covered employee
- Covered employee becomes entitled to Medicare
- Divorce or legal separation of the spouse from the covered employee
- Death of the covered employee

Qualifying event for a dependent child of a covered employee if it causes the child to lose coverage

- Loss of "dependent child" status under the plan rules

COBRA enables eligible people to continue their healthcare plan through the employer's group plan for a limited period. However, they must pay both their own and the employer's share of the plan costs, and the employer can charge an additional 2 percent of this cost as an administration fee (even though actual administration costs are often greater). For example, suppose the employer's share of an employee's monthly premium is $150, and the employee's share is $250, so the total premium amount is $400. If the employer charges the allowed 2 percent administration fee ($8), then the total cost to the employee would be $408 a month. Even though the employer no longer pays for the healthcare, this option enables most eligible people to purchase healthcare coverage for a lower price than they would get through an individual plan with similar coverage. Generally, adults can continue coverage for eighteen months, and dependent children can continue for thirty-six months. However, if an adult becomes disabled, coverage can be extended to twenty-nine months.

Like ERISA, COBRA also requires that plan administrators communicate specific information to qualified beneficiaries, and this is the area that you as a manager need to be most familiar with. To meet COBRA's requirements for communicating with plan participants and covered employees, a plan administrator must notify eligible people about COBRA coverage and related information and events, such as open enrollment and cancellation procedures. The law is very specific about the information that must be communicated to participants and the time frame in which this must happen, as detailed in *Exhibit 12j*. In most cases, the plan administrator handles this communication. However, you should be aware of these requirements because some of them involve information that should be distributed during hiring and orientation and posted in the workplace.

In addition, you may be responsible for notifying the plan administrator when an employee leaves the operation or loses healthcare coverage to ensure that plan participants receive all notices in a timely manner.

Exhibit 12j

COBRA Communication Requirements for Plan Administrators

Summary plan description (SPD) to a plan participant within ninety days of joining the plan

General notice of rights under COBRA to employees and spouses within ninety days after the employee joins the plan

(This notice must include the name, address, and telephone number of the contact person for more information on COBRA and the plan. It may be included in the SPD if a copy of the SPD is given to both the employee and spouse.)

Summary of material modification (SMM) to plan participants within the applicable time frame (which varies depending on the severity of the change)

Copy of an SPD or SMM within thirty days after a written request from a participant

Notices and instructions on continuous healthcare coverage to qualified beneficiaries within fourteen days of receiving notice of a qualifying event

When applicable, notice of denial of coverage or an extension to coverage within fourteen days of receiving the request for coverage or the extension

When applicable, notice of early termination of coverage to the participant "as soon as practicable" after the decision to terminate coverage is made

The employer must notify the plan administrator within thirty days when a covered employee:

- Terminates employment

- Loses coverage because of a reduction in hours

- Dies

- Becomes eligible for **Medicare,** a federally insured healthcare plan for people age sixty-five or older

The participant is responsible for notifying the plan administrator for other qualifying life events, such as divorce, legal separation, or loss of dependent status. In some cases, the participant may notify the employer instead, and the employer will notify the plan administrator. The participant's responsibilities must be explained in the plan's general notice of COBRA rights and the summary plan description. However, as a manager, you should be able to explain these responsibilities to employees, as well as provide a general description of how COBRA works.

Complying with HIPAA

Another amendment to ERISA, the **Health Insurance Portability and Accountability Act (HIPAA),** helps ensure people do not lose access to healthcare because of preexisting conditions, other health status factors, or limits on plan enrollment periods. HIPAA offers protection both for people who have access to group healthcare plans, such as those commonly offered by employers, and for people who purchase or apply for individual plans, which is usually done outside of the workplace.

HIPAA has three main functions:

- To give people the right to add family members to their group healthcare plan at times other than open enrollment, under certain circumstances

- To protect people from being excluded from healthcare plans or denied coverage because of preexisting conditions

- To protect people from discriminatory pricing or treatment under a plan because of preexisting conditions or other health status factors (see *Exhibit 12k*)

A **preexisting condition** is a medical condition for which a person has sought medical treatment before applying to join a healthcare plan. In the past, people who had preexisting conditions often were denied full or even partial coverage under many healthcare plans. For example, if a person had been treated for colon polyps, a plan might stipulate that any future treatment related to colon polyps and

Exhibit 12k

HIPAA Health Status Factors

Health status

Medical conditions (both physical and mental illnesses)

Claims experience

Receipt of healthcare

Medical history

Genetic information

Evidence of insurability

Disability

colon cancer would not be covered, or it might deny the person any type of coverage. If the plan accepted someone with a preexisting condition, the premiums for that person generally would be much higher than they would have been otherwise. Sometimes plans also excluded coverage for preexisting conditions for a certain time after enrollment. This period is known as an **exclusion period.**

Protection from Discriminatory Exclusions and Pricing

While exclusion periods are still allowed as long as they are applied equally to all plan participants, HIPAA limits or eliminates some of these exclusions and provides some protection against higher premiums due to preexisting conditions and other health factors. Under HIPAA, when a person joins a plan, he or she cannot be charged a higher rate because of a preexisting condition or health factor.

In addition, HIPAA does not allow plans to exclude coverage for preexisting conditions unless the person sought medical advice, diagnosis, care, or treatment for that condition within six months of enrolling in the plan. (See *Exhibit 12l.*) For preexisting conditions that fall within this six-month time frame, or **look-back period,** HIPAA limits the period during which plans can exclude coverage. However, there are exceptions for dependent children: generally, newborns, adopted children, and children placed for adoption are fully covered as long they are enrolled within thirty days of joining their families.

For everyone else, the maximum exclusion period is twelve months for people who enroll on the earliest possible enrollment date, and eighteen months for people who enroll after this date. If a person was previously covered under one or more plans without a break in coverage longer than sixty-three days, HIPAA requires that the maximum exclusion period be reduced by the number of days previously covered. For example, suppose George left his job at Chez Michelle, where he had continuous health insurance for the nine months that he worked there, to accept a position at O'Hara's. Two months before George changed jobs, he was diagnosed with high blood pressure and put on medication. The healthcare plan at his new job covers high blood pressure medication, but unfortunately, it has a twelve-month exclusion period for preexisting conditions. However, because George had health coverage at his old job—and can prove it—HIPAA requires that his exclusion be reduced by the number of covered days he had under his previous plan. Since George was covered for nine months, that amount of time is credited against the twelve-month exclusion period. Therefore, George only has to wait three months before his high blood pressure medication is covered under his new employer's plan.

Exhibit 12l

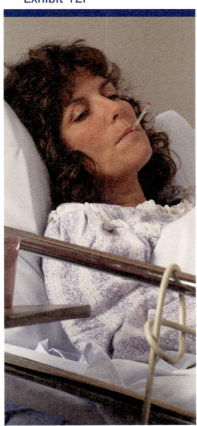

HIPAA limits exclusions from healthcare for preexisting conditions.

Exhibit 12m

EBSA Model Certificate of Group Healthcare Plan Coverage

CERTIFICATE OF GROUP HEALTHCARE PLAN COVERAGE

Important—This certificate provides evidence of your prior health coverage. You may need to furnish this certificate if you become eligible under a group health plan that excludes coverage for certain medical conditions that you have before you enroll. This certificate may need to be provided if medical advice, diagnosis, care, or treatment was recommended or received for the condition within the 6-month period prior to your enrollment in the new plan. If you become covered under another group health plan, check with the plan administrator to see if you need to provide this certificate. You may also need this certificate to buy, for yourself or your family, an insurance policy that does not exclude coverage for medical conditions that are present before you enroll.

1. Date of this certificate: _____
2. Name of group health plan: _____
3. Name of participant: _____
4. Identification number of participant: _____
5. Name of any dependents to whom this certificate applies: _____
_____
6. Name, address, and telephone number of plan administrator or issuer responsible for providing this certificate: _____
_____
7. For further information, call: _____
8. If the individual(s) identified in line 3 and line 5 has (have) at least 18 months of creditable coverage (disregarding periods of coverage before a 63-day break), check here _____ and skip lines 9 and 10.
9. Date waiting period or affiliation period (if any) began: _____
10. Date coverage began: _____
11. Date coverage ended: _____ (or check if coverage is continuing as of the date of this certificate: _____)

Note: Separate certificates will be furnished if information is not identical for the participant and each beneficiary.

U.S. Department of Labor

To help people prove that they were covered under a healthcare plan, HIPAA requires healthcare plans to provide former plan participants with a **certificate of creditable coverage,** a document showing that a person was covered under the plan and the starting and ending dates of coverage. Plan administrators must provide certificates of creditable coverage to plan participants, including employee's family members, at these times:

- When a participant loses healthcare coverage, including coverage under COBRA

- When a participant requests this certificate before coverage ends or within twenty-four months after coverage ends

The U.S. Department of Labor, Employee Benefits Security Administration (EBSA), provides a model certificate that plan administrators can use. (See *Exhibit 12m.*)

Special Enrollment Periods

Another requirement of HIPAA is to allow people to enroll in group healthcare plans at certain times other than open enrollment, called **special enrollment periods.** These periods are designed to make healthcare accessible for people who otherwise might not be able to get coverage. Special enrollment rules apply in these situations:

- When a person loses other healthcare coverage, such as when an employee has coverage through a spouse's plan, and the spouse loses his or her coverage

- When a person gets married to someone who has coverage

- When a child is born to someone who has coverage

- When a dependent child is adopted or placed for adoption with someone who has coverage

In any of these cases, the person without coverage can enroll in the plan of the family member who is covered under a group plan. If a husband and wife or a family lose coverage under one spouse's plan, the couple or family becomes eligible for coverage under the other spouse's plan. To be eligible for special enrollment, however, the employee must notify the plan administrator within thirty days of losing other coverage, if applicable, or of a qualifying event, such as the birth of a child.

Activity

Communicating Information about Health and Retirement Benefits

Assume you are a manager in an operation that provides health insurance, a retirement plan an employee assistance program, and meal and uniform benefits. Your operation has an internal human resources specialist, Darius Wilson, who acts as the plan administrator for both the health and retirement plans. Your operation's defined contribution retirement plan begins matching employee contributions after five years. Darius also is the contact person for your operation's employee assistance program.

Review each of the following scenarios and respond to each.

1 During a performance review, Sonia, a full-time employee, has confided in you that she wants to finish her college degree so she has a better chance at being promoted into management. She laments that, to go to college, she would need to reduce her work hours for two semesters, which would make her ineligible for health insurance. She says she cannot risk being without health insurance because her five-year-old daughter is on the plan. What could you tell Sonia to help her understand her health insurance rights?

2 When you ask one of your employees, Manny, how he has been, he replies that his wife's company suddenly went out of business. They were getting their health insurance through her employer's plan, and he is particularly worried because his wife is six months pregnant. What could you tell Manny to help him with this situation?

3 Valerie has been an employee with your operation for four years. She says she has many questions about the retirement plan, but she lost the benefits information given to her during orientation. She also wants to know how and when she can set up a retirement account. How could you help Valerie get the information she wants?

4 Lately, one of your employees, Alex, has seemed unusually tired and forgetful and has been making a lot of mistakes. When you talk to him about his recent behavior, he tells you he and his wife have been fighting a lot, and he has not been sleeping well. He says they are considering couples counseling, but due to their work schedules, he doubts they can find a good counselor who is available when they are. How could you help Alex get the help he needs?

Ensuring Mandatory Benefits

Even though healthcare and retirement benefits are heavily legislated, employers are not required to offer them. However, federal and state governments require some employers to provide or pay for other benefits. These include Social Security, workers' compensation insurance, unemployment compensation insurance, and in certain situations, unpaid leaves of absence. Because these programs are mandated and therefore provided by most employers, many people do not consider them to be benefits. However, employers must administer and pay for these programs as they do for many other types of voluntarily provided benefits.

As a manager, you need to be familiar with these programs so you can help employees understand them and how they relate to any voluntary benefits your operation provides. You also need to understand your operation's legal responsibilities for providing and administering these mandated benefits. One of the best known is Social Security.

Think About It...

Social Security is the only type of employment-related pension program for more than half of all American workers.

Social Security

Established by the Social Security Act of 1935, **Social Security** is a federal pension program in which most private sector (nongovernmental) employers and employees must participate. It was originally designed as a "social insurance" program to provide a minimum level of income for workers who were retired or could no longer work. Social Security has evolved to include a broad range of benefits:

- Retirement benefits—a pension for eligible workers who have retired, their spouses, and their dependents

- Survivor benefits—a pension for the spouses and dependent children of eligible workers who die before they retire

- Disability benefits—a pension for disabled workers who are younger than full retirement age (see *Exhibit 12n*)

- Medicare—a federally insured healthcare plan for people age sixty-five or older

Both employers and employees pay for Social Security benefits through a payroll tax. Employers must pay both the employer's and employee's share of this tax to the Social Security trust and deduct the correct amount from each employee's paycheck. (Self-employed people pay both the employer's and employee's shares.)

To be eligible for Social Security benefits, a person must have worked for a certain length of time and earned a minimum

Exhibit 12n

Full Retirement Age for Social Security Benefits

Birth Year	Full Retirement Age
1937 or earlier	65
1938	65 and 2 months
1939	65 and 4 months
1940	65 and 6 months
1941	65 and 8 months
1942	65 and 10 months
1943–1954	66
1955	66 and 2 months
1956	66 and 4 months
1957	66 and 6 months
1958	66 and 8 months
1959	66 and 10 months
1960 and later	67

income—or be the spouse or dependent child of someone who meets these work requirements. If a person is applying for Social Security disability benefits, then he or she must meet additional eligibility requirements.

The value of a Social Security benefit depends in large part on how much income the employee earned and when the benefit payments begin. If an employee retires early and applies to receive Social Security benefits before full retirement age, the retirement benefit amount is reduced. If the employee applies to receive Social Security after full retirement age, the retirement benefits are increased.

To receive Social Security, an eligible person must apply for these benefits with the Social Security Administration.

Unemployment Insurance

Another benefit mandated by the Social Security Act of 1935 is **unemployment insurance,** which temporarily provides a reduced level of income to employees who lose their jobs involuntarily. This benefit is intended to help people during short periods of unemployment while they are looking for a new job.

While the federal government requires unemployment insurance, it is implemented by the states. Therefore, each state has its own rules for the amount of unemployment benefits to be paid and for how long. Unemployment benefits are required to be paid for a minimum time, as long as the employee remains eligible for these benefits.

In general, to be eligible for unemployment compensation, a former employee must work for an employer for a certain period of time and must be out of work for a certain period of time. Most states also require former employees to be able and available to work and to actively look for work. (However, a few states also have temporary disability laws to help unemployed people who are not able to work.)

People receiving unemployment benefits typically are also required to register with the local unemployment office and prove they are actively looking for work.

Most states also specify certain conditions that can disqualify an employee from receiving benefits. Common reasons that disqualify former employees include:

- Being fired because of misconduct

- Turning down a job offer of suitable work

- Going on strike or not working due to a labor dispute

- Accepting certain types of income, such as workers' compensation, a retirement or Social Security pension, or Social Security payments

Unemployment insurance is funded through payroll taxes paid by employers. The amount of this tax varies by state and by employer. For example, if an employer has terminated or laid off many employees who filed for unemployment benefits, that employer's tax rate will be higher compared to employers who do not have many claims.

Laws for communicating unemployment insurance information to employees also vary by state. Some states may require that employers notify employees of their rights to unemployment insurance. *Exhibit 12o* shows a poster required by the state of Massachusetts. In addition, a federal law, the Worker Adjustment and Retraining Notification Act (WARN), requires employers who are covered by WARN and planning mass layoffs to provide those employees with information about unemployment insurance.

Exhibit 12o

Poster Required for Unemployment Insurance Notification in Massachusetts

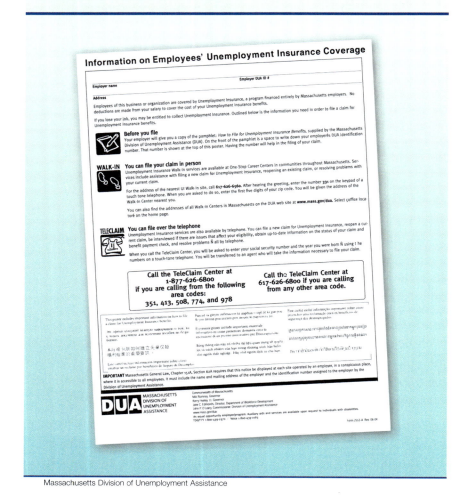

Massachusetts Division of Unemployment Assistance

Workers' Compensation

Another benefit designed to provide a basic level of income to people who are not working is **workers' compensation,** or workers' comp, a system for providing financial compensation to employees or their survivors when an employee is injured at work, becomes sick because of the workplace environment, or dies as a result of a workplace situation. Worker's compensation programs are controlled by state laws and differ from state to state.

Workers' compensation is a "no fault" system in which employers are financially responsible for taking care of their injured or ill employees, regardless of who (the employee or the employer) caused the illness or injury. For example, if an employee does not follow procedures and injures himself, the employer is still liable for workers' compensation. In essence, workers' compensation laws were designed to help take care of employees and their families and to reduce the lawsuits against, and liability of, individual companies. Generally, employers are responsible for paying for an employee's medical costs and providing a reduced income while the employee is recovering or disabled. State laws specify the amount of these costs and income, along with any limits.

Restaurant and foodservice companies typically purchase workers' compensation insurance to pay any claims. The cost of these insurance policies is calculated on the nature of the employees' work, the operation's safety record, the history of the operation's previous claims, and the operation's provision of healthcare benefits. Most State Restaurant Associations provide operations with some assistance in this matter, often by offering large group plans. However, very large companies may choose to insure themselves rather than purchase this type of insurance.

Family and Medical Leaves of Absence

Sometimes employees want or need to temporarily stop working and then return to work. When a period of time cannot be covered by paid time-off days, such as vacation time, personal days, or sick days, it is called a **leave of absence.** A leave of absence, or leave, may be short or long. Depending on the employer and the reason for the leave, employees on leave may or may not be paid their normal wages. While employers today often voluntarily accommodate employee requests for unpaid leave, the federal government and many state governments mandate unpaid leaves of absence in certain situations.

The federal **Family and Medical Leave Act (FMLA)** gives qualified employees the right to take up to twelve weeks of continuous or intermittent unpaid leave in a rolling twelve-month period (see *Exhibit 12p*) for certain medical or family-care situations. Employers also must provide certain benefits and reemployment to employees who take leaves under FMLA.

Under FMLA, employers must allow unpaid leave when employees:

- Have a serious medical condition that prevents them from working

- Need to take care of a child, spouse, or parent with a serious medical condition

- Have a newborn child or adopt a child

Exhibit 12p

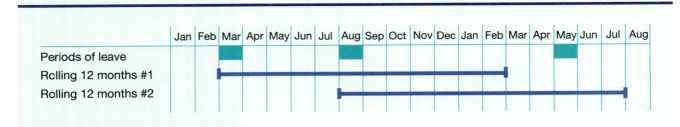

Rolling Twelve-Month Period

The FMLA defines a **serious medical condition** as "an illness, injury, impairment, or physical or mental condition that involves: inpatient care …[or] continuing treatment by a healthcare provider." The continuing treatment may be for a condition that incapacitates the employee or for which the employee must receive multiple treatments.

If the employee has health insurance through the employer, the employer must continue to provide this benefit during the leave. However, the employee must pay for any benefits he or she normally would pay, such as healthcare insurance premiums. When employees return from family or medical leave, they are entitled to the same benefits and essentially the same positions they had before taking the leave.

Not all employers and employees are covered under FMLA. Employers must comply with this act if they have fifty or more full-time employees who live within seventy-five miles of the business. To be eligible under federal law for mandatory family and medical leave, employees must have worked for the operation for one year and a minimum of 1,250 hours in the previous twelve months (approximately twenty-four hours a week).

Exhibit 12q

FMLA Poster

Your Rights
under the
Family and Medical Leave Act of 1993

FMLA requires covered employers to provide up to 12 weeks of unpaid, job-protected leave to "eligible" employees for certain family and medical reasons. Employees are eligible if they have worked for their employer for at least one year, and for 1,250 hours over

the previous 12 months, and if there are at least 50 employees within 75 miles. The FMLA permits employees to take leave on an intermittent basis or to work a reduced schedule under certain circumstances.

Reasons for Taking Leave:

Unpaid leave must be granted for *any* of the following reasons:
• to care for the employee's child after birth, or placement for adoption or foster care;
• to care for the employee's spouse, son or daughter, or parent who has a serious health condition; or
• for a serious health condition that makes the employee unable to perform the employee's job.

At the employee's or employer's option, certain kinds of *paid* leave may be substituted for unpaid leave.

Advance Notice and Medical Certification:

The employee may be required to provide advance leave notice and medical certification. Taking of leave may be denied if requirements are not met.
• The employee ordinarily must provide 30 days advance notice when the leave is "foreseeable."
• An employer may require medical certification to support a request for leave because of a serious health condition, and may require second or third opinions (at the employer's expense) and a fitness for duty report to return to work.

Job Benefits and Protection:

• For the duration of FMLA leave, the employer must maintain the employee's health coverage under any "group health plan."

• Upon return from FMLA leave, most employees must be restored to their original or equivalent positions with equivalent pay, benefits, and other employment terms.
• The use of FMLA leave cannot result in the loss of any employment benefit that accrued prior to the start of an employee's leave.

Unlawful Acts by Employers:

FMLA makes it unlawful for any employer to:
• interfere with, restrain, or deny the exercise of any right provided under FMLA:
• discharge or discriminate against any person for opposing any practice made unlawful by FMLA or for involvement in any proceeding under or relating to FMLA.

Enforcement:

• The U.S. Department of Labor is authorized to investigate and resolve complaints of violations.
• An eligible employee may bring a civil action against an employer for violations.

FMLA does not affect any Federal or State law prohibiting discrimination, or supersede any State or local law or collective bargaining agreement which provides greater family or medical leave rights.

For Additional Information:

If you have access to the Internet visit our FMLA website: http://www.dol.gov/esa/whd/fmla. To locate your nearest Wage-Hour Office, telephone our Wage-Hour toll-free information and help line at 1-866-4USWAGE (1-866-487-9243): a customer service representative is available to assist you with referral information from 8am to 5pm **in your time zone**; or log onto our Home Page at http://www.wagehour.dol.gov.

U.S. Department of Labor
Employment Standards Administration
Wage and Hour Division
Washington, D.C. 20210

WH Publication 1420
Revised August 2001

*U.S. GOVERNMENT PRINTING OFFICE 2001-476-344/49051

U.S. Department of Labor

Many state laws also apply to certain employers and employees, and in many cases, provide coverage more extensively than FMLA.

FMLA requires employers to communicate certain information at certain times. Employers are responsible for communicating employees' rights under this act by posting information about it. The Department of Labor provides posters that employers can use to satisfy this requirement. (See *Exhibit 12q*.) Employers also must provide information on FMLA or any applicable state law in the employee handbook or through handouts when requested by the employee. This information includes instructions on how to take leave under FMLA or any applicable state law and contact information for the person or department that administers this benefit.

Because family and medical leave laws are complex, many organizations designate certain people as administrators for this benefit. Usually, these administrators are human resources professionals, but they may be people at outside agencies or even managers. However, to help ensure confidentiality and impartiality, some companies do not use managers as designated contacts.

Usually when an employee wants to take leave under FMLA or any applicable state law, the employee and the designated administrator meet to discuss the reason for the leave and the employee's rights and requirements under such laws. Regardless of whether or not a meeting occurs, the employee is responsible for providing thirty days notice of the leave whenever possible. Before granting the leave, the employer may require the employee to provide certified proof of the medical condition and obtain a second or third medical opinion (if the employer pays for this consultation). In addition, when the employee is ready to return to work, the employer may request a document from the employee's physician stating that the employee is healthy enough to work.

Sometimes when employees are considering taking leave under FMLA, they will first approach their immediate supervisors. As a manager, you need to be able to direct your employees to the appropriate FMLA contact for your operation. If an employee is willing to discuss his or her need for a leave, you should be capable of accurately explaining your company's policies for paid and unpaid time off. For example, many employees do not understand what constitutes a "serious medical condition" and may request medical leave under FMLA when a few sick days or personal days would suffice. As a manager, understanding your operation's policies and applicable laws will help you ensure that your employees' rights are respected while protecting the operation's interests.

Military Leaves of Absence

The federal government also protects people who need a leave of absence to serve in the military. As discussed in Chapter 1, the **Uniformed Services Employment and Reemployment Rights Act (USERRA)** protects employees from workplace discrimination based on their obligation to, application for, or interest in military service. This act protects people enlisted in the Armed Forces, the Army National Guard, the Air National Guard, and other uniformed services.

However, the main purpose of USERRA is to ensure that military personnel are not penalized in the workplace when they return from their military duties. In some ways, USERRA provides similar protections as other federal laws, namely FMLA and COBRA. However, USERRA provides more extensive protection and applies to all employers in the public and private sectors, regardless of size.

While the employee is on leave, USERRA requires the employer to continue all of the employee's benefits as if the employee were not on leave. However, if an eligible employee serves longer than thirty-one days, the employee can opt to continue healthcare coverage through the employer, similar to COBRA, or can get coverage through the military's healthcare plan.

Under USERRA, eligible employees are entitled to return to the same job or an equivalent one when their service is finished, providing the employee meets certain conditions. These conditions are listed in the USERRA poster in *Exhibit 12r*. If the employee would have been

Exhibit 12r

USERRA Poster

U.S. Department of Labor

promoted had he or she continued working, the employer also must provide that promotion and any accompanying benefits to the employee as if he or she had not been on leave.

For example, suppose Eva worked for four years as a server in a restaurant where she was being groomed for an assistant dining room manager position. Anyone in her position might normally be promoted to this new position in about five years. Before that could happen, Eva was called to military service for one year. If she had continued working and performing at the same level, she most likely would have been promoted during the year she was on military leave. When Eva returns from service, she is guaranteed the assistant dining room manager position or an equivalent one, even if she is not quite ready to be the assistant dining room manager. In this case, her employer must provide the training to help her become qualified—basically, to help her catch up to where she would have been had she not left for military service. However, there are exceptions for employees who cannot perform their previous or equivalent jobs because of a disability incurred during military service.

When an employee returns to work after taking leave under USERRA, the employer cannot fire the employee without cause for 180 days if the employee has 31 to 180 days of service, or for one year if the employee has more than 180 days of service.

Employers are responsible for communicating information about USERRA to their employees. The Veterans Benefits Improvement Act of 2004 requires this communication to be posted, like the poster in *Exhibit 12r,* or to be distributed using other methods, such as email.

Activity

Communicating Information about Mandatory Benefits

You are a restaurant manager for an operation in a large hotel that is part of a chain. Your company employs hundreds of people in the local area and provides them with health insurance and other benefits, which are all administered by the human resources department.

Review the following scenarios and respond to each.

1 Your company's policy requires employees to use all of their paid sick days and vacation days before going on a medical leave under the Family and Medical Leave Act. One of your employees, Raymond, calls in sick with the flu, says he wants to take four weeks off to recover, and states that he wants to exercise his rights under the FMLA. Raymond does not get four weeks of paid time off each year, and he uses his sick days and vacation days as quickly as he accrues them. Is Raymond eligible for medical leave under the FMLA? If so, how would you explain to Raymond the company rules for taking medical leave? If he is not eligible, how would you explain to him why he is not?

_____

_____

_____

_____

2 Anita, a long-time employee who has worked the same schedule for years and has never expressed an interest in overtime, surprises you by asking for a permanent increase in hours. Sensing your surprise, she explains that her ex-husband has died, leaving her without child support for her two teenage children, and that the older one just entered high school and hopes to go to college in a few years. In your discussion, she mentions that her ex-husband did not have any retirement benefits or life insurance. Even though you do not know any details about her ex-husband's work situation, what could you tell her about possible benefits that may be mandated by the government for her children?

_____

_____

_____

_____

3 Juan, one of your best servers, has been called to active military duty. He tells you he just got word that he has to ship out next month. He says his tour is supposed to last six months, and he hopes to come back to work afterward. He asks if you can keep his job open and wants to know whether he will lose his seniority and vesting status in the retirement plan. What can you tell Juan about his concerns?

_____

_____

_____

_____

Keeping Current on Benefits and Related Laws

All managers in an operation need to understand the intent of the laws that govern their workplace as well as their operation's policies and procedures for complying with these laws. Because these laws are so numerous and complex—and the consequences of noncompliance can be expensive or even disastrous—all managers need to fully comprehend these laws and policies.

Ideally, every manager in an operation should be well trained in employee benefits, company policies and procedures, and workplace laws. Since these areas are so complex and benefit plans and workplace laws often change, operations should dedicate at least one management meeting each quarter to reviewing benefit programs. In larger operations, a human resources professional or lawyer may publish memos or post information to communicate changes as they occur. Carefully read any information from the human resources department, management office, or legal staff. In operations that do not offer such training or communication, managers may need to keep abreast of these changes on their own.

Regardless of the support your operation provides you as a manager, you are responsible for following your operation's policies and for making an effort to help your employees use the benefits they are legally entitled to receive. It is in your employees', your operation's, and your own best interests to learn as much as you can about your operation's employee benefit plans, policies, and procedures and the laws that govern them, and to continuously update your knowledge in these areas.

You can keep up with these issues by developing your own resources, such as:

- The U.S. Department of Labor and most states provide free or inexpensive resources, such as posters and publications. Many of these resources are available through Web sites.

- The National Restaurant Association and State Restaurant Associations send their members regular updates on legal and other issues that can affect the restaurant and foodservice industry.

- Local chambers of commerce often provide information on local, regional, or statewide regulations.

- Various human resources newsletters provide information on regulations affecting businesses.

Given the breadth and complexity of employee benefits and related legal issues, you may want to develop multiple resources.

Activity

The Hunt for Resources

Suppose you are just starting your own restaurant, and you need to develop an employee handbook. You want to hire a human resources consultant to help you do this and to help you choose a health insurance plan for your employees. However, to ensure you choose a good consultant, you want to learn as much as you can about employee benefits and the laws that govern them before you start interviewing candidates.

Research the following resources through the Internet. For each resource, list the name of the Web site or publication and the URL. Use a separate piece of paper if necessary.

1 U.S. Department of Labor Web site *www.dol.gov*—Find at least three pages or publications that relate to employee benefits administration and federal law.

_____

_____

2 Your state Web site—Find at least two pages or publications that relate to employee benefits administration and state law.

_____

_____

3 Professional organization—Find at least one professional organization that offers resources, articles, or publications related to employee benefits administration.

_____

4 One chamber of commerce Web site, preferably a local one—Find at least one page or publication that relates to employee benefits administration.

_____

5 Online human resources newsletters or Web sites—Find at least two such resources.

_____

_____

Ensuring Legal Wages

Employee benefits may be one part of a compensation package that includes incentives and wages—the most important form of compensation for most people. To ensure workers receive a fair wage for their labor, numerous laws control the minimum amount and payment of wages. In addition, many state and local governments also have enacted similar laws to ensure fair labor practices and compensation. Some of these laws are more restrictive or set different wages than federal laws. For example, some state and local governments have a higher minimum wage than federal law requires.

Ensuring a Minimum Wage

The Fair Labor Standards Act (FLSA) of 1938, as amended, serves as the cornerstone of employment law. In addition to the child labor provisions, the act provides a basic minimum wage and overtime pay for some employees and requires employers to keep certain records. Since this act was passed, many additional state and local laws have established higher minimum wages than those provided by the FLSA.

In addition, the FLSA also establishes different types of minimum wages. Most hourly positions in the United States are entitled to the basic minimum wage, but there are exceptions:

- **Tipped employees' minimum wage**—Tipped employees may be paid a lower cash wage when their tips are enough to ensure the basic minimum wage is met. (See *Exhibit 12s.*)

- **Youth minimum wage**—Employees younger than twenty years of age may be paid a lower minimum wage during their first ninety consecutive days of employment.

- **Subminimum wage**—The FLSA allows employers to pay certain people a lower minimum wage:

  - Student-learners who are placed in a job as part of a vocational education program or other education program

  - Individuals who have a reduced capacity to be productive because of a physical or mental disability

The minimum wages for tipped employees and youth are common in the restaurant and foodservice industry. The subminimum wage is not common because of the need to offer competitive wages. Also, many schools that have student-learner programs do not allow participating employers to pay a subminimum wage.

These minimum wage exceptions are allowed only under very specific circumstances. For example, to pay someone a subminimum wage, an employer needs to get a certificate issued by the Wage and Hour Division of the Department of Labor, Employment Standards Administration, and display a special minimum wage poster. When considering whether to use these special minimum wages, you should seek professional advice.

Exhibit 12s

Some tipped employees may be paid a lower minimum wage.

Compensating Employees for Overtime

In most operations, full-time employees are expected to work forty hours each week. If an employee—whether part-time or full-time—puts in more hours than are standard for the operation, these hours are known as overtime. The FLSA also ensures that hourly employees receive higher wages after working a certain number of hours each week at their usual rate.

While exempt (salaried) employees are not required under the FLSA to receive extra pay for overtime hours, hourly employees are entitled to receive overtime pay because of requirements under the FLSA. The FLSA requires that covered employees who work more than forty hours in a workweek be paid overtime wages at one-and-one-half times their normal hourly rate. For example, if an employee earns ten dollars an hour in normal wages, his or her overtime rate would be fifteen dollars an hour.

Using the Tip Credit Provision

The tip credit provision of the FLSA allows operations that employ tipped employees to choose between paying them the basic minimum wage or paying them the reduced cash wage and taking a tip credit allowed for tipped employees. This option may be considered only for employees defined by the Department of Labor as tipped employees—those who "customarily and regularly" receive more than a certain amount of income in tips each month. Currently, this amount is thirty dollars.

The basic idea of the tip credit provision is to reduce the payroll burden on some employers while ensuring that tipped employees receive at least the basic minimum wage after their tips are included. For example, if the cash wage for tipped employees is $2.13 and the basic minimum wage is $5.15, tipped employees must earn an average of at least $3.02 in tips each hour for the employer to use the full tip credit provision. If the tips do not bring the employee's hourly wage up to the basic minimum wage, the employer must pay the difference.

Employers who use the tip credit provision must do the following:

- Notify the employee in advance. Generally, operations include this information in the employment letter or employment contract.

- Be able to show that the employee receives at least the basic minimum wage when the reduced cash wage and the employee's tips are combined.

Whether using the tip credit or not, employers must allow employees to keep all of their tips, except when the operation has a valid tip-pooling or tip-sharing arrangement. Even in these arrangements, tipped employees do not have to share their tips with employees "who have not customarily and regularly participated in tip-pooling arrangements, such as dishwashers, cooks, chefs, and janitors."

However, using the tip credit provision is not that simple. Whether an operation can use the tip credit provision and if so, how wages should be calculated, are affected by rules in the following areas:

■ Service charges

■ Tips paid by credit card

■ Deductions for uniforms or equipment

■ Additional tip-pooling rules

■ Overtime rules

■ Reimbursements for damages or losses caused by the employee

■ State and local laws

Reporting Tip Income

To enable compliance with the FLSA tip credit provision and parts of the Internal Revenue Code, both employees and employers are responsible for reporting tip income. Employees must report their tips to employers, no less than on a monthly basis. They can use an IRS form to report these tips, or they can use another format as long as it contains the information required by the IRS. Employees also must report their tip income when they file their personal income tax returns.

Employers' reporting responsibilities are more complex. They must:

■ Report to the IRS the total tip income that each employee earns per year

■ Pay and withhold the applicable taxes on tip income

Some establishments also must file an annual report that discloses the total sales, credit card sales, credit card tips, and reported tips for the year. This report is filed on IRS Form 8027, "Employer's Annual Information Return of Tip Income and Allocated Tips," and is required when:

■ Tipping is customary in your operation.

■ Food and drink are served for on-site consumption.

■ More than ten employees or their equivalent are employed on a typical day.

Exhibit 12t

IRS Form 8027

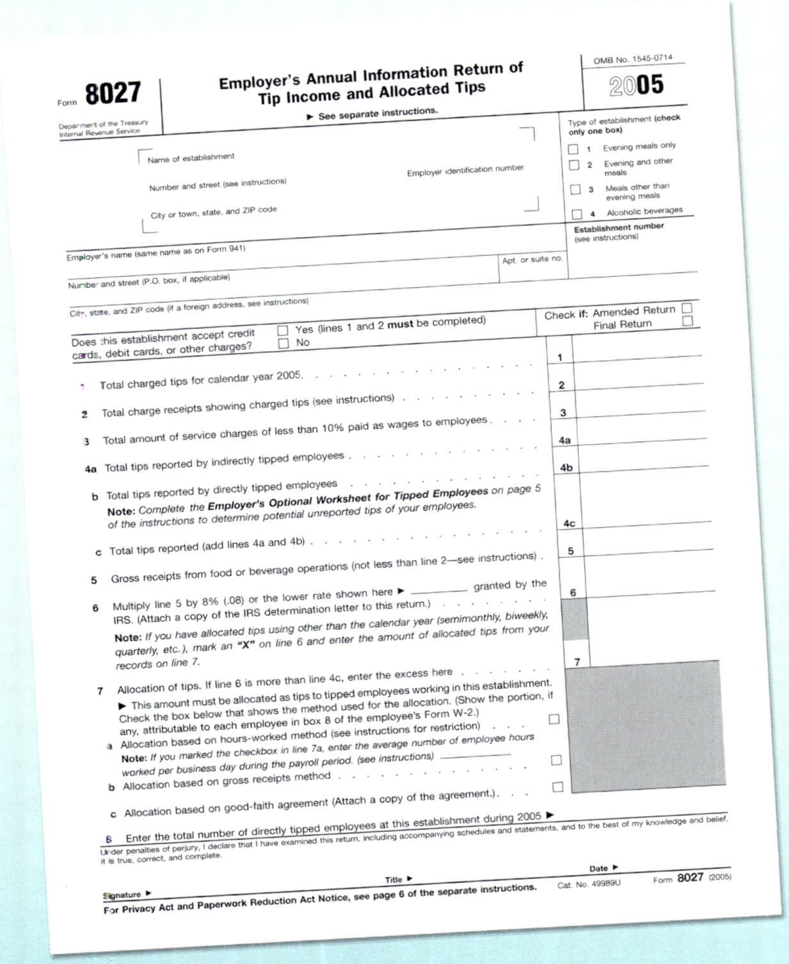
Form **8027**

Department of the Treasury
Internal Revenue Service

Employer's Annual Information Return of Tip Income and Allocated Tips

► **See separate instructions.**

OMB No. 1545-0714

2005

Name of establishment

Number and street (see instructions)

City or town, state, and ZIP code

Employer identification number

Type of establishment (**check only one box**)

☐ 1 Evening meals only

☐ 2 Evening and other meals

☐ 3 Meals other than evening meals

☐ 4 Alcoholic beverages

Establishment number (see instructions)

Employer's name (same name as on Form 941)

Number and street (P.O. box, if applicable)

Apt. or suite no.

City, state, and ZIP code (if a foreign address, see instructions)

Check if: Amended Return ☐ Final Return ☐

Does this establishment accept credit cards, debit cards, or other charges? ☐ Yes (lines 1 and 2 **must** be completed) ☐ No

1 Total charged tips for calendar year 2005 . . . . . | 1

2 Total charge receipts showing charged tips (see instructions) . . . . . | 2

3 Total amount of service charges of less than 10% paid as wages to employees . . . . | 3

4a Total tips reported by indirectly tipped employees . . . . . | 4a

b Total tips reported by directly tipped employees . . . . . | 4b

Note: *Complete the* ***Employer's Optional Worksheet for Tipped Employees*** *on page 5 of the instructions to determine potential unreported tips of your employees.*

c Total tips reported (add lines 4a and 4b) . . . . . | 4c

5 Gross receipts from food or beverage operations (not less than line 2—see instructions) . | 5

6 Multiply line 5 by 8% (.08) or the lower rate shown here ► ________ granted by the IRS. (Attach a copy of the IRS determination letter to this return.) . . . . . | 6

Note: *If you have allocated tips using other than the calendar year (semimonthly, biweekly, quarterly, etc.), mark an* **"X"** *on line 6 and enter the amount of allocated tips from your records on line 7.*

7 Allocation of tips. If line 6 is more than line 4c, enter the excess here . . . . . | 7

► This amount must be allocated as tips to tipped employees working in this establishment. Check the box below that shows the method used for the allocation. (Show the portion, if any, attributable to each employee in box 8 of the employee's Form W-2.)

a Allocation based on hours-worked method (see instructions for restriction) . . . ☐

Note: *If you marked the checkbox in line 7a, enter the average number of employee hours worked per business day during the payroll period. (see instructions)* ________

b Allocation based on gross receipts method . . . . . ☐

c Allocation based on good-faith agreement (Attach a copy of the agreement.) . . . ☐

8 Enter the total number of directly tipped employees at this establishment during 2005 ►

Under penalties of perjury, I declare that I have examined this return, including accompanying schedules and statements, and to the best of my knowledge and belief, it is true, correct, and complete.

Signature ► Title ► Date ►

For Privacy Act and Paperwork Reduction Act Notice, see page 6 of the separate instructions. Cat. No. 49989U Form **8027** (2005)

Internal Revenue Service

If an operation is required to file Form 8027 (see *Exhibit 12t*), and the total tips its employees report for the pay period or year do not add up to 8 percent of the operation's sales, the operation also must follow **tip allocation** rules. These rules require employers to allot tip income amounts to employees who reported tips of less than 8 percent of their individual sales. The employers provide these tip allocation amounts on the employee's W-2 tax form, which the employee provides to the IRS when filing an income tax return.

Although it is each employee's responsibility to accurately report tips, as a manager, you should make sure your employees understand this responsibility. If they underreport their tips, both your employees and your operation are more likely to be audited by the IRS, and the employer may be responsible for its FICA (Social Security and Medicare) tax on any unreported tips. Employees who underreport their tips may also be responsible for their share of FICA (Social Security and Medicare) tax, as well as income tax.

Another area where the IRS may be involved in both your employees' and your operation's finances is wage levies.

Ensuring Legal Garnishments and Levies

Title III of the Consumer Credit Protection Act prohibits employers from terminating or disciplining employees in some cases when a court or a government mandates their wages be paid in part to a third party. This situation occurs when a creditor obtains a court order to receive payments directly from an employee's earnings or when a government tax agency, such as the IRS, seizes wages to pay for back taxes, fines, or penalties. Payments taken by a government agency are called **levies,** and payments ordered by a court are called **garnishments.** The law also restricts the amounts of these garnishments and levies, based on the employee's income.

Ensuring Accurate Compensation

Ensuring employees receive the compensation they are supposed to receive is an important responsibility. As a manager, your responsibility is to follow your operation's policies and procedures for monitoring employee time reports and working with the **payroll administrator**—the person, department, or outside company that ensures paychecks are issued.

Payroll Administrators

The most visible function of a payroll administrator is delivering accurate paychecks on time. As part of this, payroll administrators must ensure that the correct taxes, health insurance premiums, benefit contributions, and other applicable items are deducted from each employee's wages and forwarded to the appropriate agency, company, or account. They also must ensure that any bonuses, expense reimbursements, advances, or special payments owed to an employee are added to his or her paycheck.

However, the role of a payroll administrator is not limited to ensuring the correct dollar amount on a paycheck. In many organizations, payroll administrators also ensure that employees receive accurate credits and debits for any benefits based on length of service. For example, in operations that provide paid vacation, vacation time may be based on how many days an employee has worked. The payroll administrator must track the number of days worked, so an employee can receive credit for the correct number of vacation days. When an employee uses a vacation day, it must be correctly deducted from the number of accrued vacation days.

Likewise, tracking the length of time and the dates an employee has worked is important for ensuring that he or she fulfills service or vesting requirements for certain benefits, such as a retirement benefit. The payroll administrator is often responsible for communicating this service information to benefit plan administrators. The degree and method of communication between payroll administrators and benefit plan administrators, and the accuracy of the hours reported, depends in part on the operation's payroll system.

Exhibit 12u

A timecard system is part
of a payroll system.

Payroll Systems

A **payroll system** is a method for recording and tracking employee time and issuing paychecks. It can include timecards, card readers, computers, paperwork, reports, and other resources, and can involve various people and procedures. In small operations, for example, simple timecards are often used, which employees complete and sign each day. Typically, supervisors review and sign these cards at the end of the week and then forward them to the payroll administrator. Some operations, especially larger ones, use timecard machines where employees "clock in" and "clock out," and then sign their timecards at the end of the week to certify their hours. (See *Exhibit 12u.*) Alternatively, card readers can electronically read employee identification cards and record the hours in a database.

As a manager, one of your roles is to ensure that employees are reporting the correct number of hours and crediting those hours to the right category, such as work versus personal days. In most payroll systems, managers are required to sign off on their employees' time reports to verify the information is correct. Although many managers think they only need to monitor the hours of nonexempt workers, they soon learn that reviewing the hours or timecards of salaried workers is just as important. (See *Exhibit 12v.*) Depending on how automated your payroll system is, you may need to periodically review and sign individuals' timecards and generate or review payroll reports.

Exhibit 12v

Reasons to Verify Time Reported by Salaried Workers

- Ensure the employee was at work.

- Ensure the time record accurately reflects the appropriate category—work, personal leave, sick days, unpaid leave, etc.

- Ensure the employee puts in a fair number of hours but not too many hours (which may indicate a need for additional staff or training).

- Determine whether the employee is coming in and leaving at the expected times.

- Determine whether the employee is misusing paid time off.

- Determine if the employee may have performance problems— if there is a relationship between the time put in and poor work performance.

In operations that have computerized payroll systems, these systems may be linked to larger systems that automate certain tasks, especially communication among the payroll administrator, plan administrator, and human resources personnel. For example, when a new employee is hired, a human resources professional may enter the new hire's start date, salary, personal information, and benefit selections into the computer system. When the new hire begins submitting time reports, the payroll system will automatically issue an accurate paycheck and begin tracking employee service based on the reported hours. When the employee becomes eligible for benefits that have service requirements, the system will notify the plan administrator. Alternatively, the plan administrator may periodically generate reports to identify people who will become eligible for certain plans.

Regardless of the level of automation, a payroll system must incorporate methods for keeping records as required by law. For example, the FLSA requires employers to keep certain records for each nonexempt, or hourly, employee. It also requires operations to keep other records that show how wages were figured, such as timecards, schedules, and wage rate tables, as well as records related to payroll, collective bargaining agreements, and sales and purchase records.

Payroll Administration Options

Given that payroll systems can be very complex, many restaurant and foodservice operations have outsourced the payroll administration function. Such operations have found that outside services can handle detailed payroll paperwork more efficiently and effectively with fewer errors because they specialize in this area of business. These services handle payroll, tax withholding, tax payments, tax reporting, and other details associated with payroll processing. However, managers must still review timecards or pay sheets and monitor the reported hours before submitting any information to the payroll service.

In smaller restaurant and foodservice operations, such services may not be worth the added expense. A part-time bookkeeper may be able to handle these tasks. Alternatively, smaller operations can use bookkeeping software designed especially to help with payroll administration for small businesses.

Selecting the right payroll system—often done by the human resources or financial staff of large restaurant or foodservice companies—is one of the many aspects of payroll management. Finding the best system for the size and extent of your organization involves determining what you need the system to keep track of, such as:

- Dates and hours worked
- Regular hours at different pay rates for different employees
- Overtime rates for those hours that are eligible
- Federal, state, and local taxes
- Vacation and personal time accrual and use

- Sick days

- Employees' healthcare and other insurance premiums

- Dollar value of all the benefits each employee receives

- Employee contributions to defined contribution plans, such as a 401(k)

- Plan matching contributions made by the employer

- Quarterly and annual payroll reports to various government agencies

- Garnishments and levies

- Pay advances and paybacks of these advances

- Merit or performance-determined pay and bonuses

- Expense reimbursements and other special payments

Learning about these different functions and researching the available systems and software can be a major undertaking. Some operations will hire an expert to assist them rather than risk choosing the wrong system or software. However, in other areas related to payroll, such as controlling labor costs, an operation's own employees are often in the best position to help.

Activity

Research Payroll Services

To help you appreciate the complexity of payroll administration, investigate payroll administration services on the Internet. Look at the Web sites of several companies. What types of payroll services do they provide? Do any of them have special services for small businesses? If so, what are they?

Controlling Labor Costs

Labor costs account for a large part of most restaurant and foodservice operations' total costs. Fortunately, as a manager, there are many strategies you can use to reduce and control this portion of your operation's costs. One of the most fundamental ways is to limit the wages that you pay to employees. However, setting lower pay rates is not always the best approach to building a profitable operation.

Setting Pay Rates

To be competitive in the job market, you need to offer wages and benefits that will encourage people to apply for your jobs, accept your job offers, and stay with your operation. On the other hand, you also need to keep your labor costs as low as possible. You need to balance these needs, while complying with the laws that determine wages, when setting pay rates for employees and potential employees.

Establishing competitive pay rates is an important part of compensation administration. In large companies, human resources professionals often conduct this work. For small operations, the owner or manager may determine the pay rates. In any case, it is useful to understand the process of establishing pay ranges. The first step is to consider the operation's total labor needs.

Analyzing Total Labor Needs

If you are responsible for setting your operation's pay rates, you need to analyze your operation's total labor needs before you consider how much to pay employees. You may do some of this analysis as part of a recruiting plan, but your research for setting wages should be broader. How many person hours do you need each day and for which positions and times? (A **person hour** is one hour of work done by one person.) How many people are filling these positions? What are the hours these employees work each day and each week? How many full-time employees do you need? How many part-time employees do you need? What are the total compensation costs, including benefits, for each full-time and part-time employee?

There are many other questions to address, and your research should include a look at past labor needs and forecasts for future labor needs. Based on what you find, you can determine if you need to adjust your scheduling and labor plans. For example, if past and current labor patterns show a lot of overtime costs, your operation may want to add employees and adjust the schedule.

The solutions are not always this simple, however. You need to really understand your operation, its labor market, and its staffing challenges to do a good of job analyzing your operation's total labor needs. For example, if past and current labor patterns do not show a lot of overtime costs, but exit interview data indicate employees are leaving because they are not getting enough hours, you need to investigate further. Can you give existing employees more hours without increasing total labor costs through overtime and additional benefits? If not, then you need to compare the costs of turnover against the higher costs of labor.

Researching Wage Rates

Once you have determined your total labor needs, you can consider the wages your operation can offer in the context of what other operations are offering locally and regionally. However, to be competitive in your labor market, you first need to figure out who the competitors are for your labor pool and what compensation they are offering. Remember, your competitors may include businesses other than restaurant and foodservice operations, and compensation can include employee benefits and incentives in addition to wages.

To help you learn about the compensation that other businesses offer, you can use a range of national and regional compensation surveys. These surveys typically summarize different measures of compensation for various jobs and types of establishments, such as the average wage earned by prep cooks in a casual full-service restaurant, or the types of benefits offered in the average catering operation. Many government, nonprofit, and business organizations publish wage and salary surveys. For example, the National Restaurant Association and State Restaurant Associations provide information on salary surveys, as do many career or human resources Web sites.

Whether or not you use surveys, you should still investigate the compensation offered by your competitors. There are many ways to do this; for example, you might routinely review local help-wanted advertisements to monitor any wages that are published.

Determining Your Market Position

After you have collected information about the pay ranges of your competitors and labor market, you can decide how you want to position your operation: as a low-pay, high-pay, or competitive-pay organization. From that decision, you can establish the pay ranges that you will offer for each position. However, when setting rates, you need to be mindful not only of minimum wage laws, but also of laws that prohibit discrimination in compensation.

Activity

Investigating Wages in Your Area

Individually or in teams, develop a list of ways to learn the salaries of local dishwashers, line cooks, and waitstaff. Then discuss the costs and benefits of each of these techniques for collecting information.

Exhibit 12w

Federal Laws That Prohibit Discrimination in Compensation

- Title I of the Americans with Disabilities Act (ADA)—prohibits discrimination in compensation based on a disability

- Age Discrimination in Employment Act (ADEA)—prohibits discrimination in compensation based on an age of forty years or older

- Title VII of the Civil Rights Act—prohibits discrimination in compensation based on race, color, religion, sex, or national origin

- Equal Pay Act—requires equal pay to be given to men and women for doing essentially the same work in the same establishment

Ensuring Nondiscriminatory Compensation

In addition to the minimum wage requirements, operations need to comply with various laws that prohibit employers from discriminating against people through any form of compensation—wages, employee benefits, or incentives. Several of the antidiscrimination laws mentioned in previous chapters contain provisions that prohibit this type of discrimination. (See *Exhibit 12w.*)

While Title VII of the Civil Rights Act offers some protection to people paid an unfair wage based on gender, the U.S. Congress has concluded that women have historically been paid much lower wages than men. The Equal Pay Act (EPA) of 1963, which is an amendment to the FLSA, provides protections in this area to both women and men. The EPA requires employers to pay the same compensation to men and women who do essentially the same work in the same establishment. According to the Equal Employment Opportunity Commission (EEOC), the jobs must be "substantially equal." This equality is determined by the skills, effort, responsibilities, and working conditions required to do the jobs being compared. When setting pay rates for various jobs, be sure to consider these factors; also keep in mind that there are other ways to control labor costs.

Controlling Overtime

Since labor is one of an operation's largest expenses, minimizing overtime should be one of your focal points as a manager. The process of controlling overtime costs involves careful planning, clear policies, and some flexibility to alter staffing patterns according to need—to add employees to certain shifts, or to reduce staff on other shifts.

Strategies for Monitoring Overtime

One of the common ways that employers limit overtime is to develop a policy that requires employees to get approval for overtime ahead of time. Such a policy reminds supervisors and employees that overtime is not automatic and should be used sparingly. It also reinforces the importance of good planning and awareness of labor costs.

Another way to control overtime is to have managers review timecards at the end of each shift to ensure that no employee's hours could lead to overtime later in the week. If an employee has already worked close to forty hours, you may be able to rearrange the schedule later in the week to provide time off or a shorter workday for that employee, thereby preventing overtime.

However, if reworking the schedule still leads to overtime, or if employees forget to get approval for overtime, then the operation must pay for the overtime. Although some operations try to disallow payment for overtime when it is not preapproved, this is illegal. The proper solution is to pay for the overtime, then reprimand the employee for working unauthorized overtime.

Legitimate Uses of Overtime

While reducing or limiting overtime can often be achieved with careful planning and is normally the preferred course of action, there are times when overtime is essential. Overtime can be the right choice when:

- There are unforeseen needs for extra staff due to emergencies or unplanned business.

- Coverage is needed for training employees.

- Coverage is needed for vacations and time off.

In many cases, paying existing employees to work overtime can result in better productivity than you would get with new hires or temporary workers since you do not need to train existing employees. However, this approach should be used sparingly because excessive overtime will wear out your employees and result in reduced productivity, poor morale, and increased turnover. In short-term situations, overtime can be cost effective for the operation, and it also can be a perquisite ("perk") for employees who are willing to work extra hours.

Think About It...

How was overtime planned and handled in restaurant or foodservice operations where you worked? How does your experience compare with these practices?

Summary

As a manager, you need to understand the benefits offered by your operation and the federal, state, and local laws and company policies that affect them. This understanding enables you to comply with the laws and company policies, manage benefits in a cost-effective and fair manner, and help employees take advantage of their benefits.

Mandated employee benefits include Social Security, unemployment insurance, workers' compensation, and leaves of absence in certain situations. FMLA requires you to provide twelve weeks of unpaid leave to employees who have a serious medical condition, who need to care for a family member, or who have given birth to or adopted a child. USERRA provides unpaid leave for military service and ensures that employees who serve in the military will keep their civilian jobs.

Restaurant and foodservice employers often voluntarily provide other benefits, most commonly uniform and meal benefits, healthcare plans, employee assistance programs, and retirement benefits.

Several laws govern how some of these benefits are administered. ERISA protects employees' pensions and healthcare plans. COBRA extends group healthcare coverage for people who would otherwise lose their health insurance. HIPAA helps ensure that people do not lose access to healthcare because of preexisting conditions, other health status factors, or limits on plan enrollment periods.

Every manager should be well trained in employee benefits, company policies and procedures, and workplace laws. Ideally, internal resources can help you keep abreast of changes in the laws. You also should develop your own resources for learning about these changes.

Employee benefits are part of a total compensation package. Several laws control various aspects of wages and payroll. The FLSA requires some employees to be paid a minimum wage and overtime pay and has record-keeping requirements. Antidiscrimination laws prohibit discrimination in compensation. The Equal Pay Act helps ensure pay equity between men and women. The Consumer Credit Protection Act protects the rights of employees whose wages are garnished or levied.

Your operation's policies and procedures should guide you in complying with applicable laws. You should also follow your operation's policies and procedures to ensure employees are paid the correct amount at the correct time, monitor employee time reports, and work with the payroll administrator.

Review Your Learning

1 Which action helps an employer comply with the Employee Retirement Income Security Act of 1974 (ERISA)?

   A. Posting a notice on equal opportunity rights in the workplace

   B. Providing a summary plan description to employees when they first join a plan

   C. Supplying a copy of the employee handbook to employees whenever they ask

   D. Periodically reminding employees of their rights under ERISA

2 Which action helps an employer comply with the Consolidated Omnibus Budget Reconciliation Act (COBRA)?

   A. Notifying the plan administrator when an employee experiences a life event

   B. Supplying medical claim forms to employees whenever they ask

   C. Notifying the plan administrator when an employee quits

   D. Posting a notice about medical leave in a prominent place

3 Which action helps a plan administrator comply with the Health Insurance Portability and Accountability Act (HIPAA)?

   A. Providing a certificate of creditable coverage to plan participants when they lose healthcare coverage

   B. Sending a summary annual report to all participants and written updates on their plans as needed

   C. Notifying employees whenever a preexisting condition changes their coverage or premiums

   D. Posting a notice about military leave in a prominent place

4 Which action can help you manage the costs of a meal benefit?

   A. Providing a meal allowance for employees

   B. Only allowing fifteen-minute meal breaks

   C. Posting a notice about the rules for meal breaks

   D. Monitoring the kitchen at all times

5 Which action can help you manage the costs of a uniform benefit?

   A. Providing adequate personal protective equipment

   B. Limiting how often employees can change their uniforms

   C. Obtaining uniform care instructions from the manufacturer

   D. Periodically bidding out the uniform and laundry contracts

6 Which statement best describes the tip credit provision of the Fair Labor Standards Act (FLSA)?

   A. Tipped employees younger than twenty are credited with extra tips that equal or exceed the basic minimum wage.

   B. The overtime rate for tipped employees must be equal to one-and-one-half times their normal hourly rate.

   C. The minimum wage for tipped employees plus their average tips must equal or exceed the basic minimum wage.

   D. Tipped employees must report all their tip income, or their employers are required to report an 8 percent credit to the employees' tip income.

7 Which action can help an employer comply with the Family and Medical Leave Act (FMLA)?

A. Providing proof of an employee's return to work

B. Not questioning the reason for an employee's leave

C. Posting a notice about continuing health insurance coverage

D. Consulting with an employee's physician

8 Which action can help an employer comply with the Uniformed Services Employment and Reemployment Rights Act (USERRA)?

A. Posting a notice about USERRA

B. Sending periodic notices to employees who are on leave

C. Not filling an employee's position while he or she is on leave

D. Notifying an employee's family of any change in benefits

9 What is one of a manager's key responsibilities in a payroll system?

A. Ensuring that the payroll department is issuing paychecks on time

B. Ensuring that employees are reporting the correct number of hours

C. Ensuring that each employee completed the necessary tax withholding forms

D. Generating quarterly reports and submitting them to the payroll department

10 Which is *not* a strategy for controlling overtime?

A. Schedule shifts for part-time employees to reduce required breaks.

B. Require people to get approval for overtime ahead of time.

C. Closely monitor employees' timecards and alter schedules as needed.

D. Plan schedules to keep employees' weekly hours at or below forty.

Notes

Field Project

The Employment Cycle

Introduction

Understanding the recruiting, screening, hiring, and orientation processes is critical to the process of finding and hiring new employees, particularly in an industry with a high turnover rate, such as the restaurant and foodservice industry. This research project will give you firsthand knowledge about managers' responsibilities in these areas.

This project will also give you a chance to meet industry professionals, compare practices in a variety of restaurant and foodservice operations, and develop a better understanding of the ways in which these activities are conducted. Some of the tasks involved are:

- Identifying and selecting several local restaurant or foodservice operations to research

- Collecting information about these operations through interviews, observations, site visits, and advertising

- Analyzing the information acquired and describing the results of your research in a paper

The entire project has been designed to help you assess the variety of recruiting, screening, hiring, and orientation practices used in the restaurant and foodservice industry in your local area. If you have trouble with any part of this project, ask your teacher for assistance.

Assignment

To conduct this project, first there are several decisions you need to make and then several steps to undertake.

1 Identify operations to research.

Your first task is to identify and then select at least four restaurant or foodservice operations in your area that you want to learn more about. Pick establishments from which you think you will learn the most through your visits and observations. You should include operations from different categories, such as:

- ☐ Quick service
- ☐ Casual dining
- ☐ Family oriented
- ☐ Independently owned
- ☐ Fine dining
- ☐ Business and industry foodservice
- ☐ Franchise (or centrally owned location) of a large national chain
- ☐ College foodservice
- ☐ Health care or hospital foodservice
- ☐ Private club—country, sports, urban, etc.
- ☐ Hotel or resort restaurant(s)

2 Collect information.

To learn about the recruiting, screening, hiring, and orientation processes used at each selected operation, your research should include interviews with managers or owners and site visits to observe how an operation is run. However, you should also consider other methods of gathering useful information about an operation and its procedures, including:

- ☐ Studying the menu, layout, uniforms, and other aspects

- ☐ Looking at recruiting notices

- ☐ Reading newspapers, local magazines, and other sources of information in your area for job advertisements and other pertinent information

- ☐ Asking for copies of forms or documents used by the operation

continued on next page

The Employment Cycle *continued from previous page*

☐ Researching the local labor market and other related information through the local chamber of commerce

☐ Talking to local restaurant organizations or other professional organizations

Before interviewing a manager or owner, you should develop a series of questions to ask. To make it easier to compare information across operations, use the same questions with every interview. Although you should develop your own set of questions, you might include questions such as those shown in the Exhibit to the right. When possible, also ask the manager or owner for copies of materials used in the recruiting, screening, hiring, and orientation processes.

3 Present your research.

The last part of your assignment involves preparing an analytical paper that compares the processes used in these various operations with the concepts discussed in Chapters 3, 4, and 5. In addition, if you see areas that could be improved in the operations you studied, include your recommendations in your paper. Be sure to support these recommendations with evidence from your reading or your observations. If possible, also include any supporting documentation collected from a particular establishment.

Sample Interview Questions

■ What are the most effective ways you advertise or promote openings in your operation?

■ What internal methods of recruiting are used, and how successful are these methods?

■ What kind of work experience do you look for in a potential employee?

■ What characteristics do you look for in a potential employee?

■ What questions do you ask in an interview?

■ Who conducts interviews of potential new employees?

■ Do you use a standard application form?

■ How do you handle reference checks?

■ How are hiring decisions made?

■ Are there any standard forms used in the hiring process?

■ What elements of the hiring process are established by a central human resources department?

■ Are there parts of the hiring process that strike you as unusual?

■ When you make a job offer, do you use an employment letter or contract?

■ What information do you give candidates before and after they accept a job offer?

■ How do you orient new employees to their job, company policies, and the organizational culture?

Index

Human Resources Management and Supervision

Exam Prep Guide

PEARSON

Prentice
Hall

Upper Saddle River, New Jersey
Columbus, Ohio

NATIONAL
RESTAURANT
ASSOCIATION
S O L U T I O N S ™

10 9 8 7
ISBN-13: 978-0-13-501895-8
ISBN-10: 0-13-501895-1

Contents

How to Take the ManageFirst Examination

The ability to take tests effectively is a learned skill. There are specific things you can do to prepare yourself physically and mentally for an exam. This section helps you prepare and do your best on the ManageFirst Examination.

I. BEFORE THE EXAM

A. How to Study
Study the right material the right way. There is a lot of information and material in each course. How do you know what to study so you are prepared for the exam? This guide highlights what you need to know.

1. **Read the Introduction to each *Competency Guide*.** The beginning section of each guide explains the features and how it is organized.

2. **Look at how each chapter is organized and take clues from the book.**

   - ***The text itself is important.*** If the text is bold, large, or italicized you can be sure it is a key point that you should understand.

   - *The very first page tells you what you will learn.*

     Inside This Chapter: This tells you at a high level what will be covered in the chapter. Make sure you understand what each section covers. If you have studied the chapter but cannot explain what each section pertains to, you need to review that material.

Learning Objectives: After completing each chapter, you should be able to accomplish the specific goals and demonstrate what you have learned after reading the material. The practice exam as well as the actual exam questions relate to these learning objectives.

- *Quizzes and Tests*

  Test Your Knowledge: This is a pretest found at the beginning of each chapter to see how much you already know. Take this quiz to help you determine which areas you need to study and focus on.

- *Key Terms* are listed at the beginning of each chapter and set in bold the first time they are referred to in the chapter. These terms—new and specific to the topic or ones you are already familiar with—are key to understanding the chapter's content. When reviewing the material, look for the key terms you don't know or understand and review the corresponding paragraph.

- *Exhibits* visually depict key concepts and include charts, tables, photographs, and illustrations. As you review each chapter, find out how well you can explain the concepts illustrated in the exhibits.

- *Additional Exercises*

  Think About It sidebars are designed to provoke further thought and/or discussion and require understanding of the topics.

  Activity boxes are designed to check your understanding of the material and help you apply your knowledge. The activities relate to a learning objective.

- *Summary* reviews all the important concepts in the chapter and helps you retain and master the material.

3. **Attend Review Sessions or Study Groups**. Review sessions, if offered, cover material that will most likely be on the test. If separate review sessions are not offered, make sure you attend class the day before the exam. Usually, the instructor will review the material during this class. If you are a social learner, study with other students; discussing the topics with other students may help your comprehension and retention.

4. **Review the Practice Questions,** which are designed to help you prepare for the exam. Sample questions are designed to familiarize the student with the format, length, and style of the exam questions, and represent only a sampling of topic coverage on the final exam. The performance level on sample questions does not guarantee passing of a ManageFirst Program exam.

B. How to Prepare Physically and Mentally

Make sure you are ready to perform your best during the exam. Many students do everything wrong when preparing for an exam. They stay up all night, drink coffee to stay awake, or take sleep aids which leave them groggy and tired on test day.

There are practical things to do to be at your best. If you were an athlete preparing for a major event, what would you do to prepare yourself? You wouldn't want to compete after staying up all night or drinking lots of caffeine. The same holds true when competing with your brain!

1. **Get plenty of sleep.** Lack of sleep makes it difficult to focus and recall information. Some tips to help you get a good night's sleep are:

   - Make sure you have studied adequately enough days before the exam so that you do not need to cram and stay up late the night before the test.
   - Eat a good dinner the night before and a good breakfast the day of the exam.
   - Do not drink alcohol or highly-caffeinated drinks.
   - Exercise during the day, but not within four hours of bedtime.
   - Avoid taking sleep aids.

2. **Identify and control anxiety.** It is important to know the difference between actual test anxiety and anxiety caused by not being prepared.

Test anxiety is an actual physical reaction. If you know the information when you are **not** under pressure but feel physically sick and cannot recall information during the exam, you probably suffer from test anxiety. In this case, you may need to learn relaxation techniques or get some counseling. The key is how you react under pressure.

If you cannot recall information during reviews or the practice exam when you are not under pressure, you have not committed the information to memory and need to study more.

- Make sure you are as prepared as possible. (See "Anxiety Caused by Lack of Preparation")
- Take the exam with a positive attitude.
- Do not talk to other students who may be pessimistic or negative about the exam.
- Know what helps you relax and do it (chewing gum, doodling, breathing exercises).
- Make sure you understand the directions. Ask the instructor questions *before* the test begins.
- The instructor or proctor may only talk to you if you have defective materials or need to go to the restroom. They cannot discuss any questions.
- The instructor or proctor may continuously monitor the students so do not be nervous if they walk around the room.
- Know the skills described in Section II, During the Test.

3. **Anxiety Caused by Lack of Preparation.** The best way to control anxiety due to lack of preparation is focus on the exam. Whenever possible, you should know and do the following:

- Know the location of the exam and how to get there.
- Know if it is a paper-and-pencil test or an online exam. Pencils may be available but bring sufficient number 2 pencils if taking the paper-and-pencil version of the exam.
- If it is an online exam you may need your email address, if you have one, to receive results.
- You are prohibited from using purses, books, papers, pagers, cell phones, or other recording devices during the exam.
- Calculators and scratch paper may be used, if needed. Be sure your calculator is working properly and has fresh batteries.
- The exam is not a timed; however, it is usually completed in less than two hours.
- Take the sample exam so you know what format, style, and content to expect.
- Arrive early so you don't use valuable testing time to unpack.

II. DURING THE TEST

An intent of National Restaurant Association Solutions' ManageFirst exams is to make sure you have met certain learning objectives. If you are physically prepared, have studied the material, and taken the practice exam, you should find the ManageFirst exams to be very valid and fair. Remember, successful test taking is a skill. Understanding the different aspects of test preparation and exam taking will help ensure your best performance.

A. *Test Taking Strategies*

- Preview the exam for a quick overview of the length and questions.
- Do not leave any question unanswered.
- Answer the questions you are sure of first.

- Stop and check occasionally to make sure you are putting your answer in the correct place on the answer sheet. If you are taking an online exam, you will view one question at a time.
- Do not spend too much time on any one question. If you do not know the answer after reasonable consideration, move on and come back to it later.
- Make note of answers about which you are unsure so you can return to them.
- Review the exam at the end to check your answers and make sure all questions are answered.

B. Strategies for Answering Multiple-Choice Questions

Multiple-choice tests are objective. The correct answer is there, you just need to identify it.

- Try to answer the question before you look at the options.
- Use the process of elimination. Eliminate the answers you know are incorrect.
- Your first response is usually correct.

III. AFTER THE EXAM

Learn from each exam experience so you can do better on the next. If you did not perform on the exam as you expected, determine the reason. Was it due to lack of studying or preparation? Were you unable to control your test anxiety? Were you not focused enough because you were too tired? Identifying the reason allows you to spend more time on that aspect before your next exam. Use the information to improve on your next exam.

If you do not know the reason, you should schedule a meeting with the instructor. As all NRA Solutions ManageFirst exams are consistent, it is important to understand and improve your exam performance. If you cannot identify your problem areas, your errors will most likely be repeated on consecutive exams.

IV. EXAM DAY DETAILS

The information contained in this section will help ensure that you are able to take the exam on the scheduled test day and that you know what to expect and are comfortable about taking the exam.

- Have your photo identification available.
- Anyone with special needs must turn in an *Accommodation Request* to the instructor at least 10 days prior to the exam to receive approval and allow time for preparations. *If needs are not known 10 days prior, you may not be able to take the exam on the scheduled test day.*
- A bilingual English-native language dictionary may be used by anyone who speaks English as a second language. The dictionary will be inspected to make sure there are no notes or extra papers in it.
- If you are ill and must leave the room after the exam has begun you must turn in your materials to the instructor or proctor. If you are able to return, your materials will be returned to you and you may complete the exam. If it is an online exam you must close your browser and if the exam has not been graded yet, login in again when you return.
- Restroom breaks are allowed. Only one person may go at a time and all materials must be turned in prior to leaving the room and picked up when you return; or you must close your browser and login again for online exams.
- Make-up tests may be available if you are unable to take the exam on test day. Check with your instructor for details.
- If you are caught cheating you will not receive a score and must leave the exam location.

Human Resources Management and Supervision Chapter Summaries and Objectives

Chapter 1 Building a Welcoming Work Environment and Encouraging Diversity

Summary

The restaurant and foodservice industry contains one of the most diverse workforces. In this industry, encouraging diversity means you treat *all* people—employees, vendors, and guests—in a nondiscriminatory manner; that is, without regard to race, color, national origin, and any other trait not related to that person's role at your establishment. Diversity issues and antidiscrimination policies impact every aspect of human resources, from finding and recruiting potential employees to managing employee terminations.

Creating an environment in which all people are valued has many benefits. Encouraging and honoring differences can mean a larger and better quality labor pool, a more enjoyable and productive environment, improved public relations, and most important, more customers. Promoting diversity also helps you fulfill regulatory guidelines and better positions you to defend against any claims of illegal discrimination.

Discrimination is appropriate when deciding among competing options, but making arbitrary distinctions could be unethical and illegal. Employers cannot base employment actions on characteristics protected under applicable federal, state, or local laws against discrimination. In addition, employers cannot create or allow an environment that is hostile to people based on these characteristics.

Federal law prohibits workplace discrimination based on race, color, religion, sex, national origin, age (forty or older), pregnancy, citizenship, disability, and military service. In addition, organizations that contract with the federal government, provide services or supplies as a subcontractor to a business that contracts with the government, or accept federal grants or funds may be governed by additional equal employment opportunity rules.

To promote and manage diversity, you need to be able to distinguish among stereotypes and prejudice, which should be discouraged, and cultural tendencies, which should be respected. Stereotypes are generalizations that individuals make about particular groups and the assumptions that all members of that group are the same. Stereotypes produce prejudice or bias, a general attitude toward a person, group, or organization on the basis of stereotypes unrelated to abilities. In contrast, many groups of people have cultural tendencies, or common beliefs and ways of acting. The main difference between stereotypes and cultural tendencies is that stereotypes do not distinguish between what a group of people may tend to do or believe, and what an individual actually does or believes.

Since discriminatory treatment often is illegal, allowing it to happen in your operation exposes you to the possibility of a complaint, investigation, or possible lawsuit. In addition, when discrimination and harassment are allowed, a culture of distrust and frustration is likely to develop. Employee productivity will fall, and their willingness to help each other will diminish dramatically. Morale will drop, and conflict and turnover will increase. Ultimately, these conditions will result in a poorly functioning operation.

To promote a culture of mutual respect, you need to help break down the stereotypes that people hold and manage activities that impact diversity. These activities include actively recruiting for members of minority groups, increasing cross-cultural communication among employees, educating employees about diversity and discrimination, setting and communicating expectations for positive (or at least neutral) behavior, and holding employees and the organization accountable to these expectations.

After completing this chapter, you should be able to:
- Define diversity as it relates to foodservice.
- Identify the benefits of a diverse workplace.
- List the ten categories of people protected from discrimination by federal equal employment opportunity (EEO) laws.
- Recognize federal laws that prohibit discrimination in the workplace.
- Differentiate between a cultural tendency and a stereotype.
- Identify how stereotypes and prejudices can affect a workplace.
- Recognize practices that promote diversity in the workplace.
- Describe ways to increase positive cross-cultural interaction and communication.

Chapter 2 Defining Job Descriptions

Summary

Job descriptions are documents that define the work involved in a particular assignment or position. Job descriptions are primarily intended as a tool to help an employee understand his or her job. However, they also support recruiting screening, hiring, orienting, development, training, performance programs and evaluations, salary administration, safety, union relations, and legal support.

A good job description starts with a thorough job analysis. A well-written job description includes at least the following information: (1) job identification information, which may include whether a position is exempt or nonexempt; (2) position supervisor information; (3) job summary; (4) responsibilities; and (5) job specifications. Some job descriptions also include job setting and publication information. The responsibilities should be written as duties and may include performance standards, although most operations do not do this.

A good job description avoids discriminatory language. Doing this involves writing the description honestly with a focus on the duties and bona fide occupational qualifications and using neutral language. To ensure job descriptions stay relevant, they should be reviewed periodically and updated as needed.

After completing this chapter, you should be able to:
- Define job description.
- Identify the functions of a job description.
- Identify the minimum information needed for a good job description.
- Explain how the Americans with Disabilities Act (ADA) affects the information in a job description.
- Recognize the differences between exempt and nonexempt positions.
- Recognize the importance of periodically reviewing job descriptions.

Chapter 3 Finding and Recruiting New Employees

Summary

Recruiting is an ongoing activity that encompasses many tasks. These include deciding what vacancies exist in the organization, establishing the skills and backgrounds needed in new employees, clarifying what your operation can offer to prospective employees, identifying sources of potential employees, and communicating the vacancies in the most productive way to build a talent pool of qualified people. You also need to build and maintain ongoing relationships with the sources of potential employees.

To identify when to increase recruiting efforts, you can forecast your staffing needs. Forecasting involves examining a variety of information about your operation, similar operations, and the labor market in your area. Once you have determined when to increase recruiting and for which jobs, you can identify the skills, knowledge, and abilities you want in potential employees and what your operation can offer in return.

Promoting a job opening involves marketing your recruiting message to appropriate sources of potential employees. These sources may be internal or external to your operation.

For internal recruiting, operations typically use a combination of recruiting methods, including job postings and regular employee communications. Employee referral programs often provide an incentive to current employees to refer friends and family to apply for new positions. The practice of promoting from within encourages employees to apply for other jobs within the operation.

For external recruiting, the range and number of sources depend in large part on the location of your operation. To successfully use many of the external recruiting methods, you first must build and maintain relationships with the external sources. The most productive external sources include schools, government agencies, and professional and community organizations.

In any type of recruiting effort, be sure to communicate the information in an effective way that complies with equal employment opportunity regulations. Avoid gender-specific titles and other discriminatory language, and avoid references to specific groups of people. Focus on the actual skills, knowledge, abilities, and responsibilities needed for the job. Include a diversity statement to encourage everyone who is interested in the job to apply.

To identify how successful a recruiting strategy is and whether the recruiting efforts need to be adjusted, analyze and evaluate the recruiting methods. This analysis should consider the costs of recruiting versus the benefits or results of the recruiting.

After completing this chapter, you should be able to:
- Identify information that can be used to forecast staffing needs.
- Identify common sources of potential employees in the restaurant and foodservice industry.
- Communicate a job opening to internal and external audiences.

- Describe methods for maintaining relationships with sources of potential employees.
- Avoid using discriminatory language in advertisements for job openings.
- Describe how to track and analyze the results of recruiting.

Chapter 4 Screening Potential Employees

Summary

Screening is the process of learning more about job applicants to determine how suitable they are for a job opening at your restaurant or foodservice operation. This process includes reviewing initial application documents; conducting screening interviews; administering tests, assessments, or simulations; conducting job interviews; and checking references. Some operations also conduct background checks and require applicants to undergo physical examinations or drug tests, or submit medical records, although these activities when used are usually conducted after a job offer is made. At every stage in the process, applicants are evaluated.

Throughout the screening process, it is critical to comply with employment laws regarding discriminatory language and practices. Avoiding discrimination ensures all applications have a fair chance for the job and protects your operation from claims of discrimination and lawsuits.

Several types of interviews are used during the screening process. Screening interviews, or pre-interviews, are intended to (1) gather information about the person applying for a position, (2) make him or her feel welcome, and (3) build interest in the operation. Job interviews are intended to gather additional information about an applicant and to give the applicant a realistic idea of what the job entails. Different types of job interviews and questions can be used to gather information: information gathering/skill interview questions, stress interview questions, and character/personality interview questions. These formats can be combined so different kinds of questions are asked in the same interview. Other interview formats include group interviews and successive interviews.

After completing this chapter, you should be able to:
- Describe the steps in the screening process.
- Recognize standard tools and techniques to screen job applicants.
- Identify examples of discriminatory language and practices related to screening.
- Describe typical methods for testing work skills and assessing personality traits.
- Recognize different types of interviews and when to use them.
- Develop a list of interview questions to use when screening an applicant.
- Describe common methods for checking references.

Chapter 5 Hiring and Orienting New Employees

Summary

Hiring and orientation affect many aspects of a person's critical first experiences as a new employee. Hiring involves making a job offer, processing that offer, conducting final background checks, and preparing the individual for employment. Orientation involves introducing a new employee to an operation and a job, so that he or she feels comfortable and welcome. Successful orientation programs offer many benefits, including welcoming new employees, demonstrating hospitality, ensuring consistency, and reducing turnover.

When a job offer is made, it should include details about the position, compensation, and benefits, as well as logistical information and any employment contingencies. If the operation is a union shop, the job offer should mention this. Job offers may be made orally, but the final job offer should always be documented in a letter or employment contract that the employee signs. A job offer may be contingent on the results of a final background check or health examination. Once a position is filled, you should notify the other candidates that they did not get the job.

At some point before or on an employee's first day of work, several documents need to be completed or produced to ensure that the employee can legally work for you and is added to the payroll successfully. Several other documents also need to be distributed or processed within a short time of the start date, including summary plan descriptions. These include benefit documents, such as plans and enrollment forms; job documents, such as a job description; and company policy documents, such as an employee handbook. Benefit, job, and company policy documents also should be explained orally as part of orientation.

Most of these documents need to be stored in the employee's personnel file. This confidential file also should include other employment-related documents. Personnel files should be stored in a safe and secure location.

Successful orientation programs require careful planning and often involve a range of resources. Checklists provide a way to manage the hiring and orientation process, but perhaps the most important resource is the people who will conduct the orientation activities. When an orientation is complete, you should evaluate how successful it was, so that you can make improvements to the program when necessary.

After completing this chapter, you should be able to:
- Explain the importance of orientation.
- List the information that belongs in a job offer.
- Identify documents and methods commonly used to communicate operation policies and practices.
- Describe methods for conducting final background checks.
- Recognize the types of documents that need to be produced or processed as part of hiring a new employee.
- Describe the information that belongs in a personnel file and how this file should be stored.
- Develop a checklist to manage hiring-related documents and the orientation process.

- Identify the tools, documentation, and personnel commonly involved in a successful orientation program.
- Recognize the importance of the contributors who conduct orientation activities.
- Identify a method for evaluating orientation programs.

Chapter 6 Supervising and Motivating Employees

Summary

The primary function of a supervisor is to help employees be successful. To fulfill this goal, supervisors encourage productivity and quality by planning for and creating the right environment. As part of this, they set the tone for an operation by the way they treat employees and the behavior they model. They also communicate their goals to employees and what they want employees to do.

When hourly employees are promoted to supervisory positions, they often need to adjust the way they think about their work. This adjustment includes changing their focus away from doing the visible, technical work to managing the people who do this work and building and managing employee relationships. A good habit for all supervisors to develop is to reflect on their management practices. By doing this, they can improve their own performance.

A large part of supervision is monitoring employees and enforcing standards. Supervisors should train, coach, reward, and discipline employees based on standards. To reinforce positive performance, good supervisors express their appreciation to employees. To improve poor performance, good supervisors provide corrective feedback, which should be delivered in a timely, professional, and positive manner. There are many models that can be followed when giving feedback. Some methods are asking the employee to describe any work difficulties, affirming or correcting this understanding, complimenting the employee, making suggestions for improvement, giving the employee an opportunity to respond, and asking for input on how to improve the situation. When training and coaching are not enough to bring an employee's performance up to standards, supervisors use progressive discipline as needed. Ideally, employees will be motivated enough so that this is not needed.

Supervisors are responsible for motivating their employees on a daily basis. Maslow's hierarchy of needs and the motivation-hygiene theory are two theories that explain what motivates people. Informal ways to motivate employees include acknowledging them as individuals; expressing appreciation for good work; sharing information to encourage involvement and belonging; and involving employees in various aspects of planning, problem solving, and decision making. Formal recognition and incentive programs also can motivate employees.

When planning an effective recognition or incentive program, the goals and parameters need to be clearly defined, as well as how and when to communicate results and how to celebrate the end of the program. When the program ends, it should be evaluated so that information learned can be used to improve future programs.

After completing this chapter, you should be able to:
- Describe the primary function of a supervisor.
- Recognize needs and factors that affect employee motivation.
- Identify the basis upon which employees should be trained, coached, rewarded, and disciplined.
- List communication techniques for providing feedback to employees.
- Describe techniques for motivating employees on a daily basis.
- Identify the most effective time to recognize or reward good performance.
- Identify the elements of a good employee recognition and incentive program.
- Give examples of rewards given for accomplishment.
- Give examples of incentives that motivate people to change behaviors or improve performance.

Chapter 7 Developing Employees

Summary

Employee development is an important part of every restaurant and foodservice manager's job. It is the primary method of turning adequate employees into outstanding employees. Employee development addresses the acquisition of new skills, knowledge, attitudes, and the improvement of existing ones. The employee's own goals should also be considered. The manager can help the employee determine his or her goals for improvement, but it is the employee's responsibility to make these improvements. A simple but effective process for developing employees is available.

There are many methods for developing employees. It is up to the manager and the employee to select the appropriate method(s) in light of what is available and what works best for the employee.

Employee development planning is a one-on-one situation that should be handled in privacy. Regular progress reviews and adjustments are also part of the process.

After completing this chapter you should be able to:
- Explain what employee development is and why it is important in restaurant and foodservice operations.
- Describe the important features of the employee development planning meeting.
- Describe how to set developmental goals for employees.
- List and describe the types of possible employee development methods.
- Discuss the advantages and disadvantages of each employee development method.
- Describe how to set up and implement a cross-training program.
- Describe the coaching process.

Chapter 8 Training Employees

Summary

Training is a powerful way of improving employees' skills, knowledge, and attitudes, as long as training is what is needed to correct a performance deficiency; the training actually addresses the skill knowledge gap of the employees; and an effective and affordable type of training is used. If this is not the case, then training will not be effective. Training gives an operation many benefits, such as improving skills, productivity, cohesiveness, and loyalty. It is much easier to do nothing or to provide education, but these tactics will not provide the benefits that training does. Although it takes time and money to analyze actual training needs, design good training, and develop good training, the payoff of this investment can be great.

The analysis stage is critical for aligning the training with the needs of the job and the trainees. Designing good training by following the four Ps of preparation, presentation, practice, and performance results in the most effective type of training. For instructor-led training, using a trainer who is an expert in both the subject and in enabling learning causes the training to be as effective as possible.

Training developed in-house is not the only source of good training. In fact, there are a lot of good training programs available from commercial companies, professional associations, and institutions of higher education.

After completing this chapter, you should be able to:
- Explain ways in which training can help an organization.
- Differentiate between training and education.
- Identify the elements of a successful training program.
- Explain the content that training materials should include.
- List and describe the steps of the ADDIE model of training development.
- Describe the steps of a thorough evaluation of training activity.

Chapter 9 Managing Shifts to Ensure a Quality Operation

Summary

Shift management is all about managing for quality. Without constant attention throughout every shift, quality suffers. Quality is about achieving the standards that the restaurant or foodservice operation has set. These standards are documented in the form of policy statements and checklists. There are three primary times in a shift when quality reviews are made using checklists: (1) opening or pre-shift, (2) mid-shift, and (3) shift-end or closing. At each of these times, there are checks made in many areas: facility interior and exterior, front of the house and back of the house, and fiduciary tasks.

Of course, you cannot achieve the quality level you want without having a plan and goals for each shift. An important part of shift goals is having enough staff on hand, so scheduling staff is an important part of shift management.

Shifts do not exist in a vacuum. What happens on one shift will affect the next shift and perhaps many future shifts. In order to transfer information about what happened and what was done on a shift, managers keep communication logs to record information relevant to a specific area.

After completing this chapter, you should be able to:
- Identify the purpose of using checklists in a restaurant or foodservice operation.
- Discuss the importance of planning for a shift and developing shift goals.
- Identify typical areas that should be included in longer-term goals for the operation.
- Explain why managers should inspect operating areas before a shift starts.
- Describe the purpose of communication logs.
- Identify information that is typically included in communication logs.

- Identify information that should *not* be included in communication logs.
- Recognize critical incidents.

Chapter 10 Managing Voluntary Terminations

Summary

The voluntary termination of a valued employee can be a sad and costly event, but it can lead to improvement in the operation if handled well. By conducting a good exit interview, you can learn more about the effects of the policies, practices, working conditions, and management of the operation. You can then use this information to improve the operation by addressing problem areas or capitalizing on the employee's insight about a better way of doing things. Besides assisting management in making improvements, exit interviews can benefit the employee leaving by providing closure to the employment experience and a formal way to say good-bye.

The information to be gathered during an exit interview will vary depending on your purpose for having the interview and will typically follow a format prescribed by the operation. Exit interviews may be conducted in person, by telephone, in writing, or by computer. The best and most common method is the face-to-face interview conducted by someone from the operation. These interviews may be structured or unstructured.

When planning for a face-to-face exit interview, schedule it on a day near the employee's last day of employment and conduct the interview in a private place where there are no distractions. The person interviewing the employee should not be the employee's immediate supervisor, unless all other options have been exhausted. Ideally, the exit interviewer should have interviewing experience and communication skills (including listening), question-asking skills, recording skills, and patience. The interviewer also should be able to establish the right tone.

After an exit interview, analyze the information collected. To do this, review and categorize the interview information, gather any additional information needed, and then compare the information to identify patterns. Follow your operation's guidelines for investigating and dealing with issues that could lead to legal problems.

Once you have analyzed the exit information, prioritize which issues to address. Rank information within the different categories to find out which areas need the most improvement, according to your former employees. Then consider other factors that can affect the priorities, such as legal problems that may arise, policies or business plans that may dictate priorities, and potential return on investment.

In addition to conducting an exit interview, you need to manage the termination process so everything that needs to be done before the employee leaves is taken care of. Using an employee termination checklist helps ensure nothing in this process is forgotten.

After completing this chapter, you should be able to:
- Describe the purpose of an employee termination checklist.
- Explain the benefits of exit interviews.
- Identify information that should be included in an exit interview.
- List advantages and disadvantages of different exit interview methods.
- Identify the qualities a person needs to successfully conduct an exit interview.
- Recognize the best time and place to conduct a face-to-face exit interview.
- Describe how to analyze information gathered during exit interviews.
- Prioritize the issues identified through an exit interview.
- Use information learned through exit interviews to develop action plans.

Chapter 11 Ensuring a Lawful Workplace

Summary

Laws impact every area of a restaurant or foodservice operation, from the safety and accessibility of the physical environment to the way you treat every person and most products that come into your operation. Given this broad impact and the importance of complying with laws, you as a manager need to have a clear understanding of how the laws affect your operation. Fortunately, the policies and procedures of most operations closely follow the laws. To reduce the possibility of legal problems, you should follow your operation's policies and procedures and keep abreast of changes in the law.

One of your most important responsibilities is to ensure that the food your operation serves is safe to eat. As part of this, you need to thoroughly understand food sanitation laws and your responsibility as a manager to develop and maintain a food safety management system, provide adequate training for employees, and routinely perform self-inspections to ensure your products are safe. In addition, if you have a quality food and safety system in place you will be more able to defend your operation in case of a food-related lawsuit.

You also need to ensure that your operation complies with local alcohol service regulations and employees are clear on their own responsibilities under these laws. Employees who serve alcohol should know how to do this responsibly, and all employees should know what to do if a customer becomes intoxicated. These responsibilities are essential for protecting the customers, the community, and your operation.

Other protections are offered to employees through various antidiscrimination laws. Title VII of the Civil Rights Act prohibits sexual harassment, the Pregnancy Discrimination Act protects the rights of pregnant women, and the Americans with Disabilities Act prohibits discrimination based on a disability. If someone in your operation tells you they are being harassed, you need to take prompt action to correct the situation and enforce your operation's policies.

When an employee reports an illness or disability, or is injured at work, this situation can be complex. The local health code, the ADA, and possibly OSHA's Bloodborne Pathogens Standard may cover a particular situation, so you need to understand how to handle it. If employees are exposed to blood in the workplace, you need to ensure not only that the injured employee receives adequate first aid, but also that first-aid providers and other employees know how to safely handle blood.

OSHA has many standards to protect employees on the job. One of these is the Hazard Communication Standard, which requires employers to communicate information about any potential hazards to employees, to label hazardous chemicals, and to make Material Safety Data Sheets available to employees. This OSHA standard is the one most often violated in the restaurant and foodservice industry.

Special workplace protections are required for employees who are minors. Child labor laws restrict the tasks and hours for minors. You should be familiar with these restrictions for your area.

State laws also require that you give breaks to all employees if they work a certain amount of time. These requirements vary, but certain break practices are common in the restaurant and foodservice industry.

Union labor contracts also may specify break times and other workplace practices and conditions. If your operation has union employees, you need to thoroughly understand the labor contracts in your establishment to avoid causing any grievances. You also should have a general understanding of the laws that restrict employers and unions when employees are deciding whether to become union members. However, in union shops, employees must become union members within a certain period after they are hired.

General guidelines for complying with laws include: following your operation's policies and practices; keeping current on workplace laws; monitoring employees for compliance; providing an "open door" for employees; allowing employees to exercise their rights; keeping accurate records; and posting required notices.

After completing this chapter, you should be able to:

- Identify labor laws that affect restaurant and foodservice operations.
- Recognize a manager's responsibilities in complying with sanitation laws.
- Recognize a manager's responsibilities in complying with alcohol service laws.
- Describe the impact of antidiscrimination laws on restaurant and foodservice operations.
- Define sexual harassment.
- Describe ways to respond when an employee discloses an illness.
- Identify the principles of OSHA's Hazard Communication Standard as they relate to restaurant and foodservice operations.
- Identify the impact of child labor laws on restaurant and foodservice operations.
- Recognize the impact of unions on the manager-employee relationship.
- Describe general guidelines for complying with workplace laws.

Chapter 12 Ensuring Employee Benefits and Compensation

Summary

As a manager, you need to understand the benefits offered by your operation and the federal, state, and local laws and company policies that affect them. This understanding enables you to comply with the laws and company policies, manage benefits in a cost-effective and fair manner, and help employees take advantage of their benefits.

Mandated employee benefits include Social Security, unemployment insurance, workers' compensation, and leaves of absence in certain situations. FMLA requires you to provide twelve weeks of unpaid leave to employees who have a serious medical condition, who need to care for a family member, or who have given birth to or adopted a child. USERRA provides unpaid leave for military service and ensures that employees who serve in the military will keep their civilian jobs.

Restaurant and foodservice employers often voluntarily provide other benefits, most commonly uniform and meal benefits, healthcare plans, employee assistance programs, and retirement benefits.

Several laws govern how some of these benefits are administered. ERISA protects employees' pensions and healthcare plans. COBRA extends group healthcare coverage for people who would otherwise lose their health insurance. HIPAA helps ensure that people do not lose access to healthcare because of preexisting conditions, other health status factors, or limits on plan enrollment periods.

Every manager should be well trained in employee benefits, company policies and procedures, and workplace laws. Ideally, internal resources can help you keep abreast of changes in the laws. You also should develop your own resources for learning about these changes.

Employee benefits are part of a total compensation package. Several laws control various aspects of wages and payroll. The FLSA requires some employees to be paid a minimum wage and overtime pay and has record-keeping requirements. Antidiscrimination laws prohibit discrimination in compensation. The Equal Pay Act helps ensure pay equity between men and women. The Consumer Credit Protection Act protects the rights of employees whose wages are garnished or levied.

Your operation's policies and procedures should guide you in complying with applicable laws. You should also follow your operation's policies and procedures to ensure employees are paid the correct amount at the correct time, monitor employee time reports, and work with the payroll administrator.

After completing this chapter, you should be able to:
- List and explain voluntary employee benefits common in the restaurant and foodservice industry.
- Give examples of ways to manage the costs of meal and uniform benefits.
- Recognize employer and plan administrator actions to comply with ERISA.
- Recognize employer and plan administrator actions to comply with COBRA.
- Recognize plan administrator actions to comply with HIPAA.
- List and explain mandatory employee benefits.
- Recognize employer actions to comply with FMLA.
- Recognize employer actions to comply with USERRA.
- Describe the tip credit provision of the FLSA.
- Describe ways to manage payroll administration.
- Describe ways to investigate wages paid in your labor market.
- Explain several strategies for controlling overtime in a restaurant or foodservice operation.

Human Resource Management and Supervision Practice Questions

Please note the numbers in parentheses following each question. They represent the chapter and page number, respectively, where the content in found in the ManageFirst Competency Guide.

IMPORTANT: These sample questions are designed to familiarize the student with format, length and style of the examination questions, and represent only a sampling of topic coverage.

The grid below represents how the *actual* exam questions will be divided across content areas on the corresponding ManageFirst Program exam.

Human Resources Management and Supervision	1.	Building a Welcoming Work Environment and Encouraging Diversity	8
	2.	Defining Job Descriptions	7
	3.	Finding and Recruiting New Employees	8
	4.	Screening Potential Employees	10
	5.	Hiring and Orienting New Employees	9
	6.	Supervising and Motivating Employees	12
	7.	Developing Employees	11
	8.	Training Employees	7
	9.	Managing Shifts to Ensure a Quality Operation	5
	10.	Managing Voluntary Terminations	5
	11.	Ensuring a Lawful Workplace	10
	12.	Ensuring Employee Benefits and Compensation	8
		Total No. of Questions	**100**

The performance level on sample questions does not guarantee passing of a ManageFirst Program examination. Further, the distribution of sample exam questions with their focus on particular areas of subject matter within a ManageFirst Competency Guide is not necessarily reflective of how the questions will be distributed across subject matter on the actual correlating ManageFirst exam.

1. Using what method of posting an open job utilizes today's new technology? (3, 51)
   A. Bulletin board
   B. Blind ad
   C. Radio show
   D. Web site

2. Which type of exit interview gives the best opportunity for the employee to have a feeling of closure and leave with a good feeling about the organization? (10, 254)
   A. Face-to-face
   B. Telephone
   C. Computer based survey
   D. Paper form

3. What does successive interviewing involve? (4, 82)
   A. You interview all the candidates on the same day, one after the other.
   B. An interviewee goes through a series of interviews with different people.
   C. Applicants fill out an application and have an interview with the manager immediately after submitting it.
   D. You rapidly ask the interviewee questions about different topics to add stress to the situation and see how well they handle it.

4. Why should management include honoring diversity as a criterion on the employee evaluation form? (1, 16)
   A. To make sure all stereotypes are represented within the workplace
   B. Because management needs to prove it is serious about honoring diversity and holding employees accountable to diversity policies and procedures
   C. To encourage employees to monitor and report other employees for inappropriate behavior
   D. Because restaurants are unfairly targeted for audits by the federal government for diversity compliance

5. What does a blind ad do? (3, 50)
   A. Makes financial data easily accessible
   B. Clearly promotes the companies brand
   C. Determines if applicants meet the organization's performance standards
   D. Omits the company name and other identifying information

6. Why is it important to write a job description? (2, 33)
   A. It identifies the key duties a person needs to perform.
   B. It describes the person you would like to take the job.
   C. It eliminates the need to make accommodations for a person with disabilities.
   D. It mandates when the position must be filled.

7. Why should an employer request health records or examinations after a job offer to a candidate who has disclosed his or her disability? (5, 101)
   A. To avoid discrimination
   B. To save money
   C. To be sure they know what questions to ask
   D. To reduce the amount of documentation needed

8. The responsibilities of a particular position should be specified after (2, 28)
   A. the job analysis is completed.
   B. the employee had been hired.
   C. the performance standards are set.
   D. the preferred pay range is established.

9. What are categories of jobs that fit into a defined salary range? (2, 26)
   A. Classes
   B. Grades
   C. Job specifications
   D. Job descriptions

10. Why should a manager analyze past staffing patterns? (3, 42)
    A. To forecast the need to hire additional employees
    B. To identify sources of potential employees
    C. To help develop employee referral programs
    D. To develop written job descriptions

11. What are activities designed to bring the largest number of qualified persons to apply for a job? (3, 40)
    A. Recruiting
    B. Screening
    C. Interviewing
    D. Orientation

12. According to the Competency Guide, what is a benefit of networking with schools, colleges, and technical training organizations? (3, 54)
    A. Free classes for employees
    B. A source of part-time or full-time employees
    C. Lower wages can be paid to students who are still in school
    D. Students are more available to work longer hours

13. Checklists that focus on getting the employee ready for the first day and then recording what happens on and after the first day called? (5, 111)
    A. Schedule checklist and feedback checklist
    B. New hire checklist and schedule checklist
    C. New hire checklist and orientation checklist
    D. Orientation checklist and schedule checklist

14. What is a disadvantage of employee referral programs? (3, 45)
    A. Diversity may be discouraged since people tend to refer people like themselves.
    B. It is very expensive since employees are paid a bonus.
    C. Job applicants are more familiar with your operation than most of those recruited through external sources.
    D. Candidates are usually not qualified since employees refer anyone just to receive the bonus.

15. If you make a reference phone call to ask about a potential candidate, the person giving the reference is unlikely to give negative feedback. Why can the phone call still be productive? (4, 87)
    A. You can verify that the information given on the resume is accurate.
    B. You can protect yourself from discrimination charges because you made an attempt to get more information.
    C. The way something is said; the pauses, choices of language, and the way in which to questions are answered can tell you a lot more than what is said.
    D. Candidates often provide people who like them so you can get biased information.

16. In what type of an interview would you possibly interrupt the applicant, avoid smiling, or show no response to the applicant's questions? (4, 81)
    A. Skill interview
    B. Character interview
    C. Successive interview
    D. Stress interview

17. What can using a term such as "waitstaff" instead of "waiter" or "waitress" in a job posting accomplish? (3, 60)
    A. Avoids discrimination by race
    B. Reaches a larger number of people
    C. Avoids gender specific language
    D. Discourages certain groups of people from applying

18. What is the difference between exempt and nonexempt positions? (2, 35)
    A. Exempt employees are not covered by FLSA; nonexempt employees are covered by the FLSA.
    B. Exempt employees get overtime pay; nonexempt employees do not get overtime pay.
    C. Exempt employees hold salaried positions; nonexempt employees hold hourly positions.
    D. Waitstaff are usually exempt and managers are nonexempt.

19. What is a discussion intended to determine whether to continue investing time and resources in evaluating a candidate called? (4, 70)
    A. Cost-benefit ratio debate
    B. Work simulation
    C. Job interview
    D. Screening interview

20. Why should managers evaluate orientation programs? (5, 113)
    A. To determine if federal laws are applicable
    B. To make sure the employees providing the orientation get overtime pay
    C. To revise the screening process to identify better candidates in the future
    D. To see if the participants liked the program, if it helped them become more productive and if it was cost-effective

21. How does Maslow's Hierarchy of Needs relate to managing people? (6, 124)
    A. The manager can have a pyramid style of benefits.
    B. The hierarchy of management levels needs to be understood by all employees.
    C. Employees cannot be motivated to perform better if their basic needs are not met first.
    D. When a new employee is hired his or her unique needs should be identified and documented.

22. What process involves reviewing application forms, cover letters, resumes, and other materials? (4, 69)
    A. Recruiting process
    B. Screening process
    C. Hiring process
    D. Orientation process

23. What is one reason a manager or human resources professional should review an application form? (4, 73)
    A. To determine an applicant's age and gender
    B. To evaluate an applicant's personality traits
    C. To become familiar with the applicant's work history
    D. To judge an applicant's qualifications based on national origin

24. An employer is required to make a reasonable accommodation for the known disability of a qualified applicant or employee if it does not impose "undue hardship" on the operation. What is undue hardship determined by? (5, 101)
    A. A specific list of mandatory conditions provided by the federal government
    B. The requests of the employee during his or her review
    C. A dollar amount based on the previous year's taxes
    D. The employer's size, financial resources, and nature of its operation

25. How does employee development impact the organization? (7, 152)
    A. It is expensive but necessary to perform the basic tasks required to stay in business.
    B. If it is done on the job it has no cost.
    C. Employees will function with increased production making it cost effective.
    D. It allows the organization to see which employees to terminate.

26. Which of the following can occur during both the hiring or orientation process? (5, 95)
    A. Background check
    B. Check physical abilities
    C. Complete benefit enrollment forms
    D. Conduct training

27. What is a manual that contains information on policies and procedures for an operation? (5, 98)
   A. Job description
   B. At-will statement
   C. Employment contingency
   D. Employee handbook

28. What should employers do in order to help employees improve their performance and behavior rather than firing them when there is a problem? (5, 133)
   A. Have morale building exercises at employee orientation
   B. Have new hires sign a contract saying they understand the consequences
   C. Let employees know during orientation that they will be terminated if they do not perform to expectations
   D. Use progressive discipline which begins with feedback and training and moves to more serious consequences if the employee does not improve

29. When would an incentive plan be likely to fail? (6, 140)
   A. If employees feel the goal is unrealistic for them to achieve
   B. If it is implemented during busy periods
   C. If too many employees are eligible to participate
   D. If the employees have input regarding the design of the program

30. What is a job offer? (5, 96)
   A. A letter conveying the job details
   B. A legally binding agreement with termination provisions
   C. A formal invitation to join an organization
   D. A document containing the policies and procedures

31. Why is it important to involve employees in the operation such as asking for suggestions for menu items or food safety practices? (6, 137)
   A. It motivates them.
   B. It saves money on research.
   C. It is part of employee development.
   D. It meets legal regulations.

32. An employee learns new things under the supervision and guidance of an expert. What is this an example of? (7, 163)
    A. Cross-training
    B. Informal learning
    C. Job rotation
    D. On-the-job training

33. What type of discipline begins with a compliment, then points out the problem and solutions, then ends with another positive comment? (6, 132)
    A. Progressive method of discipline
    B. Public acknowledgement method
    C. Positive reinforcement method
    D. Sandwich method of feedback

34. What type of development is it when an employee is trained on the important parts of an adjacent job? (7, 162)
    A. Apprenticeship
    B. Cross-training
    C. Mentoring
    D. Job rotation

35. According to the Competency Guide, training can have a major effect on an employee's (7, 165)
    A. physical capabilities.
    B. capability to learn certain skills.
    C. skills and knowledge.
    D. attitude in the workplace.

36. What is one of the key benefits of publicly showing your appreciation to an employee? (6, 136)
    A. You only have to do it once to cover all employees
    B. You don't have to discipline employees if you recognize them
    C. It encourages everyone to work harder to get that kind of recognition
    D. It shows the employees that the manager is a nice person to work for

37. What does an actual work assessment test allow the employer to do? (4, 70)
    A. Gather information about how well the candidate gets along with current employees
    B. Evaluate the skills of an individual under real-life or simulated conditions
    C. Have multiple people give their opinion of how well they think the person performed
    D. Do some training prior to actually hiring a new employee

38. Which type of exit interview provides visual information to the interviewer from the employee? (10, 254)
    A. Telephone
    B. Paper Form
    C. Face-to-face
    D. Computer based survey

39. Whose role is it to provide feedback and help an employee improve and grow? (7, 164)
    A. Coach
    B. Family
    C. Apprentice
    D. Co-worker

40. Which of the following statements describes the difference between training and education? (8, 178)
    A. Training is long-term and education is short-term.
    B. Training improves skills and performance and education improves knowledge.
    C. Training and education are both provided by managers.
    D. Training teaches concepts and education teaches how to do something.

41. What must happen if an employee's tips do not bring an employee's hourly wage up to basic minimum wage? (12, 348)
    A. The employer must pay the difference.
    B. The employee does not have to pay taxes.
    C. The employee should file a grievance.
    D. Other employees must share their tips.

42. What is integrative practice? (8, 186)
    A. The process of preparing the trainee to learn company policies.
    B. The process of On-the-job demonstration of new skills for food preparation.
    C. The process of conveying new information to an employee.
    D. The process of coordinating prior chunks of content into a useful whole.

43. At least how often must an employee report tips to the employer? (12, 349)
    A. Daily
    B. Weekly
    C. Monthly
    D. Yearly

44. What are the four parts of a learning objective? (8, 183)
    A. Performance, presentation, repetition, practice
    B. Preparation, presentation, practice, performance
    C. Performance, conditions, standards, repetition
    D. Conditions, preparation, presentation, repetition

45. During a training session the trainer demonstrates a skill and explains how to do it. This is an example of which of the four P's? (8, 185)
    A. Preparation
    B. Presentation
    C. Practice
    D. Performance

46. What is the benefit of an unstructured interview? (10, 254)
    A. It is easy to analyze.
    B. It provides a lot of information.
    C. Specific information can be collected.
    D. It is easy to compare responses of different employees.

47. What can be done in order to maximize benefits for the guests and minimize costs to the operation? (9, 217)
    A. Managers can create a staggered schedule.
    B. Free desserts should be offered to get employees and guests.
    C. The same number of employees should be scheduled to work each day.
    D. Only hire new employees after an existing employee has left the organization.

48. A communication log entry that says "woman found a piece of plastic in her salad" is an example of what? (9, 237)
    A. Midshift check
    B. Chef's log
    C. Critical incident
    D. HACCP log

49. What is an important part of the termination process? (10, 247)
    A. Employee orientation
    B. Collecting reference phone numbers
    C. Conducting an exit interview
    D. Recruiting new employees

50. Which of the following will help protect an operation in case of a suspected foodborne-illness? (9, 207)
    A. HACCP logs
    B. Inventory checklists
    C. Receiving checklists
    D. Z report

51. According to the health code, a manager must ask if an employee has any health conditions that may affect his or her ability to safely handle food if that employee appears to be sick but hasn't said anything about his or her health. What prevents the manager from asking about symptoms that are not related to safe foodhandling? (12, 291)
    A. The Food Code
    B. HACCP
    C. Quid pro quo
    D. ADA

52. Because sexual harassment can be hard to understand, how do most operations handle it? (11, 284)
    A. By enacting a zero tolerance policy
    B. By advocating quid pro quo
    C. By overlooking questionable sexual comments
    D. By implementing rules prohibiting any socialization

53. What rule regarding alcohol is true in all fifty states? (11, 281)
    A. Happy hours and drink promotions are restricted or forbidden.
    B. An employee should never serve alcohol to a pregnant woman.
    C. A person must be twenty-one years old to purchase alcohol.
    D. Underage servers are not allowed to bring alcohol to the table.

54. What is a document required by the Hazard Communication Standard (HCS) that provides information about the chemical content of a material and how to handle? (11, 296)
    A. A Material Safety Data Sheet
    B. A Labor Contract
    C. The Food Code
    D. The Bloodborne Pathogens Standard

55. The sous chef has a cut on his finger and is bleeding. What policy should the aider's response follow? (11, 294)
    A. Food Code procedures
    B. HACCP log rules
    C. Material Safety Data Sheet guidelines
    D. Bloodborne Pathogens Standard exposure plan

56. For most types of retirement and benefit plans, who does the federal government make responsible for ensuring the laws are followed? (12, 316)
    A. Employee
    B. Manager
    C. Plan administrator
    D. Union

57. According to the Competency Guide, why is it important to eliminate personal and judgmental comments from logs? (9, 235)
   A. Opinions cannot be defended if the logs are subpoenaed by a court of law, only facts.
   B. Managers on different shifts should not let other managers know what they are thinking.
   C. The logs become too lengthy and people tend not to read all of the information.
   D. The managers should not let employees know their management philosophies.

58. When are special enrollment periods required by the Health Insurance Portability and Accountability Act (HIPPA)? (12, 334)
   A. An employee realizes that he or she did not select the correct options
   B. An employee has a child or adopts a child
   C. An employee has had an accident that prevents him or her from working
   D. An employee has reached his or her deductible

59. According to the Competency Guide, what should a manager do if an employee works unauthorized overtime? (12, 358)
   A. Pay but also reprimand the employee
   B. Not pay the employee for the overtime
   C. Immediately fire the employee
   D. Remind the employee that it is illegal to work unauthorized overtime

60. What is an operation that integrates diversity into the mission statement promoting? (1, 13)
   A. Cultural tendencies
   B. A hostile environment
   C. Conformity
   D. Cross-cultural interaction

Human Resources Management and Supervision Answer Key to Practice Questions

1.	D	26.	C	51.	D
2.	A	27.	D	52.	A
3.	B	28.	D	53.	C
4.	B	29.	A	54.	A
5.	D	30.	C	55.	D
6.	A	31.	A	56.	C
7.	A	32.	D	57.	A
8.	A	33.	D	58.	B
9.	B	34.	B	59.	A
10.	A	35.	C	60.	D
11.	A	36.	C		
12.	B	37.	B		
13.	C	38.	C		
14.	A	39.	A		
15.	C	40.	B		
16.	D	41.	A		
17.	C	42.	D		
18.	C	43.	C		
19.	D	44.	C		
20.	D	45.	B		
21.	C	46.	B		
22.	B	47.	A		
23.	C	48.	C		
24.	D	49.	C		
25.	C	50.	A		

Human Resources Management and Supervision Explanations to the Answers for the Practice Questions

Question #1
Answer A is wrong. A bulletin board posting would be considered low tech.
Answer B is wrong. A blind ad omits the company's name and other identifying information.
Answer C is wrong. Radio ads have been in use for decades.
Answer D is correct. Posting ads on a Web site is a high tech solution utilizing today's technology.

Question #2
Answer A is correct. A face-to-face interview allows the employee to receive and give feedback, say what is important to him or her, and depending on the relationship with the interviewer, help them feel closure.
Answer B is wrong. A telephone interview does not allow the employee to pick up on nonverbal cues.
Answer C is wrong. A computer based survey allows limited input from the employee and has no two-way communication.
Answer D is wrong. A paper form asks for specific information and the employee may not be able to provide information they want to give. They also do not receive feedback.

Question #3
Answer A is wrong. This addresses the interviewing schedule, not the type of interviewing done.
Answer B is correct. A series of interviews is called successive interviewing.
Answer C is wrong. This answer merely tells the time frame.
Answer D is wrong. This is stress interviewing.

Question #4

Answer A is wrong. Stereotypes should be discouraged and removed where possible.

Answer B is correct. Employees need to know what behavior is expected of them and to be held accountable for their actions. Management shows commitment to diversity by including diversity criteria in the employee evaluation.

Answer C is wrong. Managers need to prevent the situation where employees feel responsible for reporting other employees' behavior.

Answer D is wrong. It is important to meet federal regulations, but restaurants are not targeted for audits.

Question # 5

Answer A is wrong. Blind ads do not make financial data accessible.

Answer B is wrong. See Answer D.

Answer C is wrong. A performance standard evaluation would take place after the employee has been hired.

Answer D is correct. Blind ads omit the company name and other identifying information.

Question #6

Answer A is correct. It is important to stay neutral by describing just the duties and not show any preference to a person or type of person.

Answer B is wrong. See answer A.

Answer C is wrong. The job description should not be written in such a way that it purposely prevents people from being eligible if a reasonable accommodation could be made.

Answer D is wrong. The job description should describe the duties of the job and does relate to time. Information about when the job needs to be filled can be provided with the description when it is posted.

Question #7

Answer A is correct. If an employer asks for these records and the person is not offered the job, it may appear the information in them was used to make the decision.
Answer B is wrong. This information does not cost the employer money.
Answer C is wrong. Health related questions are not allowed prior to hiring so there is no need to request the documents prior to that.
Answer D is wrong. The documents are not needed prior to making a job offer so there is no reason to request them.

Question #8

Answer A is correct. A job analysis includes a detailed breakdown of duties, skills and knowledge needed and environmental conditions of the job.
Answer B is wrong. The person who will be performing the job cannot be selected until the requirements are known.
Answer C is wrong. Performance standards cannot be set until all duties are known.
Answer D is wrong. The duties and qualifications to perform the job need to be known before the pay can be established.

Question #9

Answer A is wrong. Classes are clusters of jobs that have common information bases or skill areas.
Answer B is correct. Grades are categories of jobs that fit into a defined salary range.
Answer C is wrong. Job specifications are the qualifications a person should have to do the job.
Answer D is wrong. Job descriptions define the work involved in a particular assignment or position.

Question #10
Answer A is correct. Human resource professionals and managers normally analyze the past staffing needs of their business and other information to forecast when they will need to hire additional employees.
Answer B is wrong. Identifying sources of potential employees is part of promoting job openings.
Answer C is wrong. Employee referral programs are part of the recruiting process.
Answer D is wrong. Job descriptions are written based on the duties and responsibilities required by the position.

Question #11
Answer A is correct. Recruiting is a series of activities designed to bring the largest number of qualified person to apply for a job.
Answer B is wrong. Screening occurs after you have recruited candidates.
Answer C is wrong. Interviewing occurs after recruiting.
Answer D is wrong. Orientation occurs after a person is hired.

Question #12
Answer A is wrong. Schools provide businesses with an opportunity to create internships and sponsor events.
Answer B is correct. Educational institutions and organizations provide sources of employees.
Answer C is wrong. Wages are determined by federal and state minimum wages, in addition to local demand.
Answer D is wrong. Due to educational demands, students are less likely to be available than other workers.

Question #13
Answer A is wrong. There is no schedule or feedback checklist.
Answer B is wrong. The new hire checklist is used to record what happens after the first day but there is no schedule checklist.
Answer C is correct. The new hire checklist is used prior to the first day and the orientation checklist is used after hire.
Answer D is wrong. There is no schedule checklist.

Question #14
Answer A is correct. It is important to reach a large population to get a representation of different types of people.

Answer B is wrong. Even if there is a bonus paid, it is usually more cost and time effective than other forms of recruiting.

Answer C is wrong. If applicants are familiar with the organization it would be a benefit, not a disadvantage.

Answer D is wrong. A bonus is usually not paid unless a referral is hired or at least makes it through a screening process.

Question #15
Answer A is wrong. Information on the resume is not usually reviewed. Different information is sought.

Answer B is wrong. Getting information does not exempt you from discriminatory responsibilities.

Answer C is correct. The cues you receive from the other person can tell you a lot about how this person feels about the candidate as an employee and person.

Answer D is wrong. You do not want biased information.

Question #16
Answer A is wrong. A skill interview asks questions about an applicant's work experience, former employers, and job challenges.

Answer B is wrong. A character interview assesses an applicant's personality and whether the person will work well in your operation.

Answer C is wrong. Successive interviewing is a serial interviewing process.

Answer D is correct. Stress interviews are designed to put applicants in a stressful situation to reveal how they handle stress. Some techniques used are not smiling, unresponsiveness, and interrupting the applicant.

Question #17

Answer A is wrong. The terms "waiter" or "waitress" have nothing to do with a person's race.

Answer B is wrong. The term does not specify male or female but it does not cause more people to see the posting.

Answer C is correct. The term "waitstaff" does not imply gender therefore avoiding any possible discrimination issues.

Answer D is wrong. The term relates to any gender so anyone with the correct qualifications will not be discouraged from applying.

Question #18

Answer A is wrong. Exempt positions are not covered by the FLSA, but nonexempt employees are.

Answer B is wrong. Exempt means you are not covered by law requiring overtime pay.

Answer C is correct. Salaried positions are exempt. Hourly positions are nonexempt.

Answer D is wrong. Waitresses are usually nonexempt (hourly) and managers are exempt (salaried).

Question #19

Answer A is wrong. A debate about the cost-benefit ratio would relate to the process, not an individual.

Answer B is wrong. Work simulation is when you recreate actual working conditions to evaluate skills.

Answer C is wrong. The discussion is to determine whether to complete a job interview or not.

Answer D is correct. A screening interview is the initial determination whether to continue looking at this person as a possible employee.

Question #20
Answer A is wrong. The federal laws need to be considered prior to conducting an orientation program.
Answer B is wrong. You are looking at the results of the orientation process, not the hours involved. This could be part of a cost-benefit comparison.
Answer C is wrong. The success of the orientation process evaluates how well new hires are assimilated into the culture and organization and become productive. The interview process should identify if the screening process was not effective.
Answer D is correct. The purpose of an orientation program is to make the new people productive as quickly as possible.

Question #21
Answer A is wrong. Maslow's theory relates to the different levels of people's needs, not benefits.
Answer B is wrong. The theory does not relate to levels of management.
Answer C is correct. Maslow's theory states that people cannot be motivated on one level until the lower level of needs are met.
Answer D is wrong. Maslow's theory addresses different types of needs, not individual needs.

Question #22
Answer A is wrong. Reviewing documents is the first phase of screening.
Answer B is correct. The screening process includes reviewing documents, conducting screening interviews, assessing skills, more interviewing to determine appropriateness for the job, and investigating backgrounds.
Answer C is wrong. The hiring process is done after the screening and interviewing.
Answer D is wrong. The orientation process occurs after the person has been hired.

Question #23

Answer A is wrong. Judging an applicant based on age or gender is discriminatory.

Answer B is wrong. Personality tests and character interviews are used to evaluate personality.

Answer C is correct. One of the many reasons to review an application is to become familiar with the person's work history, background, and skill level.

Answer D is wrong. Judging an applicant based on national origin is discriminatory.

Question #24

Answer A is wrong. It is not possible to list every possible situation and what would or would not be reasonable for your organization.

Answer B is wrong. If the requests would cost a lot of money or be difficult to implement depending on the size, financial resources, and nature of the operation, then it would be considered a hardship. Timing of the request is irrelevant.

Answer C is wrong. The financial resources, not just tax information, the size of the organization and the structure of the business, must also be considered.

Answer D is correct. Undue hardship is deemed as an action requiring significant difficulty or expense when considered in light of factors such as an employer's size, financial resources, and the nature and structure of its operation.

Question #25

Answer A is wrong. Employee development trains for aspects beyond the basic skills.

Answer B is wrong. On-the-job training affects productivity and there is high risk wrong methods will be learned.

Answer C is correct. In return for providing development opportunities for the employee and paying the costs, the operation will function with increased productivity.

Answer D is wrong. The purpose of development is to benefit the employees and operation. It would be a waste of money to train employees who may potentially be terminated.

Question #26
Answer A is wrong. Background checks are done during the hiring process only.

Answer B is wrong. Physical abilities can be checked only during the hiring process.

Answer C is correct. Benefit enrollment forms can be done during either the hiring or orientation process.

Answer D is wrong. Training only occurs during orientation.

Question #27
Answer A is wrong. A job description defines the duties and responsibilities of a specific position.

Answer B is wrong. This is a notification to the employee that either the employee or employer can end the employment relationship at any time for any reason.

Answer C is wrong. An employment contingency contains results of transcripts, background checks, medical and drug tests.

Answer D is correct. An employee handbook is a manual or document that contains policies and procedures for an operation.

Question #28
Answer A is wrong. The employees' morale may not be the problem.

Answer B is wrong. Employers need to communicate with employees to let them know what is expected and how they can achieve it.

Answer C is wrong. Threatening the employee does not improve performance and behavior.

Answer D is correct. Progressive discipline gives the employee an opportunity to improve behavior before any serious consequences occur.

Question #29
Answer A is correct. If employees do not feel they can meet the goal they will not try for it.

Answer B is wrong. It may be easier for employees to meet the goal during busy times.

Answer C is wrong. Incentive programs are usually available to all employees.

Answer D is wrong. If employees have input into the program they will probably believe in it.

Question #30
Answer A is wrong. An employment letter is a letter conveying job details.
Answer B is wrong. An employment contract is a legally binding agreement with termination provisions.
Answer C is correct. A job offer is a formal invitation to join an organization.
Answer D is wrong. An employee handbook contains policies and procedures.

Question #31
Answer A is correct. Allowing people to give their opinion makes them feel productive, useful, and fulfills esteem needs.
Answer B is wrong. Employee opinions would not replace research if it was needed.
Answer C is wrong. Employee input to the operation is not considered part of employee development.
Answer D is wrong. There are no legal regulations saying employees need to give input to the operations.

Question #32
Answer A is wrong. Cross training is where employees learn important aspects of adjacent jobs.
Answer B is wrong. Informal learning is where employees learn from other employees and through trial and error. The other employees are not necessarily experts.
Answer C is wrong. Job rotation is where employees are assigned to other jobs for a period of time to better understand the original job and the organization as a whole.
Answer D is correct. On-the-job-training is when an employee learns something under the supervision of an expert.

Question #33
Answer A is wrong. Progressive discipline gives the employee warning and support to improve his or her behavior and performance.
Answer B is wrong. Public acknowledgement is a type of motivator.
Answer C is wrong. Positive reinforcement is a type of motivator.
Answer D is correct. Sandwich method of feedback begins with a compliment, then points out the problem and solutions; and ends with another positive comment.

Question #34

Answer A is wrong. An apprenticeship is when a person studies under a master craftsman.

Answer B is correct. Cross-training is when employees learn important parts of adjacent jobs so they can fill in for absent employees and peaks in demand.

Answer C is wrong. Mentoring is when one employee helps another reach his or her goals.

Answer D is wrong. Job rotation is when employees are assigned to other jobs in the organization.

Question #35

Answer A is wrong. Training cannot totally counteract an employee's physical capabilities.

Answer B is wrong. Some people cannot learn certain things because it is beyond their capabilities.

Answer C is correct. Training is good only for improving skills and knowledge.

Answer D is wrong. While training can have a small effect on attitude, other work factors have a much greater effect and will overcome the effects of training.

Question #36

Answer A is wrong. Public recognition is not done to recognize large groups of people but rather to acknowledge someone in front of others.

Answer B is wrong. Recognition is a motivator but it does not mean there will not be a need for discipline in a different matter.

Answer C is correct. Recognition for one person can motivate others because they know they are appreciated.

Answer D is wrong. Public recognition is to show appreciation and let others know that person is appreciated. It should not focus on the manager.

Question #37

Answer A is wrong. Work assessment involves shadowing or completion of actual tasks under real-life or simulated conditions to evaluate the skills of an individual.

Answer B is correct. See Answer A.

Answer C is wrong. This could be part of group or successive interviews.

Answer D is wrong. The assessment is to evaluate the person's current skill level.

Question #38

Answer A is wrong. A telephone interview does not allow the employee to pick up on non-verbal cues.

Answer B is wrong. A paper form does not allow the interviewer to pick up on non-verbal cues.

Answer C is correct. A face-to-face interview allows the interviewer to receive and evaluate non-verbal cues.

Answer D is wrong. A computer based survey does not allow the interviewer to pick up on non-verbal cues.

Question #39

Answer A is correct. A coach provides feedback and makes suggestions for change, thus helping the employee improve and grow.

Answer B is wrong. Family typically is not involved in workplace coaching.

Answer C is wrong. An apprentice works under a master craftsperson to learn a skill.

Answer D is wrong. A co-worker should not be responsible for monitoring a fellow employee.

Question #40

Answer A is wrong. Training is short-term and education is long-term.

Answer B is correct. Training improves skills and performance and education broadens knowledge.

Answer C is wrong. Training is provided by managers and trainers and education is provided by teachers.

Answer D is wrong. Training teaches how to do something and education teaches concepts.

Question #41

Answer A is correct. The employer must ensure the employee receives minimum wage with the salary and tips combined.

Answer B is wrong. The employer needs to pay taxes on any money earned.

Answer C is wrong. Tipped employees are protected by federal law so the union should not have to file a grievance.

Answer D is wrong. Some organizations may have a policy of shared tips but it should be documented and not change from one policy to another.

Question #42

Answer A is wrong. This is step 1 of the classic model of training or preparation.

Answer B is wrong. This is step 4 of the classic model of training or performance.

Answer C is wrong. This is step 2 of the classic model of training or presentation.

Answer D is correct. In the integrative practice, there is no new content; instead, the learner is expected to integrate prior chunks of content into a useful whole.

Question #43

Answer A is wrong. An employee can report tips on a daily basis but can also wait longer.

Answer B is wrong. An employee can report tips on a weekly basis but can also wait longer.

Answer C is correct. An employee must report tips on at least a monthly basis.

Answer D is wrong. Tips must be reported on at least a monthly basis.

Question #44

Answer A is wrong. See answer C for the parts of a learning objective.

Answer B is wrong. See answer C for the parts of a learning objective.

Answer C is correct. Performance, conditions, standards, and repetition are the parts of a learning objective.

Answer D is wrong. See answer C for the parts of a learning objective.

Question #45

Answer A is wrong. Preparation is getting the trainee ready to learn.
Answer B is correct. Presentation is where skills are demonstrated.
Answer C is wrong. Practice is where the employee has a chance to practice the task.
Answer D is wrong. Performance involves ongoing observation and feedback on the employee's routine performance.

Question #46

Answer A is wrong. Unstructured interviews are hard to analyze because there is a lot of information and they can cover a large range of topics.
Answer B is correct. Unstructured interviews can result in a large range of topics and allow the employee to bring up whatever he or she wants.
Answer C is wrong. Structured interviews ask specific questions.
Answer D is wrong. It is difficult to compare different employees' responses since they may not cover the same topics.

Question #47

Answer A is correct. A staggered schedule allows employees to start and stop at varying times as needed.
Answer B is wrong. Offering free desserts to employees in not an effective way to manage the operation's costs.
Answer C is wrong. Employees should be scheduled to work so there is adequate help when needed but not idle employees.
Answer D is wrong. You should hire employees so there is enough time to train them before another employee leaves.

Question #48

Answer A is wrong. A midshift check is when a manager reviews the operation at various stations during a shift.
Answer B is wrong. The chef's log records information about covers, customer reactions to specials, recipe ideas, unusual equipment performance, and reminders for the next shift.
Answer C is correct. Critical incidents are events that need to be recorded for historical purposes in case of a potential claim or lawsuit.
Answer D is wrong. The HACCP log is used to record ongoing monitoring and corrective actions in operations.

Question #49

Answer A is wrong. An employee orientation takes place after hiring an employee and is not part of the termination process.

Answer B is wrong. Reference phone numbers are used for screening an employee being considered for a position.

Answer C is correct. An exit interview is conducted when an employee is leaving an operation and is part of the termination process.

Answer D is wrong. A new employee may need to be recruited to fill an open position but this is not part of the terminated employee's exit process.

Question #50

Answer A is correct. The HACCP logs are used to record ongoing monitoring and corrective actions in operations that use a HACCP system to manage food safety.

Answer B is wrong. Inventory checklists assess levels of supplies and track property.

Answer C is wrong. Receiving checklists are used to verify receipt and condition of goods as received.

Answer D is wrong. A Z report is run after zeroing out a cash register.

Question #51

Answer A is wrong. The Food Code has recommendations to prevent foodborne illnesses.

Answer B is wrong. HACCP is a system to control hazards throughout the flow of food.

Answer C is wrong. Quid pro quo is when one person asks for or expects an action of sexual nature as a condition of employment.

Answer D is correct. The Americans with Disabilities Act makes it illegal to discriminate against anyone because of a disability.

Question #52

Answer A is correct. A zero tolerance policy does not leave room for interpretation, because anything that could be considered offensive is prohibited.

Answer B is wrong. Quid pro quo is a form of sexual harassment where employment is impacted by sexual activity.

Answer C is wrong. Ignoring an issue is not a way to handle it.

Answer D is wrong. People are never prohibited from interacting.

Question #53
Answer A is wrong. Happy hours are only forbidden or restricted in some states.
Answer B is wrong. Refusing to serve a pregnant woman would be sex discrimination.
Answer C is correct. The drinking age is 21 years old in every state.
Answer D is wrong. Different states have different laws about underage servers selling or serving alcohol.

Question #54
Answer A is correct. A MSDS must be made available for any hazardous material.
Answer B is wrong. A labor contract is a written agreement of employment terms between the union and the employer.
Answer C is wrong. The Food Code regulates businesses to prevent foodborne illnesses.
Answer D is wrong. The Bloodborne Pathogens Standard minimizes the risk of exposure to bloodborne diseases.

Question #55
Answer A is wrong. The Food Code is the federal government's recommendations for foodservice regulations to prevent foodborne illnesses. It is not a first-aid response code.
Answer B is wrong. The HACCP log is used to record monitoring and corrective actions in operations that use a HACCP system to manage food safety.
Answer C is wrong. The Material Safety Data Sheet provides information about the chemical content and safe handling of materials that are potentially hazardous.
Answer D is correct. The Bloodborne Pathogens Standard Exposure plan documents operating procedures to eliminate or minimize an employee's exposure to another's blood.

Question #56
Answer A is wrong. The employee is not responsible for the organization's compliance to laws.
Answer B is wrong. The manager is responsible for making sure the employees get the information they need to know, but is not responsible for ensuring the laws are met.
Answer C is correct. The plan administrator is responsible for knowing the laws and making sure the company complies.
Answer D is wrong. The union is not responsible for the organization's compliance to laws. They may get involved if they believed the company was not complying, impacting the employees.

Question #57
Answer A is correct. Only facts should be documented since they may need to be defended.
Answer B is wrong. Managers should communicate their opinions to each other but not in the logs that could be used in court.
Answer C is wrong. Any pertinent information should be included regardless of length.
Answer D is wrong. Logs are not an appropriate place for managers to share their management philosophies.

Question #58
Answer A is wrong. You cannot change an enrollment unless there is a specific situation that changes your family status.
Answer B is correct. The child may be added to the parent's plan when born or adopted.
Answer C is wrong. See answer A.
Answer D is wrong. See answer A.

Question #59
Answer A is correct. The proper solution is to pay for the overtime then reprimand the employee for working unauthorized overtime.
Answer B is wrong. It is illegal to not pay the employee.
Answer C is wrong. The employee may not have known the overtime was unauthorized. They should be reprimanded.
Answer D is wrong. It is not illegal to work unauthorized overtime.

Question #60

Answer A is wrong. Beliefs and habits create cultural tendencies.
Answer B is wrong. A hostile environment results when diversity is not accepted.
Answer C is wrong. Diversity is lost when people conform and become the same.
Answer D is correct. By incorporating diversity into the mission statement and policies and procedures, it encourages meaningful interaction among diverse background

Human Resources Management and Supervision Glossary

Active managerial control   a proactive approach to addressing common risk factors responsible for foodborne illness. It requires continuously monitoring employees to ensure they are following policies and procedures

ADDIE   the acronym for a five-step model used to ensure all the necessary issues in designing and developing training have been considered. The five steps are analyze, design, develop, implement, and evaluate

Affirmative action programs   programs that actively take positive steps to eliminate existing, remedy past, and prevent future discrimination

Americans with Disabilities Act Accessibility Guidelines for Buildings and Facilities (ADAAG)   standards designed to help architects, business owners, and others understand and comply with the Access for Disabled People under Title III act

Annuities   regular payments that continue for a specified period of time

Applicants   the people who have applied for an open job

Arbitrator   a third party used to settle grievances that cannot be resolved by management and union representation. (Also called **mediator**)

Attitudes   feelings about facts or situations that influence behaviors, such as liking to help people or disliking being interrupted

Back of the house (BOH)   the kitchen and other areas where customers do not go

Banquet and catering log   a record kept by banquet or catering staff of guest counts, special needs, information about equipment needs, problems, changes requested by the customer, and staffing requirements

Bargain in good faith   the requirement that employers and unions make a genuine attempt to reach agreement during negotiations

Beneficiary   someone who is entitled to receive a benefit under a plan

Bias   a general attitude toward a person, group, or organization on the basis of judgments unrelated to abilities. (Same as **prejudice**)

Bleeding the register   see **cash drop**

Blind ads   public ads for new employees which omit the company name and other identifying information

Bloodborne Pathogens Standard   a standard for minimizing risks against bloodborne diseases for employees who work with sharp knives and equipment and may cut themselves

Bona fide occupational qualifications (BFOQ)   the realistic range of skills or credentials needed to perform the essential functions of the job

Candidates   the applicants who possess minimum job qualifications and are being considered for a job opening

Cash drop   counting all the cash and depositing some of it in the safe. (Also called **bleeding the register**)

Certificate of creditable coverage   a document showing that a person was covered under a plan and the starting and ending dates of coverage

Chef's communication log provides a place for the chef to record information about **covers**, recipe ideas, customer reactions to specials, allergic reactions, unusual equipment performance, reminders for the next shift, and efficiency and effectiveness of the back-of-the-house staff

Child labor laws special laws for children and youth

Chunk manageable modules of learning

Class cluster of jobs that have common information bases or skill areas

Classical model of training each chunk goes through four steps: preparation, presentation, practice, and performance (Also called **four-step training method**, **job instruction training**, **four P approach**)

Coaching a formal program through which an employee is matched with an experienced employee or supervisor (coach) who helps the employee achieve career goals or increase skills and knowledge

Collective bargaining the process union and company representatives use to renegotiate the terms of a labor contract when it is about to expire

Communication log documents in which information about what happens on a particular shift is recorded for the purpose of sharing information with the next shift and future shifts

Compensation package a combination of benefits, wages, and incentives

Competencies the general capabilities needed to perform a duty

Consolidated Omnibus Budget Reconciliation Act (COBRA) requires optional healthcare coverage to be offered to some employees after employment ends

Conventional indemnity plans see **fee-for-service plans** (Also called **traditional health insurance**)

Cost-benefit relationship a comparison of the total direct and indirect recruiting costs against the number (and sometimes quality) of applicants produced

Covers number of people fed during a meal period

Critical incident events that need to be recorded for historical purposes in case of a potential claim or lawsuit

Cross-cultural interaction meaningful communication among employees from diverse cultures and backgrounds

Cross-training a method through which employees learn a job related to their own, often one that is "upstream" or "downstream" in a process

Cultural tendencies tendency for groups of people to do some things based on beliefs and habits

Day part see **service period**

Deductible minimum out-of-pocket expenses

Defined benefit (DB) a retirement benefit in which the employee is guaranteed certain payments upon retirement; the payout, or final value of the benefit, is defined

Defined contribution (DC) a benefit that guarantees certain payments will be made into an account owned by an individual employee; that is, the employer's or employee's contribution is defined

Design document a report documenting the objectives for a training event and organizing the chunks and sequence of training

Designated first-aid provider an employee appointed to provide first aid (Also called **first aider**)

Developmental goals   same as **employee development goals**

Dining room log   see **dining room manager's communication log**

Dining room manager's communication log   a place to record information about weather, customer service patterns, dramatic changes in cover counts, balance between reservations and walk-ins, guest complaints, and anything that affected business during that shift (Also called **reservation log** or **dining room log**)

Discrimination   the ability to notice differences

Dissatisfiers   another name for hygiene factors in the motivation-hygiene theory by Frederick Herzberg (Also called **maintenance factors**)

Diversity   the differences among people

Dram shop law   a regulation that varies from state to state but which holds the server, and the restaurant or foodservice operation, liable for serving liquor to an already intoxicated person or someone who is underage

Ego needs   another name for esteem needs in Maslow's hierarchy of needs

Employee assistance programs (EAPs)   provide counseling and other services to individuals and families to help them deal with a wide range of problems that impede their ability to function effectively at work (Also known as **referral programs**)

Employee benefit plan   a program that describes the non-wage compensation or services an employee is eligible to receive and the circumstances under which the employee will receive them (Also called **plan.**)

Employee development goals   the skills, knowledge, and attitudes that need to be gained or improved in order to eliminate or reduce a performance gap (Same as **developmental goals**)

Employee development process   identifying developmental goals, determining how to make improvements, and evaluating the results

Employee development program   any organized series of actions that are intended to reduce a gap in an employee's skills, knowledge, or attitudes

Employee goals   goals beyond job performance, such as getting a certification, moving ahead in life, finding a better job, or improving a personal situation

Employee handbook   a manual or document that contains the policies and procedures for the operation

Employee performance goals   goals that focus on the tasks that an employee must be able to perform as part of his or her job

Employee referral programs   programs where a bonus or reward is provided to current employees who refer candidates

Employee Retirement Income Security Act of 1974 (ERISA) designed to protect employee pensions and healthcare plans from incompetent, unethical, and unfair administration; ensuring benefits promised to employees are actually there when the employees need them

Employment at will   employers can fire anyone for any reason

Employment contract   a legally binding agreement that includes additional terms of employment, such as termination provisions, and removes an otherwise "employment at will" relationship between the employer and the employee (Sometimes called **employee agreement**)

Employment letter   a letter conveying the job details and starting information to the potential employee

Enrollment   when an employee signs up for a benefit plan

Essential functions   key duties that an individual must be able to perform in order to do a job

Esteem needs   the fourth level of needs, which focuses on how people feel about themselves and how they perceive what others feel about them, such as self-esteem, self-respect, and respect of others, in Maslow's hierarchy of needs (Also called **ego needs**)

Exclusion period   a certain time after enrollment in a healthcare plan that excludes coverage for preexisting conditions

Executive orders (EOs)   proclamations issued by the President of the United States, with implementing regulations issued by federal agencies such as the U.S. Department of Labor

Exempt   positions not covered by the Fair Labor Standards Act (FLSA), which specifies a minimum wage and when overtime pay is required; salaried positions

Exit Interview   an interview with the employee who is leaving to determine what things about the operation could be improved and, for voluntary terminations, why the employee is leaving

External sources   potential employees who come from outside your operation, such as people referred by employment agencies or recruited through advertising, open houses, and networking activities

Family and Medical Leave Act (FMLA)   gives qualified employees the right to take up to twelve weeks of continuous or intermittent unpaid leave in a rolling twelve-month period for certain medical or family-care situations

Fee-for-service plans   plans administered by insurance companies that directly pay service providers (physicians, hospitals, etc.) or reimburse the plan participants (Also called **traditional health insurance** or **conventional indemnity plans**)

Fiduciary   dealing with managing income

First aider   see **designated first-aid provider**

Flexible spending accounts (FSAs)   special accounts that allow employees to contribute a certain amount of income before taxes to their individual account that can be used only to pay for certain medical expenses that are not covered by the employee's healthcare plan (Also called **Health Savings Accounts (HSAs)**

Flow of food   the path food takes through your operation

Foodborne illness   a disease carried or transmitted to people by food

Food Code   the federal government's recommendations for foodservice regulations to prevent foodborne illnesses

Food safety management system   a group of programs and procedures designed to control hazards throughout the flow of food
Forecast   to predict when additional employees will need to be hired based on analyzing the past staffing needs of the business

Four P approach (or four Ps)   see **classical model of training**

Four-step training method   see **classical model of training**

Front of the house (FOH)   the dining room or where customers are

Garnishments   payments ordered by a court to be taken directly from an employee's earnings

Grade   category of jobs that fit into a defined salary range

Grievances   complaints filed against an employer for breaking the terms of the labor contract

Group interview   multiple people from the operation interview one applicant

Group plan   a benefit plan that provides essentially the same benefit to multiple people, such as life insurance or healthcare; usually purchased through the workplace

Hazard Communication Standard (HCS) standard for communicating information about workplace hazards to protect employees from both physical hazards, such as explosions, and health hazards, and medical conditions caused by exposure to chemicals

Health code local laws designed to ensure food safety

Health Insurance Portability and Accountability Act (HIPAA) ensures people do not lose access to healthcare because of preexisting conditions, other health status factors, or limits on plan enrollment periods

Health maintenance organizations (HMOs) plans that are almost entirely prepaid through premiums; the service providers are part of the HMO

Health savings accounts (HSAs) see **flexible spending accounts (FSAs)**

Hostile environment an environment in which someone is exposed to unwelcome, intimidating, offensive, or antagonistic behavior that interferes with his or her ability to perform a job and is based on a protected characteristic

Hourly positions covered by the Fair Labor Standards Act (FLSA), which specifies a minimum wage and when overtime pay is required; nonexempt positions

Hygiene factors defined in the motivation-hygiene theory by Frederick Herzberg as work situations that can make employees unhappy and prevent them from doing a good job These include working conditions, company policies, hours, equipment, fair pay, health benefits, time off, working relationships, and supervision style (Also called **maintenance factors** or **dissatisfiers**)

Immutable characteristics characteristics such as race and sex that cannot be changed

Incentive program program designed to entice employees into meeting specified goals by offering some kind of reward

Individual plan   a benefit plan for one person or one family; usually purchased outside of the workplace

Instructional design   a systematic process of developing instruction based on adult learning principles

Integrative practice   a practice at the end of several chunks in which there is no new content; rather, the learner is helped and then expected to integrate the prior chunks into a useful whole

Internal sources   potential employees that come from within your operation, such as existing employees you promote or people referred by employees

Interview schedule   a standard list of questions used for every candidate who interviews for the same position in order to protect you from possible liability and to make sure you get all the information you want

Intranet   internal computer network

Involuntary termination   the operation asked the employee to leave

Job analysis   aspects of a job that include (1) detailed breakdown of the duties involved in a position, (2) skills, knowledge, attitudes, and experience a person should bring to the position, and (3) environmental conditions of the job

Job description   a document that defines the work involved in a particular assignment or position

Job instruction training   see **classical model of training**

Job interview   interview with the potential supervisor and/or other employees to gather additional information about an individual and to give the individual a realistic idea of what the job entails

Job offer   a formal invitation to join an organization as an employee on a certain date to perform a described range of duties for a specific salary or hourly rate and benefits package

Job postings   notices about jobs placed on a bulletin board in areas frequented by employees or on an internal Web site (intranet)

Job specifications   the qualifications a person should have to do a job

Knowledge   information stored in a person's mind, such as facts, concepts, rules, and procedures

Labor chart   helps calculate the number of hours for which individual employees are scheduled (Also called **staffing chart**)

Labor contract   a written agreement of the terms of employment that a union negotiates for its members

Layoffs   terminations due to economic factors or reasons other than performance

Learning objectives   thorough descriptions of the skills, knowledge, and attitudes to be learned These are a guide to the preparation of the learning and as the basis for the evaluation of the learning

Leave of absence   a period of time that cannot be covered by paid time-off days (vacation time, personal days, or sick days)

Levies   payments taken directly from an employee's earnings by a government agency to pay from back taxes, fines, or penalties

Life events   events that change a family, such as birth, adoption, marriage, divorce, or death

Longevity   length of stay (in a job)

Look-back period   the six month time frame prior to enrolling in a healthcare plan in which the plan can check for a preexisting condition

Maintenance factors   another name for hygiene factors in the motivation-hygiene theory by Frederick Herzberg (Also called **dissatisfiers**)

Manager's communication log   a record of information that affects the operation in general but may also contain information recorded in other types of logs

Manager's report   a detailed report of all financial transactions for the day

Mandated   required by federal or state governments

Maslow's hierarchy of needs   a theory by psychologist Abraham Maslow that human beings have five basic needs that arise or evolve in a specific hierarchy, or order As soon as one need is fulfilled, a person is motivated to fulfill the next higher need

Material Safety Data Sheet (MSDS)   a document that provides information about the chemical content of a material, instructions for its safe handling, and emergency information for treating someone who has been exposed

Mediator   see **arbitrator**

Medicare   a federally insured healthcare plan for people age sixty-five or older

Minors   people younger than eighteen years of age

Motivation factors   defined in the motivation-hygiene theory by Frederick Herzberg as opportunities for esteem, accomplishment, contribution, responsibility, acknowledgement, recognition, and growth (Also called **satisfiers**)

Motivation-hygiene theory   a theory by Frederick Herzberg that identifies different sets of factors that can motivate and demotivate employees (Also called **two-factor theory**)

Mystery shoppers   people who visit an establishment as regular customers and rate employee performance

Needs assessment   determining the needs of trainees by looking at their readiness for training and their existing skills and knowledge; and comparing them to the ideal employee

Negligent hiring   the failure to ensure, through background checks, that the person is a safe and competent person for the position

Negligent training   a lack of training or inadequate training

Networking   the practice of building and maintaining ongoing communication with individuals who you can help and who can help you

New hires   people newly employed by an operation

New hire checklist   a checklist that focuses on getting the employee and operation ready for the employee's first day on the job

Nonexempt   position covered by the Fair Labor Standards Act (FLSA), which specifies a minimum wage and when overtime pay is required; hourly position

Occupational Safety and Health Administration (OSHA)   an agency within the Department of Labor that enforces the Occupational Safety and Health Act (OSH Act) and develops detailed regulations and standards

Open-ended questions   questions that enable answers to be provided in an unstructured way

Open enrollment period   a limited time during which employees can change their plan or their coverage under a plan

Open house   a designated time for people to visit your operation

Operating standards   ways of doing things correctly and in the manner that management wants them done

Orientation   the process of providing an introduction to the organization and the job so employees know what to do and how to do it

Orientation buddies   persons who serve as mentors or guides to new employees during orientation

Orientation checklist   a checklist that records what happens on the first day of employment and during follow-up meetings

Orientation kit   a collection of documents used in orientation programs such as organization charts, work schedules, copies of menus and promotional materials, and contact information

Overtime   hours worked after which nonexempt employees must be paid 1.5 times the regular hourly rate

Participant   someone who is a member of a plan

Payroll administrator   the person, department, or outside company that ensures paychecks are issued

Payroll system   a method for recording and tracking employee time and issuing paychecks

Performance standards   how well and possibly how often or how quickly a duty must be completed

Pensions   regular payments that continue until the retiree dies

Person hour   one hour of work done by one person

Personnel file   a confidential file that contains documents related to hiring, training, evaluating, promoting, and, if necessary, disciplining an individual

Perquisites (perks)   incidental benefits such as formal training, flexible scheduling, and opportunities for advancement

Physiological needs   the most basic needs relating to the body, such as food, water, air, or sleep, in Maslow's hierarchy of needs

Plan administrator   a designated person or group of people responsible for handling the administrative tasks for a plan, such as processing forms and communicating notices

Plan provider   the company offering a benefit, such as an insurance company

Point-of-sale (POS) system   a computer-based system for recording orders, sending them to the kitchen, printing bills, and recording information for management reports

Postshift meeting   a gathering of shift personnel at the end of the shift to discuss what happened during the shift

Postshift review   feedback about accomplishments, failures, and behavior

Potable water   water that is safe to drink or use as an ingredient in food

Preexisting condition   a medical condition for which a person has sought medical treatment before applying to join a healthcare plan
Preferred provider organizations (PPOs)   managed care plans in which service providers discount the cost of their service in exchange for more patients and timely payment

Preinterview   screening interviews intended to (1) gather information about the person applying for a position, (2) make him or her feel welcome, and (3) build interest in the operation

Prejudice   a general attitude toward a person, group, or organization on the basis of judgments unrelated to abilities (Same as **bias**)

Premium   monthly fee for healthcare plans

Preshift meeting   a gathering of the shift crew to verify readiness and communicate important information before a shift begins

Primary care physicians   typically general practitioners or internists

Primary needs   social, safety, and physiological needs in Maslow's hierarchy of needs

Production sheet   a document that explains what food will be prepared for a shift

Progressive discipline   system in which the employee has plenty of warning and support to improve his or her behavior and performance

Promoting from within   promoting current employees into open positions

Protected categories   categories protected by federal laws against discrimination. These categories are race, color, religion, sex, national origin, age (forty or older), disability, pregnancy, citizenship, and military service.

Protected classes   individuals who share one of the characteristics of the protected categories (Same as **protected groups**)

Protected groups - individuals who share one of the characteristics of the protected categories (Same as **protected classes**)

Qualified beneficiary   a person entitled to COBRA continuation coverage

Qualified plan   retirement plans or accounts that have tax advantages and follow certain IRS rules for contributions and withdrawals

Quid pro quo   from the Latin phrase meaning "this for that," quid pro quo harassment is when one person asks for or expects an action of a sexual nature from another person as a condition of that person's employment or advancement

Realistic job preview   a realistic expectation for the position and operation that helps the applicant understand if your operation is one in which he or she wants to work and will be successful

Reasonable accommodation   alternate ways defined by the Equal Employment Opportunity Commission as "a change in the job application process, a change in the way a job is performed in the work environment, or a change to other parts of the job that enables a person with a disability to have equal employment opportunities"

Reasonable care defense   defense against a lawsuit that requires proof your establishment did everything that could be reasonably expected to ensure food was safe to serve

Recruiting   a series of activities designed to bring the largest number of qualified persons to apply for a job

Reservation log   see **dining room manager's communication log**

Return on investment (ROI)   the profits of a program or event against the costs of implementing it; used to evaluate recruiting activities

Role model   one who sets an example for employees to imitate

Safety needs   the second level of needs, dealing with things that make us feel secure or safe, such as shelter or stable income, in Maslow's hierarchy of needs

Salaried   exempt positions where the compensation is based on a set salary rather than an hourly wage

Satisfiers   another word for motivation factors in the motivation-hygiene theory

Scope of a job   the range of responsibilities a person is expected to undertake

Screening   reviewing the skills, experience, attitudes, and backgrounds of people who have applied to work at your operation

Screening interview   discussion intended to determine whether an individual meets basic requirements before the business invests more time and resources in evaluating him or her for a job opening

Self-actualization   the fifth and highest level of needs, which is the realization of one's own potential, in Maslow's hierarchy of needs

Self-insured   employers insure their employees and pay all of the covered healthcare costs

Serious medical condition   defined by the FMLA as "an illness, injury, impairment, or physical or mental condition that involves: inpatient care… [or] continuing treatment by a healthcare provider"

Service   days or time spent at work

Service period   breakfast, lunch, or dinner (Also called **day part**)

Sexual harassment   unwelcome behavior of a sexual nature that has the effect of interfering with the employee's job performance

Side work   work in addition to the main job of serving customers, such as stocking stations and filling salt and pepper shakers

Skill gap   a gap between the skills the employee presently has and the skills that are needed

Skills   intellectual or physical actions that help accomplish a goal, such as baking a cake or planning a menu

Social needs   the third level of needs, involving people's need to be with others, such as love, belonging, and friendship, in Maslow's hierarchy of needs

Social Security   a federal pension program in which most private sector employers and employees must participate

Sources   places, organizations, and individuals you can draw on to find new employees

Sous chef   the person in charge of a kitchen or shift who works for the executive chef

Special enrollment periods   certain times, other than open enrollment, when people who might not otherwise be able to get healthcare coverage can enroll in a plan

Staffing chart   see **labor charts**

Staggered schedule   staff members start and stop at varying, overlapping times

Standard operating procedures (SOPs)   procedures to define what steps people should take in certain circumstances to handle unusual situations or routine day-to-day procedures

Standards   the levels of quality, speed, food safety, or hospitality that employees are expected to demonstrate while completing their work

State dislocated worker units   state government agencies created by Title III of the Job Training Partnership Act to help workers affected by layoffs with job retraining and placement services

Stereotypes   generalizations that individuals make about particular groups that assume that all members of that group are the same

Strike   an order to all union members at one or more locations to stop working

Structured interview   interview designed to collect specific information

Subminimum wage   wage lower than minimum wage allowed for student-learners who are placed in a job as part of a vocational education program or other education program or individuals who have a reduced capacity to be productive because of a physical or mental disability

Subpoenaed   legally required to be produced in a court of law

Successive interviewing   a series of interviews as part of the screening process

Summary annual report   a summary of the annual report that was filed with the government

Summary of material modification (SMM)   a document, required by ERISA, that explains changes in a plan or summary plan description

Summary plan description (SPD)   a document that explains the plan benefits, identifies the plan administrator, and describes participants' rights and responsibilities under the plan

Summary plan documents   documents that relate to and describe the administration of benefits

Task analysis   a thorough description of all the elements of the job or work, including tools and equipment, cultural and historical impact, safety and sanitation, and impact on customers and other parts of the operation

Tax deferred   tax is not paid until you withdraw money from an account

Termination checklist   a document that lists all the termination requirements and has space for the appropriate manager to sign when these tasks have been completed

Tip allocation   income allotted by employers to tipped employees that earn less than 8 percent of their individual sales

Tipped employees   those who "customarily and regularly" receive more than a certain amount of income in tips each month

Tipped employees' minimum wage   tipped employees may be paid a lower cash wage when their tips are enough to ensure the basic minimum wage is met

Traditional health insurance　see **fee-for-service plans** (Also called **conventional indemnity plans**)

Two-factor theory　another name for the motivation-hygiene theory by Frederick Herzberg

Undue hardship　an action that is excessively costly, extensive, or substantial in relation to an employer's size and financial resources, or that would fundamentally alter the nature or operation of the business

Unemployment insurance　a benefit mandated by the Social Security Act to temporarily provide a reduced level of income to employees who lose their jobs involuntarily

Uniformed Services Employment and Reemployment Rights Act (USERRA)　protects employees from workplace discrimination based on their obligation to, application for, or interest in military service

Union dues　fees to help pay for the administration of the union

Union shop　where all employees are required to join the union and pay union dues as a condition of employment

Union steward　a union representative

Unions　organizations designated by employees to negotiate their employment terms, such as wages, benefits, discipline, and job security

Unstructured interview　interview designed to provide an opportunity for the employee to bring up a wide range of subjects; whatever the employee wishes to address or topics that come up naturally during the interview

Validation　comparing the content of the training and its evaluation methods to the actual job of a master performer in order to determine whether they are in sync

Vested　entitled to a benefit

Voluntary termination the employee decided to leave

Whistleblowers employees who report a violation or possible violation

Work schedule a list of who reports for what shift on what days for what duty

Workers' compensation financial compensation to employees or their survivors when an employee is injured at work, becomes sick because of the workplace environment, or dies as a result of a workplace situation

Wrongful termination when employees are fired for arbitrary, unproven, or discriminatory reasons

Youth minimum wage Employees younger than twenty years of age may be paid a lower minimum wage during their first ninety consecutive days of employment

Z report a report generated after zeroing out a register or cash drawer

Zero tolerance policy a policy against harassment that does not tolerate harassment in any form by any person; all persons are responsible for stopping harassment whenever it occurs and should report it